THE CORFU INCIDENT
OF 1923

THE CORFU INCIDENT OF 1923

MUSSOLINI AND THE LEAGUE OF NATIONS

BY JAMES BARROS

PRINCETON, NEW JERSEY
PRINCETON UNIVERSITY PRESS
1965

Copyright © 1965 by Princeton University Press
All Rights Reserved

LC Card: 65-14305

Publication of this book has been aided
by the Robb Fund
of Princeton University Press

Printed in the United States of America
by Princeton University Press

TO MY PARENTS

ACKNOWLEDGMENTS

TO THANK the people who make a study possible is an old and pleasant tradition in the academic community. First and foremost, I would like to express my warmest thanks to Professors Leland M. Goodrich and René Albrecht-Carrié of Columbia University, as well as to Professor Ivo Lederer of Yale University, whose criticisms of the manuscript and encouragements made it a far better book. Mr. Gordon H. Evans, who also read the manuscript, offered valuable advice and criticism.

Access to unpublished archival materials was made possible by the following: Lord Scarsdale very kindly made available to me the personal papers of his uncle, Lord Curzon; Mr. Julian Amery, M.P., opened for examination and allowed quotation from the diaries of his father, Mr. Leopold S. Amery; and The Dowager Lady Keyes permitted me to examine and quote from the letters of her husband, Admiral Sir Roger Keyes. In Geneva, access to the Archives of the League of Nations and permission to quote from League materials was kindly arranged by Mr. A. C. Breycha-Vauthier, Director of the United Nations Library. In Rome, Professors Mario Toscano and Renato Mori put at my disposal the unpublished Archives of the Italian Foreign Ministry dealing with the Corfu Incident. In Athens, the unusual permission to examine the Foreign Ministry Archives was given by the Greek Government. Lastly, examination of American diplomatic materials was made possible by the Foreign Affairs Division of the National Archives of the United States in Washington, D.C. Thanks are especially due to the Director of the Archives Division of the Greek Foreign Ministry, Mr. Constantine Hadjithomas, and to his assistants, Epaminondas Ekonomidis and Constantine Pantelidis, as well as to the historian, Angelo Papacosta, for their valuable assistance. The archival research mentioned above was made possible by a Fulbright award to Greece during the academic year 1961-1962.

I would also like to express my appreciation to the following

Acknowledgments

people: Lord Baldwin of Bewdley for permission to quote his father's letter to Lord Curzon; Mrs. Anne Crawshay for permission to quote the letters of her father, Lord Tyrrell, to Lords Curzon and Crewe; Lady Crewe for permission to quote her husband's letters to Lord Curzon; Mr. Arthur Norris Kennard for permission to quote his father's letter to Lord Curzon; Dr. Basil Laourdas and the Institute for Balkan Studies in Salonika for permission to reproduce chapter three, which had originally appeared as an article in the 1961 issue of *Balkan Studies*; the Marquess of Salisbury for permission to quote the letter of his uncle, Lord Robert Cecil, to Lord Curzon; Lord Scarsdale for permission to quote the letter from his uncle, Lord Curzon, to Lord Crewe cited in James Pope-Hennessy, *Lord Crewe, 1858-1948; the Likeness of a Liberal* (London: Constable and Co., Ltd., 1955); and lastly, Mrs. Virginia Thesiger for permission to quote the letter of her uncle, Sir Ronald W. Graham, to Lord Curzon.

Before ending, a special note of thanks is due to my wife for her critical judgment in helping to revise the manuscript and for the unenviable job of typing it.

JAMES BARROS

Dartmouth College
Hanover, New Hampshire
December 1964

CONTENTS

ACKNOWLEDGMENTS	vii
ABBREVIATIONS	xiii
CHRONOLOGY OF EVENTS: JULY-DECEMBER 1923	xv
INTRODUCTION	xix

I. THE CONFERENCE OF AMBASSADORS — 3

Negotiations Establishing the Conference of Ambassadors — 3
The Conference of Ambassadors as an Institution — 11
Establishment of the Conference's Commission of Delimitation — 16

II. THE TELLINI MURDER — 20

Prior Greek Warnings — 20
The Murder and Subsequent Investigations — 22
Theories on Tellini's Murder — 29

III. THE ITALIAN ULTIMATUM — 33

Mussolini's Reaction to the Tellini Murder — 33
Montagna's Attitude — 35
Montagna's Communications and Mussolini's Reaction — 37
Italy's Diplomats and Mussolini — 40
Events in London and Paris — 47
Events in Athens — 50
Reactions in Italy to Tellini's Murder — 54
Mussolini's Demands — 56
The Greek Reply — 65

Contents

Prior Italian Naval Preparations	67
Last Minute Moves	70

IV. MUSSOLINI VERSUS THE LEAGUE OF NATIONS — 74

Solari Blunders at Corfu	74
Reactions in Athens	80
Reactions in Geneva	83
Reactions in London and Paris	85
Geneva: the First Encounter	90
Threats to Leave the League	98
A Special Courier: Giovanni Giuriati	104
Curzon's Decision to Support Greece's Appeal	107
Paris Assures Rome	113
Greece Accepts the Conference's Note of Protest	117
The Anglo-French Dilemma	122

V. THE LEAGUE OF NATIONS AND THE CONFERENCE OF AMBASSADORS — 124

Avezzana's Advice	124
Greek, British, and French Proposals for a Solution	128
Activities in Geneva	132
The Conference of Ambassadors Convenes	142
Reaction to the Conference of Ambassadors' Meeting	150
The Council's Overtures to the Conference	157
The Conference's Communication Causes Disquiet in Geneva	169
Reports from Geneva to Athens and Rome	171
British Military Weakness	176
Italian Military Weaknesses	181
Whitehall Retreats	184

Contents

VI. SETTLEMENT BY NEGOTIATION AND COMPROMISE — 188

- A Compromise Formula Devised — 188
- Mussolini's Qualified Acceptance of the Conference's Note — 201
- Instructions to Lord Robert Cecil — 212
- Mussolini's Qualified Acceptance Announced to Conference — 221
- Reports to Athens and Rome — 225

VII. CRUCIAL DAYS: SEPTEMBER 12-13 — 230

- Struggling for a Formula — 230
- Impressions of the Meeting — 234
- Pressure for an Evacuation Date — 236
- British Pressure and Mussolini's Decision — 239
- Avezzana's Declaration — 244
- Mussolini's Reaction — 248
- The League Withdraws from the Dispute — 254
- The Commission of Inquiry in Epirus — 258
- Mussolini's Instructions — 265

VIII. SURRENDER — 268

- The Conference's Decision: Greece Must Pay — 268
- Curzon Agrees to the Conference's Decision — 279
- The Conference's Note to Greece — 283
- Athens Concedes — 286
- Rome Thwarts Continuation of Investigation — 291

CONCLUSION — 297

APPENDICES

A. Text of the Conference of Ambassadors' Message to the Council of the League of Nations, September 5, 1923 — 315

Contents

B. Text of Avezzana's Declaration to the Conference of Ambassadors, September 13, 1923 — 316

C. Memorandum by Sir Eric Drummond on the Corfu Incident, September 14, 1923 — 317

D. Note of the Conference of Ambassadors to the Greek Government, September 27, 1923 — 321

BIBLIOGRAPHY — 323

INDEX — 331

ABBREVIATIONS

Amery Papers	The personal papers and diaries of Leopold S. Amery, London, England.
Bulletin Périodique de la Presse Grecque, etc.	Ministère des Affaires Étrangères (France), *Bulletin Périodique de la Presse*....
Curzon Papers	The personal papers of Lord Curzon, Kedleston, Derby, England.
DBrFP	*Documents on British Foreign Policy 1919-1939*; First Series (London: H. M. Stationary Office, 1947-1960), 9 vols.
DDDIG	Ministère des Affaires Étrangères (Greece), *Documents Diplomatiques. Différend Italo-Grec: Août-Septembre 1923* (Athènes: Macris, 1923).
DDI	Ministero degli Affari Esteri, *I Documenti Diplomatici Italiani*, Settima Serie (Roma: Libreria dello Stato, 1955), 2 vols.
FRUS, 1919	*Foreign Relations of the United States, 1919* (Washington: Government Printing Office, 1934), 2 vols.
FRUS, PPC	*Foreign Relations of the United States, 1919, The Paris Peace Conference* (Washington: Government Printing Office, 1942-1947), 13 vols.
Greek Archives	Archives Division of the Royal Greek Ministry of Foreign Affairs, Athens, Greece.
Italian Archives	Archives Division of the Italian Ministry of Foreign Affairs, Rome, Italy.

Abbreviations

Keyes Papers	The personal papers of Admiral Sir Roger Keyes, Tingewick House, Buckingham, England.
L.N.	League of Nations.
League of Nations Archives	League of Nations Archives, United Nations Library, Palais des Nations, Geneva, Switzerland.
NA	National Archives of the United States, Washington, D.C.

CHRONOLOGY OF EVENTS:
July-December 1923

July 24	Italian fleet recalled to Taranto on instructions from Rome.
July 29	A conversation is held in Rome between the Minister of Marine, Grand Admiral Thaon di Revel, Admiral Emilio Solari, and Captain Antonio Foschini, in which the former laments the decline of Italian prestige.
July-August	Conversations are held between military officials and career officials of the Italian Foreign Ministry as to what measures to take in the case of any Greek reaction to an Italian proclamation of sovereignty over the Dodecanese Islands. The decision taken after these conversations is to occupy Corfu, and the necessary military preparations are pushed forward during August.
August 27	General Enrico Tellini and his staff are murdered near the Greek-Albanian frontier, but in Greek territory.
August 29	Italian ultimatum is presented to the Greek Government.
August 30	The Greek Government rejects the Italian ultimatum.
August 30	Mussolini decides to adhere to the Conference of Ambassadors' projected note of protest to Greece over the Tellini murder.
August 31	Italian naval units bombard and occupy the island of Corfu.
August 31	The Conference of Ambassadors' note of

Chronology of Events

protest is presented to the Greek Government.

September 1 — Greece appeals to the League of Nations.

September 2 — Greece accepts the Ambassadorial note of protest and proposes that an international commission be appointed to investigate the Tellini murder.

September 4 — Greek proposals to settle the Italo-Greek dispute are presented to the League Council by the Greek delegate, Nikolaos Politis.

September 5 — Salandra, on instructions from Mussolini, denies competence of the League Council to handle the Italo-Greek dispute.

September 5 — The Conference of Ambassadors, meeting at Paris, assumes Greek responsibility for the Tellini murder and communicates its decision to the League Council.

September 6 — The Council of the League of Nations submits for the consideration of the Conference of Ambassadors eight suggestions as a means of giving satisfaction to the demands of the Conference as a consequence of the Tellini murder.

September 7 — A second note covering the demands of the Conference and the Italian Government is transmitted to the Greek Government.

September 9 — Greece agrees to execute all the requests for sanctions and reparations demanded by the Conference of Ambassadors.

September 10 — On instructions from the Foreign Office, Lord Robert Cecil does not press the

Chronology of Events

League's competence in the Italo-Greek dispute.

September 10-13   After long and difficult negotiations the Conference of Ambassadors and the Italian Government devise a formula for the evacuation of Corfu.

September 17   The Commission of Inquiry, sent by the Conference to investigate the Tellini murder, arrives in Epirus.

September 17-18   The League Council acquiesces to the role assumed by the Conference of Ambassadors in settling the Italo-Greek dispute.

September 22   The Commission of Inquiry forwards to the Conference of Ambassadors its first report, which is ambiguously worded.

September 25   Acting on the strength of the Commission of Inquiry's first report, the Conference decides to award Italy 50 million Italian lire.

September 26   Lord Crewe is instructed by Lord Curzon to accept the Conference's decision.

September 27   Italian troops evacuate Corfu.

September 27-29   A delay by the Greek Government in transferring the 50 million lire causes the Italian ships to anchor off Corfu for several days.

September 29   Greece under protest agrees to pay Italy the 50 million Italian lire demanded by the Conference of Ambassadors.

September 30   The Commission of Inquiry forwards to the Conference of Ambassadors its second report.

Chronology of Events

September 30-
November 30
Agreement between the Conference representatives over how the investigation into the Tellini murder is to continue proves impossible.

December 12-13
The first and second reports of the Commission of Inquiry are forwarded by the Conference to the Greek and Albanian Governments, as well as to the League of Nations.

INTRODUCTION

DURING the interwar period the League of Nations appeared to many as the only hope for averting a repetition of the great disaster which had shaken Europe and the world from 1914 to 1918.

What many well-wishers of the League failed to realize, however, was that the organization established at Geneva was not as great an innovation in international relations as they thought. If they had looked carefully they would have seen that a more exact description of the structure and powers of the organization was given by its French name, *La Société des Nations*, than by its English equivalent.

Supporters of the organization often refused to admit that though the League could play a valuable role in international politics, it was still the foreign offices and chancelleries, especially those of the Great Powers, that were of paramount importance. They blinded themselves to the fact that the nature of international politics had not substantially changed with the establishment of the League, and that in foreign relations the desire to further the interests and well-being of one's country was still the order of the day.

Therefore, the League's seeming impotence during the Corfu dispute was a great shock to many of its supporters. They felt that the League and its principle had been betrayed and that the seeds of a future disaster had been planted. Whether these assumptions were correct will be examined in the following pages. The divergent positions taken by the Great Powers towards Italy and the League of Nations will be considered, as will the interpretation of the League by the Great Powers, especially the manner in which the League complemented their foreign policy requirements. The way in which the Corfu dispute was finally settled, and the actual role played by the League of Nations and the Conference of Ambassadors in

Introduction

helping to bring the dispute to a peaceful conclusion, will conclude the study. Throughout, the relations between Mussolini and the career officials of the Italian Foreign Ministry will be touched upon. In essence, this study wishes to throw light on the handling of disputes during the League period and by doing so to attempt to discover the possibilities and limitations of political settlement under the auspices of an international organization.

Lastly, a few words should be said about sources. The only studies of the incident, prior to my own, were made in the 1920's. They are mostly French and German doctoral dissertations based on no documentary material except the public records of the League of Nations; they are cited in the bibliography. There were six parties to the affair: Britain, the Conference of Ambassadors, France, Greece, Italy, and the League of Nations, and I have examined the complete papers of four of these—those of the Conference of Ambassadors (never before used *in toto*) and the Archives of the League of Nations, Italy, and Greece. I might add that in the case of the last three special permission was needed before the papers could be examined.

In an attempt to use as much Italian documentary material as possible an examination was made of the Corfu dossiers in the Italian Foreign Ministry Archives. These materials, however, proved in general to be identical with those published in the seventh series of the *Documenti Diplomatici Italiani*, used in this study. Since this latter Italian publication includes documents from other Italian Government Ministries and departments it gives a fuller picture of Italian actions than does an examination of the Foreign Ministry Archives. Nevertheless, the Foreign Ministry Archives did yield several interesting documents not reproduced in the *Documenti Diplomatici Italiani*, and where these have been used they are clearly cited in the footnotes.

In the case of Greek documentary materials, the Corfu dossiers of the Royal Greek Foreign Ministry were also examined. These dossiers naturally included reports to Athens from Greek

Introduction

diplomatic and consular missions overseas, and instructions from Athens to these same missions. Of special interest in the Foreign Ministry Archives were the police, judicial, and other official reports on the murder and the actions taken by the Greek authorities to apprehend the Tellini assassins. After the defeat of Greece during the Second World War, all these papers in the Greek Foreign Ministry as well as archives in other Greek Government Ministries were closely examined by the Italian occupation authorities, undoubtedly in an attempt to throw more light on the Tellini murder. These researches, however, uncovered no evidence to link the Greek Government either directly or indirectly with the murder of General Tellini.

In the case of Great Britain, the Foreign Office operates under the fifty-year rule, so that their archives on the incident will not be open until 1973 at the earliest. To surmount this obstacle I examined as many private archives as possible, and special permission was given to examine the papers of the Foreign Secretary then, Lord Curzon, the First Lord of the Admiralty, Leopold S. Amery, and Admiral Sir Roger Keyes. Unfortunately, the papers of Stanley Baldwin, then Prime Minister, cannot be seen for many years to come, while the papers of other British cabinet ministers and military personages either contain no materials or are closed to researchers. As to the French, their archives are open only up to 1896 and the French Foreign Ministry has no intention of opening its archives beyond this period for many years to come.

THE CORFU INCIDENT
OF 1923

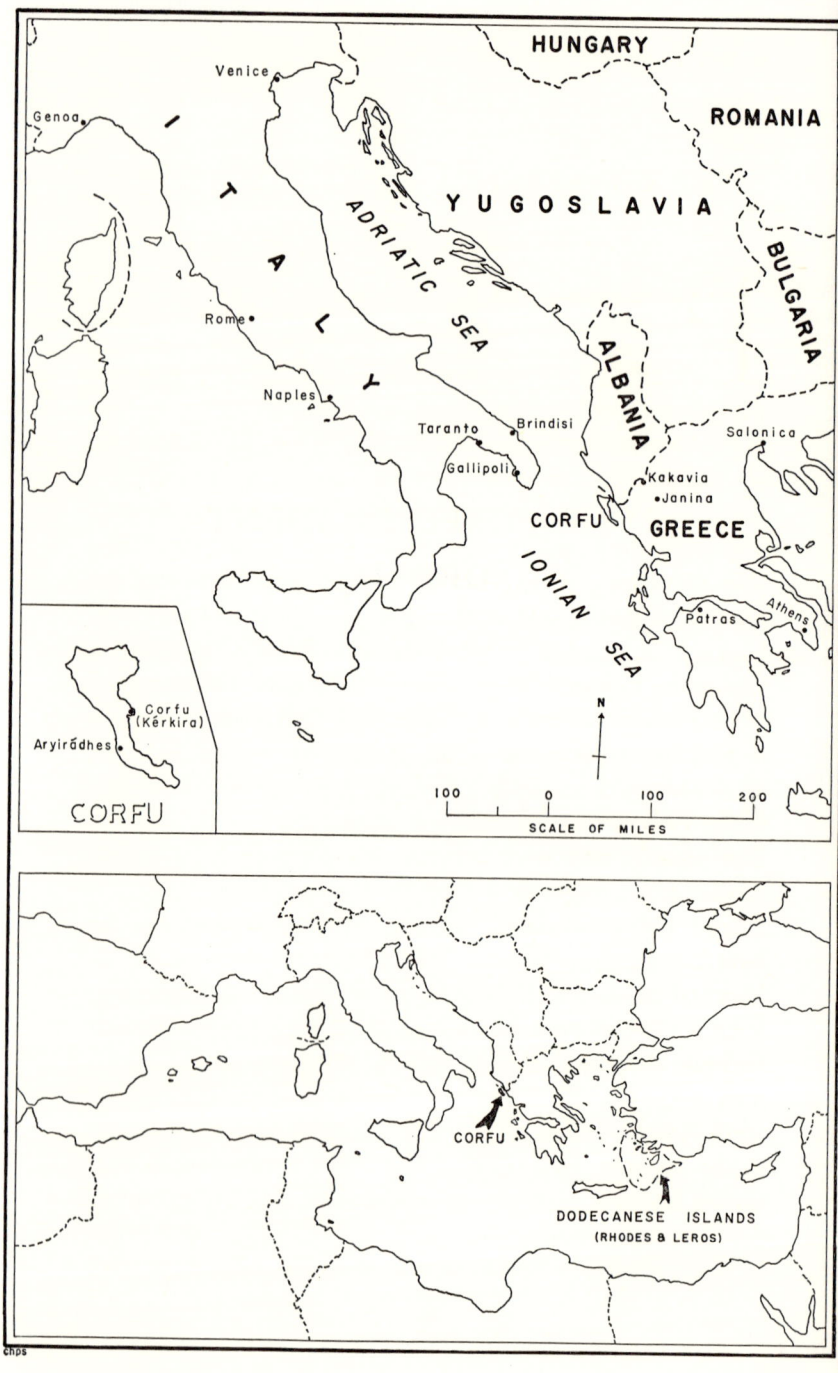

CHAPTER I

THE CONFERENCE OF AMBASSADORS

NEGOTIATIONS ESTABLISHING THE CONFERENCE OF AMBASSADORS

PRIOR to the First World War, conferences of ambassadors were a commonly accepted diplomatic institution for the negotiation and settlement of disputes. Thus the Conference of Ambassadors, the institution that played so important a role in solving the Corfu Incident of 1923, was no novelty. The Conference had its beginnings on July 1, 1919, three days after the signing of the Versailles Treaty. At a meeting of the Supreme Council held at the Quai d'Orsay, Prime Minister Georges Clemenceau proposed that the Council "nominate a Committee to watch the execution of the Treaty with Germany when ratified." Clemenceau added that "the Committee was to have no executive power but should superintend the work of all Commissions dealing with the details of the provisions of the Treaty ... [furthermore it] would report to the Council from time to time what progress was being made and what further action might be needed."

Lord Balfour declared that he intended to nominate Sir Eyre Crowe, then Assistant Under-Secretary for Foreign Affairs and member of the British Delegation to the Peace Conference. Clemenceau's nominee was M. André Tardieu, French Delegate Plenipotentiary to the Peace Conference and Chairman of the Central Territorial Committee of the Conference, while Baron Makino proposed Mr. Otchiai, Secretary-General of the Japanese Delegation at the Peace Conference. It was agreed, however, to postpone nominations until the following day since both Secretary of State Robert Lansing and Foreign Minister Tommaso Tittoni of Italy were not prepared to offer

The Conference of Ambassadors

any nominations.[1] On the following day Mr. John Foster Dulles was named as the American representative to the Committee, while Italy appointed Vittorio Scialoja.[2]

The Committee on the Execution of the Clauses of the Treaty, now established by the Supreme Council, was understood to be merely a temporary arrangement. Thus the Committee at an early date turned its attention to the creation of a more permanent organ having authority on any question raised once the Versailles Treaty came into force.[3] This organ, subsequently established as the Conference of Ambassadors, originated in an American proposal which the Committee had examined in three of its sessions and unanimously adopted.[4]

Paragraph 1 of the American proposal called for a special committee to study and follow up all questions "concerning the interpretation and the execution of the treaty with Germany." This excepted those questions specifically confided by

---

[1] Minutes of the Meeting, July 1, 1919. *FRUS, PPC*, VII, pp. 1-2; *DBrFP*, First Series, I, pp. 1-2. According to Frances Kellor and Antonia Hatvany, *Security against War* (New York: Macmillan Co., 1924), I, pp. 88-89, the Conference of Ambassadors owed "its existence, in all probability, to Mr. David Lloyd George." After the rejection of the League Covenant by the United States and with it the attempt to have "it share the responsibilities of bringing about European equilibrium, he conceived the idea of submitting questions of a political nature arising from the Versailles Treaty, not to the League of Nations . . . but to the Conference of Ambassadors, where the American representatives could 'unofficially observe,' and where, perhaps step by step, the United States would be drawn into a closer commitment to European Affairs." This theory is patently false, as the following pages will show —unless Clemenceau was acting in Lloyd George's behalf, which seems improbable. No less false is the statement that "Great Britain . . . probably made the original proposal of creating the Conference of Ambassadors." Gerhard P. Pink, *The Conference of Ambassadors (1920-1931)* (Geneva Studies, Vol. XII, Nos. 4-5, 1942; Geneva: Geneva Research Centre, 1942), p. 26.

[2] Minutes of the Meeting, July 2, 1919. *FRUS, PPC*, VII, p. 14; *DBrFP*, I, p. 11; Commission to Negotiate Peace to the Acting Secretary of State (Phillips), July 4, 1919. *FRUS, 1919*, I, p. 1.

[3] *FRUS, PPC*, XIII, p. 7.

[4] Note for the Supreme Council from the Commission on the Execution of the Clauses of the Treaty, July 23, 1919. *Ibid.*, VII, p. 362. The original French text is to be found in *DBrFP*, I, p. 231.

The Conference of Ambassadors

the Versailles Treaty either to the League of Nations, or to the Commissions on Reparations and on Military, Naval, and Air Control, or to some other organ. Established at Paris, the Committee if it so wished could also convene at other locations. The governments represented on the Committee were to be provided with "common and coordinated bases for information and interpretations," and in case of necessity with proposals relating to the matters defined above. At the earliest opportunity the Allied and Associated Powers were to make known the delegates, diplomatic or other, empowered to represent them in the projected Committee. These delegates in turn could be supported by technical advisers, depending upon the substance of the questions to be considered.

The relationship between the Committee, the governments, and the commissions authorized to execute the Treaty was to be regulated in the following manner: (1) commissions would report to the Committee all questions settled by them and the local German authorities or other authorities with whom they might be in contact; (2) the members of the Committee were empowered by their respective governments to send instructions to the commissions, to the Allied and Associated Governments, and to the representatives of the German Government when any disagreement arose in the field, *other than one of principle*. In the latter case the Committee, after a collective examination, would propose solutions to the governments. The governments in turn would notify their commissions in the field and the diplomatic representatives of the Allied and Associated Governments stationed in Berlin of the decisions and measures of execution. The Committee would also receive copies of the decisions for its information. The Allied and Associated Governments were to determine the relationship between the Committee and the Secretary-General of the League of Nations, in order that all steps taken to execute the Treaty would conform "to the principles and ideals which are the basis of the League." At the signing of the other peace treaties, in order to ensure "their execution under the same

The Conference of Ambassadors

conditions," an organ, composed of the same persons, would be established.[5]

On July 28, almost four weeks after its establishment, the Committee forwarded the American draft recommendation to the Supreme Council for its action.

Lord Balfour, with foresight, questioned whether there would not be some confusion between the proposed new committee and the League of Nations. A Permanent Committee at Geneva and another at Paris "might lead to disputes."

Tardieu declared that Lord Balfour's doubts were adequately answered in paragraph 1 of the Committee's draft resolution. This clearly spelled out the Committee's field of jurisdiction and its relationship with the League and other organs. He felt there was no "risk of overlapping." In addition, according to paragraph 5 of the draft resolution, the Allied and Associated Powers would determine what relationship would exist between the proposed committee and the League of Nations.[6]

Balfour declared he was satisfied but raised a further question, whether the Council had any objection to the appointment of ambassadors as delegates to the projected committee. This question was interpreted by the American Mission at the Paris Peace Conference as "made . . . [undoubtedly] with the idea that the committee would merely serve as a clearing house between commission[s] functioning in Germany and the Allied and Associated Governments."[7]

Tardieu answered this query by directing Lord Balfour's

[5] Italics added. Draft recommendation. *FRUS, PPC*, VII, pp. 362-364. The original French text is to be found in *DBrFP*, I, pp. 231-232.

[6] Lord Balfour was not alone in his confusion. Throughout the 1920's and 1930's it was to be voiced by numerous British M.P.'s. Great Britain, *Parliamentary Debates*, Fifth Series, House of Commons, *Official Report*, Vol. 161, March 19, 1923, col. 2066-2067; *ibid.*, Vol. 169, February 14, 1924, col. 1126-1127; *ibid.*, Vol. 169, February 18, 1924, col. 1287-1288; *ibid.*, Vol. 170, February 25, 1924, col. 23; *ibid.*, Vol. 174, May 28, 1924, col. 384; *ibid.*, Vol. 175, June 26, 1924, col. 578; *ibid.*, Vol. 175, June 30, 1924, col. 908-910; *ibid.*, Vol. 175, July 9, 1924, col. 2229; *ibid.*, Vol. 235, February 12, 1930, col. 381.

[7] American Mission (Polk) to the Acting Secretary of State (Phillips), October 25, 1919. *FRUS, PPC*, XI, p. 654.

The Conference of Ambassadors

attention to the draft recommendation. Though there was no specific need to appoint ambassadors, there was at the same time no provision against their appointment.

With no further questions and no dissents, the Supreme Council agreed to adopt the draft resolution submitted. Thus a Co-ordinating Committee to deal with questions of interpretation and execution of the Versailles Treaty was set up.[8]

Near the middle of October, the French delegation feared that the ratification of the Treaty and its subsequent execution would find the Allied and Associated Powers unprepared. They thought it "advisable to ascertain whether the International Commissions provided for . . . [were] nominated and ready to operate."[9] The French proposal did not specifically mention which particular "International Commissions" it had in mind. The Supreme Council, however, at its meeting of October 15 agreed that the Committee on the Execution of the Treaty should furnish to the Council a "list of the Commissions to be appointed in these first weeks," after the coming of the Treaty into force.[10]

The pressure was now mounting to see that the Allied and Associated Powers were adequately prepared to execute the Treaty when it came into force. It was only natural, therefore, that the following day the American Mission at Paris should report to the Secretary of State that nominations for the Committee to Co-ordinate the Interpretation and Execution of the Clauses of the Treaty with Germany were on the agenda for the next meeting of the Council. The Mission desired to "know as soon as possible who is to be the American representative."[11]

At that next meeting of the Supreme Council on October

---

[8] Minutes of the Meeting, July 2, 1919. *Ibid.*, VII, pp. 356-357; *DBrFP*, I, pp. 225-226.

[9] Note of the French Delegation dated October 13, 1919. *Ibid.*, VIII, p. 665; *ibid.*, pp. 966-967.

[10] Minutes of the Meeting, October 15, 1919. *Ibid.*, pp. 645-646; *ibid.*, pp. 961-962.

[11] American Mission (Polk) to the Secretary of State, October 16, 1919. *Ibid.*, XI, p. 653; *FRUS, 1919*, I, pp. 14-15.

The Conference of Ambassadors

18, the United States, France, and Italy were not prepared to designate their representatives.[12] Four days later Italy appointed Count Lelio Bonin Longare, its Ambassador in Paris, with Professor Pagliano as alternate delegate. France nominated its Foreign Minister, M. Stephen Pichon, with M. Philippe Berthelot, the Secretary-General of the Quai d'Orsay, as alternate delegate.[13] England and Japan had previously designated their respective Ambassadors, Lord Derby and Mr. Matsui.[14] This left only the United States unrepresented. Such a situation, Secretary of State Lansing explicitly informed Frank L. Polk of the American Mission, could not be remedied "until we ratify the treaty, and until it becomes clear whether ratification of such appointments must be made by the Senate."[15] Polk stressed this point to the Supreme Council several times.[16]

The composition of the Committee now firmly established with the exception of the American delegate, the French and Italian delegates on the interim Reparations Committee began to propose "to extend the scope of the committee so as to constitute a consultative body to consider matters of importance arising out of the Treaty." The British delegate, however, took exception to this proposal declaring "that he was

[12] Minutes of the Meeting, October 18, 1919. *Ibid.*, VIII, p. 694; *DBrFP*, II, p. 21.

[13] Minutes of the Meeting, October 22, 1919. *Ibid.*, p. 732; *ibid.*, p. 46.

[14] American Mission (Polk) to the Secretary of State, October 16, 1919. *FRUS, PPC*, XI, p. 653; *FRUS*, 1919, I, pp. 14-15.

[15] Secretary of State (Lansing) to the American Mission (Polk), November 6 [8], 1919. *Ibid.*, p. 660; *ibid.*, p. 19. However, as early as October 18, 1919, the Acting Secretary of State, Phillips, had made it clear that the United States was prepared to "act accordingly," and requested from the American Mission information as to the need in the way of assistants and clerical force, for the anticipated Committee. *Ibid.*, p. 654; *ibid.*, p. 15.

[16] According to the Minutes of the Meeting of the Supreme Council of October 18, 1919, Polk informed the Council that "prior to ratification the United States was not authorized to be officially represented," on the Reparations Commissions. This point he reiterated on October 23, when he declared "that the United States could not be represented on any Commissions prior to the ratification of the Treaty by the Senate." *Ibid.*, VIII, pp. 692, 749; *DBrFP*, II, pp. 19, 54.

The Conference of Ambassadors

against resurrecting the ghost of the Supreme Council after it had departed."[17]

France continually sought to extend the powers of what was to be the Conference of Ambassadors. The extension was finally realized in the Conference's handling of the Corfu dispute four years later.

The French position throughout the Versailles negotiations was opposed to the more limited American interpretation. Tacitly supported by the British, the Americans felt that the contemplated Conference of Ambassadors was no more than a co-ordinating committee dealing with questions "relating to the interpretation and execution of the Treaties."[18]

No less adamant was the American view that the future Conference of Ambassadors could not under any circumstances "become a continuation of the Supreme Council."[19] This point of view Polk never failed to impress upon his colleagues at meetings of the Supreme Council.[20] England first attempted to implement it in the Conference of Ambassadors after the entry of German troops into the neutral zone of the Rhineland, in March of 1920.[21]

During this minor crisis France attempted to use the Conference of Ambassadors as one more instrument in the furtherance of her policy of *sécurité* against a defeated Germany. She proposed that the Conference sanction counter measures against this blatant German violation of the Versailles Treaty. As President Alexander Millerand put the French case: "the Conference of Ambassadors charged with the interpretation of the Treaty and also charged with watching over its execution, is *ipso facto* qualified to examine all measures that may be

[17] American Mission (Polk) to the Acting Secretary of State (Phillips), October 25, 1919. *FRUS, PPC*, xi, p. 654.
[18] Minutes of the Meeting, November 10, 1919. *Ibid.*, ix, p. 76; *DBrFP*, ii, p. 261.
[19] Secretary of State (Lansing) to the American Mission (Polk), November 6 [8], 1919. *Ibid.*, xi, p. 660; *FRUS, 1919*, i, p. 19.
[20] Minutes of the Meeting, October 28, and December 5, 1919. *Ibid.*, viii, p. 786, and ix, p. 475.
[21] See Lord Derby's remarks at the Conference of Ambassadors' meeting on March 18, 1920. *DBrFP*, ix, p. 175.

The Conference of Ambassadors

necessary to ensure its execution."[22] None of his colleagues could agree with this interpretation, Ambassador Bonin Longare of Italy included.[23]

Millerand's interpretation of the powers of the Conference prompted Scialoja two days later in London to ask Lord Curzon somewhat caustically "on which side of the English Channel decisions could be taken." Within four years the Italian attitude towards the Conference was to be vastly different. The Foreign Secretary's retort was "that of the two bodies the one in Paris and the other in London, the latter was best qualified to reach decisions."[24] Annoyed at Millerand's highhanded interpretation, Curzon lost no time and that same evening informed Lord Derby in Paris, "you should resist this claim, which has no legitimate foundation, by every means in your power."[25] The following day Lord Curzon made it clear to his colleagues that "it might sometimes be difficult to distinguish between what were matters of detail and what were matters of principle," though in his mind, "there was no doubt that the conference in London dealt with the latter."[26] Time and the requirements of national policy, however, would (in the Corfu crisis as well as on other occasions) find the British Government twisting and turning like a pirouetting ballerina, in its attitude towards the Conference of Ambassadors.

[22] Minutes of the Meeting, March 20, 1920. *Ibid.*, p. 194.
[23] *Ibid.*, pp. 195-196.
[24] Minutes of the Meeting, Allied Representatives, March 22, 1920. *Ibid.*, VII, pp. 587-588. After the conclusion of the main session of the Paris Peace Conference on January 21, 1920, the Allied Representatives retired to London. At London, the sessions were divided on February 27, 1920 in much the same way that the sessions of the Paris Peace Conference had been split into the Council of Four and the Council of Five, or Council of Foreign Ministers. At London the main allied council sessions continued to sit at the Prime Minister's residence at 10 Downing Street. At the same time a complementary Conference of Foreign Ministers and Ambassadors met in Lord Curzon's room at Whitehall. This was what Curzon was referring to as "the other [body] in London."
[25] Lord Curzon to Lord Derby, March 22, 1920. *Ibid.*, IX, p. 223.
[26] Minutes of the Meeting, Allied Representatives, March 23, 1920. *Ibid.*, VII, p. 600.

The Conference of Ambassadors

THE CONFERENCE OF AMBASSADORS AS AN INSTITUTION

On December 13, 1919, the Conference of Ambassadors was formally established during a meeting at London on the basis of a draft resolution offered by Lloyd George with Clemenceau's concurrence. The resolution stipulated that after the termination of the Peace Conference "large questions of policy" were to be handled by direct contact between the governments themselves. On the other hand, "questions of detail" were to be handled by a "Conference of Ambassadors." Though Viscount Chinda of Japan acceded in behalf of his government, Scialoja of Italy and Ambassador John W. Davis of the United States merely accepted the resolution for transmission to their respective governments.[27]

Davis' act had already been determined by the action of the United States Senate which had rejected the Versailles Treaty in November. This prompted President Wilson to order withdrawal of all American representatives on any Commissions, the projected "Committee of Ambassadors" included.[28]

By January 7, 1920, Ambassador Hugh C. Wallace cabled Secretary of State Lansing that his attendance "would be of advantage should the United States ratify the treaty at an early date." He therefore requested instructions concerning his "part in the meeting of the so-called Committee of Ambassadors."[29] In response to this cable Lansing voiced no objections to Wallace's "attending unofficially and as an observer" on condition that his colleagues would offer no objection to his "attending the meeting in such capacity."[30] Hence, throughout the life span of the Conference of Ambassadors, the United

[27] Minutes of the Meeting, December 13, 1919. *FRUS, PPC*, IX, pp. 856-858; *DBrFP*, II, p. 778; Davis (London) to the Secretary of State, December 13, 1919. *FRUS, 1919*, I, p. 29.

[28] Secretary of State (Lansing) to the American Mission, November 27, 1919. *FRUS, 1919*, I, pp. 21, 22.

[29] Wallace (Paris) to the Secretary of State (Lansing), January 7, 1920. *Ibid.*, p. 32.

[30] Secretary of State (Lansing) to Wallace (Paris), January 9, 1920. *Ibid.*, p. 32.

The Conference of Ambassadors

States Ambassador found himself in the unique position of being "an intermittent observer."[31]

On January 21, 1920, the Council of Foreign Ministers decided to call into being the Conference of Ambassadors set up by the Supreme Council. Curzon pointed out, though, that the Conference was never intended to handle the projected Turkish Peace Treaty (Sèvres), which was a question reserved exclusively for the attention of the Supreme Council.[32] The Conference held its first meeting on January 26, 1920; it was to hold its last one eleven years later on March 30, 1931. During that period it was to have 327 sessions and to adopt 2,957 resolutions.[33] It sat at the Quai d'Orsay and was served by an experienced and skilled secretariat headed by a secretary-general,[34] who in his communications used a very formal stationery inscribed "Conference of Ambassadors—Office of the President."[35]

By international usage the representative of the host country presides over any international conference. Therefore the Conference was often chaired by the President of the French Republic, who was the de jure president of the Conference. Though he often took decisions as the representative of France, he also signed the notes and other materials as President of the Conference of Ambassadors. By custom, however, the French President was represented by someone else in the French delegation,[36] a situation that France used to great advantage during the Corfu crisis. Thus, Jules Cambon, the great diplomatist, acted in place of the French President as President of the Conference, while M. Jules Laroche, of the political section of the Quai d'Orsay, and other members of the French delegation represented the official French view.

[31] *FRUS, PPC*, XIII, p. 8.

[32] Minutes of the Meeting, January 21, 1920. *Ibid.*, IX, pp. 1005-1008; *DBrFP*, II, pp. 963-965; Wallace (Paris) to the Secretary of State (Lansing), January 31, 1920. *FRUS, 1919*, I, p. 35.

[33] *FRUS, PPC*, XIII, p. 8.

[34] The first two secretaries-general were Jules Cambon and René Massigli, both of whom figured prominently in the Corfu crisis. Pink, p. 18.

[35] Kellor and Hatvany, I, p. 89.   [36] Pink, p. 42.

The Conference of Ambassadors

In the matter of representation the only exception made was in the case of Belgium when the Conference on February 2, 1920, resolved that "on account of its special situation as a Power bordering upon Germany, and taking part in the occupation of the Rhineland, Belgium shall be qualified to participate in the deliberations of the Conference of Ambassadors upon all questions for which the Conference shall consider the presence of a Belgium Delegate *advisable*."[37]

The Conference was unique in a number of other respects. It had added assistance from both ad hoc and established organs. It received advice and reports from naval counselors of the four principal powers. It established a Technical Geographic Committee to help with delimitation and territorial questions. A Financial and Editing Committee and a Technical Committee on Railroads also rendered assistance to the Conference in their appointed fields. Lastly, the Conference collaborated with the Allied Military Committee of Versailles. This committee had been granted the power, by a decision of the Heads of Government on December 13, 1919, to deal exclusively with the military problems relating to the Treaty's execution.[38]

The Conference's actions were taken in four forms: (1) resolutions, which were decisions without appeal and which could be questioned only by the governments permanently represented in the Conference; (2) declarations, which were grave acts in that they engaged the general policy of the ex-Allied States; (3) protocols, which concerned questions dealing with the application of the treaties and were signed by the ambassadors and plenipotentiaries; (4) the *procès-verbaux* of the meetings of the Conference.[39] The last was to be used as a face saving device for Italy during the Corfu crisis.

---

[37] Italics added. As quoted in Catherine S. Kadragic, *International Delimitation of Albania, 1921-1925* (Unpublished Ph.D. dissertation, Columbia University, 1956), p. 7. The statement by Kellor and Hatvany, I, p. 89, that there were "no representatives of small states," in the Conference of Ambassadors is wrong, as the above clearly shows.

[38] *FRUS, PPC*, XIII, p. 8; Pink, pp. 125-161.

[39] *Ibid.*, p. 8.

The Conference of Ambassadors

As pointed out, the Conference of Ambassadors set up by the Supreme Council was not a totally novel feature in European diplomatic development. Prior to the First World War, conferences of ambassadors had been instituted many times.[40] These pre-World War One conferences of ambassadors differed in a number of ways from the Conference of Ambassadors established by the negotiations at Versailles. When established, these pre-World War One conferences "were given a definite task," which was "either narrow or wide." In contrast, the Conference of Ambassadors that sat at the Quai d'Orsay for eleven years entailed "a greater and more general task ... the execution of the Peace Treaties of 1919 and 1920," and, by cooperation with other institutions, the creation of a new Europe.[41]

The previous conferences had their "basis in a new agreement valid specifically for each conference";[42] therefore they were ad hoc arrangements. The only point of similarity between the earlier conferences and the Conference of Ambassadors was that they all adhered to the cardinal principle of European diplomacy, "the preponderance of the Great Powers."[43] For in practice conferences of ambassadors were nothing more than formalized meetings of the Great Powers in concert. The necessity to solve certain pressing issues, which could not be handled effectively either by ministerial meetings or bilateral negotiations and in which a consensus and agreement among the Great Powers had to be found, led to their development. They were convenient and, depending upon the problem to be solved, an absolutely indispensable method for negotiating and settling disputes that touched or threatened Great Power interests. In a sense, conferences of ambassadors were self-constituted high courts of political adjudication and appeal. Prior to the First World War, in an age dominated by traditional diplomacy with its intricate and delicate negotiations, they proved to be the perfect instruments for secret agreements and compromise. It would be no exaggeration to

[40] Pink, pp. 15-16.
[41] *Ibid.*, p. 16.
[42] *Ibid.*, p. 17.
[43] *Ibid.*, p. 17.

The Conference of Ambassadors

say that they contributed largely to safeguarding the peace of Europe before the outbreak of the First World War.

But, most important, the Conference of Ambassadors at the Quai d'Orsay was unique as compared to all previous ambassadorial conferences primarily in its organizational patterns. Its secretariat and the organizations that either cooperated with the Conference or emanated from it were arrangements which prior conferences had never enjoyed.

During its eleven years the Conference of Ambassadors attempted to be something more than a mere assemblage of representatives of the Great Powers sitting at the Quai d'Orsay for the express purpose of solving the technical questions that arose out of the peace treaties of the Paris Peace Conference.

The Conference negotiated with governments, sent out missions, and made agreements. Like the League of Nations, it was never officially considered to be a subject of international law,[44] but it often operated as a de facto if not a de jure subject of international law.

Throughout its existence the Conference had "a tendency to become an international organ where, if not all, at least many threads of European administration, legislation and the settlement of disputes would meet."[45] Certainly in the Corfu crisis

[44] In 1925, the League of Nations appeared before the Cour de Justice Civile in Geneva, claiming that it was "un organisme international . . . en vertu des principes généraux du droit public international et des dispositions du Pacte, des privilèges, et immunités, qui l'exemptent de la juridiction des tribunaux locaux." Schidlin v. Bureau International du Travail soit la Société des Nations, *La Semaine Judiciaire, Journal des Tribunaux*, 47, p. 250. For further discussion on this point see Guenter Weissberg, *The International Status of the United Nations* (New York: Oceana Publications, 1961), pp. 5-9. As to the confusion that arose when attempts were made to define and characterize the Conference of Ambassadors see Pink, pp. 19-23.

[45] Pink, pp. 18, 113. For a contrary view see F. P. Walters, *A History of the League of Nations* (London: Oxford University Press, 1960), pp. 244-245, who writes that merely because the Conference of Ambassadors was made up of representatives from a number of states this did not of itself entitle it to be termed international. The Conference of Ambassadors set up by the Great Powers to serve their interests, and responsible only to these powers, "had no shadow of claim to such a description."

The Conference of Ambassadors

and in the delimitation of the Albanian frontiers it acted in that manner. In the latter case, the competence of the Conference to delimit the Albanian frontiers was not based on the peace treaties, since Albania was not one of the contracting states, but on the ability of the Conference to successfully overstep its allotted fields of endeavor.

ESTABLISHMENT OF THE CONFERENCE'S COMMISSION OF DELIMITATION

The establishment of Albania after the Balkan Wars (1912-1913) left the delimitation of its borders as one of the unresolved issues facing the Great Powers when Europe went to war in 1914. The northern Albanian border had been established by the London Conference of Ambassadors.[46] Its delimitation commission ceased working December 12, 1913, with the arrival of winter.[47] The southern delimitation commission on the other hand, had by its "Protocol of Florence," of December 17, 1913, established a boundary line. This line ran in a general southwest-northeast direction from Ptelia, near Cape Stylos, to Lake Prespa, passing about 40 kilometers north of Janina.[48] The outbreak of war the following summer suspended the work of both commissions in their task of delimiting the border in loco.[49]

With the termination of hostilities, the Albanian Government on several occasions appealed to the Paris Peace Conference for a settlement of its boundaries,[50] but without success. Then on May 15, 1920, in the agreement of Kapishtica, the Albanian and Greek Governments promised "qu'elles se conformeront à la décision de la Conférence qui déterminera

[46] Protocol of London. *Permanent Court of International Justice*, Series C, Tome 11, No. 5, p. 265.

[47] Ernst C. Helmreich, *The Diplomacy of the Balkan Wars, 1912-1913* (Harvard Historical Studies, XLII; Cambridge: Harvard University Press, 1938), p. 429.

[48] *Permanent Court of International Justice*, Series C, Tome 11, No. 5, p. 266.

[49] Luigi Villari, *Italian Foreign Policy under Mussolini* (New York: Devin-Adair Co., 1956), p. 20.

[50] Pink, p. 107.

The Conference of Ambassadors

définitivement la ligne des frontières."[51] Unfortunately, the Allied Powers at Paris, harassed by more pressing problems, reached no decisions as to the frontiers.

A month after signing of the Kapishtica agreement, the French handed over to Albanian authorities the district of Koritsa. This area, which had been in French possession since 1916, was assigned to Albania by the London Conference of Ambassadors in 1913, though it was also claimed by Greece.

In August, a convention signed between Tirana and Rome led to an Italian evacuation of all areas held by Italy on the Albanian mainland. On Albania's northern and eastern borders, however, which had been drawn but not delimited in loco in 1913, Yugoslav troops occupied areas on the Albanian side of the 1913 line. In these areas disturbances persisted.[52]

With Albania's frontiers still unfixed and border disputes increasing, the British Government on June 6, 1921, after consultation with the French and Italian Governments, proposed in a memorandum to the Conference of Ambassadors that the latter fix the new frontiers of Albania.[53] In the debates that subsequently took place in the League Council on June 25, the extension of the Conference's competence was actively supported by Yugoslavia and Greece.

During this Council meeting called by Tirana, the Albanian delegate maintained that his country's frontiers, as established by the London Conference of Ambassadors in 1913, were still valid, and therefore requested that the Council dispatch a Commission of Inquiry to Albania. The Greek and Yugoslav representatives, however, contended that the London decisions of 1913 had been nullified by later events, and accordingly their frontiers with Albania had to be redefined. They felt that the institutions best qualified for this task were the Supreme Council of the Allies or its organ, the Conference of

[51] A. F. Frangulis, *Mémoire sur l'Albanie et l'Épire du Nord* (Athènes: Imprimerie Nationale, 1921), pp. 33-34.
[52] *Survey of International Affairs 1920-1923*, by Arnold J. Toynbee (London: Oxford University Press, 1925), p. 344.
[53] *Permanent Court of International Justice*, Series C, Tome 11, No. 5, p. 303.

The Conference of Ambassadors

Ambassadors sitting in Paris. The Council's decision was not to take action on the question of Albania's frontiers, since the Ambassadors' Conference had already taken up the question and was discussing it at that very moment. It merely recommended that the Conference come to a decision as quickly as possible.[54] Greece was sorely to regret this action, for it was "the first instance where the Council formally deferred to the Conference of Ambassadors concerning a matter before that body." Even more important, it established "the principle that whenever a controversy is under consideration by the Conference of Ambassadors it is inadvisable for the Council to act."[55]

The Albanian representative, however, refused to accept the Conference's competence and reserved the right to reopen the whole question at the next meeting of the League Assembly.

By August, Tirana was lodging a second protest with the Council against "alleged Jugoslav incursions" into northern Albania. This protest as well as the question of Albania's frontiers was referred by the Council to the League Assembly. The Assembly's final decision, on October 2, recommended that Albania accept the Conference of Ambassadors' decision, suggesting at the same time that the Council dispatch to Albania the Commission of Inquiry which Tirana had requested in June.

Rising tensions during October and November between Albania and Yugoslavia moved London, on November 7, to request the Secretary-General of the League, to convene a meeting of the Council "to consider [the] situation and to agree upon measures to be taken under Article 16 [of the Covenant] in the event of the Serb-Croat-Slovene Government refusing or delaying to execute their obligations under the Covenant."[56]

On November 9, two days after the dispatch of this message to the Secretary-General, the Conference of Ambassadors

---
[54] *Survey of International Affairs 1920-1923*, p. 344.
[55] Kellor and Hatvany, I, p. 196.
[56] *Survey of International Affairs 1920-1923*, pp. 344-345.

The Conference of Ambassadors

determined the Albanian frontiers on the basis of the lines laid down in 1913, and appointed a delimitation commission whose task was to mark out the boundary in loco.[57] This decision by the Conference to delimit the Albanian borders on the basis of the lines drawn up by the London agreements of 1913 and to appoint a delimitation commission to mark the border in loco was subsequently acceded to by Albania, Greece, and Yugoslavia. In the case of Yugoslavia, the Conference's decision was accepted only under protest and because of *force majeure*.[58]

The Conference's Commission of Delimitation after preliminary meetings at Paris and Florence arrived on the spot March 7, 1922. The approach of winter forced it to suspend operations on December 11, 1922, and it did not commence work again until May 1, 1923.[59] The relationship of the Commission and its Italian President, General Enrico Tellini, to the Greek Government and the Greek delegate attached to the Commission was extremely strained throughout.

The Greek delegate felt that General Tellini in particular was prejudiced against Greece and partial to the Albanian point of view.[60] This feeling was undoubtedly reinforced by the Ambassadorial Declaration of November 9, 1921, a declaration which gave to Italy a special position in Albania and stipulated "that any modification in the frontiers of Albania constitutes a danger for the strategic safety of Italy."[61]

As the Conference was preparing its reply to Greek accusations against its Commission and president, word arrived in Paris that General Tellini and other members of the Italian Mission attached to the Commission had been murdered at Kakavia near the Albanian-Greek frontier, but within Greek territory. The incident had occurred—the crisis was now to begin.

[57] L.N., *Official Journal*, 2nd year, 1921, p. 1195.
[58] *Survey of International Affairs 1920-1923*, p. 346.
[59] Vannutelli (Paris) to Mussolini, August 30, 1923. *DDI*, p. 141.
[60] Vannutelli (Paris) to Mussolini, August 30, 1923. *Ibid.*, pp. 140-141.
[61] L.N., *Treaty Series*, 12, No. 333, p. 382.

CHAPTER II

THE TELLINI MURDER

PRIOR GREEK WARNINGS

UPON his arrival in Albania, General Tellini proposed and the Conference of Ambassadors agreed that while he and the Italian delegates would delimit the Albanian-Greek frontier, the English and French delegates would supervise the delimitation of the Albanian-Yugoslav frontier.[1]

The area in which the Commission of Delimitation was working was renowned for rampant banditry. Because of the primitiveness of the region and the local passions, the power and authority of both the Greek and Albanian gendarmerie were limited. Anarchy and blood feuds were common to the area.[2]

As early as May 1921, the Greek press was complaining about the incursions of Albanian bands into Greek territory. At that time the instigation of the incursions was attributed to France, whose suspected support of the Kemalist forces in Anatolia did little to endear her to the heart of the Greeks.[3]

By August 16, 1923, bandit infiltration into Greek territory for "acts of robbery and plunder" had increased. In order "to avert serious consequences that would not fail to result from the frequent repetition of similar acts," the Greek Foreign Ministry, in a *note verbale*, invited the Albanian Legation in Athens "to intercede with its Government so that a vigorous supervision [of the border] may prevent in the future the formation and infiltration into Greek territory of armed bands of every kind."[4]

In its reply six days later the Albanian Legation complained

---

[1] Vannutelli (Paris) to Mussolini, August 30, 1923. *DDI*, p. 140.
[2] Margaret Hasluck, *The Unwritten Law in Albania*, ed. J. H. Hutton (Cambridge: The University Press, 1954), pp. 219-260.
[3] *Bulletin Périodique de la Presse Grecque*, No. 63, pp. 2-3.
[4] *DDDIG*, p. 5.

The Tellini Murder

that no specific details had been given in the Greek note as to the date, locality, and types of crime perpetrated on Greek territory by "the alleged Albanian bandits." It had, nevertheless, cabled its Government requesting it "to proceed towards an active inquiry." In conclusion, the legation expressed the belief that "mutual interest" imposed on both countries the obligation to do everything possible "not only to redress errors," but also to prevent any acts which might foster difficulties in the relations between the two nations.[5]

The immediate Greek reply, on August 23, enumerated four specific Albanian bands which according to the local Greek authorities were operating in the Epirus area. Prophetically, it cautioned the Albanian Legation against "the grievous consequences that could result, if severe measures of the Albanian Government do not put an end to these outrages."[6]

In the meantime, in Epirus itself, the Governor General, aware of the danger from brigands, advised the Italian Consul not to depart without escort for Santi Quaranta (Sarandë), where he intended to embark for Brindisi.[7] Moreover, on August 27, the Greek Foreign Ministry presented to the Albanian Legation an even more detailed note describing the composition and the operations of these bands. It complained that the raids had intensified "in spite of repeated protests by the Greek Government." According to the Greek Government, the operations of these bands were "tolerated by certain subordinate Albanian agencies." As on the earlier occasion the legation was invited "to intercede with its Government for the cessation of these unfriendly intrigues, which are likely to have the most serious repercussions in the good neighborly relations between the two countries."[8]

That same day, while these exchanges were taking place, General Tellini and his staff were murdered.

---

[5] *Ibid.*, pp. 5-6.

[6] *Ibid.*, p. 6.

[7] Report of the Inter-Allied Control Commission in Epirus, September 30, 1923. George Glasgow, *The Janina Murders and the Occupation of Corfu* (London: The Anglo-Hellenic League, 1923), p. 19.

[8] *DDDIG*, p. 7.

The Tellini Murder

THE MURDER AND SUBSEQUENT INVESTIGATIONS

Three days before this exchange of notes, Tellini had informed the Greek and Albanian delegations that on August 27 a reconnaissance would take place in the Drin Valley. He had designated the Greek frontier post of Kakavia and 9 o'clock in the morning as the place and time of rendezvous. The Greek delegate, Colonel Dimitrios Botzaris, in preparing for the reconnaissance, ordered the Greek topographic and liaison officers to meet him on the appointed day at 8 A.M. at Kakavia. He also requested that horses be sent to Kakavia because of the nature of the terrain to be surveyed.[9] The movement of these horses was later interpreted as the "first sign" the assassins had as to "the next passage of the Commissions."[10]

On the appointed morning of August 27, at 5:30 A.M., the Albanian delegation led the departure from Janina for Kakavia. The Greek delegation, composed of Colonel Botzaris and Captain Tsinganos, followed at about 6:00 A.M. Last came the Italians—General Tellini; Major Corti, the delegation's physician; Lt. Mario Bonaccini, Tellini's aide-de-camp; the chauffeur, Farnetti Remizio; and the Albanian interpreter, Thanassi Ghèziri, an Epirote of Leskovik. A significant reversal of this original formation occurred shortly after departure. It did not go unnoticed in subsequent comments by the Greek press.

About 45 minutes after leaving Janina, Colonel Botzaris' Ford had a motor failure somewhere between the 16th and 17th kilometer markers. A few minutes passed before the Lancia bearing the Italian delegation appeared. Seeing the Greek auto disabled, General Tellini dispatched his aide-de-camp, Lt. Bonaccini, to ask Colonel Botzaris if he required any assistance. Assurances by the Colonel's chauffeur that he could manage alone plus Tellini's belief that there was no need

[9] Colonel Botzaris' Report, September 5, 1923. Pierre Lasturel, *L'Affaire Gréco-Italienne de 1923* (Paris: L'Ile de France, 1925), pp. 42-43.
[10] Captain de Limperany's Report, Secretary of the Delimitation Commission to the Conference of Ambassadors, August 30, 1923. *Ibid.*, p. 48.

The Tellini Murder

to stop prompted the Italian delegation to continue the journey.[11]

The Italian auto thus moved into second position with the Greeks now in the rear. Colonel Botzaris was obliged to wait while the needed repairs were made, and, though the nephew of the Archbishop of Janina appeared on the scene, it proved impossible to switch vehicles.[12]

With the repairs completed the journey was again commenced but now at top speed to make up for lost time. Arriving at Kalpaki, at the 34 kilometer marker, Colonel Botzaris telephoned ahead to the commandant of the military post of Kakavia. He requested that the other delegations be informed that he would be delayed. He also recommended that the Italian and Albanian delegations begin with the reconnaissance of the area with the Greek officers, Captain Lambropoulos, a topographer and Captain Spyropoulos. The latter, who had been detached from the 5th Army Corps as a liaison officer, would replace him provisionally. Botzaris' only request was that horses and a guide be left so that he could join the other delegations quickly upon his arrival at Kakavia.[13]

Continuing his journey Colonel Botzaris at about 10:00 A.M. arrived at a spot called Zepi, lying between kilometer markers 53 and 54 on the Janina-Kakavia road. This was a point where the road turned and crossed a very thick woods. There, he found himself, as he subsequently wrote, "devant un spectacle

---

[11] Testimony of Colonel Botzaris to the Inter-Allied Commission of Control. See, Γρηγόριος Δαφνῆς, Ἡ Ἑλλάς μεταξύ δύο Πολέμων 1923-1940 ('Αθῆναι: Ἴκαρος, 1955) [Grigorios Dafnis, *Greece between Two Wars 1923-1940* (Athens: Ikaros, 1955)], I, p. 86. Colonel Botzaris' Report, September 5, 1923. Lasturel, p. 43. The Report of the Commandant of the Gendarmerie of Epirus, Colonel Platis, to the Minister of the Interior, September 22, 1923, is somewhat incorrect as to what time the delegations left Janina. *DDDIG*, p. 111. A statement by the Albanian Legation in Rome on August 29, 1923, that in order of departure the "Albanian mission went first followed by the Italian mission, the Greek mission being last," is factually incorrect. *The Times* (London), August 31, 1923, p. 8.

[12] Colonel Botzaris' Report, September 5, 1923. Lasturel, p. 43.

[13] Colonel Botzaris' Report, September 5, 1923. *Ibid.*, pp. 43-44; Colonel Platis' Report, September 22, 1923. *DDDIG*, p. 111.

The Tellini Murder

tragique." General Tellini, Major Corti, Lt. Bonaccini, the chauffeur Remizio, and the interpreter Ghèziri had all been slain.[14]

After the passage of the Albanian auto in the vanguard, the assassins had skillfully barred the way by placing several large tree branches at a turn in the road where maneuver was difficult. Thus the Italian Lancia had been forced to either slow up or stop. This clearly showed that the ambush had been "cleverly prepared."[15]

Realizing the enormity of the crime, Botzaris immediately retraced his steps to Han Delvinaki, about five kilometers down the road, where a battalion of the 5th Army Corps was encamped. Orders were immediately given to pursue the culprits. All frontier posts were alerted. A request was transmitted to the authorities at Janina to detain all passengers and drivers of automobiles coming from Argyrocastro in Albania. Finally, in an action later criticized by the Inter-Allied Commission of Inquiry, the Albanian delegation was requested to remain at Kakavia though no reason for this request was given.[16] The Albanians were not given the facts until the

[14] Colonel Botzaris' Report, September 5, 1923. Lasturel, pp. 44-45.
[15] Captain de Limperany's Report, August 30, 1923. *Ibid.*, p. 48.
[16] Colonel Platis' Report, September 22, 1923. *DDDIG*, p. 111; Colonel Botzaris' Report, September 5, 1923. Lasturel, p. 45.

The Inter-Allied Commission of Inquiry in its second report felt that the attempt by Colonel Botzaris to conceal the crime from the Albanians was unfortunate. Since Kakavia was only 40 km. from Argyrocastro and 10 km. from Zepi, the scene of the crime, if the Albanians had been promptly informed they could have taken "immediate measures" by telephoning the Albanian police authorities in Argyrocastro. Therefore, action on both sides of the border and "the network of vigilance thus constituted and reinforced would have led to the discovery of the culprits, who would have had less chance of escaping pursuit."

The British delegate, Major Harenc, felt however that Colonel Botzaris' action was taken "lest the inhabitants of the Albanian villages near the frontier, in which he perhaps knew there were some of the accomplices of the crime, might take steps to conceal the authors of the assassination and prevent their detection." Harenc based this observation on personal experience in Asia Minor. Glasgow, p. 21.

In his report written well before the Inter-Allied Commission of Inquiry arrived in Epirus and about a week after the murder, Botzaris stated that he informed the Albanian delegation "not to depart from

The Tellini Murder

following morning, August 28. By 11:00 A.M. Botzaris had returned to the scene of the crime at Zepi. Precautions were taken to see that no one disturbed the bodies or other evidence until the arrival of the proper officials from Janina, who would examine the evidence and search the surrounding area.[17]

These precautions the Inter-Allied Commission of Inquiry subsequently criticized as being "not precise enough." For by the evening of the 27th "the branches [which the assassins had used to bar the road] had disappeared and were burnt by the soldiers of the neighboring Greek posts, although there was no shortage of fuel in the brushwood surrounding the post itself." The branches, if saved, might have provided fingerprints which would have been extremely valuable at any subsequent trial.[18]

Botzaris now hastened to inform the other local authorities and the government in Athens of what had occurred.[19] The immediate and frantic reply of the latter was an appeal that the

---

there [Kakavia], because I do not know the extent and the objectives of the criminal *mise en scène*." Colonel Botzaris' Report, September 5, 1923. Lasturel, p. 45.

The Commission also felt that, though orders were given in time by the Greek authorities for alerting the frontier posts and pursuing the assassins, these same authorities did not "appear to have assured themselves personally of the execution of the orders given by themselves or by their subordinates." Content with merely verbal reports, the Greek authorities therefore were later "unable to give the Commission an emphatic assurance that the steps taken by the commandants of the detachments, to pursue the culprits were adequate to the situation."

On the other hand, the Commission felt it was "perhaps proper to see above all in this negligence a defect in the training of the Greek army." Second Report of the Inter-Allied Control Commission, September 30, 1923. Glasgow, p. 22. In her pro-Fascist and pedestrian account, Muriel Currey, *Italian Foreign Policy, 1918-1932* (London: I. Nicholson and Watson, Ltd., 1932), p. 103, states that when the Greek car reached the scene of the tragedy, "there was . . . by that time no trace of the murderers, nor was proof ever produced that any serious effort was made to discover them." This is false, as the above clearly shows. Other details about the Tellini murder recounted by Currey are factually wrong.

[17] Colonel Botzaris' Report, September 5, 1923. Lasturel, pp. 45-46.
[18] Second Report of the Inter-Allied Control Commission, September 30, 1923. Glasgow, p. 20.
[19] *DDDIG*, p. 8.

The Tellini Murder

local authorities "take the most energetic ... [and] exceptional measures for the discovery and arrest of the authors of the odious crime."[20]

The commander of the gendarmerie for all of Greece, Colonel Demosthene Florias, and numerous other legal, police, and medical officials on orders from the Minister of the Interior left Athens for Janina by destroyer to assist in the investigation and pursuit of the assassins.[21] The destroyer undoubtedly was used as a quicker means of transportation because of the poor roads that existed at that time between Athens and Janina.

In Janina by 1:30 P.M., through army authorities, the commander of the gendarmerie of Epirus, Colonel Platis, was informed of what had occurred. He hurried to convey the ghastly news to the Governor General and the Procureur of Janina, Mr. Exarchopoulos. The first Italian official to learn of what had transpired was Mr. Andrea Liverani, the secretary of the Italian Consulate, who was informed by Colonel Platis on instructions from the Governor General. Within two hours Colonel Platis, Liverani, the Procureur of Janina, the Examining Magistrate, Mr. Constantinidis, and several physicians and other personnel departed for Zepi, where they arrived by 6:30 P.M.[22] At this time the preliminary examination began.

The examination conducted immediately established that none of the victims' valuables had been removed. Thus theft was ruled out as the motive for the crime. As Colonel Platis wrote subsequently, he found himself faced by "un crime politique."[23] All investigators agreed to this.[24]

---

[20] *Ibid.*, p. 9.

[21] Report of Colonel Florias to the Minister of the Interior, October 14, 1923. *Ibid.*, p. 109; *The Times* (London), August 30, 1923, p. 8.

[22] Colonel Platis' Report, September 22, 1923. *Ibid.*, p. 112. Captain de Limperany in his report to the Conference of Ambassadors on August 30 felt that the authorities in Janina had organized too slowly. If one takes into consideration the details that first had to be ironed out before the competent officials could leave, two hours does not appear excessive. Lasturel, p. 49.

[23] Colonel Platis' Report, August 22, 1923. *DDDIG*, p. 117.

[24] Captain de Limperany's Report, August 29, 1923. Lasturel, p. 47;

The Tellini Murder

Captain de Limperany stated to the Conference of Ambassadors, on August 30, that the object of the crime was to stop the work of the Commission. His feeling that the action "was aimed in particular against the Italian delegation" was never substantiated. Subsequent events cast doubts on its validity.[25]

An examination of the surrounding area by Colonel Platis and his assistants revealed footprints and cartridge cases from German repeating rifles. A trail and footprints stretching from the scene of the crime towards the Albanian border were followed and lost in the dense forest. In Colonel Platis' opinion the assassins numbered about eight or nine and had used this same trail not only to flee the murder scene but also to approach it.[26] It was the feeling of all high Greek police officials that the assassins had sought refuge in Albanian territory, which was only three-quarters of an hour away.[27]

An exhaustive investigation on August 28 and 29 failed to yield further evidence.[28] On August 30, Colonel Florias and other officials dispatched from Athens by destroyer arrived on the spot and the investigation was intensified. On Florias' recommendation,[29] the government offered a reward of one million drachmas for information leading to the discovery of the culprits.[30] His conduct of the investigation produced, by September 2, two shepherds, eyewitnesses to the crime, who furnished valuable testimony.[31]

Simultaneously, interrogation of innumerable individuals by the Examining Magistrate, Mr. Constantinidis, and the Procureur of Janina, Mr. Exarchopoulos, uncovered other wit-

---

First Report of the Inter-Allied Control Commission, September 22, 1923. *Ibid.*, p. 146; Second Report of the Inter-Allied Control Commission, September 30, 1923. Glasgow, p. 18.

[25] Captain de Limperany's Report, August 30, 1923. Lasturel, p. 49.
[26] Colonel Platis' Report, September 22, 1923. *DDDIG*, pp. 113-114.
[27] Colonel Platis' Report, September 22, 1923. *Ibid.*, p. 114; Colonel Florias' Report, October 4, 1923. *Ibid.*, p. 110.
[28] Colonel Platis' Report, September 22, 1923. *Ibid.*, pp. 114-115.
[29] Colonel Florias' Report, October 4, 1923. *Ibid.*, p. 109.
[30] *The Times* (London), September 5, 1923, p. 10.
[31] Colonel Florias' Report, October 4, 1923, *DDDIG*, p. 110; *The Times* (London), September 5, 1923, p. 10 and September 6, 1923, p. 10.

The Tellini Murder

nesses to the crime who supplied additional information.[32] Based on a long investigation and forwarded to the Inter-Allied Commission of Inquiry, their final report, on September 27, alleged "that the crime had been hatched at Argyrocastro [Albania] and executed by assassins at the instigation of Albanian individuals and eventually by Albanian authorities."[33]

Somewhat similar charges were echoed by Colonel Platis, who was convinced "that the murder had been committed by an Albanian band," and that the only problem was to determine "the names of the members and the chief of the band in question."[34] Subsequently these charges were denied by the Albanian Government in its official Red Book.[35] To this

[32] *DDDIG*, pp. 117-121. The fact that the members of the Albanian delegation of the Delimitation Commission were never questioned by the Examining Magistrate was criticized in the second report of the Inter-Allied Control Commission, September 30, 1923. Glasgow, p. 20.

[33] *DDDIG*, p. 122.

[34] Colonel Platis' Report, September 22, 1923. *Ibid.*, p. 117. The Greek theory that the assassins could be Albanians was first reported to Mussolini by the Italian Minister in Athens, Montagna, on August 30. His closing comment to the Duce was that it would be desirable for Albania to cooperate in the investigation and possible capture of the assassins since they could have "taken refuge on Albanian territory." Montagna (Athens) to Mussolini, August 30, 1923. *DDI*, p. 138. This report from Athens to the Duce brought to the attention of the Italian Minister, Carlo Durazzo, in Durazzo. Mussolini to Durazzo (Durazzo), August 31, 1923. *Ibid.*, p. 147. Almost simultaneously another cable to Mussolini from the Italian chargé d'affaires in Paris quoted an offer by his Albanian colleague to assist in proving the political character of the Tellini murder. Vannutelli (Paris) to Mussolini, August 29, 1923. *Ibid.*, footnote, p. 147. Mussolini instructed Vannutelli to accept the Albanian offer. Mussolini to Vannutelli (Paris), August 31, 1923. *Ibid.*, p. 147. Unfortunately none of the above cables appears to have affected Mussolini in the actions that he had already instituted vis-à-vis Greece.

[35] État Albanais, Bureau de la Presse, *Deux Documents sur la crime de Janina* (Tirana, 1923); Text. Lasturel, pp. 116-132. The publication of the Red Book by the Albanian Government contained, according to the Greek Foreign Ministry, "insults against the Greek people and Greek Army to which it [the Red Book] attributed the crime." When the request that the Albanian Government "disapprove [the Red Book] . . . and . . . punish the director of the Press Bureau" brought an unsatisfactory reply, the Greek Minister, Mr. Naos Panourias, informed the Albanian Government that on orders from his government he

The Tellini Murder

day the name and the nationality of the assassins of General Tellini and his staff have never been ascertained.

THEORIES ON TELLINI'S MURDER

Most discussions or analyses of Tellini's murder revolve around the theory that it was an act motivated by political considerations. Some, for example, felt that the murder of General Tellini was instigated by Mussolini because of the general's alleged anti-Fascist inclinations and his dislike of the Duce. This theory, however, cannot be substantiated by any documentary evidence.[36] Indeed, it appears that the Tellini murder was as great a shock to Mussolini as it was to others. Of course, one can make analogies and point to the subsequent murder in May of 1924 of the deputy Giacomo Matteotti, leader of the reform Socialists, as an indication of how far the Duce was willing to go. Though it cannot be denied that an assassination, like that of Matteotti, was a perfectly acceptable *modus operandi* for Mussolini and the Fascists, is the analogy really valid? In the Tellini case Mussolini and the Fascists would always have had to consider the army's reaction if they were discovered or implicated in the murder. Would not the risks have been too great for them in 1923? Discovery by the army that Tellini, who was a respected war hero, had been assassinated under Fascist instigation would have been too serious a risk to run so early in the Fascist regime. Certainly, during this period the army was more than capable of overthrowing

---

would leave though it was not to be interpreted as a break in relations. *Le Messager d'Athènes*, December 13, 1923, p. 4. The "resignation" of the director of the Press Bureau (*ibid.*, December 14, 1923, p. 4) and the issuance of a *démenti* by the Albanian Government (Text. *Ibid.*, December 17, 1923, p. 4) caused the Greek Government to reverse its actions and brought the incident to a close. Atherton (Athens) to the Department of State, December 27, 1923. File 765.68/132, Record Group 59, NA.

[36] Δαφνῆς [Dafnis], pp. 105-109. The publication of the interwar Italian Diplomatic Documents has produced no evidence to support this theory. Since the publication of Italian interwar archives was motivated by a number of considerations including embarrassment to the Fascist and right wing parties in Italy, the existence of such material would probably have been published.

The Tellini Murder

the Duce, who had been in power only ten short months and was still attempting to consolidate his position in Italy. By 1924, however, things were somewhat different, and though the assassination of Matteotti caused an uproar it came to naught, for the reform Socialists were not the Italian Army, and liquidation of a deputy, though a reprehensible act, was not as risky a business as being implicated in the liquidation of a respected general. Yet in 1923, as Count Carlo Sforza relates, "not a few people in Italy ended by believing in the hypothesis that Mussolini himself had organized the massacre which gave him the opportunity for a brilliant exploit."[37]

If one accepts the theory that the murder was committed for political motives, and all investigators came to this conclusion, can it be assumed that the accidental breakdown of Colonel Botzaris' vehicle and the resultant reversal of positions, with Colonel Botzaris bringing up the rear rather than General Tellini, subjected Tellini to an ambush originally prepared for Botzaris?[38]

If it is assumed that it was really Botzaris who was the intended victim rather than Tellini, the motive could have been an Albanian desire to remove from the scene the one individual whose constant objections and obstructionist tactics were felt by certain persons to be harmful to their interests and to those of Albania.

This assumption appears plausible if one keeps in mind that several months later on December 17, 1923, a similar but unsuccessful attempt was made on Colonel Botzaris' life.[39] Botzaris, "not possessing any tangible proof," refused to accept the theory that the intended ambush had been organized by an Albanian band.[40] The Albanian Government similarly

[37] Count Carlo Sforza, *Contemporary Italy*, trans. by Drake and Denise De Kay (New York: E. P. Dutton and Co., 1944), p. 349; Count Carlo Sforza, *L'Italia dal 1914 al 1944* (Rome: Mondadori, 1946), p. 177.

[38] Lasturel, pp. 172-173. See the comments of the Greek press. *Bulletin Périodique de la Presse Grecque*, No. 79, p. 3.

[39] *Le Messager d'Athènes*, December 17, 1923, p. 4.

[40] *Ibid.*, December 28, 1923, p. 4.

The Tellini Murder

denied this theory,[41] and Botzaris was also unwilling to believe that the unsuccessful ambush was "a new edition of the crime of Kakavia."[42]

If Tellini had been the intended victim it is unlikely that he would have been attacked by Albanians under orders from Tirana, who, if discovered, had everything to lose by such an act. This is especially true if the Greek charge that Tellini was partial to the Albanians was correct, a charge that cannot be lightly dismissed. Indeed, it was in Albanian interests to have Tellini live, for Italy was Albania's main supporter against Greek and Yugoslav territorial ambitions. On the other hand, there are some Greeks who argue that the Tellini attackers were Albanians who had a grudge against Tellini from the time he had served with the Italian forces in Valona and who hoped that the murder would strain Italo-Greek relations so that Albania would profit by acquiring even greater Italian support for her struggle against the Greeks. What role, however, was or was not played by the Albanian Government or private individuals must await examination of materials in Tirana, though undoubtedly these materials will not be accessible for some time to come.

Certainly in Athens the murder of General Tellini and his staff was received with genuine shock. It cannot be doubted after an examination of their archives that the Greeks felt that the murder was a disaster and that the culprits had to be captured regardless of their nationality. If the crime was committed by Greeks it was done without the knowledge or consent of the Greek Government. It is conceivable that the attack against Tellini, regardless of his partiality, could have been an act of revenge by Greeks resident in Albania whose villages were included in Albanian territory by Tellini's demarcation of the border. This possibility was admitted by the Greek Foreign Minister in a conversation with the French chargé d'affaires.[43] But again, no concrete evidence to substantiate this supposition exists.

[41] *Ibid.*, December 22, 1923, p. 4.
[42] *Ibid.*, December 18, 1923, p. 4.   [43] *Infra*, Chapter IV.

The Tellini Murder

There is of course one last possibility: that the Tellini murder had no political basis and that the attackers "were a group of bandits in close proximity to the imperfectly defined frontier."[44] Though the evidence seems to make this theory unlikely and all observers dismissed it at the time, it warrants examination. The area was in semi-anarchy. Robbery, ambush, and violence were common events. Therefore it is quite possible that the murder of Tellini and his staff was motivated by robbery, and the realization that important personages had been killed and that it would be incriminating to possess their valuables may explain the murderers' sudden flight into the woods leaving behind the personal belongings and valuables of the men they had slain.

Even after four decades the two important questions of who murdered Tellini and why remain unanswered. Archival materials will probably never yield this secret. Assassination, by its very nature, is an odious crime in which the desire of planners and assassins alike is not to leave to posterity a record of their deed. Instead, verbal agreements and communications are used which leave no record and make the task of subsequent researchers almost impossible. Thus any attempt to make a judgment about the identity of the assassins or the reasons for the deed would be purely speculative in nature. It would tend to arouse passions and antagonisms in an area that can well do without them.

Even in late August of 1923, the identity and nationality of the assassins proved to be of no importance. Of primary importance were the reactions that news of the crime produced in Rome and in the Italian Legation at Athens, and the reverberations of what followed—Mussolini's occupation of Corfu on August 31, 1923.

[44] Kenneth Edwards, *The Grey Diplomatists* (London: Rich and Cowan, Ltd., 1938), p. 83.

CHAPTER III

THE ITALIAN ULTIMATUM

MUSSOLINI'S REACTION TO THE TELLINI MURDER

WORD of what had happened to the Tellini Mission first reached Mussolini via the secretary of the Italian Consulate at Janina, Andrea Liverani, whose telegram arrived in Rome at 6:15 on the evening of August 27.[1] Almost simultaneously another cable was dispatched by Captain de Limperany, secretary of the Commission of Delimitation, to the Conference of Ambassadors in Paris to inform them of the tragic news.[2] The events that were now to move with such breath-taking speed were to be centered in three cities, Rome, London, and Paris. Throughout the first days the advantage of initiative was to be in the hands of Rome, while the latter two capitals would be saddled with the unappetizing role of merely reacting to actions already instituted in Rome.

Mussolini's reaction at the arrival of the tragic news from Janina was "immediately violent, intransigeant," according to an eyewitness, the chief of the Near Eastern Division of the Foreign Ministry.[3] His cable in the early morning hours of August 28 to the Italian Minister in Athens, Giulio Cesare Montagna, is revealing. The Duce felt that "immediate and ex-

[1] Liverani (Janina) to Mussolini, repeated to Athens, August 27, 1923. *DDI*, p. 125. On November 16, 1923, in a speech before the Italian Senate, Mussolini stated that due to a delay in communications he did not receive word of the Tellini murder until the evening of August 28. What prompted him to alter the date on which he had received word of the murder is unexplainable. *Scritti e Discorsi di Benito Mussolini* (Milano: Ulrico Hoepli, 1934), III, p. 266.

[2] Captain de Limperany (Janina) to the Conference of Ambassadors, August 27, 1923. Attached to file 768.7515/54, Record Group 59, NA.

[3] Raffaele Guariglia, *Ricordi 1922-1946* (Napoli: Scientifiche Italiane, 1950), p. 28.

The Italian Ultimatum

emplary punishment of the culprits is indispensable because of the deep horror which will be aroused in Italy and abroad" that Italian officers, part of an international commission on a peaceful mission entrusted to them by the Great Powers, had been brutally murdered. Therefore, he instructed Montagna to make "the most energetic protest" to the Greek Government. At the same time Montagna was to reserve the right to reparations which would be due to Italy and which would be claimed after all the facts had been ascertained in detail.[4]

Concurrent with this cable to Montagna another was sent to the Italian Embassies in Paris and London stating, "that which has happened notwithstanding lack of injury to other delegations represents an affront against the prestige of the Allied Powers." Mussolini thus urgently requested that they convey the terrible news to the governments to which they were accredited. In closing, he stressed his reliance on the solidarity of both England and France. He urged that both Italian missions convince their respective host nations to instruct quickly their legations in Athens "to join with the forcefulness dictated by the gravity of the event" in the steps that would be undertaken by the Italian Legation.[5]

Although Mussolini was undoubtedly excited there is nothing in the substance of the above telegrams that warrants criticism. The instructions issued to Montagna in Athens were of a type that would have been issued by any government in a similar situation. Similarly, the cable to the Italian missions in Paris and London was in no way out of the ordinary. On the contrary, the second cable was a request for Great Power solidarity regarding what the Duce considered to be an "affront against the prestige" of the Great Powers. The crucial question, however, was what subsequent steps Rome would instruct its legation in Athens to take. The reports of the Italian Minister in Athens were to trigger these instructions.

[4] Mussolini to Montagna (Athens), August 28, 1923. *DDI*, p. 127.
[5] Mussolini to Della Torretta (London) and Vannutelli (Paris), August 28, 1923. *Ibid.*, p. 127.

The Italian Ultimatum

MONTAGNA'S ATTITUDE

If it is a cardinal principle of diplomatic practice that one should always be as precise as possible, eschewing all personal animosities towards the host government, it should be noted that the Italian Minister in Athens did not follow this most important rule.

Minister Montagna had first arrived in Athens in 1919. During the period 1922-1923 he also served as Italian delegate at the Lausanne Conference. Here the Allied Powers and the Kemalists negotiated the treaty that brought peace to the eastern Mediterranean and an end to Greek dreams of expansion into Asia Minor. His dislike for the Greek Revolutionary Government, then in office and unrecognized by the Powers, was quite apparent at the Conference.[6]

A proposal was made by the Italian chargé d'affaires in Athens, De Facendis, to take a new tack in Greece.[7] Since the proposal involved a rapprochement with the revolutionary government Montagna declared it useless. It was of no value for Italy to trouble herself with the "ill-humor of men who today govern Greece against the will of the country," he cabled Mussolini.[8]

In Athens, Montagna's attitude toward the Greek Government was an open secret that did not go unreported by his diplomatic colleagues. The American Minister, Ray Atherton, cabled the Department of State on September 2, after the occupation of Corfu: "There is every probability of growing unconfirmed [reports or rumors?] that Italy's precipitant action had

---

[6] After the defeat of the Greek Army in Anatolia in August and September 1922 a group of young army officers led by Colonels Nikolaos Plastiras and Stylianos Gonatas overthrew the government. A Commission of Inquiry was appointed by the Revolutionary Committee to fix the blame for the Anatolian debacle. The arrest, trial, conviction, and execution of three ex-Premiers, two ex-Ministers, and the former Commander-in-Chief caused a painful impression throughout Europe.

[7] De Facendis (Athens) to Mussolini, repeated to Lausanne, June 28, 1923. *DDI*, p. 67. Montagna's opinion was asked for by the Secretary-General of the Foreign Ministry. Contarini to Montagna (Lausanne), June 30, 1923. *Ibid.*, p. 69.

[8] Montagna (Ouchy) to Mussolini, July 2, 1923. *Ibid.*, p. 70.

The Italian Ultimatum

been based throughout on the reports of Montagna to his government colored by his personal antagonism toward present day Greece."[9] Atherton noted that a similar view had been voiced by the British chargé d'affaires, Sir Charles Bentinck, who was inclined "to believe that [the] extreme antagonism of Montagna toward present Greek authorities has led him to overstress his reports to [the] Italian Government. . . . [Bentinck] has advised London accordingly."[10] If one keeps all of the above in mind, the contents of the cables that Montagna was now to send to Mussolini and which were to affect his thoughts so deeply become explainable and make the reactions and the events that are to follow more understandable.[11]

---

[9] Atherton (Athens) to the Department of State, September 2, 1923. File 765.68/21, Record Group 59, NA.

[10] Atherton (Athens) to the Department of State, September 2, 1923. File 765.68/22, Record Group 59, NA.

[11] On September 1, after the Corfu occupation, the attention of the Greek Foreign Ministry, much to Montagna's embarrassment, was drawn to the Greek press. Montagna claimed that the Greek press was inciting public opinion against him and accusing him of being primarily "responsible for the hostile attitude of Italy against Greece." Montagna (Athens) to Mussolini, September 1, 1923. *DDI*, p. 151. Montagna's relationship with the Greek press left a great deal to be desired. As early as May, during the Lausanne Conference, he had protested to Eleutherios Venizelos about the attacks of the Greek press directed against his "person for the action that I display [at] Lausanne as Italian delegate." Montagna felt that they had been inspired by the Greek delegation. Venizelos deplored the attacks and gave assurances that he would contact Athens in order to have the attacks cease. Montagna (Lausanne) to Mussolini, May 19, 1923. *Ibid.*, p. 32.

In his dispatches Montagna made no attempt to disguise his feelings toward the Greek Government. It was a government, he cabled Mussolini on September 3, whose "yoke [is] stained with the blood of their tyranny." Montagna (Athens) to Mussolini, September 3, 1923. *Ibid.*, p. 168. On the other hand, Montagna's "over-excited condition" did not go unnoticed by the Yugoslav Minister who emphasized it to his American colleagues on the same day that Montagna was filing the above cable to Rome. Atherton (Athens) to the Department of State, September 3, 1923. File 765.68/22, Record Group 59, NA.

The mistrust of the Greek Foreign Ministry toward Montagna increased to such an extent during the crisis that rather than deal with him directly (as when it wished to inform him that the Greek fleet had been ordered to retire from the Athens area in order to avoid any possible conflict between Italian and Greek naval units) it had the

The Italian Ultimatum

MONTAGNA'S COMMUNICATIONS AND MUSSOLINI'S REACTION

Montagna's first cable reached Rome at 2:00 A.M. on August 28, half an hour after Mussolini's first cables had already been transmitted. Its relationship to the events that were to follow is witnessed by the fact that the Duce was to cite this very cable to the Italian Embassies in London and Paris when his demands to Greece were brought to their attention.[12]

The cable was essentially a description of a visit by an official of the Greek Ministry of Foreign Affairs who presented himself at the legation to inform Montagna of the Tellini murder and "to express the grief of the Greek Government." Rather than seeing the official personally, which would perhaps have been in order, Montagna delegated the task to a subordinate member of his staff. The official attempted "to minimize the gravity of the crime [by] insinuating that the murder . . . [had] been committed near the frontier and perhaps by brigands"—a reasonable interpretation if one keeps in mind

---

news conveyed to him through the British and French chargés d'affaires. This procedure, Montagna declared to them, he found "strange and incomprehensible" since the Greek Government could have contacted him by normal diplomatic means. He added that if normal channels were not used he would consider that the news had never been delivered. Both chargés d'affaires agreed, and after they informed the Foreign Ministry an official was appointed to communicate the news directly to Montagna. Montagna cabled the Duce that the whole episode was an attempt to "craftily establish intervention by third parties in our affairs" by giving an "impression about relations with the Royal [Italian] Legation different from reality and . . . [attempting] to ignore the existence of the Royal [Italian] Representative." Montagna (Athens) to Mussolini, September 6, 1923. *DDI*, p. 191.

Montagna's relations with the Greek Government during this period deteriorated a great deal. As the chief of the Press Section of the Greek Foreign Ministry made it clear, the Greek Government "would be prepared to deal directly [in an] amicable arrangement of the conflict with the Italian Government at Rome debarring from the negotiations the Royal [Italian] Legation at Athens looked at presently under the circumstances as inimically inspired towards Greece." Montagna (Athens) to Mussolini, September 6, 1923. *Ibid.*, pp. 191-192.

[12] Mussolini to Della Torretta (London) and Vannutelli (Paris), August 29, 1923. *DDI*, p. 136.

The Italian Ultimatum

the history of the area. Montagna, however, immediately felt this should be excluded a priori because they were "dealing with *well-known bands subsidized by the [Greek] Government.*" For this dramatic assertion one can devise no explanation except Montagna's basic and initial antagonism toward the Greek Government. Nevertheless, this assertion turned out to be of paramount importance, for within the coming hours it was to greatly influence Mussolini's thoughts. Montagna continued by stating: "This circumstance if confirmed would eliminate every doubt about the *political nature of the crime.*" This was a further point that was to influence the Duce that warm August night.

Continuing his comments, Montagna felt that the crime should not go unpunished "even in consideration of moral responsibilities"—an observation that did not fail to register with the excited Mussolini. Lastly, he emphasized that the rank of the deceased Tellini and the fact that he was the president of an International Commission emanating from the Conference of Ambassadors "can only force our allies to behave [in a manner] dictated by the moral solidarity [which] is incumbent upon them."[13]

Montagna's second telegram reached Rome an hour after his first, at 3:00 A.M. on August 28. After quoting in full a cable transmitted to the Royal Consulate at Janina requesting more details about the Tellini murder, Montagna drew Mussolini's attention to reports recently filed by General Tellini. In particular he noted "the paragraphs concerning the menacing and arrogant behavior of the Greek delegate [Colonel Botzaris] which now assume a symptomatic character." His "first impression," Montagna continued, "is that we are dealing with a crime [which] has a political basis, due in great part to the systematically hostile attitude to us of the Greek authorities and

---

[13] Italics added. Montagna (Athens) to Mussolini, August 27, 1923. *DDI*, p. 126.

In all the literature about the crime at Kakavia, as well as in all the investigations that followed the crime, Greek and non-Greek, no mention or even inference was made that the armed bands of the Epirus area were subsidized by the Greek Government.

The Italian Ultimatum

to the perfidious anti-Italian propaganda actively encouraged by the current Greek Government for internal politics especially in Epirus."[14] Montagna made no attempt to enlarge upon this charge or to substantiate it either by offering concrete evidence or by referring to prior dispatches filed to Rome covering these particular points. On July 19, however, the Italian chargé d'affaires, De Facendis, had emphasized to Rome the hostility shown by certain Greek officials toward Italy.[15] Montagna, not wishing to close without one parting shot, noted the manner in which the news reached the Royal Consulate at Janina, "merely by the Commander of the local gendarmerie."[16]

Having received only these two cables, aside from the original cable notifying him of Tellini's murder, Mussolini retired for the night. The dawn of a new day brought about a crystallization of his thoughts. In a note written in his own hand Mussolini recorded these thoughts for posterity. First, a thought transposed from Montagna's cable, the *"crime [is] political, desired by armed bands in the pay of Greece."* Second, there is a "sensitiveness" in the Tellini Mission. Here Mussolini was undoubtedly alluding to the importance that Italy attached to Tellini's mission because Rome was committed to supporting Albania against Greek and Yugoslav territorial ambitions. Third, the Greek Government is not diplomatically recognized. Fourth, since this same government "does not give guarantees hence [it has] to give necessary reparations." Lastly and most crucial, "While waiting, the Italian Government draws up its requests [that] it may have guarantees and reparations and as a measure of retaliation *Italy occupies by force of arms the island of Corfu.*" A marginal annotation by another hand noted that this last had been for the moment suspended by Mussolini.[17]

The Duce had now decided on his course of action: "he

[14] Montagna (Athens) to Mussolini, August 27, 1923. *Ibid.*, pp. 125-126.
[15] De Facendis (Athens) to Mussolini, July 19, 1923. *Ibid.*, p. 91.
[16] Montagna (Athens) to Mussolini, August 27, 1923. *Ibid.*, p. 126.
[17] Italics added. Mussolini, morning of August 28, 1923. *Ibid.*, p. 128.

The Italian Ultimatum

wanted the occupation of Corfu."[18] All the diplomatic notes and hurried replies that followed were gestures meant merely to impress the unknowing and gullible with his feigned sincerity. Europe was seeing a type of diplomacy which was to reach its zenith and its most cynical form in the coming decade.

In the early afternoon of this same day Mussolini, in a note somewhat similar to the one above, recorded six of the seven demands that would be cabled within a matter of hours to Montagna for presentation to the Greek Government. The demands Mussolini desired were: an apology on the part of the highest Greek military authority; a funeral service in the Roman Catholic Cathedral in Athens, attended by all the members of the government; a criminal investigation to be completed within five days after the arrival of the Italian military attaché, Colonel Ferdinando Perrone; capital punishment for all the culprits; an indemnity of 50 million Italian lire payable within five days (though in a moment of generosity Mussolini had first written eight days and had then corrected it to five). Lastly, honor was to be shown the Italian flag.[19]

To set the stage for the events that were soon to follow, secret priority cables were sent by the Duce to the Prefects of Bari and Lecce ordering them to make the necessary preparations to stop all cable-telegraphic communications directed to Greece unless otherwise instructed. But the Duce's confusion and unsureness over his next steps were manifested, during these early hours, in the composition of the cable. The request at first was to have been effective "from tomorrow at mid-day," August 29. It was then to be effective as of midnight the 28th, and finally, in a postscript in Mussolini's own hand, it was to be delayed forty-eight hours or until August 30.[20]

ITALY'S DIPLOMATS AND MUSSOLINI

The incidents that occurred between Mussolini and the career officials at the Palazzo Chigi illustrate the position to

[18] Guariglia, p. 28.
[19] Note by Mussolini, August 28, 1923. *DDI*, p. 128.
[20] Mussolini to the Prefects De Vita (Bari) and D'Arienzo (Lecce), August 28, 1923. *Ibid.*, p. 128.

The Italian Ultimatum

which professional diplomatists were relegated in their relation vis-à-vis the political leadership during the interwar years. It was a situation that was not peculiar to Italy but endemic throughout the chancelleries of Western Europe.[21]

The first weeks after his assumption of power in October 1922, the Duce "brought little but uncertainty," to the career officials of the Palazzo Chigi. Prior to achieving power, Mussolini's statements had suggested "that at the very least he would try to startle the diplomatic world with a series of melodramatic gestures."[22]

Seemingly grandiose, Mussolini's foreign policy aims were actually very much in keeping with earlier Italian desires. Like his predecessors, the Duce thought the time was ripe for Italian moves in Southeast Europe. The dissolution of Austria-Hungary, the military defeat of Germany, and the collapse of Russia had removed from the scene the three nations that had played so important a political role in Southeast Europe prior to 1914, nations that in the past had helped to curb Italian actions in that part of the world. With Italy territorially enlarged, her northern frontiers secure, and the Austrian menace removed, Rome desired that Italy's political influence also be increased, to be commensurate with her greater role in world affairs. Thus, one of the essential points of Italian policy—now pursued by Mussolini—was the establishment of Italian control of the Adriatic and ultimately of the Mediterranean. Though economic moves were of importance, political and strategic considerations dominated the implementation of this objective. Moves in this direction had already been made by Italian statesmen before the Duce's advent to power, for instance the war with Turkey over Libya (1911-1912) and political commitments gained from the Allies during the course of the First World War (the Treaty of London of April 1915 and the Treaty of St. Jean de Maurienne of April 1917).

[21] Gordon A. Craig and Felix Gilbert (eds.), *The Diplomats: 1919-1939* (Princeton: Princeton University Press, 1953), passim.
[22] H. Stuart Hughes, "The Early Diplomacy of Italian Fascism: 1922-1932," in Craig and Gilbert, p. 214.

The Italian Ultimatum

Therefore the immediate objectives of the new Fascist government were quite clear: first, the settlement of the Fiume question, which, unsolved since 1919, had greatly strained Italo-Yugoslav relations, and second, the establishment by Rome of a paramount position in Albania. By this latter action it was hoped that the eastern shores of the Strait of Otranto would come into Italian hands, and thus exit from and entrance into the Adriatic would be under firm Italian control, turning this body of water into an Italian lake.

But the aims of Mussolini and his predecessors did not go unchallenged. Yugoslavia, for one, viewed these designs as a menace to her interests and had no wish to renounce her own claims in the north Adriatic. This clash in the north repeated itself farther down the coast in Albania. Here the situation was complicated by Yugoslav territorial ambitions in Albania. Naturally, Belgrade looked with alarm on any projected Italian hegemony in Albania, or on an Albania under strong Italian influence.

Greece also shared Yugoslavia's attitude. Though Athens had no direct interest in the north Adriatic, she did have territorial demands on southern Albania, known also as northern Epirus, and on Italy because of its continuing occupation of the Greek-populated Dodecanese Islands in the eastern Mediterranean. Likewise, she desired to thwart any Italian control of the eastern shores of the Otranto Strait and of exit from and entrance to the Adriatic. This situation was in turn complicated by French interests in the region. The Quai d'Orsay's desire was to establish groupings of smaller states, a move which would support France's general policy of maintaining the frontiers and hence the status quo legalized by the Paris Treaties of 1919. In the Balkans, Yugoslavia appeared to be the hub around which such a grouping could be established. Paris therefore did everything possible to strengthen Yugoslavia and to help settle difficulties between Yugoslavia and her neighbors. Rome on the other hand instinctively felt that this policy was an intrusion into an area where she had many more interests than France. She viewed any grouping of Balkan states under

The Italian Ultimatum

French patronage with Yugoslavia as its nucleus as a possible menace to her eastern seaboard. Rome considered a Balkan grouping to be a replacement of the former Austro-Hungarian menace, establishing a potentially strong antagonist in any Adriatic adventures. Italian policy therefore was to do everything possible to frustrate this Balkan grouping. In this task Rome was fortunate to find an immediate ally in Bulgaria. Since Bulgaria was one of the defeated states, her acceptance of the French scheme would have been a denunciation of Bulgarian irredentism with respect to Yugoslavia and Greece and an acceptance of the territorial and nationality clauses of the Treaty of Neuilly. It would have required that Sofia put an end to comitadjis raids, allegedly made to protect Macedonian Bulgars against Greek and Yugoslav oppression, raids if not encouraged, at least tolerated by Sofia.

Though Bulgaria was for Italy a natural ally against Yugoslavia and Greece, other tensions within the area lent assistance to Italy's designs. For instance, Greece was politically isolated and economically exhausted after her ill-fated invasion of Turkish Anatolia—an invasion whose consequences would rankle in Greece for years to come and make impossible for almost a decade a Greek-Turkish rapprochement. Though Greek-Yugoslav relations were correct, the old warmth had disappeared and Belgrade's desire for some sort of an access to the Aegean led to increasing anxieties in both countries.

In Danubian Europe the Balkan situation was again repeated, this time in an Italian-Hungarian alliance. Here French attempts to organize a grouping of smaller states to maintain the territorial status quo legalized by the Paris Treaties of 1919 was resisted by Italy. To Rome, this grouping, though less of a direct menace than the Balkan one, was nevertheless considered a French attempt at hegemony in Eastern Europe. Hungary as one of the defeated states found herself in a position similar to that of Bulgaria: unable to accept a role in any such grouping without undercutting her own policies. Thus she viewed Italy as an understanding friend and a potential supporter in rectifying her borders and in liquidating some of

The Italian Ultimatum

the more onerous clauses of the Treaty of Trianon. To the Italian satellites of Bulgaria and Hungary, Austria must also be added. Rome could not view with indifference the disappearance of her new northern buffer. She found unattractive the idea of sharing a common frontier with a powerful Germany, enlarged further by the absorption of Austria. Thus reduced to a minor status in Europe and denied Anschluss with Germany by the Versailles Treaty, Austria fell almost naturally under Italian protection. Rome's historic dream of the Italian flag waving in the Brenner Pass and a weak Austria under Italian influence had, by the time Mussolini assumed power in October 1922, become reality.

However, the Duce's inexperience in, and ignorance of, foreign affairs required him—at least at the very beginning—to depend upon the advice of the career official. Before Mussolini's arrival the man who "wielded the real power" was the Secretary-General, Salvatore Contarini.[23] Contarini was once described as "thinking two moves ahead of his diplomatic adversaries. Though his methods are often tortuous, he plays safe."[24] His power, methods, and influence within the Foreign Ministry were such that they have been styled "Contariniana."[25] During this early period he attempted to restrain the Duce and to convince him that one of the traditional prerequisites for a successful Italian foreign policy was friendship with Great Britain.[26]

[23] G. A. Borgese, *Goliath; the March of Fascism* (New York: The Viking Press, 1937), p. 254.

[24] Gunther (Rome) to the Department of State, October 15, 1923. File 765.68/127, Record Group 59, NA. For other laudatory descriptions of Contarini's ability, see H. Stuart Hughes, "The Early Diplomacy of Italian Fascism: 1922-1932," in Craig and Gilbert, pp. 216-217. Count Carlo Sforza, *Contemporary Italy*, trans. by Drake and Denise de Kay (New York: E. P. Dutton and Co., 1944), p. 347, who had appointed Contarini felt that he "had the soul of a rabbit under a proud Sicilian physiognomy. Contarini was of service only in arranging things rather poorly after they had begun to go awry." Sforza was probably piqued with Contarini, for though he himself left on Mussolini's assumption of power, Contarini remained and did not leave the Foreign Ministry until 1925, when he finally broke with the Duce.

[25] Guariglia, pp. 12, 14.   [26] *Ibid.*, pp. 12-15, 24.

The Italian Ultimatum

The Italian career diplomats, like Max Weber's ideal bureaucrat, were apolitical. Yet at the same time they recognized that the "internal solidarity" and "unpredictability" of the Duce's government gave "them leverage for negotiation abroad," to better realize Italian foreign policy aims.[27] Though they were always apprehensive of the Duce they "felt sure that time and training, and advancement in manners under their supervision, would strip the words [of the Fascists] of all danger, leaving just that zeal for aggressive rhetoric that may prove usable, from time to time, in that competition of nations."[28]

The ends desired both by the career officials at the Palazzo Chigi and by Mussolini were the same: "Italy great and respected, substantially enlarged in territory and influence." Where they differed was in the methods or the means to be used. The career officials were more modest, realizing the inadequacies of Italy's strength both financial and military. They recognized as chimerical the belief that Austria, Hungary, and Bulgaria could ever be reliable allies. Therefore, in their dealings with Mussolini they continually impressed upon him the sine qua non of Italian foreign policy—friendship with Great Britain.[29]

It was this very policy that the Duce challenged by his eruptive action at Corfu—an entanglement from which the career officials at Rome, London, Paris, and Geneva would have to extricate him. Once his decision to occupy Corfu militarily had been taken, no one at the Palazzo Chigi "was given the means to canalize through normal measures the solution of the incident."[30]

An important circumstance was the fortuitous absence from

[27] H. Stuart Hughes, "The Early Diplomacy of Italian Fascism: 1922-1932" in Craig and Gilbert, p. 266.

[28] Borgese, p. 254.

[29] H. Stuart Hughes, "The Early Diplomacy of Italian Fascism: 1922-1932" in Craig and Gilbert, p. 266.

[30] Guariglia, p. 28; Legatus [pseudonym—Roberto Cantalupo?], *Vita Diplomatica di Salvatore Contarini* (Roma: Sestante, 1947), p. 91.

The Italian Ultimatum

Rome of Contarini, who appears to have been on a holiday.[31] The only person competent enough to draw up the demands to Greece "was not consulted."[32] His reaction upon learning of the Corfu occupation was one of alarm and condemnation. He immediately withdrew to his home at Anzio, informing Rome that he could not participate "in such statesmanship." Asked to return to Rome, Contarini refused. Only later did he return to the Palazzo Chigi, when the situation between Italy and the Great Powers had become so strained that Mussolini turned to him for assistance.[33] In view of Mussolini's volatile character one can certainly question whether his "impetuosity in the Greek affair would have been restrained and his energies directed into other safer channels of action,"[34] if Contarini had been present.

When Baron Romano Avezzana, the Ambassador in Paris, appeared at the Palazzo Chigi after August 27, and before the Corfu occupation, he found the Foreign Ministry deserted of officials.[35] The importance of their absence, as that of Contarini, is speculative in light of the events that were to follow.

---

[31] All sources agree that Contarini was absent during this period. Count Carlo Sforza, *L'Italia dal 1914 al 1944* (Roma: Mandadori, 1946), p. 176, places him on the island of Ischia. Mino Caudana, *Il Figlio del Fabbro* (Roma: Centro Editoriale Nazionale, 1960), I, p. 289, states he was at Cortina d'Ampezzo. See also Gunther (Rome) to the Department of State, October 15, 1923. File 765.68/127, Record Group 59, NA; Borgese, p. 255; Legatus, pp. 91, 92; *The Times* (London), September 8, 1923, p. 8.

[32] Sforza, *L'Italia dal* . . . , p. 176.

[33] Legatus, pp. 92-93. On the other hand, the declaration of the American Embassy that Contarini "was away during the whole of the Greco-Italian crisis," is incorrect. Gunther (Rome) to the Department of State, October 15, 1923. File 765.68/127, Record Group 59, NA. Also incorrect is Sforza, *L'Italia dal* . . . , p. 176, who writes that Contarini did not wish to go to Rome, thinking that the Corfu debacle would cause the Duce's government to topple. Contarini, according to Sforza, failed to realize that "with passive opposition one can save one's soul not Italy." In the Italian diplomatic documents Contarini's name appears on September 7, 1923, though he may have arrived earlier to join his colleagues in the task of trying to solve the dispute.

[34] Gunther (Rome) to the Department of State, October 15, 1923. File 765.68/127, Record Group 59, NA.

[35] Sforza, *L'Italia dal* . . . , p. 177.

The Italian Ultimatum

EVENTS IN LONDON AND PARIS

Unaware of the diplomatic moves that were unfolding in Rome, the Italian Ambassadors in Paris and London, true to the instructions issued by Mussolini, appeared at their respective foreign offices.

In London, Marchese Pietro Tomasi della Torretta presented himself at Whitehall and informed the Under-Secretary of State, Sir William Tyrrell, of the "horrible massacre." Tyrrell "displayed anger" at the news. In the conversation that followed, Della Torretta requested "complete British solidarity" with the steps that his government would instruct its legation in Athens to take. Mistakenly, Tyrrell informed him that, prior to his arrival, the British Embassy in Paris had informed the Foreign Office of the Italian chargé d'affaires' urgent request for a meeting of the Conference of Ambassadors. The chargé desired that it deal with an urgent event and decide on an inquiry, the decision to be communicated to the Greek Government. Tyrrell had agreed to this meeting and authorized the British representative to act accordingly. He then added, to Della Torretta, that it would be unnecessary to telegraph the British representative in Athens as desired by the Italian Government.

Admitting his ignorance of any events unfolding in Paris, Della Torretta emphasized to Tyrrell that Mussolini's instructions had been "imparted in a precise and explicit manner," requesting British solidarity with the action that the Italian Government would undertake in Athens. When Tyrrell hesitated, Della Torretta added "that Italy alone was capable of obtaining from Greece full satisfaction for the grave crime perpetrated against Italy and reparations for the injury caused to her prestige." However, because of the international character of the Tellini Mission, his government believed that it could count on British solidarity in support of any action that it took in Athens. On the other hand, Della Torretta added that any Italian action would be independent of whatever was agreed upon in Paris, of which he had not the slightest information.

The Italian Ultimatum

Della Torretta, therefore, was basing Italian actions and rights to reparations on the firm rule of international law traceable to the Vattel thesis that "whoever ill-treats a citizen indirectly injures the State."[36] At the same time, however, he wished to get British support because of the international character of the Tellini Mission. Such support would not be essentially for international but for Italian demands. He was willing to admit, however, that separate demands could be instituted by the Conference of Ambassadors because of the international character of the Tellini Mission.

To Della Torretta's persuasive arguments Tyrrell succumbed and promised to dispatch the required instructions to Athens. He added that they would be sent the next day [August 29] after receiving prior authorization from the Foreign Secretary, Lord Curzon, who was on the Continent. Tyrrell felt sure that Curzon would approve the necessary instructions, which were being sent to him as a mere formality.[37]

The ambassador had thus succeeded in implementing the instructions issued by the Duce, who enthusiastically approved "fully the language used by Torretta to Tyrrell which corresponds exactly to the point of view of the Royal [Italian] Government."[38]

Della Torretta's successes in London were not to be repeated in Paris. The Italian chargé d'affaires, Count Luigi Rey Vannutelli, presented himself at the Quai d'Orsay, and in a conversation with Peretti de la Rocca, the Director of Political Affairs, requested similar action—that the French Government adhere to the steps to be undertaken by the Italian Minister at Athens.

Peretti replied that France was ready to do so, "but not

[36] The quote continues, "the sovereign of the injured citizens must avenge the deed and, if possible, force the aggressor to give full satisfaction or punish him, since otherwise the citizen will not obtain the chief end of civil society which is protection." Emmerich de Vattel, *Le Droit des Gens; ou, Principes de la Loi Naturelle* (London, 1858), Livre II, section 71.

[37] Della Torretta (London) to Mussolini, August 28, 1923. *DDI*, p. 129.

[38] Mussolini to Vannutelli (Paris), August 30, 1923. *Ibid.*, pp. 138-139.

The Italian Ultimatum

separately," a major qualification. Any action of this type, he felt, had to be carried out in concert with the Conference of Ambassadors, of which the Tellini Mission was a "dependent organ."

Vannutelli stressed that the atrocious nature of the crime "justified manifestations of immediate solidarity." Peretti was not to be shaken. He drew Vannutelli's attention to a number of precedents to the Tellini murder, though none as serious, in which "every initiative was deferred to the Conference of Ambassadors."[39] With France involved in occupation of the Ruhr, and relations with England strained over it, Peretti's tack was therefore quite clear. He wished to forestall any possible Balkan difficulties. His interpretation, therefore, "had the object of giving to the considered *démarches* an inter-Allied character and thus avoiding a direct conflict between Italy and Greece, which would be of heavy consequences."[40]

The Prime Minister, Raymond Poincaré, immediately had London agree to Peretti's interpretation.[41] His next step was to have Italy agree. As a result, Della Torretta's success in London proved to be fleeting.

The simultaneous receipt of Captain de Limperany's cable officially informing the Conference of Ambassadors of the Tellini murder galvanized Poincaré into action. He urgently convened the secretaries of the British, French, Italian, and Japanese delegations. A draft note was prepared for Poincaré in his capacity as President of the Conference of Ambassadors, to be delivered to the French Minister in Athens. The minister was invited to make a joint *démarche* with his Italian and British colleagues to the Greek Government. The purpose of the *démarche* was: "to protest in the name of the Allied Powers represented on the Conference of Ambassadors, with all the vigour that the gravity of the circumstances permit, against the odious and unprecedented crime, victims of which [were] on Greek territory, several members of an Inter-Allied

[39] Vannutelli (Paris) to Mussolini, August 29, 1923. *Ibid.*, p. 132.
[40] Jules Laroche, *Au Quai d'Orsay avec Briand et Poincaré, 1913-1926* (Paris: Librairie Hachette, 1957), p. 174.
[41] *Ibid.*, p. 174.

The Italian Ultimatum

commission invested by the Conference of Ambassadors with a mission of pacification." Secondly, the Greek Government was to be asked: "to proceed without delay in an inquiry with a view to establishing the responsibilities, and to make known to it [the Conference] that the Powers reserve to themselves to present eventually any demands for sanctions and for reparations that will appear necessary to them."[42]

At the last moment the British chargé d'affaires in Paris, Sir Eric Phipps, demurred, feeling that he could not adhere to the second "request for penalties and reparations without first consulting his government." He promised a reply once he had secured instructions from London, which he felt would arrive the following day [August 29]. To the harassed Vannutelli, who was without instructions and faced with a rapidly changing situation because of Poincaré and Peretti's quick action, there was no other choice than to turn to Rome for instructions. He especially desired to know how to deal with the projected draft note of protest by the Conference.[43]

His request for further instructions would bring no immediate response. Events unfolding in Rome and Athens were to monopolize the Duce's attention; he had to issue instructions of a more pressing nature.

EVENTS IN ATHENS

In Athens, the day following the Tellini murder, at the time when Della Torretta was presenting himself at Whitehall, and Vannutelli himself at the Quai d'Orsay, Montagna, following the instructions issued to him by Mussolini, presented himself at the Greek Ministry of Foreign Affairs.

On being received by Apostolos Alexandris, the Foreign Minister, he made it clear that his visit "should not be in any way interpreted nor represented as a sign of change in the relations between the two governments." Warming to his task he did not hesitate to inform Alexandris that the "gravity of the fact, which I am going to discuss with . . . [you does] not

[42] File 763.72119/12020, Annex A, Record Group 59, NA.
[43] Vannutelli (Paris) to Mussolini, August 29, 1923. *DDI*, p. 133.

The Italian Ultimatum

make me hesitate to put momentarily aside questions of form even of political complexion."

After what Montagna modestly described as "a short and impressive synthesis" in which he "put in evidence the serious responsibilities of the Greek people and Greek Government in the ghastly crime," he stated to Alexandris "in a harsh, red-hot and indignant tone," Mussolini's instructions. At this point Alexandris, who was disconcerted, attempted "to provoke discussion." Montagna refused to yield to any discussion, "reporting to him sharply that we insist upon immediate exemplary punishment of the murderers," and that Italy reserves the right "to ask ample reparations after ascertaining the facts." Alexandris made no attempt to dispute Montagna's statement nor did he object to the demands, but merely "limited himself to reiterating the regret and condolence of the Greek Government," for the tragic events that had occurred. Continuing, Alexandris stated the measures the government had taken in an attempt to capture the perpetrators of the crime which was strongly deplored and condemned by the Greeks.

Montagna, playing his role to the hilt, replied "coldly" that he would convey to his government, at Alexandris' own request, the declarations made. The interview now over, Montagna could not help "noticing with a point of irony that it was necessary that I bring myself to him [Alexandris] in order to learn the grief of the Greek Government." Alexandris' immediate retort was that he had not come to see Montagna for fear of not being received by him.

Later the conversation was continued at the Italian Legation. Alexandris came to inform Montagna that the Revolutionary Government had ordered that police and judicial officials be sent to Janina "in order to direct and intensify the actions initiated for the arrest of the murderers." His statement that the culprits would be immediately shot when captured caused Montagna to observe that there was need to control the judicial procedure and judgment. For Montagna there had to

The Italian Ultimatum

"be no doubts to the identity of the criminals," in order "to avoid an easy and not unlikely substitution of innocents."

Missing no opportunity to make a point, Montagna, in closing the interview, warned Alexandris against the "deplorable consequences of [any] hostile behavior against us." He pointed to the behavior of the local press, whose "perfidious and systematic anti-Italian propaganda," he considered "good under the circumstances to contain and above all not to excite." The government, he felt, should not allow the press to issue "unfounded and tendentious news," particularly if the Italian Legation "was not allowed to correct and refute" this news.[44]

Montagna's preoccupation with the Greek press was again accentuated in a meeting that same afternoon with his American colleague. The latter reported that Montagna "took [a] very serious view of this matter [Tellini's murder] as he has frequently warned the Greek authorities of the danger [of] permitting anti-Italian propaganda."[45]

Though the second interview with Alexandris had ended, Montagna's work for the day had just begun. To confirm the representations made to Alexandris a *note verbale* to be transmitted to the Greek Foreign Ministry on the following day was drawn up. A copy was also sent to Mussolini.

The note repeated the declarations made by Montagna. It then turned to a summation of his statements, "on the basis of information received from authorized and competent sources," regarding the murder of the Italian delegation.

The murderers, according to the note, were "une bande d'irréguliers grecs," though no evidence was offered to substantiate this point. It went on to demand that those guilty of the crime be quickly arrested and subjected to immediate and exemplary punishment, care being taken to protect the innocent. The execution of this condition would not in any way absolve "the extremely grave responsibility of Greece in re-

[44] Montagna (Athens) to Mussolini, August 28, 1923. *Ibid.*, pp. 129-130.
[45] Atherton (Athens) to the Department of State, August 28, 1923. File 768.7515/44, Record Group 59, NA.

The Italian Ultimatum

spect of this crime, which was undoubtedly committed for political motives."

Continuing, the note observed the "spirit of goodwill and justice,[46] in which the Tellini Mission had done its work, having won the admiration and sympathy of all people and officials with whom it had come into contact. However, there was one exception to this general feeling, the note remarked, "the evidence on this point is quite definite—this attitude of respectful approbation was always lacking and there alone open or ill-concealed manifestations of opposition and hostility and even incitement to hatred were observed,"—an obvious allusion to the Greek Government. The Italian Legation, however did "not consider it necessary for the moment to insist on this point." The Greek Government, it added, could "not help being aware of the circumstances referred to."

In closing, the note energetically protested against the Tellini murder, which was committed well within Greek territory "et presque sous les yeux des autorités Helléniques." The note reserved all rights to reparations to which Italy was entitled because "of the grave responsibility of the Greek Government in this deplorable matter."[46] Montagna was stressing not so much Greek territorial responsibility as Greek culpability, an unsubstantiated but far more serious charge.[47]

The Greek reply, on August 30, began by stating that the Greek Government shared "entirely the sentiment of indignation expressed" in the Italian note on the Tellini murder. It observed that once informed of the crime, the Greek Government immediately took all measures possible to "facilitate the search and arrest of the culprits," whose guilt would be ascertained by the investigation already in operation. With a touch

[46] Manley O. Hudson, "How the League of Nations Met the Corfu Crisis," *World Peace Foundation*, vi, No. 3 (1923), pp. 199-200. The French text in *DDDIG*, pp. 10-11, is somewhat incorrect.

[47] Though thirty-eight years have passed since the Tellini murder, the culpability theory is still expressed in pro-Fascist accounts. There is absolutely no evidence to warrant the statement by Luigi Villari, *Italian Foreign Policy under Mussolini* (New York: Devin-Adair Co., 1956), p. 21, that "there is every reason to believe that the outrage had been organized with at least the connivance of certain local Greek officials."

The Italian Ultimatum

of irony the note stated that it could undoubtedly count on the active collaboration of the Italian Legation "which would possess on this subject information from trustworthy sources as it made mention in its *note verbale*." What had "especially attracted" the Greek Government, it added, was "the information, according to which the Italian Delegation, could have been attacked par une bande d'irréguliers grecs." Since the Greek Government lacked "similar information" it requested that the Italian Legation give any details which "would be of a nature to facilitate the work of the inquiry already begun." Since it also lacked any information that would substantiate the fact that the murder had been committed "sous les yeux des autorités Helléniques," it denied this charge categorically. In conclusion, it appealed to the Italian Legation "to communicate to it immediately all details that will be at its disposition and which could facilitate the task of the Greek authorities."[48]

REACTIONS IN ITALY TO TELLINI'S MURDER

In Italy meanwhile, on August 28, the public announcement of the Tellini murder produced the "greatest indignation." The tone of the Italian press from the anti-Fascist *Corriere della Sera* to the Fascist mouthpiece *Il Popolo d'Italia* was the same.[49] On the following day the Italian crowds reacted to the "disastrous influence" of the press.[50] In Trieste, Turin, Florence, Genoa, and Bologna, violent demonstrations occurred, directed against Greek-owned establishments and Greeks resident in Italy. In Naples and Catania, Greek Consulates were also attacked.[51] The outbursts continued on the 30th. At Turin the outbursts took on an anti-French flavor.

[48] *DDDIG*, p. 13.

[49] Muriel Currey, *Italian Foreign Policy, 1918-1932* (London: I. Nicholson and Watson, Ltd., 1932), p. 104. For Italian press comments see *Corriere della Sera*, August 29 and 30, 1923, p. 1.

[50] Pierre Lasturel, *L'Affaire Gréco-Italienne de 1923* (Paris: L'Ile de France, 1925), p. 60.

[51] *Ibid.*, pp. 60-62. In Rome, however, things were comparatively quiet. *The Times* (London), August 31, 1923, p. 8.

The Italian Ultimatum

There were shouts of "Abbasso la Francia" and demonstrations before the French Chamber of Commerce and the French Consulate, much to the Duce's annoyance.[52]

The demonstrations appear to have been spontaneous and there is no evidence to show complicity either by Mussolini or by members of his government.[53] They were outbursts probably due to the humiliation and frustration, real or imagined, that most Italians felt because their national pride had suffered by Italy's failure to gain its postwar demands. The Tellini murder had been the last straw. Hence the official communiqué after the occupation of Corfu was on firm ground in declaring that "the Government was in entire unity with the feelings of the country."[54]

Protesting to the Italian Legation against the anti-Greek demonstrations and the actions of the Italian press, the Greek Government requested the legation to intercede "with an eye to the adoption of proper measures to put an end to the regrettable incidents."[55]

To Montagna, this legitimate Greek note of protest only made a "pretense [of the] profound impression produced on the Greek Government," by the anti-Greek demonstrations in Italy. His own recommendation to the Duce was to disregard it entirely.[56] Mussolini disagreed with him even though Corfu had by this time been occupied. He instructed Montagna to point out to Athens that proper measures had been taken to insure Greek safety and requested him to demand a cessation of the anti-Italian campaign of the Greek press.[57]

The Greek Foreign Ministry's reply noted the assurances of the Italian Government that "all necessary measures had been taken . . . with a view to preventing the renewal of the re-

[52] Mussolini to the Prefect Palmieri (Turin), September 6, 1923. *DDI*, p. 192.
[53] Lasturel, p. 62. [54] Quoted in Currey, p. 104.
[55] *DDDIG*, p. 16.
[56] Montagna (Athens) to Mussolini, September 1, 1923. *DDI*, pp. 151-152.
[57] Mussolini to Montagna (Athens), September 2, 1923. *Ibid.*, pp. 162-163. For the Italian note of September 3, 1923, to the Greek Ministry of Foreign Affairs see *DDDIG*, pp. 23-24.

The Italian Ultimatum

grettable incidents." It stated it could not disregard the gravity of the acts which constituted "grave violations of treaties and international customs" and involved "unquestionably the responsibility of the Italian authorities." In closing, the Greeks could not help but observe that cessation of press attacks was a two-way street.[58]

Montagna's reaction to the Greek note, as might be expected, was negative. He cabled Rome that he considered the note "inspired by the usual bad faith" and written "in a rather arrogant tone in contrast with the moderation and rigid correctness of our communication."[59]

MUSSOLINI'S DEMANDS

As August 28 came to an end, the tempo of exchanges between Rome and Athens quickened. First, Mussolini cabled to Montagna the amount of "reparations to be considered the minimum consistent with the grave offense of which Greece is rendered liable to Italy." The seven demands enumerated were essentially the same as those the Duce had already noted, though there was one addition and certain refinements.

Montagna was instructed to request: (1) an apology in the fullest and most official manner to be presented to the Italian Government via the Italian Legation by the highest Greek military authority; (2) a solemn funeral for the victims of the murder at the Roman Catholic Cathedral in Athens to be attended by all the members of the Government; (3) honor to be rendered the Italian flag on the very day of the funeral ceremony by units of the Greek fleet (excluding torpedo boats, which were to be anchored) in the presence of the Italian navy in Phalerum Bay outside Athens; (4) an investigation by the Greek authorities with the assistance of the Italian military attaché, Colonel Perrone (the Greek Government was to be fully responsible for Perrone's safety and was to facilitate the task entrusted to him in every way, the investigation to be

---
[58] *DDDIG*, pp. 35-36.
[59] Montagna (Athens) to Mussolini, September 8, 1923. *DDI*, p. 206.

The Italian Ultimatum

concluded within five days after receipt of the Italian demands); (5) capital punishment for the culprits; (6) an indemnity of 50 million Italian lire ($2,270,000 in 1923); (7) military honors to be paid to the corpses on the occasion of their transferral to an Italian vessel at the Greek port of Preveza. This last demand was previously unrecorded.

The Duce requested that Montagna insist upon a Greek reply of full acceptance within twenty-four hours of the receipt of the Italian demands by the Athens government.[60] On the remote possibility that the Greek Government might accept the Italian demands, arrangements were made to conduct Colonel Perrone from the port city of Patras to Preveza.[61] Whether Mussolini framed his demands in order to make them unacceptable to the Greeks is unclear. At any rate complete acceptance of the demands by Greece would, at little cost, have been something of a diplomatic coup. Though the Duce was unsure of what Athens' reaction might be, military measures were taken in case of the possible rejection of the demands. The Governor of Rhodes, for example, in the Italian-held Dodecanese, was alerted that a naval division would leave "this very evening towards Leros, where it will wait further instructions."[62]

At the same time, Mussolini, somewhat belatedly, informed King Victor Emmanuel III of the demands transmitted to Montagna at Athens for presentation to the Greek Government. The Duce commented ominously that "in agreement with the Ministers of War and Marine, [I have] taken the disposition of a military character necessary in order to be in a position to cope with the unfolding of events in a

---

[60] Mussolini to Montagna (Athens), August 29, 1923. *Ibid.*, pp. 133-134. Antonio Foschini, "A trent anni dall' occupazione di Corfu," *Nuova Antologia*, Anno 88, Fasc. 1836 (Dicembre 1948), p. 404, infers that the ultimatum "was drawn up easily and rapidly" by the Director-General of Political Affairs, Mario Arlotta, who had previously served in Athens as naval attaché.

[61] Mussolini to Montagna (Athens), August 29, 1923. *Ibid.*, p. 134.

[62] Mussolini to Lago (Rhodes), August 29, 1923. *Ibid.*, p. 135.

The Italian Ultimatum

manner consonant with national dignity and prestige."[63] The King assented to these actions.[64]

At the time the demands were received, on the afternoon of August 29, at Athens, the Italian Embassies at London and Paris were also informed of the demands, with instructions that they be brought to the attention of the host government. The "reparations requested . . . represent, if immediately consented to, the minimum which public opinion of our country, profoundly offended and exasperated at the news of the savage massacre, expects," cabled Mussolini.[65]

By eight in the evening Montagna delivered to the Greek Foreign Minister, Apostolos Alexandris, the Italian demands in a *note verbale*.[66] Alexandris declared that he would immediately transmit it to his government. Montagna's only comment was that he expected a reply within twenty-four hours, that is, by eight o'clock the following evening [August 30]. Montagna cabled Rome that Alexandris had "feigned indifference" when the Italian note was presented. He then added significantly that neither the British nor the French chargé d'affaires had received instructions to join his actions.[67]

Upon receipt of the Italian demands, the Greek cabinet was immediately convened.[68] In a statement to the press the Prime Minister, Colonel Stylianos Gonatas, explained that the demands did not have "the character of an ultimatum," and that the note delivered by the Italian Minister contained various demands, some of which were acceptable; others had to be modified, while still others were completely unacceptable. However, since the Tellini outrage had been committed in Greek territory the government was willing to give to the

---

[63] Mussolini to Vittorio Emanuele III (Racconigi), August 29, 1923. *Ibid.*, p. 135.

[64] Vittorio Emanuele III (Racconigi) to Mussolini, August 29, 1923. *Ibid.*, p. 137.

[65] Mussolini to Della Torretta (London) and Vannutelli (Paris), August 29, 1923. *Ibid.*, p. 136.

[66] Hudson, pp. 201-202; *DDDIG*, pp. 11-12.

[67] Montagna (Athens) to Mussolini, August 29, 1923. *DDI*, p. 137.

[68] Ἀπόστολος Ἀλεξανδρῆς, Πολιτικαί Ἀναμνήσεις (Πάτραι, 1947) [Apostolos Alexandris, *Political Recollections* (Patras, 1947)], p. 106.

The Italian Ultimatum

Italian Government full satisfaction to its *amour propre*, in so far as this was compatible with Greek dignity. Furthermore, the Greek Government was "willing to award to the families of the victims ... a reasonable indemnity." As to the departure of the Italian military attaché for Janina, Gonatas declared that Colonel Perrone could not assist in the investigation "as such participation would mean intervention in internal affairs."[69]

Of course it is conceivable that Gonatas, aware of Greece's weakened state, was playing for time in the hope of British or French support. Thus, to have acknowledged the note as an ultimatum would have been a tactical mistake. At the same time, however, his being a military man and unaware of diplomatic subtleties may explain his denial that the note was an ultimatum.[70]

The observations of both the foreign and the Greek press were somewhat more incisive than Colonel Gonatas'. The

[69] Montagna (Athens) to Mussolini, August 30, 1923. *DDI*, pp. 139-140; *The Times* (London), August 31, 1923, p. 8. Colonel Perrone was subsequently recalled. *The Times* (London), September 3, 1923, p. 10.

[70] Why the Prime Minister, Colonel Gonatas, did not consider the Italian note an ultimatum remains something of a mystery. According to Sir Harold Nicolson, *Diplomacy* (2nd ed.; London: Oxford University Press, 1950), p. 242, an ultimatum does not necessarily mean war, "It is often merely 'the last word' before negotiation is broken off. It generally takes the form of a written intimation that unless a satisfactory reply is received by a certain hour on a certain date certain consequences will follow." Sir Ernest M. Satow, *A Guide to Diplomatic Practice*, ed. Nevile Bland (4th ed.; London: Longman, Green and Co., 1957), p. 105, states that an ultimatum "ordinarily but not always implies a threat to use force, if the demand is not complied with." However, a more detailed examination is to be found in L. Oppenheim, *International Law*, ed. H. Lauterpacht (7th ed.; London: Longman, Green and Co., 1952), II, p. 295, who divides ultimatums into *simple* or *qualified*. The *simple* ultimatum does not include any indications of the measures envisaged by the Power transmitting it. On the other hand, a *qualified* ultimatum indicates measures envisaged, whether reprisals, occupations, war, etc. The Italian note therefore appears to fall under the category of a *simple* ultimatum. But it should have been obvious to the Greek authorities that any note containing a series of demands, with a twenty-four hour time limit, sent by one of the Great Powers to a smaller Power, has implied sanctions attached and was therefore an ultimatum.

The Italian Ultimatum

analogy between the Austrian demands to Serbia in 1914 and the Italian demands to Greece was too strong not to be brought up.

The Italian "demands . . . ," the London *Times* wrote, "do not appear to be inspired wholly by a desire for justice. Some of them are expressly designed to inflict the bitterest humiliation upon Greece and others—among them the amount of money indemnity—seem to be altogether excessive." Continuing, it observed that, "There is not evidence even that the criminals were Greek at all."[71] The tone of the Greek press was the same. The demands from Rome were not a request for satisfaction of wounded dignity, wrote the *Eleftheron Vima*, but simply an attempt "to humiliate Greece and its national prestige and to violate its sovereignty."[72]

Montagna's own impressions from Athens were that the Greek Government was trying to obtain support from Paris and London "for the purpose of containing or minimizing our action." The hope of a collective action with other powers, he cabled the Duce, was virtually a dead letter since the British chargé d'affaires had received instructions to limit himself only to supporting a note of protest by the Conference of Ambassadors to the Greek Government.[73]

Similar instructions had also been transmitted by Whitehall to its chargé d'affaires at Paris, Sir Eric Phipps, who was ordered to accept in full the projected text of the Conference's note of protest to the Greek Government. This left only Vannutelli without instructions. He urgently asked Mussolini whether or not he should also adhere.[74]

The British and the French, therefore, appeared to be acting in unison after a decision on Poincaré's initial appeal to collectivize the problem had been delayed. The delay was neces-

[71] August 31, 1923, p. 9.
[72] August 31, 1923. As quoted in *Bulletin Périodique de la Presse Grecque*, No. 79, p. 3.
[73] Montagna (Athens) to Mussolini, August 30, 1923. *DDI*, pp. 137-138.
[74] Vannutelli (Paris) to Mussolini, August 30, 1923. *Ibid.*, p. 139.

The Italian Ultimatum

sitated by Phipps' hesitation in accepting the projected draft note before he had received clearance from Whitehall.

Before the arrival of either of these cables signifying a developing British and French modus vivendi, Mussolini had also decided to adhere to the projected Ambassadorial draft note of protest. By this concession Mussolini was admitting that the Tellini murder also affected the Conference of Ambassadors, that the dispute also had an inter-allied character. Unknowingly the Duce was also establishing the channel through which the dispute would be solved, in a way that would save his face. This decision, however, was due less to Mussolini's diplomatic acumen than to the accidental presence of a career official, the vacationing Italian Ambassador from Paris, Baron Camillo Romano Avezzana, who "persuaded him to concede" to the Ambassadors' Conference.[75]

Therefore, Mussolini's instructions to the impatient Vannutelli, in the early morning hours of August 30, were to accept the projected draft note of protest "even if it does not contain mention [of] reparations and sanctions." With his mind already made up and his plans already in operation, what the Conference was going to request from Greece was immaterial to him. Italy would participate within the Conference of Ambassadors in the deliberations that would inevitably follow since the Tellini Mission was a dependent of the Conference. The government at Rome would attend "precisely [because] of the inter-allied function which in [a] subordinate line covers the victims." At the same time it was to be understood that by so doing it was not renouncing the fundamental rights that belonged to it. Nor was it trying to evade "the duty of acting directly in order to exact reparations owed it by the most grave injury caused to the entire Italian nation in the person of officials and soldiers who before every other quality had that of Italian citizens." All this Vannutelli was to bring to the attention of the Quai d'Orsay, because from it flowed Italy's

[75] Sforza, *L'Italia dal* . . . , p. 177.

The Italian Ultimatum

"request for [the] reparations and sanctions presented by Montagna to the government at Athens."[76]

Mussolini admitted the right of the Ambassadorial Conference to intervene since Tellini and his staff had acted as their agents. At the same time he maintained the Vattel thesis, which Della Torretta at London had expressed to Sir William Tyrrell—that the wrong committed to Tellini was a wrong committed to the Italian nation. In this respect the Duce's argument was founded on firm legal principles.

Vannutelli's dual assignment was to bring to the attention of the Quai d'Orsay Italy's demands to Greece and her adherence, with all its qualifications, to the projected note of protest by the Conference of Ambassadors.

Officially informed by Vannutelli of the Italian demands to Greece, Peretti de la Rocca, the Director of Political Affairs at the Quai d'Orsay, merely noted them and stated he would immediately transmit them to Poincaré. It appeared, Vannutelli cabled, that within the British Embassy at Paris the reaction of the chargé d'affaires, Sir Eric Phipps, was one of great surprise at "the grave initiative taken by Italy without previous concert with [the] Allied Powers."[77]

Vannutelli was quite correct, for on certification of the news Phipps immediately telephoned Jules Laroche at the Quai d'Orsay. He informed him that after the Italian demands, which he described as a "coup de la grosse Bertha italienne," it seemed useless to collectivize action on the dispute in the Conference of Ambassadors by firing "le petit fusil de la Conférence."[78] By collective action of the Great Powers Poincaré had hoped to prevent possible complications between Italy and Greece in the Balkans at a time when France's attentions were focused on the Ruhr. The realization of this hope appeared to be slipping through his fingers.

Poincaré, desperately wishing to save a deteriorating situation, acted with vigor and dispatch. He got in touch with the

---
[76] Mussolini to Vannutelli (Paris), August 30, 1923. *DDI*, pp. 138-139.
[77] Vannutelli (Paris) to Mussolini, August 31, 1923. *Ibid.*, p. 142.
[78] Laroche, p. 174.

The Italian Ultimatum

Foreign Office. As a result, the latter again consented to collective action through the Conference of Ambassadors "declaring that in this case it denied to Mussolini the right of acting separately."[79]

This British withdrawal and subsequent readherence "only after insistence on the maintenance of the principle of inter-allied intervention," was brought to the Duce's attention by the ever watchful Vannutelli.[80]

As to Italian adherence to the projected note of protest by the Conference of Ambassadors, Peretti, after consultation with Poincaré, informed Vannutelli that France considered the government at Rome "free to take separately those measures in which it believes vis-à-vis Greece." But he still insisted on the thesis assumed in his first conversation with Vannutelli several days before—that France in an analogous case would have followed the procedure of giving exclusive jurisdiction to the Conference of Ambassadors. Vannutelli's thesis was that recourse to the Ambassadors' Conference was a prerogative belonging to the individual state "while direct protection [of the] citizen's life . . . in every circumstance is the duty of each government." Vannutelli's concluding observation in his cable to Mussolini was that this Italian view was finally beginning to seep through to the French press "in spite of the Minister of Foreign Affairs [Poincaré], who endeavors to reverse it preferring [the] inter-allied authority of the Conference of Ambassadors to the direct and individual Italian national action."[81]

In London, on presenting the Italian demands to Tyrrell, Della Torretta was informed that the Foreign Office was already aware of them. The only point Tyrrell admitted not being aware of was the demand for a reply by Athens within twenty-four hours. Della Torretta noted to Sir William that given the gravity of the facts the Italian demands represented the minimum that his country could ask under the present circumstances. Tyrrell agreed with this observation. Della

---
[79] *Ibid.*
[80] Vannutelli (Paris) to Mussolini, August 31, 1923. *DDI*, p. 142.
[81] Vannutelli (Paris) to Mussolini, August 31, 1923. *Ibid.*, p. 143.

The Italian Ultimatum

Torretta personally thought it would be desirable for the Greek Government to prove its good sense by quickly accepting the Italian demands. He felt if this were not done greater trouble could follow. The latter statement provoked no comment from Tyrrell. Sir William then drew Della Torretta's attention to the note of protest forwarded to Athens by the Conference of Ambassadors. Della Torretta observed to Sir William that Italian action was natural and independent from whatever was devised by the Conference of Ambassadors. Tyrrell agreed "fully" with this observation. As in his prior conversation with Tyrrell, Della Torretta was justifying Italian actions under the Vattel thesis. Sir William's reserve throughout the interview, as he subsequently explained, was an attempt to avoid committing Lord Curzon in any way.

After his interview with Tyrrell, Della Torretta had the impression that, following the first instructions sent to the British chargé d'affaires at Athens to support Montagna's protests over the Tellini murder, the Foreign Office had had second thoughts. With the Conference of Ambassadors now involved in the question, he thought the Foreign Office wished to keep any actions within the sphere of the Conference.[82] Della Torretta's impressions were correct.

---

[82] Della Torretta (London) to Mussolini, August 30, 1923. Italian Archives.

On August 31, the day following his interview with Della Torretta, and before news reached London of the Italian bombardment and occupation of Corfu, Sir William wrote Lord Curzon: "I think it is only right to let you know that I have scrupulously refrained from expressing any opinion to the Italian Ambassador in my daily interviews on the measures which his government are contemplating as a consequence of the massacre of the Italian Delegation. I have of course expressed to him horror and indignation at the cruel fate which has overtaken the Italian Mission, but as regards his communications I have confined myself to stating that I will transmit them to you. I have taken up the same attitude with the French chargé d'affaires, as I have been most anxious to avoid committing you in any way.

"I am being bombarded with telegrams from Bob Cecil and am informing him that he will hear from you. I would therefore suggest if you approve our telegram to him you will send it either direct from Paris or via Aix if you decide on acquainting the Prime Minister with your decision." Sir William Tyrrell (London) to Lord Curzon, August

The Italian Ultimatum

Pressured by Great Britain and desiring to collectivize the action of the Great Powers, Poincaré acted once again. While the Ambassadorial note of protest was on its way to the French Legation in Athens for presentation to the Greek Government, Poincaré was demanding from Rome the withdrawal of the Italian demands submitted on August 29th.

Poincaré's *démarche* would prove to be a hopeless gesture, for it was already too late and his note to Rome would cross with the news that the Italian fleet had already bombarded and occupied the island of Corfu.[83]

THE GREEK REPLY

In Athens at 8 o'clock on the evening of August 30, within the time limit set by Montagna the previous day, an official of the Greek Foreign Ministry appeared at the Italian Legation and submitted a *note verbale* embodying the Greek reply to the Italian demands.[84]

The Greeks in their reply "protested against the allegation" that Greece was "guilty of an offense against Italy." It could not "in fact be seriously alleged that such an offense could have been committed by the Hellenic Government, either intentionally or through negligence," since it had no animosity toward the Italian Mission, which was merely doing its duty. Nor could the government "be accused of negligence in connection with the safety of the Mission," as it had placed special troops at the disposal of the Mission and the local authorities had organized patrols because of the presence of Albanian brigands. Furthermore, no doubts had ever been expressed to the Greek Government as to the personal safety of either General Tellini or any other member of his staff.

The Greek Government accordingly took exception to the tenor of the Italian note "that the Hellenic Government is guilty of a serious offense against Italy," and regarded this

---

31, 1923. Folder marked "Letters to Curzon M-Y, 1923," Box 65, Curzon Papers.

[83] Laroche, p. 174.

[84] Montagna (Athens) to Mussolini, August 30, 1923. *DDI*, p. 141.

The Italian Ultimatum

charge as unfounded. Therefore, it was impossible to accept points 4, 5, and 6 of the Italian note. These points, the Greek Government felt, would "outrage the honor and violate the sovereignty of the State."

However, since the "abominable crime was committed on Greek territory against subjects of a friendly State" the government expressed its willingness to accept the following points: that regrets be expressed to the Italian Government "in the most complete and official form" by the general officer commanding at Athens to the Italian Minister; that funeral services be held at the Roman Catholic Cathedral in Athens attended by all members of the government; that honors to the Italian flag be paid by a detachment of the Athens garrison which could come to the Italian Legation and salute the flag, "paying all customary honors"; and that solemn military honors be paid to the murdered victims at the Greek port of Preveza upon their transferral to an Italian vessel.

The Greek note furthermore declared its "willingness to grant, as a measure of justice, an equitable indemnity to the families of the victims." Colonel Perrone, the Italian military attaché, would also be welcome to assist the inquiry by providing any information that would facilitate the discovery of the murderers.

In closing, the note expressed the hope that the government at Rome would "recognize the justice" of the Greek view "as well as its desire to give satisfaction to the Italian Government in the most equitable way possible." If this did not prove true and the Italian Government was "unwilling to recognize the satisfaction given as adequate," the Greek Government would "in accordance with the provisions of the Covenant of the League of Nations . . . appeal to the League and undertake to accept its decision."[85]

In brief, the Greek Government rejected outright three of the original seven demands, accepted two, and modified two others. Montagna's observations were that the ruling circles

[85] Hudson, pp. 202-204; *DDDIG*, pp. 14-15.

The Italian Ultimatum

appeared to be exhibiting a "marked indifference" which made one "think that they will not yield notwithstanding my perfectly clear warning of the gravity of the situation." On the other hand, he observed they could be relying upon "the support of others."[86]

Montagna had reason to believe that the Yugoslav Minister was inciting the Greek Government in its present course of action. The minister had stated to Montagna that Italy was offending Greek sovereignty by some of its demands and would galvanize world opinion against herself. The Yugoslav Minister could not help but compare the Italian demands to the Austrian ultimatum to Serbia in 1914 which provoked the World War, an idea that had also appeared in the Greek press. These assertions Montagna had energetically denied.[87]

PRIOR ITALIAN NAVAL PREPARATIONS

A few minutes after midnight on August 30, within an hour after the arrival of the news from Athens that the demands had been rejected and that the Greek Government would resort to the League, orders were issued from Rome to Admiral Emilio Solari, Commander of the Italian Navy, "to proceed at once to the occupation of Corfu."[88]

The Minister of Marine, Grand Admiral Thaon di Revel, later had grave misgivings about these orders since any Greek or, especially, British naval reaction would have isolated the Corfu task force from the Italian mainland. The possibilities of aid to the latter were practically nil, since an Aegean task force

[86] Montagna (Athens) to Mussolini, August 31, 1923. *DDI*, p. 146.
[87] Montagna (Athens) to Mussolini, August 31, 1923. *Ibid.*
[88] Antonio Foschini, *La Verità sulla Cannonate di Corfù* (Roma: Giacomaniello, 1953), p. 37. The Italian Navy had already been moved into position to strike at Corfu some hours earlier. At 4:35 P.M. on August 30, orders were issued to Admiral Solari to proceed to the Italian port of Gallipoli on the eastern shore of the Gulf of Taranto. At 10:35 P.M. Montagna's cable about the rejection of the Italian demands by the Greek Government was received in Rome. Fifty minutes later, at 11:25 P.M., orders were issued to Admiral Solari to proceed with the occupation of Corfu. Minister of Marine, Thaon di Revel, to Admiral Solari, September 30, 1923. *DDI*, p. 270.

The Italian Ultimatum

under the command of Rear-Admiral Angelo Frank was far to the southeast in the Dodecanese.[89]

Prior Italian planning and the present measures to deal with the new and unexpected situation had merged. Almost a month before, on July 24, the day the Lausanne Treaty with Turkey was signed, the Italian fleet had been recalled to Taranto and Admiral Solari had been instructed by the Minister of Marine, Thaon di Revel, to report to Rome. In a conversation which ensued on July 29 between Thaon di Revel, Admiral Solari, and Naval Captain Antonio Foschini, the minister indicated "with a sense of bitterness" the necessity of raising Italy's prestige, which had fallen so low: Dalmatia had been deserted, Albania evacuated. "After Yugoslavia and Albania, it appears the moment for Greece may perhaps have arrived," he observed to Solari and Foschini.[90]

Di Revel's desire to resurrect Italy's fortunes, to achieve world-wide status, to attain prestige by some sort of symbolic act, had already attracted Mussolini's attention. Only a little earlier the Duce had proposed to send a naval squadron to take solemn possession of the Dodecanese. He was dissuaded from doing so only with reluctance and ill-humor by the career officials at the Palazzo Chigi. The gesture, they argued, would would be both provocative and ridiculous, since Italy had been in occupation of the islands for more than a decade.[91] What connection there was—if any—between Mussolini's ill-fated

[89] Guariglia, p. 28. Guariglia feels that the minister's remarks were well taken and demonstrated the basic weakness in Italian possession of the Dodecanese. The islands were useful in so far as Italy was able to construct a naval force powerful enough to operate solely in the eastern Mediterranean, without any danger to the defenses of the mainland or Africa. Without this naval force, the islands were a military liability, especially if Italy's meager naval forces had to cover both the mainland and the islands. Mussolini thought that British friendship could still be preserved in spite of the Corfu occupation. The point he missed was that Italian strength in the Mediterranean "had remained more or less the same" when he took upon himself this venture which could have created war with England. *Ibid.*, pp. 28-29.

[90] Foschini, p. 25.

[91] Guariglia, pp. 25-28; Luigi Salvatorelli and Giovanni Mira, *Storia del Fascismo* (Roma: Novissima, 1952), p. 202.

The Italian Ultimatum

proposal and the comments that Thaon di Revel was now to make to Admiral Solari and Captain Foschini is difficult to say.

Minister di Revel explained to both naval officers that the real motive for the concentration of naval units at Taranto was the deteriorating relations with Greece. By Article 15 of the Treaty of Lausanne, Turkey had renounced in favor of Italy the Dodecanese Islands, acquired by Italy during the Italo-Turkish war of 1911. Greece, however, claimed the same islands. Greek-Italian relations were further strained by the work of General Tellini. These two controversies, fanned by the Greek press, "had already provoked public manifestations against Italy," which the government in Athens did nothing either to prevent or restrain.[92]

In this "so red-hot" atmosphere, Di Revel concluded, any Italian proclamation of sovereignty over the Dodecanese contemplated for late August, after the ratification of the Lausanne Treaty, was sure to produce in Greece "uproars and disorders of provocatory character." Italy however, "was not disposed to tolerate damages harmful to national dignity," and had decided to react "immediately and vigorously in an exemplary manner, in order to obtain the proper reparations." To establish "the modality of the military operations to accomplish the object," a meeting was to be held with other military officials, but directed by the officials of the Palazzo Chigi. The talks that followed were under the direction of Mario Arlotta, formerly stationed in Athens as naval attaché and now Director-General of Political Affairs. The "coercive measures" to be applied to Greece "in order to obtain reparations" in case of any "offense" were decided upon only after long discussion.

Simultaneous actions were to take place in the Aegean and Ionian Seas. Corfu, in the Ionian Sea, was to be occupied "in order to hold it as a pledge" until Italian demands were satisfied. To the east, in the Aegean, naval units operating from the island of Leros, suited for the task because of its central location and natural harbor facilities, would threaten Athens.[93]

[92] Foschini, p. 26.   [93] *Ibid.*, p. 27.

The Italian Ultimatum

Because the major share of the work fell on the naval establishment, Thaon di Revel stipulated that all naval preparations were to be finished by August and that secrecy was to be maintained. Arrangements were therefore pushed forward not only within the navy but also with other interested government departments.

Spies were sent to Corfu to gather information. Their reports clearly showed that it was poorly garrisoned, lacking naval support, and hence virtually defenseless. With the Turkish ratification of the Lausanne Treaty on August 20, Di Revel informed Admiral Solari that on August 30, immediately after the Greek ratification, Italy would proclaim its full sovereignty over the Dodecanese. Thus he ordered all units to be in full readiness.[94]

On the evening of August 29 instructions from Thaon di Revel to Solari ordered the departure of the Aegean task force under the command of Rear-Admiral Angelo Frank. It left Taranto by midnight. Passing out to sea so as to avoid detection from the Greek coast, the task force steamed at full speed eastwards towards Leros, where it arrived on August 31. Admiral Solari's force followed Frank's within twenty-four hours, its destination the island of Corfu.[95]

LAST MINUTE MOVES

As the last scene in this tragic drama was being played out,

[94] *Ibid.*, p. 28. It appears that as early as August 13, 1923, a report by Naval Lieutenant Lorenzo Daretti clearly showed that Corfu was poorly defended. This was corroborated by a report from the military attaché at Athens. Whether Lt. Daretti was one of the spies sent to Corfu is unclear. Minister of Marine, Thaon di Revel to Admiral Solari, September 30, 1923. *DDI*, p. 271. The events described above therefore answer the question as to how the Italian fleet was able to mobilize so rapidly in late August of 1923. This question has generally been tied to the thesis that Mussolini had a hand in the Tellini murder. Sforza, *Contemporary Italy*, p. 349; Sforza, *L'Italia dal . . .* , p. 117.

[95] *Ibid.*, pp. 36-37. Attempts at security proved somewhat ineffective. According to a Paris dispatch of August 30, a message from Turin to the *Petit Parisien* reported Italian fleet concentrations at Taranto, though the Italian press had severe orders not to report it. *The Times* (London), August 31, 1923, p. 8.

The Italian Ultimatum

a personal and somewhat pathetic telegram was sent by the Greek Foreign Minister, Alexandris, to the Duce. Alexandris assured the Duce that the murderers were not Greeks, and that the Greek Government was willing to pay an indemnity to the victims' families since the crime had been committed on Greek territory. He also asked him not to insist on the payment of money as a penalty since it offended Greek "national pride." Unfortunately the minister's cable, as was expected, fell on deaf ears.[96]

Several hours after the transmission of Admiral Solari's orders to proceed to Corfu, the King was informed by Mussolini that the Greek reply corresponded "in essence to the rejection of the Italian request." He therefore had arranged "for the departure of adequate naval forces and for the occupation of a pacific and temporary character of the island of Corfu." To the King, the Duce now quoted the message that at 6:30 that same morning would be flashed to all Italian diplomatic missions abroad:

> "To the just demands formulated by Italy following the barbarous massacre of the Italian Military Mission committed in Greek territory, the Hellenic Government has replied in terms that correspond in essence to the complete rejection of the same.
>
> "Such an unjustified attitude places upon Italy the necessity of recalling the Hellenic Government to a sense of its responsibility.
>
> "I have therefore communicated the order for the landing on the island of Corfu of a contingent of Italian troops.
>
> "With this measure of a temporary character Italy does not intend an act of war but only to defend its own prestige and to manifest its inflexible will to obtain the reparations due it in conformity with custom and international law.
>
> "The Italian Government hopes that Greece does not commit any act that may modify the pacific nature of the measures.

[96] Ἀλεξανδρῆς [Alexandris], p. 106.

The Italian Ultimatum

"The above does not exclude the sanctions that the Conference of Ambassadors will be taking [in view] of the fact that the assassinated Italian Delegation formed part of the mission for the delimitation of the Albanian frontiers which [mission], presided over by the lamented General Tellini, was an agent of the same Conference."[97]

While all this was occurring, another city, Geneva, which up to this point had remained silent, now entered the picture. On the afternoon of August 30, before the rejection of the Italian demands became known, the Italian diplomat, Bernardo Attolico, serving as Assistant Secretary-General of the League, sent confidentially via the Italian Consul at Geneva a request as to "what dispositions it would be expedient to adopt" in the case Greece or some other state addressed itself to the League by invoking either Articles 11 or 15 of the Covenant.[98]

The Duce, now faced with action on another front and one that throughout the last few days had not even entered his thoughts, queried Attolico whether the official communiqué could be considered as a submission to the League.[99] Not wishing to surrender his legal prerogatives to the Conference of Ambassadors, the Duce was even more unlikely to give in to the League of Nations.

In London in the early afternoon of August 31, the American chargé d'affaires, Post Wheeler, was reporting that the Foreign Office regarded the Tellini murder "with considerable anxiety" owing to an unconfirmed report that Rome had presented to Greece a five-hour ultimatum for full acceptance of the Italian demands, with the threat to occupy Corfu. "In view of the potential naval importance of this island, a serious situation would result from such a step," Wheeler warned Washington.[100] Later that same afternoon Della Torretta informed the

[97] Mussolini to Vittorio Emanuele III (Racconigi), August 31, 1923. *DDI*, p. 143.
[98] Eles (Geneva) to Mussolini, August 30, 1923. *Ibid.*, p. 140.
[99] Mussolini to Attolico (Geneva), August 30, 1923. *Ibid.*, pp. 141-142.
[100] Wheeler (London) to the Department of State, August 31, 1923. File 768.7515/48, Record Group 59, NA.

The Italian Ultimatum

Foreign Office "that orders have been given for the occupation of Corfu."[101]

Mussolini's first act of aggression had been consummated. At a time when the collective note of protest by the Conference of Ambassadors was speeding towards Athens and Poincaré's *démarche*, the request for the withdrawal of Italy's demands, was being transmitted to Rome, the Duce had already made his move.

Europe was receiving its first glimpse of what Ortega y Gasset would later describe as a "type of man who does not want to give reasons or to be right, but simply shows himself resolved to impose his opinions. This is the new thing: the right not to be reasonable, the 'reason of unreason.'" To Ortega y Gasset, man in the second decade of the twentieth century was seeing a new phenomenon—the use of "direct action." Whereas formerly the use of force had been the *ultima ratio* in defense of what the individual thought were his rights, an inversion of the order had occurred and the proclamation of violence as the *prima ratio* or more strictly *unica ratio* was the order of the day.[102]

---

[101] Wheeler (London) to the Department of State, August 31, 1923. File 765.68/11 or 768.7515/50, Record Group 59, NA.

[102] José Ortega y Gasset, *The Revolt of the Masses* (New York: W. W. Norton and Co., 1932), pp. 80-82.

CHAPTER IV

MUSSOLINI VERSUS THE LEAGUE OF NATIONS

SOLARI BLUNDERS AT CORFU

WELL aware that unnecessary military actions at Corfu on the part of the Italian fleet might complicate the diplomatic situation, the career officials at the Palazzo Chigi succeeded in getting Mussolini to issue instructions to Admiral Solari to avoid the use of force and the occurrence of incidents involving the island's population.[1]

Solari, however, was ill-suited to the delicate task assigned. Instead of arriving at Corfu at about 10:00 in the morning he arrived at 3:30 in the afternoon, a delay of five and one-half hours.[2] The morning hour would have been more suitable,

[1] Raffaele Guariglia, *Ricordi 1922-1946* (Napoli: Scientifiche Italiane, 1950), p. 29. The instructions issued by the Palazzo Chigi were to take possession of Corfu "without employing force." Antonio Foschini, *La Verità sulle Cannonate di Corfù* (Roma: Giacomaniello, 1953), p. 52.

[2] Minister of Marine, Thaon di Revel to Admiral Solari, September 30, 1923. *DDI*, pp. 270-271. Foschini, p. 39, states that for security reasons Admiral Solari approached Corfu by the southern channel rather than by the shorter northern channel. The former was deep and wide, while the latter was narrow and dangerous if mined. However, Di Revel subsequently pointed out to Admiral Solari that an approach by the northern channel, provided the ships were proceeding at 15 miles an hour, should have brought him to Corfu at 10:00 in the morning. Even an approach by the southern channel, Di Revel noted, should have delayed him no more than one and one-half hours, so that he should have anchored off the island by 11:30 A.M. As to the precautions against Greek attack, Di Revel found this unjustified since the Italians had the element of surprise and by different intelligence reports Solari knew that there were no Greek naval units stationed on the island. His caution therefore was questionable. If the delay in departure from Gallipoli, the minister observed, was caused by a wait for the arrival of other smaller naval units, this also was unjustified once orders had been issued to Solari to depart for Corfu. Thus it appears that Solari's delay in departing once orders had been given him to do so, as well as his approach by the southern channel, all

Mussolini versus the League

considering all the preliminary arrangements to be completed with the local authorities before the island could be occupied.

By his late arrival Solari reduced the number of daylight hours available and made it difficult to complete the occupation of the island before nightfall. The occupation of the island was to commence at four in the afternoon with the landing of troops. Time therefore became of the essence, and Captain Foschini was sent ahead to deliver to the Corfu authorities Admiral Solari's surrender conditions.[3] This desire to occupy the island before nightfall was to lead to the shedding of blood and was to complicate an already complicated situation. Upon his arrival at Corfu (Kérkira), the capital city of the island, at about 3:00 P.M. Captain Foschini was immediately received by the Prefect, Mr. Petros Euripéos.

Though the testimonies of Euripéos and Captain Foschini are contradictory on a number of points, a general reconstruction of the negotiations is still possible. According to Euripéos, Captain Foschini stated that the island would be peacefully occupied within half an hour. He requested the Greek authorities not to resist or to place any obstacles in the way of the occupation unless they wished to assume the responsibility for the results of such action.[4] Though Foschini subsequently denied this,[5] Admiral Solari's typewritten declaration to the Corfu authorities appears to have been altered. Instead of the text reading "the occupation will begin in two hours," it was altered to read "30 minutes."[6] Euripéos faced by a completely unexpected situation, invited the chiefs of the other government departments to be present, as well as the military commander of the island. Because he did not understand Italian the Prefect

---

added up, Di Revel wrote, to an unwarranted delay of five and one-half hours. Minister of Marine, Thaon di Revel to Admiral Solari, September 30, 1923. *DDI*, pp. 270-271.

[3] Foschini, p. 39.

[4] Report of the Prefect of Corfu to the Ministry of Foreign Affairs, September 6, 1923. *DDDIG*, p. 32. Hereafter cited as Euripéos' Report.

[5] Report of Captain Foschini to Admiral Solari. *DDI*, footnote p. 153. Hereafter cited as Foschini's Report.

[6] Italian text. *DDDIG*, p. 34.

Mussolini versus the League

also requested the presence of the Italian Consul, Mr. Schelini.

After a translation of Admiral Solari's declaration by the Italian Consul, Euripéos informed Foschini that without instructions from his government it was impossible for him to surrender the island. He therefore requested a delay of a few hours in order to communicate with Athens.[7] This reasonable request was refused by Foschini "for obvious military reasons."[8] According to Foschini the military commander of the island then threatened resistance and was warned of the consequences of such an act. Euripéos then desired, Foschini states, to confer with the other government officials, who had by this time gathered in the Prefecture, the purpose of the meeting being to induce the military commander "to reason." To this request Foschini readily agreed.[9]

The conference decided that Euripéos was to seek from Foschini a short delay in order to communicate with the government in Athens, the request Foschini had already refused. The Prefect was also to ask the conditions of surrender, which had not yet been delivered, and a definition of the occupation, that is, whether it was civil or military. Finally, if Foschini refused to agree to the requests, the Prefect was to declare that since Corfu did not possess military forces he could oppose the occupation with only passive resistance. That is to say, he would not hand over the city without instructions from the authorities in Athens, but would bow before superior force.[10] Returning from the meeting, the Prefect, according to Foschini, stated that the military commander "had reaffirmed his intention to oppose the landing, notwithstanding the contrary pressure of the others."[11]

Foschini, however, refused to give Euripéos any information concerning the conditions of the occupation, and only at the last moment when leaving the Prefecture did he hand him the surrender conditions.[12] As to a delay of two hours, Foschini

[7] Euripéos' Report, September 6, 1923. *DDDIG*, p. 32.
[8] Foschini's Report. *DDI*, footnote p. 153. [9] Foschini, pp. 40-41.
[10] Euripéos' Report, September 6, 1923. *DDDIG*, p. 32.
[11] Foschini, p. 41.
[12] Euripéos' Report, September 6, 1923. *DDDIG*, p. 33. The surrender

again refused. Foschini explained to the Prefect that two hours had already elapsed from the time he had arrived and delivered to him Admiral Solari's declaration. Any further delay could not "be allowed because the occupation had to be completed before evening."[13] Eurípéos states he again protested and declared to Foschini that the old island fortress sheltered 7,000 refugees and 350 hospitalized Armenian children and included a military hospital.[14] Though Foschini denied that it was ever made clear to him that refugees were situated in and around military sites, he did admit that Eurípéos "alluded vaguely to the fact that Greek refugees were spread everywhere in the city."[15]

Departing, Foschini reaffirmed the desire of the Italian naval authorities for a peaceful occupation of the island and noted that any resistance by the garrison would obligate the ships, which by now had anchored outside of the city, to fire.[16] Foschini then added that at 4:00 P.M. three blank shots would be fired at three-minute intervals. If at that time no white flag was raised surrendering the island, shelling would commence.[17]

Foschini's last act before leaving the island was to dispatch a letter written by Admiral Solari to the Foreign Consuls. In

---

conditions that Captain Foschini handed the Prefect were as follows: the Greek flag was to be lowered and the Italian flag raised in its place; the Italian flag would be saluted by the Italian ships in the harbor with a 21-gun salute; the command of the island was to be taken over by Rear-Admiral Bellini; the military barracks were to be surrendered with disarmed Greek troops and police inside; all military arms, munitions, and arms depots and other military equipment were to be surrendered; the Greek garrison was to be centralized in a single barracks and disarmed; Greek officers and troops would be forbidden to circulate; barracks were to be provided for the Italian troops of occupation; there was to be an immediate suspension of all wire, wireless, post, and telephone communication; lastly, there was to be Italian control of all communication and transport. Italian text. *DDDIG*, p. 35.

[13] Foschini's Report. *DDI*, footnote p. 153.
[14] Eurípéos' Report, September 6, 1923. *DDDIG*, p. 33.
[15] Foschini's Report, *DDI*, footnote p. 154; Foschini, p. 40.
[16] Foschini, p. 42.
[17] *Ibid.* In the writings of Foschini and Eurípéos there is a discrepancy as to time. Foschini, it appears, is using European Central Time and Eurípéos local Corfu time.

Mussolini versus the League

the letter Solari stated that he had been directed "to proceed to the pacific occupation of Corfu." However, if the Greeks resisted he would occupy the island "with force." The note originally gave all foreign nationals on the island "two hours" to meet at their respective consulates. Foschini changed the time allotted to "thirty minutes."[18]

Before leaving the Prefecture Foschini warned the military commander that the full responsibility for any resistance would fall on his shoulders. He reiterated that any shelling would be restricted to military objectives.[19]

When no white flag was raised at the appointed time, the Italian bombardment of the city commenced. In seven minutes Solari fired thirty-five shells. Rather than have the city destroyed the Prefect ordered the white flag raised. The appearance of the white flag put an end to the bombardment. Throughout the shelling as well as in the landing of the troops no Greek resistance was offered. During the intense shelling sixteen people were killed and over three times that number wounded.[20]

Solari had blundered. In a subsequent critical review of his naval operations at Corfu, Minister of Marine Thaon di Revel felt that the reduction of the time limit for the Foreign Consuls from two hours to thirty minutes was most injudicious, considering the task the Consuls had been assigned. The pacific occupation of the island mentioned in the note to the Foreign Consuls, Di Revel noted, made it clear that no force was to be resorted to in order to occupy the island unless resistance was offered. The pacific occupation of Corfu was also counselled by prior reports describing the weakness of the garrison about

[18] *Ibid*. The text of the letter from Admiral Solari to the Consuls resident in Corfu is in *DDI*, footnote p. 144.

[19] Foschini, p. 42.

[20] Euripéos' Report, September 6, 1923. *DDDIG*, p. 33. The list of the dead, mostly refugees from Asia Minor, is attached to Euripéos' Report.

Guariglia, p. 29, states that because of some shot from the island, Admiral Solari "proceeded to that unlucky [and] useless bombardment that rendered more complicated the solution of the incident." This is incorrect. There were no shots fired from Corfu at the Italian ships.

Mussolini versus the League

which Solari had been informed, as well as by the report of the military attaché in Athens [Colonel Perrone] "who had confirmed the non-existence of artillery on the island." The verbal resistance [*la resistenza verbale*] of the Corfu military commander, Di Revel observed, did justify intimidation such as the landing of troops supported by the firing of blank shots from smaller-caliber cannons. Even the shelling of the forts would have been justified, provided it had been done in a way that would not cause damage to persons or property. However, there was no justification, the minister strongly maintained, for the considerable number of shells fired, much less for the use of the larger-caliber cannon. Lastly, the presence of refugees in the old fortress, which was known to Admiral Solari through previous reports, should have caused him to avoid it as a target.[21] Word of what had transpired at Corfu sent Mussolini into a rage.[22]

Contarini later admitted to the British Ambassador, Sir Ronald W. Graham, that the shelling of Corfu "was entirely contrary to Mussolini's wishes and instructions," and that Solari was given "an extremely warm time" by the Duce when he reported back to Rome.[23] As Italy's League of Nations rep-

[21] Minister of Marine, Thaon di Revel to Admiral Solari, September 30, 1923. *DDI*, p. 271. In the light of the above document, Di Revel's supposed comment to Foschini that "*given the circumstances you were not able to act differently*" appears questionable. Foschini, p. 52.

[22] Raffaele Guariglia in an interview with the writer in Rome, August 1961.

[23] Sir Ronald W. Graham (Rome) to Lord Curzon, September 28, 1923. Folder marked "Letters to Curzon G-L, 1923," Box 65, Curzon Papers.

On September 2, Mussolini cabled to Admiral Solari his complete satisfaction with the way in which the Corfu operation had been carried out. He considered the sacrifice of life to have been due to the "criminal carelessness" of the Greek military commander. Mussolini to the Minister of Marine, Thaon di Revel, repeated to Paris, London, Washington, Athens, and Geneva, September 2, 1923. *DDI*, p. 163. This was the same attitude maintained in an interview, in Rome, with Captain Foschini some days after the occupation of Corfu. Foschini, pp. 53-56. In the light of the above evidence it would have been difficult for the Duce to admit in public that his own naval commander had blundered.

Mussolini versus the League

resentative succinctly put it, the bombardment which the "Italian Government had not ordered," could have been "avoided by a more prudent and cautious military commander."[24] World opinion, which at first had sided with Italy over the brutal murder of General Tellini and his staff, now turned its sympathy to the tragic victims at Corfu.[25]

REACTIONS IN ATHENS

In Athens, news that the Italian fleet was demanding the surrender of the island first reached the head of the Revolutionary Committee, Colonel Nikolaos Plastiras. He immediately hurried to the telegraph office to order resistance. Plastiras was followed by the Prime Minister, Colonel Stylianos Gonatas, and the Foreign Minister, Alexandris, who in their turn hurried to the telegraph office to prevent Colonel Plastiras from issuing any precipitate orders.[26]

The Prime Minister and the Foreign Minister undoubtedly realized that Greece was in no position to offer resistance. Burdened as she was by the influx of well over a million Greek refugees from Asia Minor, exhausted by almost ten years of continuous warfare, unrecognized by the Great Powers, in the midst of a constitutional crisis, and divided politically, any act of resistance would have been national suicide. Gonatas' and Alexandris' dash to the telegraph office was in the nick of time, for when they arrived Plastiras had already started to dictate an order to the Corfu authorities to resist. Thwarted, Colonel Plastiras protested but was persuaded that any armed clash in which Italian troops would be killed would furnish Musso-

[24] Antonio Salandra, *Memorie Politiche, 1916-1925* (Milano: Garzanti, 1951), p. 102.

[25] Guariglia, p. 29.

[26] Στυλιανός Γονατᾶς, Ἀπομνημονεύματα 1897-1957 (Ἀθῆναι, 1958) [Stylianos Gonatas, *Memoirs 1897-1957* (Athens, 1958)], p. 273; Ἀπόστολος Ἀλεξανδρῆς, Πολιτικαί Ἀναμνήσεις (Πάτραι, 1947) [Apostolos Alexandris, *Political Recollections* (Patras, 1947)], p. 107; Γρηγόριος Δαφνῆς, Ἡ Ἑλλάς μεταξύ δύο Πολέμων 1923-1940 (Ἀθῆναι: Ἴκαρος, 1955) [Grigorios Dafnis, *Greece between Two Wars 1923-1940* (Athens: Ikaros, 1947)], I, p. 77.

Mussolini versus the League

lini with an excuse for a permanent occupation of the island.[27]

The dash to the telegraph office had not ended the day's events in Athens; at 5:00 o'clock the same afternoon Minister Montagna transmitted to Alexandris a *note verbale* which embodied Mussolini's proclamation of the occupation of Corfu, flashed at 6:30 that morning to all Italian Missions abroad.

When presented the note Alexandris was "visibly impressed," Montagna cabled Rome. Probably in an attempt to ascertain if further moves were contemplated, he asked Montagna, if the action was completed. Montagna, as in previous meetings over the last few days, played his role to the hilt, and replied "in correct form but coldly" that he had nothing to add to the note he was transmitting. Montagna "cut short" Alexandris' attempt to engage in an "inopportune discussion," declaring to Alexandris that he was merely a faithful executor of his government's orders and could not consent to criticism of his government. Not wishing to close the interview without the last word, Montagna added that he had come to deliver the note himself as an "act of courtesy."[28] Half an hour later Montagna assured the American Minister that "the arrival of the Italian fleet in Corfu in no way meant annexation, but rather occupation of the island until Greece made suitable amends to Italy." He then added ominously that the Government at

[27] *Ibid.* It appears that on his way to the telegraph office Colonel Plastiras stopped off at the American Legation and informed Minister Atherton that he would order the Corfu authorities to resist in order "to protect Greek honor." Atherton (Athens) to the Department of State, August 31, 1923. File 765.68/10, Record Group 59, NA. Later that same day Atherton reported that he had been "informally advised that [the] Greek Government did not and would not issue bellicose orders to the garrison at Corfu," though the Greek fleet had been ordered to take on war supplies. Atherton (Athens) to the Department of State, August 31, 1923. File 765.68/12, Record Group 59, NA.

[28] Montagna (Athens) to Mussolini, August 31, 1923. *DDI*, p. 148. For the text of Mussolini's proclamation see Mussolini to Vittorio Emanuele III (Racconigi), August 31, 1923. *Ibid.*, pp. 143-144. For the actual *note verbale* see *DDDIG*, pp. 17-18. The Greek Foreign Ministry pointed out that the Italian fleet had arrived at Corfu prior to the delivery of Montagna's note. Atherton (Athens) to the Department of State, August 31, 1923. File 765.68/12, Record Group 59, NA.

Mussolini versus the League

Rome would no longer tolerate Greece's "antagonistic attitude" towards Italy, and that in "his opinion graver events might follow unless satisfaction was forthcoming."[29]

Mussolini's successful *fait accompli* and the smell of gunpowder at Corfu had produced a far more confident Montagna than the one who had visited the British Legation that same morning. At that meeting with the chargé d'affaires, Sir Charles Bentinck, Montagna, "in a very excited frame of mind," insisted that "Italy would not permit the case to be referred to the League of Nations as it must be settled between the two governments direct[ly]."[30] Though Italy, because of French support, was to achieve the first objective, events unfolding in London, Paris, and Geneva would make it impossible for her to achieve the second. Already steps toward a collectivization of measures for dealing with the dispute were being taken in Athens.

No sooner had Montagna left Alexandris than he was followed by the French chargé d'affaires, Count Balny d'Avricourt. By prearrangement with Montagna and the British chargé, Sir Charles Bentinck, Avricourt transmitted to Alexandris the Conference's note.

The note energetically protested against the Tellini murder, demanded an immediate inquiry, and reserved the right to present demands for any sanctions and reparations that might be necessary.

Montagna had observed to the Duce that this step should make Greece realize that she was faced by Great Power "moral solidarity" with Italy.[31] What Montagna failed to see was that Greek acceptance of the note might put Italy, not Greece, in the position of resisting the Great Powers, especially if Rome persisted in trying to settle the dispute on its own terms.

When presented with the Ambassadorial note of protest,

[29] Atherton (Athens) to the Department of State, August 31, 1923. File 765.68/12, Record Group 59, NA.

[30] Atherton (Athens) to the Department of State, August 31, 1923. File 765.68/12, Record Group 59, NA.

[31] Montagna (Athens) to Mussolini, August 31, 1923. *DDI*, pp. 148-149. For the text of the note see *DDDIG*, p. 17.

Mussolini versus the League

Alexandris stated that the Greek Government had already begun an inquiry into the Tellini murder and that it would submit itself to any eventual demands for sanctions and reparations desired. He pointed out, however, that Greece's responsibilities did not necessarily proceed from the fact that Tellini had been murdered in Greek territory. In order to show that the Greek Government had exercised "due diligence" under international law in its protection of General Tellini, Alexandris observed that the general had always refused a military escort; that the Greek Government had often protested to the Albanian Legation over the incursion of Albanian armed bands in Greek territory; and that just before the Tellini murder troops had been sent into Epirus to check the incursions. The minister felt that the crime had been perpetrated by Albanian or Greek Epirotes, the latter being persons whose villages had been allotted to Albania in the delimitation of the border and who were "exasperated in seeing themselves cut off from their country."

Turning to the Italian action at Corfu, Alexandris described it as a "warlike act," to which Avricourt replied that it was merely a coercive act and had nothing to do with war. Even if this were so, Alexandris observed, the Greek Government had decided to appeal to the League of Nations.[32] The day's events in Athens had ended. In Geneva, London, and Paris they had just begun.

REACTIONS IN GENEVA

In Geneva, Nikolaos Politis, the chief of the Greek delegation to the League of Nations, appeared at Lord Robert Cecil's hotel suite and informed the chief British delegate that he was going to bring the Corfu matter to the League Council under Article 15 of the Covenant. On the other hand, he did not mention that he would "ask for the application of sanctions under Article 16." Lord Robert replied that he was entitled to

[32] Montagna (Athens) to Mussolini, September 1, 1923. *Ibid.*, p. 151; Avricourt (Athens) to Poincaré, August 31, 1923. Attached to file 768.7515/61, Record Group 59, NA.

Mussolini versus the League

bring the matter before the Council but said nothing further. Faced by an entirely unexpected situation, he cabled Whitehall for instructions.[33]

Across the city, the chief of the Italian delegation, Antonio Salandra, who before the Corfu occupation had telegraphed Mussolini his full support, was also busy.[34] There was no doubt that the question would reach the League, Salandra cabled the Duce. Especially, he continued, since both the Council and the Assembly were in session and Greece, like every other nation, had the right to appeal to them. Because of this and "in order to avoid that Italy be cited befort the League of Nations as [a] defendant" it appeared "preferable" that Rome, in submission to Article 15, take the initiative and communicate directly to the League Council, which was "preferable to the Assembly." Rome was to keep in mind, he cautioned, that Greek participation in any Council proceedings would be inevitable. If Mussolini agreed with his recommendation, Salandra remarked, he was to reply immediately. He also suggested that the note to the Council should include the point that Italy's action was not an "act of war." In closing, he appealed for the "latest decisions" since the question had absorbed the attention of everyone at Geneva.[35]

Mussolini's reply, also repeated to the Italian Embassies in London and Paris, was that he did "not consider [it] opportune to make for the present any communication to the Council of the League of Nations." If Greece, however, appealed to the League, Salandra was instructed, on the basis of the Duce's Corfu proclamation and with "such expedients" as he deemed fitting, "to give special stress" to the fact that Italy's action was not an "act of war." Since the murdered officers were agents of the Conference, he was also to stress the role the Conference of Ambassadors had already taken and would have "yet to take in [the] determination of sanctions." These

[33] Lord Robert Cecil, *A Great Experiment* (New York: Oxford University Press, 1941), pp. 148-149.

[34] Salandra, p. 101.

[35] Salandra (Geneva) to Mussolini, August 31, 1923. *DDI*, pp. 147-148.

Mussolini versus the League

two points, Mussolini continued, would have the object of obtaining a rejection of the Council's competence, since the question was not covered by the Covenant of the League of Nations; exclusion of the Council's competence would defer the question to the Conference of Ambassadors; deferring to the Conference would suspend every decision by the League Council until the Conference would have acted.[36]

The Duce in the days to come would succeed in implementing all these points. Salandra's original recommendation would be disregarded. This would not be his first setback with Mussolini. Even his recommendation that Italy describe its action at Corfu as not being an "act of war" was perverted in a way he never intended.

REACTIONS IN LONDON AND PARIS

In the Italian Embassy in London, Della Torretta, following instructions received from Rome, appeared at the Foreign Office and read to Sir William Tyrrell Mussolini's Corfu proclamation. Tyrrell limited himself to replying that he would transmit the Duce's proclamation to Lord Curzon, who was still on the Continent. In the conversation that now followed Sir William declared to Della Torretta, in no uncertain terms, that his "government in this lawless act" was working "strenuously towards world revolution."[37] When asked by Tyrrell how the Italian Government could "reconcile the action undertaken with its obligations [in] respect [to] the Covenant of the League of Nations," Della Torretta replied "evasively."

To enlighten Mussolini concerning English feelings and politics, Della Torretta cabled that the League had in Britain

[36] Mussolini to Salandra (Geneva), September 1, 1923. *Ibid.*, p. 150. Mussolini's message crossed with a cable from Salandra sent in the early morning hours of September 1. Salandra, informed that the Greeks definitely would refer the question to the League, again brought to Mussolini's attention the advantage of acting first. If authorized to do so, Salandra proposed to submit a report "drawn in compliance" with the Duce's Corfu proclamation. Salandra (Geneva) to Mussolini, September 1, 1923. *Ibid.*, p. 150.

[37] Wheeler (London) to the Department of State, September 1, 1923. File 765.68/26, Record Group 59, NA.

Mussolini versus the League

a "great protector in public opinion and the press," and that Lord Robert Cecil, a member of the cabinet and Britain's chief delegate at Geneva, was a "fanatical supporter" who worked unceasingly to strengthen the League and to further its prestige. Because of this, it was possible that Cecil, either in the Council or in the Assembly of the League, might make some move facilitated by a Greek appeal which would find in England a "consentient public opinion and press."[38] The ambassador's remarks about British public opinion and especially as to the British press were correct. With the lone exception of the *Daily Mail*, British press comment about Italy's actions at Corfu was "severe."[39]

In a priority cable the Duce instructed Della Torretta to make a *démarche* at the Foreign Office over England's apparent attitude and especially over the actions of the British press, which was inciting the "live indignation [of] Italian public opinion." This was to be done, Mussolini added, in order to avoid any changes in the "friendly relations between [the] two people."[40] The specter of the British Navy was beginning to cast its shadow in the halls of the Palazzo Chigi.

The following morning, September 1, when the American

---

[38] Della Torretta (London) to Mussolini, August 31, 1923. *DDI*, p. 149.

[39] Wheeler (London) to the Department of State, September 1, 1923. File 765.68/26, Record Group 59, NA. The editorial and cartoon attacks of the *Daily Mail* against Lords Curzon and Cecil reached appalling lengths. See the *Daily Mail*, September 1 through 10, 1923. A "hysterical campaign" was unleashed against Lords Curzon and Cecil and the Foreign Office for their support of the League, which the *Daily Mail* described as "war mongering." Sir Harold Nicolson, *Curzon: the Last Phase, 1919-1925* (New York: Harcourt, Brace and Co., 1939), p. 371.

The violent anti-Italian attacks of the *Daily Chronicle* may be explained in part by the fact that it was owned by the Greek financier and munitions dealer, Sir Basil Zaharoff. Luigi Villari, *Italian Foreign Policy under Mussolini* (New York: Devin-Adair Co., 1956), p. 23. The Italian press was to get its *quid pro quo* in November 1924, over British actions in Egypt following the murder by Egyptian nationalists of the grand Sirdar of the Egyptian army, Sir Lee Stack. *Oriento Moderno*, IV, Nr. 12 (1924), footnote p. 772.

[40] Mussolini to Della Torretta (London), September 1, 1923. *DDI*, p. 155.

Mussolini versus the League

chargé d'affaires Wheeler appeared at Whitehall, Tyrrell opined "this is the life or death of the League itself. If Italy refuses to make the question an international one she will be walking out of the League which must take action anyway. The situation then would be most serious." Sir William's attitude was that the Italian action was "an overt act" which constituted a "deliberate crime" and called for a "penalty." Speaking personally and without having heard from Lord Curzon, Tyrrell thought that Great Britain "would welcome a suggestion" from Washington that both governments express their disapproval of Italy's actions by withdrawing their ambassadors from Rome. The suggestion should most fittingly come from across the Atlantic, Sir William observed, since the United States was a great power with interests in Western Europe and yet was "detached from its present complications." Such a move could not help but have a great effect and would find support in both countries. Even France might join this move, he added, provided it affected favorably and not unfavorably "her position in the Ruhr compared with which at present everything else in Europe seems of minute importance to her."[41]

In the isolationist atmosphere of Coolidge Washington, Tyrrell's suggestion had not the slightest chance of success. "I regard Tyrrell's suggestion," cabled Acting Secretary of State William Phillips, "as a purely personal one and not therefore representing the reasoned view of the British Government." Furthermore, he observed, since the issue had already been submitted to the League "it would be indecorous for this government to take any independent action at this moment."[42]

Though at this point Britain's future line of action was unresolved, across the channel France's policy was already determined. The Ruhr, which in Tyrrell's conversation with Wheeler had merely been touched upon, was the deciding

[41] Wheeler (London) to the Department of State, September 1, 1923. File 765.68/26, Record Group 59, NA.
[42] Phillips to Wheeler (London), September 3, 1923. File 765.68/26, Record Group 59, NA.

Mussolini versus the League

factor in determining French actions. If the Corfu issue could come before the League Council, Poincaré reasoned, could not Germany also attempt to bring before the Council the French occupation of the Ruhr—an occupation executed by French and Belgian troops on January 11, seven and a half months before? Although the Quai d'Orsay felt the Corfu and Ruhr occupations were "juridically" different, "a similar application could find favorable ears." A secondary consideration was that Italy from the beginning had supported the Franco-Belgian occupation of the Ruhr and had continued to do so after Curzon's note of August 11 protesting the French occupation. This was no time to alienate Italian support. These two factors added up to a French decision "to take refuge behind the Conference of Ambassadors," which had already been accepted by Italy and would soon be accepted by Greece.[43] A stipulation by Poincaré's cabinet which complicated the French task was that any settlement should spare Mussolini "anything smacking of humiliation."[44]

This policy, however, put France in a difficult position. The Quai d'Orsay could not neglect the attitude of reprobation toward Italy assumed by states either friendly to France or allied with her: Belgium, Poland, and the States of the Little Entente. Poincaré therefore had to move carefully, and the experienced Jules Laroche was appointed to implement his policies. Laroche, in turn, planned with Jules Cambon, the veteran diplomatist, the tactics to be followed.[45] Cambon, because of his important position as President of the Conference

[43] Jules Laroche, *Au Quai d'Orsay avec Briand et Poincaré, 1913-1926* (Paris: Librairie Hachette, 1957), p. 175.

[44] Henry de Jouvenel, "France and Italy," *Foreign Affairs*, v, No. 4 (1927), p. 538. At the same time Poincaré and the Quai d'Orsay were deciding French policy, the Italian Ambassador in London drew Mussolini's attention to France's actions in the League of Nations over the Ruhr occupation. France, he cabled the Duce, had for many months succeeded in avoiding any submission of the Ruhr controversy to Geneva, notwithstanding the hostile activity of Lord Robert Cecil and the greater part of the English press. Della Torretta (London) to Mussolini, September 1, 1923. *DDI*, p. 157.

[45] Laroche, p. 175. Laroche had served in Rome for fifteen years under Camille Barrère and spoke fluent Italian.

Mussolini versus the League

of Ambassadors, "could be relied on with his well-known experience to manage everything."[46] These two men, supported by their colleagues, René Massigli and Henri Fromageot, would dominate the discussions in the coming secret meetings of the Conference of Ambassadors, turning the conversation now this way, now that, in order to achieve French policy aims. Geneva was also not forgotten. France's League delegate, Gabriel Hanotaux, received continuing instructions from Poincaré to be the peacemaker in the Council, to seek formulas of delay and compromise, and to maintain "friendly contact" with the Italian delegation.[47]

The French position, however, was surmised by Lord Curzon;[48] M. Giuseppe Motta, the Swiss Federal Counsellor for Foreign Affairs;[49] Italy's League delegate, Antonio Salandra;[50] and undoubtedly by others. It was also known to Mussolini. He has "no delusions about France's attitude," wrote the British chargé d'affaires at Rome, Sir Howard W. Kennard, to Lord Curzon, "which he uses quite cynically for propaganda purposes." On the other hand, Kennard continued, "if France finally has to commit herself in any way against Italy, I think that there will be an outburst of feeling against her here far greater than there now is against us."[51] France's support of

[46] Jouvenel, p. 538.   [47] Salandra, p. 103.
[48] Della Torretta (London) to Mussolini, September 3, 1923. *DDI*, p. 178.
[49] Garbasso (Berne) to Mussolini, September 2, 1923. *Ibid.*, p. 165. The Italian Minister had called on Motta to discuss the anti-Italian attitude of the Swiss press. Motta explained that Switzerland, as a small country, was always "alarmed" when force was used by a great Power against a small Power, and this attitude was mirrored in her press. The Counsellor observed that perhaps in no other country in the world had the League of Nations as much prestige as in Switzerland; it was situated in Geneva, and Switzerland had become a member state only after a nation-wide referendum. Therefore, Motta continued, Swiss public opinion saw in Italy's actions a weakening of the League. Motta also felt that Articles 12 and 15 of the Covenant were applicable in the dispute. For a review of the Swiss press during the crisis see *Bulletin Périodique de la Presse Suisse*, No. 179, pp. 8-9.
[50] Salandra, p. 104.
[51] Sir Howard W. Kennard (Rome) to Lord Curzon, September 7, 1923. Folder marked "Letters to Curzon G-L, 1923," Box 65, Curzon Papers.

Mussolini versus the League

Italy never wavered, and after the incident was closed the Quai d'Orsay was informed by François Charles-Roux, its chargé d'affaires in Rome, that Mussolini "was conscious of the service that it [France] had rendered to him."[52] French national interests had required that the Quai d'Orsay pull the Italian chestnuts out of the fire.

GENEVA: THE FIRST ENCOUNTER

In Geneva, on the morning of September 1, at the fourth meeting of the League Council, the President, Viscount Kikujiro Ishii of Japan, announced that the Secretary-General had received for distribution to the Council certain documents in reference to the Italo-Greek dispute. The documents, he remarked, were being translated and would be distributed immediately. Consideration of the matter by the Council, Ishii observed, was of great urgency. However, in order to give every delegate time to study the documents, he suggested that the Council meet at 4:00 P.M. to consider them. This proposal was readily agreed to by the Council.[53] Politis' appeal under Articles 12 and 15, in line with instructions from Athens, was immediately communicated to Rome by the ever alert international civil servant, Attolico, via the Italian Consul in Geneva.[54]

The Greek appeal made no mention of the bombardment and occupation of Corfu. It merely described the Italian ultimatum and the Greek reply, texts of which were attached to Politis' appeal. Obviously Politis' instructions to appeal to the League had preceded the Corfu action.[55]

At noon, at a private meeting of the Council, Salandra stated that he had no knowledge of the contents of the documents and requested that they be distributed at a private meeting. Then, Salandra observed, the Council could decide if the discussion should be public or private. This observation pro-

[52] Laroche, p. 177.
[53] L.N., *Official Journal*, 4th year, 1923, p. 1274.
[54] Eles (Geneva) to Mussolini, September 1, 1923. *DDI*, p. 154.
[55] L.N., *Official Journal*, 4th year, 1923, pp. 1412-1413.

Mussolini versus the League

voked a discussion between Salandra and Lord Cecil over the nature of the Council's discussions and whether the Greek representative should be present before any decision was made. Salandra's feelings were that the Council should not hear the Greek representative on the matter of the publicity of the meeting, which was a "pure question of procedure." He felt that the spirit of the Covenant was that any state in a dispute with another state had the right to be represented on the Council when the dispute was aired even though it was not a member of the Council. He did not believe that there was a dispute between Italy and Greece regarding the meeting's being public or private; only the Council "was sovereign in this matter." Salandra's tack was quite clear, to attempt as much as possible to keep any discussion behind closed doors in order to feed as little fuel as possible to an aroused world public opinion. It was finally decided that a preliminary meeting in private would be held in the presence of the Greek delegate and that the Council would later decide on what publicity would be given to any further discussion of the question.[56] The first Cecil-Salandra skirmish had ended.

Salandra's observations to Rome were that any further decisions at Geneva depended mostly on the attitudes of the English and French delegates, Lord Robert Cecil and Gabriel Hanotaux. It was necessary that both of them and especially Cecil, who in the morning session had shown an uncertain attitude and had even made difficulties about a closed session, "receive from their governments instructions to support as much as possible our line of action."[57] The support that Salandra envisaged did not appear, and the attacks of Lord Cecil increased in volume and intensity.

Before the afternoon session convened, Politis, in an attempt to settle the dispute, sought out Salandra and expressed the desire that the question be disposed of "rapidly by means of direct agreement between the two countries" which the Council would easily ratify.

[56] *Ibid.*, p. 1276.
[57] Salandra (Geneva) to Mussolini, September 1, 1923. *DDI*, pp. 154-155.

Mussolini versus the League

Salandra gave no indication of either agreement or concession. Politis then requested that his overtures be communicated to Rome; these overtures, Salandra observed to Mussolini, should therefore be regarded as "official." Salandra's impression after his talk with Politis was that the Greek Government would be satisfied by "some attenuation" of the conditions which Italy had demanded in its ultimatum.[58]

At the afternoon meeting Politis took his chair at the Council table. The Greek appeal was read and at Lord Cecil's request Articles 12 and 15 of the Covenant. Politis, who was held in high esteem by his Italian counterpart,[59] now began the formal presentation of the Greek complaint.

It was only with the "greatest regret," Politis announced to the Council, that Greece felt compelled to use the right given to it under the Covenant. This regret was natural, he observed, for two reasons: one, Greece had just passed through a major crisis—here Politis was alluding to Greece's ill-fated Anatolian venture—and certainly wished to avoid a new crisis; two, it was a dispute which involved a great Power with whom Greece always desired, and still desired, to maintain the friendliest relations. As to the dispute itself, Politis felt he could add little in the way of facts. The Greek Government, he declared, "had the right and duty" to appeal under Article 15 and to submit the matter to the Council. Because acts of violence were subsequently committed he asked whether it was not a case contemplated under Article 16 of the Covenant, which he then quoted.

He was quite aware that a communiqué from Rome described the actions at Corfu as "pacific acts of a temporary character." He observed, however, that it did not seem to lie "with the author of an act to describe it." "Acts," Politis continued, "must be judged objectively, and it is for the Council to judge the acts regarding which Greece has the right to complain." The Greek Government, he declared, desired to give every satisfaction compatible with its *amour propre* and

[58] Salandra (Geneva) to Mussolini, September 1, 1923. *Ibid.*, p. 160.
[59] Salandra, p. 102.

with the dignity of Italy. It was also willing to profit by any doubts that existed as to the nature of the acts committed by Italy at Corfu so as not to take the initiative in requesting the application of sanctions under Article 16 of the Covenant. The facts, Politis continued, required that the Council render a settlement as envisaged in Article 15, section 3, of the Covenant. The Greek Government was desirous of submitting itself to any arrangement possible and he believed agreement could be reached. If Italy, like Greece, was willing to conform with the provisions of the Covenant by which both nations were bound there was one more course to pursue: to restore the status quo ante and to desist in the use of force, which had already been wrongly applied against Greece. Politis declared in the most "solemn manner" that Greece was "ready to accept and execute in good faith any proposals made to her by the Council" in order to satisfy Italian desires. By this proposal and with Italy's good will an agreement would be "possible, satisfactory and rapid." He desired it for the well-being of both countries and for the League, which he considered "the only safeguard for international order." The League was being subjected "to a rude test," he concluded, by the events of the past seventy-two hours and this was a "unique occasion" for the League to show "with the consent and good will of the two parties" that it was "in a position to fulfill its duties and that it is still worthy of the trust which had been placed in it."

One of Politis' important points was good will, but Salandra, under instructions from Rome, was in no position to reciprocate. "No Italian Government could have acted otherwise," Salandra declared to the Council. The blow that had been struck at the "public conscience" of Italy made it necessary to take the steps that were taken to "safeguard its honour." According to the Greek representative, Salandra observed, Greece did not intend to appeal to the League under Article 16 of the Covenant; nevertheless that article had been cited. As instructed by Mussolini he cautioned the Council that Article 16 could not be applied to Italy since the official communiqué from Rome made it clear that the Italian Govern-

Mussolini versus the League

ment "did not intend to commit an act of war." No nation in this situation, he continued, could tolerate the application of sanctions under Article 16. He invited Politis not to mention Article 16 but to restrict himself to other articles of the Covenant. As to the Greek representative's facts in reference to the Corfu action, he found himself at a disadvantage since he possessed "no direct information" from Rome. Likewise, he lacked instructions as to whether the Italian Government "considers itself able or unable to accept the appeal" which the Greek Government had addressed to the League.

In line with his instructions he now began to question the Council's competence. Another body, he noted, was dealing with the matter—the Conference of Ambassadors. The latter organ was certainly competent since the murdered officers had been its agents. Can the League, he queried, act before the results of the inquiry which the Conference would certainly initiate to ascertain the murderers of its agents are known? There were certain precedents in which the Council had refrained from action when the case was before the Ambassadorial Conference. Hence, Salandra asked, to what extent can the Council deal with a question which is before the Conference of Ambassadors. In concluding, he asked if the Council would grant him a recess so he could receive instructions from his government in order to reply to the Greek appeal.

Without orders and faced by a difficult situation, Lord Cecil was equal to the task. He made it clear that the matter facing the Council was the most serious that had ever been before it since the League's inception. It was difficult to comprehend, Cecil observed, how the violent occupation of a portion of someone else's territory could "be regarded as a pacific measure." He also had difficulty in understanding how this could be "differentiated from an act of war." Personally, he recognized no distinction between a great Power and a small Power. All states, he noted, were "equally amenable to the obligations" they undertook by signing the Covenant of the League. There could be no differentiation in the "sanctity of a contractual obligation" on the basis that it had been agreed to by a powerful or less powerful individual. Since Salandra was without instructions, Lord Cecil proposed that the Italian and Greek representatives should "give assurances that there would be no further acts of war or of violence pending further discussion of the matter" when instructions would be received from Rome. Cecil did not think the objection to the Council's lack of jurisdiction was sound. The Conference of Ambassadors, he observed, was merely an organ on which some of the governments at the League Council were represented. Unless these governments had instructed their representatives in the Council not to undertake the question or deal with it—and Lord Cecil admitted having received no such instructions—he could not fathom on what ground the Council could abstain from dealing with the matter merely because it had "been or is thought to have been discussed by our Governments in another capacity."

There was no doubt, the chief British delegate observed, that the matter in hand was "one of those cases which is quite clearly within the scope of Article 15," not to mention Articles 12 and 16 of the Covenant. Here was a dispute that was likely to lead to a break. This was separate from the difficulties that could arise under Articles 12 and 16. Like Politis, Cecil did not wish to raise the issue of the latter article at the present time, since it was a matter which affected not only Greece and Italy "but the whole system on which the League of Nations is built." Regardless of anyone's views on Articles 12 and 16 there was no doubt in his mind that the matter came clearly within the scope of Article 15. Whether the question "may or may not affect" another organ on which some of the states represented at the Council also sat was immaterial to him and had no bearing whatever on the "obvious, plain, grammatical, verbal meaning of the provisions of Article 15." At the moment he could see no grounds on which the Council could refuse the Greek appeal "without entirely forfeiting its right to the confidence of the world and entirely evading its position as created by the Covenant." As far as he was con-

Mussolini versus the League

cerned he was prepared "here and now" to reply to Salandra's queries in the negative. Cecil's talk had ended but the attack on Italy and Salandra's position did not cease.

To the Swedish representative, Karl Hjalmar Branting, who in the coming weeks was to be one of Italy's and Salandra's bitterest opponents, fell the task of expressing the feelings of the smaller Powers. The small States, Branting noted, whose representatives had spoken to him, felt that the "situation as regards the very existence of the League of Nations is extremely serious." The Council, he observed, had a duty to interject itself into any relationship between states which could threaten the foundation of the Covenant. It could not take into consideration what the Conference of Ambassadors contemplated doing and was duty bound to delve into the matter as quickly as possible. Neither could the Council delay its decision, as it was obligated to say something regarding this regrettable incident. Branting therefore allied himself with the views of Lord Cecil in the "conviction they would be supported almost unanimously by all the small States of Europe." These states, Branting continued, "have a vital interest in ensuring that a breach of the provisions of the Covenant should not be allowed to pass without protest and energetic steps being taken."

Salandra, in reply to Cecil, agreed that all states, great and small, were obligated to abide by the Covenant. Yet he wished to make it clear that he had spoken in the name of Italy, not "Italy as a great Power." His country, whether a great or small Power, had "regard for its dignity and prestige, and would defend them if necessary against the world." He noted that in the Greek appeal there was no request for a status quo ante. There was a difference, he cautioned, between a restoration of the previous condition and an invitation to the Council to discuss the whole question. Did or did not Politis make this proposal? This was an important point since he had to inform Rome in order to receive instructions. He still reserved the preliminary question of the Council's competence, asking the Council to profit by the delay and to appoint a committee to

Mussolini versus the League

examine the question of jurisdiction, which had to be settled before any discussion could begin about the application of Article 15.

Politis, in his reply, "thought that between Members of the League of Nations there was no longer any place for measures such as an ultimatum and coercion." Under Article 12, he noted, the member states entered into a "solemn undertaking" to follow judicial or political procedures before the Council. There were no other alternative procedures. Italy, however, had employed other means. The matter was therefore outside the bounds of the Covenant. To be once more within the terms of the Covenant it was necessary to have a speedy settlement of the dispute, to restore the status quo ante and to cease all measures of coercion, simultaneously placing the matter before the Council so that it could "remove the cause of the dispute." Politis felt that the question of competence could not arise. States, like Greece, which were not represented on the Conference of Ambassadors could "not recognize as legal the jurisdiction of that body." If in the past Greece had submitted itself to decisions by that body it was only because of *force majeure*. On the other hand, by yielding to the Council, Greece was "acting in obedience to a legal decision" and conforming to the terms of the Covenant to which it was a signatory. World public opinion, he emphasized, would be shocked if the matter, after being brought before the Council in accordance with the Covenant, "were to slip from the hands of the Council without the plaintiff having the opportunity of appearing before the Conference of Ambassadors." This situation would produce "inequality" between the two states. Greece was prepared to submit itself in advance to any decision of the Council, "but makes all reservations in the event the question remains in the hands of the Conference of Ambassadors."

With the discussion finished the Council adopted a resolution sponsored by Lord Cecil, assenting to a postponement of the debate and expressing the hope that during the interval both states would commit "no act which might aggravate the

Mussolini versus the League

situation." Salandra reserved the right to raise the question of the Council's competence at the next meeting.[60]

THREATS TO LEAVE THE LEAGUE

In his cable to Rome, Salandra pointed out that though Politis' statements had been "hostile" they had also been "skillfully moderate" towards Italy and deferent towards the Council's authority and the League of Nations. He also brought to Mussolini's attention the sphinx-like silence of M. Hanotaux and the French delegation. Salandra was well aware of the feelings of his colleagues, and of the anti-Italian attitude which all too obviously pervaded the halls of the Palais des Nations. Therefore, he felt it his duty to warn the Duce that the Italian thesis, that the question was not covered by Articles 12 and 15 of the Covenant, was "untenable," and any attempt to sustain it would meet the hostility of a unanimous Council. If, Salandra continued, the thesis "has to be absolutely supported, permit me to ask Your Excellency to entrust another delegate to sustain it." His own opinion was that the question of the competence of the Ambassadorial Conference "however weak can be supported." However, even this approach, he warned Mussolini, would fail unless London and Paris instructed their Geneva delegates to support it, since Branting and Cecil as well as other delegates were opposed to this line. Therefore, he requested "explicit instructions" in the probable case the Council declared itself competent and entered into an examination of the merits of the question.[61]

[60] L.N., *Official Journal*, 4th year, 1923, pp. 1277-1282. The Athens Government had informed the American Legation that it intended taking no aggressive actions for forty-eight hours. It hoped "that outside pressure would be brought to bear" on Rome so that she would refer the whole question to the League. The Greeks felt that if they made no move after this forty-eight hour period Italy would continue in permanent occupation of the island. Atherton (Athens) to the Department of State, August 31, 1923. File 765.68/12 Section 2, Record Group 59, NA.

[61] Salandra (Geneva) to Mussolini, September 2, 1923. *DDI*, pp. 161-162. The Assembly showed its displeasure by refusing to include an Italian among its twelve Vice-Presidents, the only instance when a

Mussolini versus the League

Salandra's pleas for Anglo-French support at Geneva had already prompted Mussolini to cable the Italian Missions in London and Paris. Both missions were advised to act "without delay" in persuading their host governments to instruct their representatives in Geneva "to favor our side." They were to make it clear that League interference would have no other object than to further complicate the situation and delay a speedy settlement of this "grave question." Certainly, he noted, quick settlement was everyone's wish. They were also to make it clear that "the dignity and honor of Italy" were involved and that the offense extended to all the Allied Powers who were members of the Delimitation Commission. Any hostile Anglo-French attitude at Geneva, the Duce warned, would in the end be harmful to the League "*and could conduce Italy to review its position in the same Society.*" Whitehall and the Quai d'Orsay were to be informed that the principles involved in the dispute did not permit the Italian Government to consider the question as one that fell under the articles of the Covenant and therefore within the competence and subject to the judgment of the League of Nations. Rome, moreover, found it impossible to consent to any discussions between Greece and Italy as equals "in a question of national honor." This was understandable since England and France had themselves refused to recognize the Athens government, revolutionary in origin and composed of men who had dipped their hands in blood.[62]

These same points were to be made by Salandra, especially in discourse with his French and English colleagues at Geneva. In discussions outside the Council meetings, he was to emphasize that submission of the Italo-Greek question to the Council would establish a dangerous precedent. It would bind states in

---

permanent Member of the Council was not chosen. F. P. Walters, *A History of the League of Nations* (London: Oxford University Press, 1960), p. 247.

[62] Italics added. The italicized sentence was added to the telegram by Mussolini. Mussolini to Della Torretta (London) and to Vannutelli (Paris), September 2, 1923. *DDI*, pp. 159-160.

Mussolini versus the League

the future to defer to an international organ each and every delicate question that involved national honor and prestige. These points, the Duce remarked, he had brought to the attention of the French and British representatives in Rome. The Italian thesis, Mussolini observed to Salandra, was being entrusted to his "lofty patriotism" and was to be sustained without hesitation. Any hesitation, he cautioned, could cause the position and the international prestige of Italy to diminish and would cast doubts on Italian solidarity towards its own position. Lastly, delay in Geneva was of "capital importance" in order to gain time to see what would come from Italian overtures in London and Paris.[63]

Along with these cables Mussolini also instructed Salandra to communicate the contents of his Corfu proclamation to the League. This communication, coupled with an official declaration, was to make it clear that Italy did not consider referring the question to the League of Nations, nor did it intend for the moment to do so since the question did "not deal with a dispute contemplated in the Covenant." The Corfu action was an attempt to "protect the prestige" and "national institutions" of Italy, a right, he added parenthetically, with which the League did not have the right to intervene. In ending, the Duce noted that the Italian measures were not of a "warlike character" nor did they constitute an act of war or threat of war. He did not consider these measures to be—a phrase he repeated for accentuation—within the competence of the League. Salandra's communication to the League, he cau-

[63] Mussolini to Salandra (Geneva), Avezzana (Paris), and Della Torretta (London), September 3, 1923. *Ibid.*, pp. 169-170. The above telegram was also repeated to the King. Mussolini to Vittorio Emanuele III (Racconigi), September 3, 1923. *Ibid.*, p. 169. A possible delaying tactic of referring the question of the Council's competence to the Permanent Court of International Justice was brought to Salandra's attention. A note from the Italian Minister at The Hague cited the precedent in the dispute over the German minority in Poland, where the Council had asked the advice of the Court as to whether it was competent. This procedure, Rome noted to Salandra, could gain Italy time without causing any change in the status quo. Mussolini to Salandra (Geneva), September 3, 1923. *Ibid.*, p. 168.

Mussolini versus the League

tioned, was to be exclusively informative in character and was an act of courtesy towards the Council.[64]

The last point in Mussolini's cable, that the Italian actions at Corfu were pacific and provisional in character, he attempted to justify to Salandra and all Italian Missions abroad. Occupations like that of Corfu, he cabled, were "fully established in international law." The impossibility for an injured state to obtain just satisfaction by peaceful means, and its subsequent recourse to violent measures might appear to be war but is not in fact action of a "warlike character." These measures merely constitute acts of "self-protection" of one's interests. One of the various coercive means not understood to be warlike was the temporary occupation of someone's territory. The Duce then cited precedents to substantiate his proposition. France had occupied the island of Mytilene in 1914 in order to compel the Ottoman Government to assume its responsibilities toward certain French firms. The latest recourse to this type of action was by the United States in its occupation of the Mexican port of Vera Cruz. The Italian occupation of Corfu, he observed, was the least harmful means open to Italy. Under international law it could have resorted to pacific blockade; bombardment of a fortified area; the occupation of Greek ports; the seizure of Greek customs houses; the confiscation of ships, goods, or credits of the Greek State or its citizens. Actions of this nature in the past were numerous. In 1884 France, in order to obtain an indemnity owed to French citizens, bombarded the Chinese arsenal of Fu-cao and blockaded the island of Formosa. Again in 1893, France blockaded the Siamese port of Menam. There were blockades of the Greek coast in 1896 and of Crete in 1897 in order to prevent an armed conflict between Greece and the Ottoman Empire. In 1902, Germany, England, and Italy blockaded the Venezuelan coast and bombarded the fort of San Carlo to compel payment of foreign debts. In 1913, the Great Powers blockaded the coast of Montenegro to force the evacuation of Scutari in Albania. In 1882, England bombarded Alex-

[64] Mussolini to Salandra (Geneva), repeated to all Diplomatic Missions Abroad, September 1, 1923. *Ibid.*, p. 156.

Mussolini versus the League

andria and landed troops. As late as 1916, the French Admiral Dartige du Fournet landed troops at Athens and bombarded the coast. Lastly, Corfu and various other Aegean islands were occupied in 1916 by the Allied Powers without war breaking out with Greece. All these precedents were to be used by the Italian diplomats as guides in any discussion of the question, and were also to be furnished to the local press.[65]

The Duce's cable, however, raised more problems than it solved. It was true that coercive measures of a similar type had been employed in the past, but none of the other territories involved were in the same legal position as Corfu. Corfu and the adjacent island of Paxo as well as their dependencies under Article 2 of the second Treaty of London of March 29, 1864, between Great Britain, France, Russia, Austria-Hungary, Prussia, and Greece, were to "enjoy the advantages of perpetual neutrality."[66] This treaty was still operative in August and September 1923.[67] To be sure, Italy, not being a signatory and

[65] Mussolini to all Diplomatic Missions Abroad and to Salandra (Geneva), September 1, 1923. *Ibid.*, pp. 157-158. The same legal exposition with added examples was reported in the *Corriere Italiano*, September 2, 1923. As quoted in *Bulletin Périodique de la Presse Italienne*, No. 207, p. 3. The analogy of the Italian action at Corfu and the American action at Vera Cruz was "vigorously condemned" in Washington. It was pointed out that the Tampico incident, which led to the American seizure of Vera Cruz, was an outrage carried out by Mexican soldiers in uniform and it was assumed that they were acts ordered by the Mexican authorities. On the other hand, the murderers of General Tellini and his staff were unknown. *The Times* (London), September 6, 1923, p. 10.

[66] Edward Hertslet, *The Map of Europe by Treaty* (London: Butterworths, 1875), III, p. 1592. This treaty had been preceded by the first Treaty of London between the Great Powers on November 14, 1863, which neutralized under Article 2 all the Ionian Islands. Under Article 3 it was also stipulated that all fortifications on the islands would be destroyed upon the withdrawal of British troops and the union of the islands with Greece. *Ibid.*, II, p. 1571. The transition from the first Treaty of London to the second was accomplished by the London Protocols of January 25, 1864, between Great Britain, France, Russia, Prussia, and Austria-Hungary. Great Britain. Foreign Office, *British and Foreign State Papers*, 54, pp. 34-35.

[67] Under the moribund Treaty of Sèvres, Great Britain and France renounced all special rights of supervision and control that devolved upon them in relation to Greece under the first Treaty of London, and

Mussolini versus the League

never adhering to the treaty neutralizing Corfu, was not legally obligated to guarantee its neutrality. The question that can be asked, however, is whether Italy was obligated to respect the neutrality of the island. The point can be made that by entering the European Concert of Nations, Italy placed herself in a position where she had to face rights which were superior to hers.[68] Certainly her record up to 1923 gives support to this argument, for though Italy was not a party to the treaty, neither did she ever object to it, nor attempt to circumvent it. One could even say that the faithful execution of the treaty by all parties and respect for it by others for almost sixty years[69] had made the neutralization of Corfu and respect for its neutrality part of the public law of Europe.

Italy, on the other hand, argued that Britain and France had established a precedent by their use of the island, during the First World War, as a military base. The whole question could not arise since her actions were not an act of war, but simply coercive measures. If neutralization implied the prohibition of acts of war on neutralized territory, Rome theorized, it certainly did not exclude a territorial occupation which had no warlike object. From any point of view, it observed, the occupation of Corfu without a warlike object was "not in contradiction with international law" and was "accordingly perfectly legitimate."[70]

---

as regards the Ionian Islands under the second Treaty of London. L.N., *Treaty Series*, xxviii, 1924, pp. 247-248.

This was reiterated in the Treaty of Lausanne. However, Greece did not ratify the Lausanne settlement until February 11, 1924, and Great Britain, Japan, and Italy only on August 6, 1924. *Ibid.*, p. 223. Therefore, the second Treaty of London of March 29, 1864, was still in force in August and September, 1923.

[68] Albert Philippe, *Le rôle de la Société des Nations dans l'Affaire de Corfou* (Lille: Librairie Robbe, 1924), p. 81.

[69] The neutrality of Corfu was respected by the Powers in their blockade of Greece in 1887 and by the Greeks in their blockade of Epirus during the Greco-Turkish War of 1897. *Ibid.*, footnote p. 83. Philippe could have added that it was respected by the Powers in their Greek blockade of 1896 and in their blockade of Crete in 1897. The Greeks in turn respected it during both Balkan Wars, 1912-1913.

[70] Pierre Lasturel, *L'Affaire Gréco-Italienne de 1923* (Paris: L'Ile de

Mussolini versus the League

The question that this thesis left unanswered was whether or not acts of a coercive nature could be justified under the Covenant of the League of Nations. Was not the League of Nations an attempt to establish a new world order? Did not the League of Nations' Covenant provide for juridical and political procedures which all signatories had to follow, in all situations? Was not the very essence of the League an attempt to prevent wars or acts of this very nature?

A SPECIAL COURIER: GIOVANNI GIURIATI

Fully aware of the dangerous situation developing in Geneva, Salandra desired to give Mussolini "an impression live and direct." As courier for this important assignment he chose Giovanni Giuriati, delegate to the Assembly of the League and Minister without portfolio in the Duce's cabinet. Selection of Giuriati for this "delicate mission" was based on long friendship and on the fact that he was a member of the cabinet and personally close to Mussolini. A poorer choice could not have been made; for Giuriati was an ultra-Nationalist of the first order and if Salandra's intention in dispatching Giuriati was to produce a new tack in Rome, his selection was most unwise.[71] Giuriati departed by train from Geneva on the night of September 1, with a verbatim report of the Council's proceedings.[72] He arrived in Rome on the morning of September 3.[73]

France, 1925), pp. 181-182. Britain and France in the past had considered neutralized territory like Belgium inviolable. The German declaration in 1914 that their invasion of Belgium was not intended as a hostile act but was in self-defense was dismissed by both countries. Neutralized territory, they felt, was inviolable by customary international law as well as by the Fifth Hague Convention of 1907, which applied permanently to territory neutralized by treaty. The Corfu occupation differed from Germany's actions in Belgium in that Italy was never a signatory to the treaty neutralizing Corfu, while Germany was a signatory to the treaties neutralizing Belgium. Quincy Wright, "The Neutralization of Corfu," *American Journal of International Law*, 18, No. 1 (1924), p. 104.

[71] Salandra, p. 105.
[72] *The Times* (London), September 3, 1923, p. 10.
[73] *Ibid.*, September 4, 1923, p. 10.

Mussolini versus the League

On the day of Giuriati's arrival in Rome, Salandra cabled from Geneva that on the previous day, September 2, an unofficial and private meeting was held by the representatives of the small Powers led by the world-renowned Norwegian delegate, Fridtjof Nansen. These states, he reported, contemplated taking the Corfu question directly to the Assembly. "Friendly or at least moderate elements," he noted, wished to avoid this event which would certainly have unfortunate consequences for Italy.

The agitation by the small Powers, Salandra warned, would induce the Council to press its competence all the more. He then frankly admitted to Mussolini that after he and Vittorio Scialoja, Italy's former Foreign Minister, had carefully studied the Covenant, he was "forced to observe that no provision [of the] Covenant excludes [the] Council, [or the] Assembly [from] question[s] of national honor." It was the "unanimous" opinion of the Council and Assembly delegates, he continued, that to renounce its proper competence in the Greco-Italian question would be a "complete weakening" of the League. He felt delaying tactics based on the argument that it was necessary to await the results of measures initiated by the Conference of Ambassadors had some possibility of success. This approach would be preferable, especially if the Italian delegation's firm attitude persuaded the "directing organs" that they would thus avoid more serious Italian actions. The behavior of the British delegation, Salandra remarked, was "hostile and cold," while the French demonstrated "sympathy at least by words" and attempted to avoid aggravation of the question. Because of the "gravity of the situation" he desired "precise instructions" the next morning [September 4].[74]

Regardless of what Salandra may have wished or desired, Giuriati, upon his arrival in Rome, in a conversation with Mus-

[74] Salandra (Geneva) to Mussolini, September 3, 1923. *DDI*, pp. 170-171. Though Salandra may have studied the Covenant with Scialoja, the latter felt differently about the matter. Vittorio Scialoia, "La Società della Nazioni e il conflitto italo-greco," *Rivista di Diritto Pubblico e della Pubblica Amministrazione in Italia*, Serie II, Anno XVI, Fascicolo 1 (Gennaio 1924), pp. 69-74.

Mussolini versus the League

solini and Guariglia, "maintained the suitability" of leaving the League of Nations. According to Guariglia he based his arguments on grounds "pseudo-juridical besides political." He argued that the League had not fulfilled its obligations towards Italy and repeated the Latin maxim, *Inadempienti non adempitur* (one does not pay one's duty to those who have not paid theirs).

Guariglia was present at the meeting in his capacity as chief of the newly established "Corfu" office. The task of Guariglia and his subordinates was to avoid the Duce's bad temper, which might lead to an Italian withdrawal from the League. He also wished to persuade Mussolini to agree to any compromise formula arranged in Paris and Geneva for settling the dispute. Guariglia naturally argued against Giuriati's recommendations. Mussolini, however, said nothing and just listened.[75]

How instrumental Giuriati's arguments were in shaping Mussolini's future course of action is debatable. The Duce had in large measure already made up his mind before Giuriati's arrival in Rome, and the latter's arguments probably did nothing to induce the Duce to think twice about the course of action he was determined to pursue. The instructions that Giuriati carried back to Salandra in Geneva were as follows: Sustain the principle of the absolute non-competence of the League in the Corfu dispute since the question involves national honor. He was to base his reasons on instructions already sent to him. Secondly, Salandra was to declare that in case the Council did not accept the Italian point of view, Italy, finding herself in a position offensive to her prestige and national interests, "would be forced in spite of herself to withdraw from the League of Nations." The Italian Ambassadors in London and Paris were also asked to inform verbally the host governments of Italy's decision and were to indicate the grave situation that could arise. They were to make it clear

---

[75] Guariglia, pp. 29-30. The idea of a special office to deal with the Corfu dispute was Guariglia's. Raffaele Guariglia in an interview with the writer in Rome, August 1961.

that Italy would not feel responsible for such a situation, and that it would not regard its withdrawal from the League as any greater inconvenience than its presence in it. Both ambassadors were cautioned, however, to phrase their words in such a way as to avoid the interpretation that Italy's actions were a hostile act against either England or France. Lastly, they were to allow to both governments room for maneuver, in case they wished to instruct their Geneva representatives to support the Italian thesis, so as to avoid Italy's decision to leave the League should its thesis not be accepted.[76]

CURZON'S DECISION TO SUPPORT GREECE'S APPEAL

Any chance for British support had vanished long before. In London, Whitehall's first recommendation to Lord Curzon, who was still vacationing on the Continent, was that England, as one of the Powers guaranteeing the neutrality of Corfu, had the special right to intervene. The Foreign Secretary, however, termed their arguments "a legal quibble" and declined to act on the theory proposed.[77]

Lord Curzon returned to London after meeting Prime Minister Stanley Baldwin, vacationing in France, and with Poincaré in Paris on September 2. He arrived at Victoria Station on the night of September 2, after a rough passage from Bagnolles de l'Orne in Normandy. The trip probably added little to his good disposition. He was met by two officials from the Foreign Office, who accompanied him to St. Pancras Station. After seeing the latest dispatches he commented, "Yes . . . there can be no doubt about it. The machinery of the League must be put into motion. Telegraph to Bob Cecil instructing him to go full steam ahead."[78] The instructions were cleared with Prime

[76] The actual instructions to Salandra have never been found. However, in the cable cited below the text is related. Mussolini to Avezzana (Paris), Ruspoli (Brussels), Della Torretta (London), Paulucci De Calboli (Madrid), Cobianchi (Rio de Janeiro), Salandra (Geneva), and Vittorio Emanuele III, September 3, 1923. *DDI*, pp. 173-174.
[77] Wheeler (London) to the Department of State, September 5, 1923. File 765.68/75, Record Group 59, NA.
[78] As quoted in Sir Harold Nicolson, *Curzon . . .* , p. 370.

Mussolini versus the League

Minister Baldwin at Aix-les-Bains before being sent to Lord Cecil.[79]

The cable to Cecil emphasized that the Greek reply to the Italian ultimatum was a virtual acceptance of the Italian demands with the exception only of the request for an indemnity and the salute by the Greek fleet. Athens was, of course, obligated to offer full compensation for the odious crime committed on her territory. On the other hand, the Italian note appeared to have been "somewhat precipitate, while their subsequent action in seizing Corfu has placed them definitely in the wrong." The cable continued by stating that it was the "strong desire of His Majesty's Government to support the League on the first occasion on which a small Power has appealed to it against the high-handed actions of a great Power." It ended by assuring Cecil that he could "rely on the support of His Majesty's Government in upholding the Covenant."[80] When he received his instructions, Cecil in Geneva was "extremely grateful . . . for the loyal and energetic support," that Lord Curzon had given him.[81]

It should be added that Curzon's decision to support League action was not an attempt to embarrass the French over their occupation of the Ruhr.[82] Nor was it motivated by any personal dislike for the Italian leader.[83]

The Italian demands and the subsequent occupation of Corfu had upset Curzon a great deal.[84] His decision, however,

[79] Wheeler (London) to the Department of State, September 3, 1923. File 765.68/27, Record Group 59, NA.

[80] Letter. Sir Harold Nicolson to Mr. Post Wheeler, chargé d'affaires of the United States Embassy, London, England, September 4, 1923. American Embassy, XVII, 1923, section marked "Graeco-Italian dispute, file 800." Record Group 84, NA; Wheeler (London) to the Department of State, September 4, 1923. File 765.68/64, Record Group 59, NA.

[81] Lord Robert Cecil (Geneva) to Lord Curzon, September 4, 1923. Folder marked "Letters to Curzon A-F, 1923," Box 65, Curzon Papers.

[82] Sir Harold Nicolson in an interview with the writer in London, July 1961.

[83] Lord Curzon to Sir Ronald W. Graham (Rome), October 9, 1923. Folder marked "Copies of Letters written by Curzon, 1921-1923," Box 65, Curzon Papers.

[84] Sir Harold Nicolson in an interview with the writer in London, July 1961.

Mussolini versus the League

to support League action and his instructions to Cecil were completely out of step with traditional British interpretation of the League. To the British, the League was "a co-operative association of independent states"[85] where all nations met to air their grievances. "Collectivists" like Lord Cecil who wished to make the League the very center of world affairs were unrepresentative of the Baldwin cabinet, where the "traditionalist" school predominated. The latter viewed the League as only one more instrument of national policy. To the traditionalists the League was useful only in supplementing the older and more conventional methods of diplomacy. Curzon's support of League action would have been acceptable to the traditionalists only in so far as it did not involve England in any positive commitments which were outside her immediate interests.[86] In the days to come this very problem is posed by Italy's intransigence, and Curzon's subsequent retreat becomes inevitable. This same struggle between traditionalists and collectivists repeated itself in the Foreign Office. Here, the "war party" was represented by Sir Harold Nicolson, the Chief of Greek Affairs, and Sir Ronald Lindsay, the Assistant Under-Secretary. The traditionalists were represented by Sir William Tyrrell, who had little faith in the League and felt that by appealing to it England would be forcing a showdown. Sir William's motto was "avoid trouble."[87]

On the day following the Foreign Secretary's return to London the Italian Ambassador appeared at Whitehall and had a long and "extremely cordial" interview with Curzon. It was to be the only meeting between the two until after the incident was settled. Curzon began by expressing to Della Torretta his indignation over the murder of General Tellini and his staff. He then stated that it was not his desire to criticize the attitude

[85] Alfred Zimmern, *The League of Nations and the Rule of Law, 1918-1935* (2nd ed. rev.; London: Macmillan Co., 1939), p. 346.

[86] For an excellent discussion of the traditionalist and collectivist attitudes towards the League see Arnold Wolfers, *Britain and France between Two Wars* (New York: Harcourt, Brace and Co., 1940), pp. 321-364.

[87] Sir Harold Nicolson in an interview with the writer in London, July 1961.

Mussolini versus the League

of the Italian Government in the situation that had developed. Yet at the same time he attempted to explain the reasons why British public opinion had taken such a decidedly anti-Italian attitude. Lord Curzon enumerated the principal arguments employed by the British press.

Della Torretta replied that British press criticism was groundless and attempted to correct for Curzon what he considered to be false information. As previously instructed, he then handed Curzon the Duce's Corfu proclamation with an official declaration attached. The declaration made it clear that Italy did not intend to refer the question to the League since it did not deal with a dispute contemplated under the Covenant. Her actions were an attempt to protect her prestige and national institutions and were not warlike measures, acts of war, or threats of war.

The Foreign Secretary "exhibited" a great deal of sorrow over the Italian decision not to refer the question to the League. He pointed out to Della Torretta that the League existed precisely in order to settle conflicts of this very nature. With the text of the Versailles Treaty in hand, he attempted to show the ambassador that the Covenant did not exclude from its purview conflicts of national honor and prestige, as alleged by the Italian Government.

Della Torretta in a long retort then set forth all the arguments Mussolini had previously cabled to him: intervention by the League would merely complicate the matter; a hostile attitude by England might force Italy to reconsider her position in the League; Greece was not an "equal" and because of its revolutionary origins and past deeds was a government that England still did not recognize; deferral to the Council would establish the precedent of referring all questions of national honor and prestige to an international organ.

Curzon replied that it was well known that English press criticism across the political spectrum wished League intervention. The policy of the present Conservative Government was founded on this demand and fully appreciated it. He observed that it was not England but Greece that had raised the ques-

Mussolini versus the League

tion with the Council, and once this was done it was impossible to stop the course of events. To have instructed Lord Cecil to support the Italian position, as desired by Rome, "would have provoked the fall of the Ministry."

Della Torretta returned Curzon's attention to the British press, which, he complained, was arousing strong resentment in Italy. The Foreign Secretary expressed sorrow over this situation. He explained that when the Italo-Greek incident occurred there was no one of authority present in the Foreign Office. Therefore, the press did not receive any "special direction or undergo any influence." He drew the ambassador's attention to the fact that the British press had been unanimous in deploring the murder of the Italian Mission and in recognizing Italy's right to compensation. He added, however, that given the great position that the League held in the eyes of the British public it was to be expected that the British press, as spokesman of British opinion, would uphold the rights of the League, even if these rights were contested by Italy. Curzon then read some reports of the Italian press which he considered not representative of current Anglo-Italian relations. He deplored especially the *Messaggero*, which even before the present crisis had used language which was neither friendly nor moderate.

Della Torretta now shifted his attack and in a lengthy discussion attempted to introduce the general relationships between the two countries. Curzon, however, resisted this shift. He refused to admit that the cordial relationships, established by months of hard work, "could be compromised by a mere movement of Italian public opinion," excited because Britain favored impartial adjudication of the dispute by the League. He insisted that to thwart League action in working out a settlement would constitute for the British Government "a renunciation of its principles and would contribute to the end" of the League of Nations. Great faith, he added, had been placed in the League by the British people, who wished to see it prosper. The conversation dragged on without arriving at a result favorable to Rome. Curzon emphasized to Della

Mussolini versus the League

Torretta that in maintaining the League's right to intervene England was not being motivated by personal gain. This, he observed, was far different from the French position, which was governed by events in the Ruhr.

Della Torretta's observations to Rome were that Britain, as was to be expected, favored League action; that in its own mind no hostile action was intended toward Italy; and, at least for the moment, the political attitude of England in the present Italo-Greek dispute did not extend beyond the limits of the League of Nations. From the conversation Della Torretta also gathered the impression that Curzon would not cancel Council action in the dispute even though he was greatly preoccupied by the contingency of "our eventual withdrawal" from the League of Nations.[88]

On the following day, September 4, Della Torretta again returned to the Foreign Office bringing the instructions issued to Salandra at Geneva. Tyrrell informed him that the information would be forwarded to Lord Curzon that night. Sir William hastened to repeat Curzon's views of the previous day: that the League was first invested with the dispute by Greece; once in motion League action could not be stopped; lastly, for reasons already explained, Great Britain could not declare itself against the competence of the League, though Britain's attitude toward Italy was friendly and not hostile. Della Torretta's own feelings were that Curzon could not be induced to change his mind. He cautioned Rome that from information that had come to his notice it appeared that the Dominions also demanded that the issue be maintained in the League of Nations. He observed that Dominion policy, led by South Africa's Jan Christiaan Smuts, made the League its "essential stronghold."[89] The reaction of Curzon and the Foreign Office had not been what Rome had desired. However, across the channel Poincaré and the Quai d'Orsay gave Italy's overtures a warmer and more sympathetic hearing.

[88] Della Torretta (London) to Mussolini, September 4, 1923. *DDI*, pp. 177-178.
[89] Della Torretta (London) to Mussolini, September 4, 1923. *Ibid.*, pp. 181-182.

Mussolini versus the League

PARIS ASSURES ROME

In Paris, Italy's chargé reported that the Greek Legation had made repeated overtures to the Quai d'Orsay to obtain French support for its Geneva appeal. Laroche assured Vannutelli that Poincaré had recommended to the Greek Legation that its government "come to terms directly with Italy" and urged Greece to desist from any act that might modify Italy's pacific intentions. The Press Bureau, Vannutelli observed, in line with French policy was trying to make a distinction between the Corfu and Ruhr occupations. As to Curzon's conversation with Poincaré, Laroche had declared to him that it was "brief and limited itself to an exchange of views on the situation," without any conclusions being reached. Though he would do everything possible to check the accuracy of this disclosure, Vannutelli felt that it was not likely that Poincaré's mind could be changed by a sudden visit from Curzon. This was especially true, he added parenthetically, if one took Poincaré's personality into consideration. France's attitude, he concluded, continued to be friendly. Because of this he brought to Laroche's attention a Rome communiqué that expressed Italy's gratitude for France's support.[90]

On September 3, the day after his arrival in Paris, the Italian Ambassador, Baron Camillo Romano Avezzana, reported that he had assurances from the Quai d'Orsay that the French delegation would support the Italian point of view at Geneva. He warned, however, that France would not act to oppose a Council resolution expressing a desire for a quick and friendly settlement of the dispute. The French delegation, he was told, also had instructions to check the small Powers and to "prevent them from meddling in the dispute."[91]

[90] Vannutelli (Paris) to Mussolini, September 2, 1923. *Ibid.*, pp. 158-159. In a prior telegram on September 1, Vannutelli had informed the Duce of the moderate and sympathetic tone of the French press. He also reported that it was the general impression that France aimed to support Italy in order to detach her from England, for support in the reparations problem. Vannutelli (Paris) to Mussolini, September 1, 1923. *Ibid.*, pp. 149-150.

[91] Avezzana (Paris) to Mussolini, September 3, 1923. *Ibid.*, pp. 171-172.

Mussolini versus the League

Later that same day Avezzana also had a very "long and exhaustive conversation" about the whole situation with Poincaré. The latter assured Avezzana that it was his intention to support Italy loyally and unconditionally in order that it might receive full satisfaction. He disclosed that he had transmitted to the French delegation at Geneva the text of a telegram from the French chargé d'affaires at Rome, which included all the arguments produced by Mussolini as to the noncompetence of the League of Nations. Poincaré frankly admitted to Avezzana that he was completely in the dark as to the attitude of the British Government. Though Cecil had already declared that the Council was competent to handle the dispute it was Poincaré's opinion that Cecil's views and those of Lord Curzon did not always coincide. In his brief conversation with Curzon, the latter had alluded to the Italo-Greek dispute. Curzon, however, had "spoken rather of the Conference of Ambassadors than of the League of Nations." Avezzana thanked Poincaré for French support. He warned, however, that Italy did not intend to renounce its rights to secure directly from Greece satisfaction for the murder of its officials. He stressed that this would still be Italian policy even in the case the dispute was forwarded from the League to the Ambassadorial Conference. "It was inconceivable," he explained to Poincaré, "that Italy had occupied Corfu in order to obtain reparations through others." It was also the height of insolence, he remarked, that Greece should submit herself to the suggestions of others "rather than to those of the Italian Government." Poincaré agreed. He then asked Avezzana if his government had looked into the legal aspects of the Corfu occupation. He thought that since the second Treaty of London of 1864 was still operative the issue of the neutrality of Corfu might be raised at Geneva and it would be well if Rome were prepared to reply.[92]

Avezzana's discussion with Poincaré was fully approved by

[92] Avezzana (Paris) to Mussolini, September 3, 1923. *Ibid.*, p. 176.

Mussolini versus the League

Mussolini, especially his distinction between reparations by the Conference and reparations desired by Italy.[93]

At the same time that Avezzana was talking to Poincaré, the American chargé d'affaires, Sheldon Whitehouse, was reporting to Washington that the Quai d'Orsay "has been and is still very reserved." Representations, he reported, had been made to Athens urging the Greeks to come to terms with Italy and to avoid any actions that might "aggravate the situation." No similar representations, he added, had been made to Rome. Laroche, Whitehouse continued, had told him that the Athens reply to the Italian ultimatum had been "very stupid." He also disclosed that a meeting of the Conference of Ambassadors would be called to consider the Greek reply to the Ambassadorial note of protest of August 31. In any such meeting Whitehouse assumed he was to "maintain a discreet silence."

When queried by Whitehouse on what the Conference would do, Laroche replied, "take sanctions." Asked if Rome would agree to sanctions of the Conference replacing her own, Laroche merely "shrugged his shoulders." The latter also seemed very "skeptical" as to any benefits that might be derived through League intervention. His greatest worry appeared to be Belgrade, where any Yugoslav intervention "would only make matters worse in Italy." Whitehouse's own opinion was that the French Government was "very embarrassed" and would attempt to take as small a part as possible in the dispute. Yet, at the same time, it would go as far as possible in order to "avoid offending Italian susceptibilities with a view of course to the Ruhr." "Analogues [sic] considerations," he concluded incisively, "make [the] French loath to have the question brought before the League."[94] The instructions immedi-

[93] Mussolini to Avezzana (Paris) repeated to London, September 5, 1923. *Ibid.*, p. 182.

[94] Whitehouse (Paris) to the Department of State, September 3, 1923. File 765.68/23, Record Group 59, NA. On September 6, three days after Whitehouse filed his cable to Washington, the Yugoslav Minister in Paris was assuring the Greek Minister, Athos Romanos, that the French Government disapproved of Mussolini's procedures. On the other hand, in its desire "de ménager [la] susceptibilité italienne" it would like to see the Ambassadors' Conference take charge of the

Mussolini versus the League

ately sent to Whitehouse upon receipt of his report were to maintain a "discreet reserve" if the question came before the Conference of Ambassadors.[95]

The Franco-Italian entente that had developed, dictated by mutual interest, was soon affected by events unfolding in Athens between the Greek Government and the Conference of Ambassadors.

---

solution of the conflict instead of the League of Nations. It was Poincaré's opinion, the Yugoslav Minister disclosed, that the Conference would obtain more promptly the evacuation of Corfu which at the moment "parait [la] question capitale." Romanos (Paris) to the Foreign Ministry, September 6, 1923. French text. Greek Archives.

Whether the above comments of the Yugloslav Minister were a French attempt to assuage Belgrade's feelings is difficult to say. During the early days of the conflict the Yugoslav Minister in Athens made no attempt to hide his anti-Italian feelings and his sympathy for the Greek Government. Montagna (Athens) to Mussolini, September 3, 1923. *DDI*, pp. 167-168. He had warned at that time that any sign of Italian mobilization would also force Yugoslavia to mobilize. Atherton (Athens) to the Department of State, September 3, 1923. File 765.68/22, Record Group 59, NA. In Belgrade the government placed restraints on the press though it followed the Italo-Greek conflict closely. Dodge (Belgrade) to the Department of State, September 4, 1923. File 765.68/36, Record Group 59, NA.

After the conflict had been solved, the Italian Legation in Belgrade reported that the Yugoslav attitude throughout the conflict had been "very correct." Summonte (Belgrade) to Mussolini, October 8, 1923. *DDI*, p. 279 and footnote. In all probability, during this period, with France occupied in the Ruhr, Paris was in no position to assist Yugoslavia should she have any difficulties with Italy. Therefore, the Quai d'Orsay's probable advice to Yugoslavia was to show moderation towards Rome. Since the Corfu and Fiume questions had arisen at the same time, Yugoslavia was in no position to protest French actions at Geneva, because France was her strongest supporter. At the same time, a pressing need for quiet and internal peace were undoubtedly a factor inducing Yugoslavia to show moderation towards Mussolini. In passing, it should not be forgotten that the policy of the then Yugoslav Foreign Minister, Momčilo Ninčić, was largely governed by the desire to be conciliatory towards Italy in order to solve the Fiume question and all other outstanding Italo-Yugoslav problems. For a review of the Yugoslav press during the crisis see *Bulletin Périodique de la Presse Yugoslave*, No. 47, pp. 4, 8.

[95] Phillips to Whitehouse (Paris), September 4, 1923. File 765.68/23, Record Group 59, NA.

Mussolini versus the League

GREECE ACCEPTS THE CONFERENCE'S NOTE OF PROTEST

In Athens, on September 2, the Greek Government in a *note verbale* accepted the Ambassadorial protest that had been presented by the French chargé d'affaires, several days before. This acceptance, however, was a *volte-face*. On August 31, when the note had been delivered, Prime Minister Gonatas had declared that Greece recognized only the League of Nations, to which it had turned prior to the Corfu occupation.[96]

The Greek reply began by expressing to the Conference the government's "profound sorrow" over the murder of General Tellini and his staff. It also wished to make known to the Conference the "unanimous and spontaneous" reprobation by the Greek Government, people, and press of the Tellini outrage. The note then described the military, police, and judicial measures taken to "ensure the prompt arrest of the culprits," whose punishment would be exemplary as promised the Italian Minister some days before. Regardless of who may be the authors of the crime, the note observed, "one is obliged to consider them insane criminals" since the murder of officials of this type could only be the "act of a madman." Criminal madness, the note continued, knows no geographical or nationality limits. The Greek Government, the note remarked, was as interested as the Conference of Ambassadors in shedding more light on the murder and hoped to do so through the inquiry already instituted. It thought, however, that much better results could be secured by the institution of a special commission composed of three representatives of the Great Powers. This commission, it observed, would be able to investigate in territory outside the jurisdiction of the Greek authorities; the Albanian frontier was very close to the scene of the murder and the assassins could have taken refuge there.

The second half of the note stated that the Greek Govern-

[96] Ἰωάννης Α. Πεπόνης, Νικόλαος Πλαστήρας, Στὰ Γεγονότα, *1909-1945* (Ἀθῆναι, 1947) [John A. Peponis, *Nikolaos Plastiras and the Events of 1909-1945* (Athens, 1947)], I, p. 386; Montagna (Athens) to Mussolini, September 1, 1923. *DDI*, p. 156.

Mussolini versus the League

ment could not "refrain from expressing its profound shock" at the Italian ultimatum and "protested with the greatest energy" against Italy's subsequent occupation of Corfu. Lastly, the Greek Government asked the Ambassadors' Conference to "use all its influence" with Rome to bring about the withdrawal of the Italian demands and an end to the Corfu occupation. On the other hand, if it were proved that the Greek Government was in any way responsible for the Tellini murder, it was willing to pay "all reparations" judged just by the Conference of Ambassadors.[97]

This note of acceptance was soon followed by a second *note verbale*. It informed the three Allied Legations in Athens that since the League Council was occupied with the dispute following Greece's appeal, the chief Greek delegate at Geneva had been instructed to propose an inquiry at Epirus. The inquiry would be under the control of the British, French, and Italian representatives, supported by one or two neutral members of the League Council.[98]

Montagna found the first *note verbale* "wordy" and cabled Rome that the second half of the note was "dedicated to arguments extraneous" to the Ambassadorial note of protest.[99] At a meeting at the Italian Legation, Montagna made it clear to the French and British chargés d'affaires that there was a distinction to be drawn between actions instituted by Italy vis-à-vis Greece and those instituted by the Conference. The former, he observed, have an "indisputable superiority" over the latter. He declared to both that the complaints in the second half of the first Greek note had nothing to do with the Conference's note of protest and were "on the contrary out of place." He insisted that reservations be lodged with the Greek Foreign Ministry on this point. This action was opposed by both his colleagues. The French chargé d'affaires added that any reservations could be formulated in Paris by the Conference of Ambassadors, to whom the note was actually addressed. Foiled in his attempt at reservations, Montagna

[97] *DDDIG*, pp. 21-22.   [98] *Ibid.*, p. 23.
[99] Montagna (Athens) to Mussolini, September 3, 1923. *DDI*, p. 174.

Mussolini versus the League

turned their attention to a phrase contained in the concluding paragraph of the note. This phrase, "in compliance with the contents of the note submitted in its name," Montagna felt, was false, for "no passage and no expression of the collective note justified such a shrewd affirmation" which tended to invalidate before the Conference the Italian request for sanctions and reparations. Agreement on this particular phrase was reached and the French chargé d'affaires hurried to the Greek Foreign Ministry to obtain a replacement for the objected phrase.[100] The replacement was made and the corrected note accepted.

The reaction of Politis in Geneva to the first *note verbale* was one of distinct displeasure. Submission to the Conference complicated the whole situation by weakening his position at Geneva, he cabled Athens. The question of the League's competence as against the Conference's, raised by Salandra, which he had fought with the support of Cecil and Branting, had every chance of being resolved in favor of the League and consequently to "our advantage," he observed. Affected by Italy's aggressive attitude, various representatives "had arranged" to proclaim at the earliest occasion their intention to withdraw from the League if the conflict were not left to the Council's investigation. Politis felt that the acceptance of an investigation and the determination of reparations by the Conference had done nothing to counter the dangerous Italian thesis as to the League's non-competence. Even more important, the note to Paris contradicted the government's previous position, which had been to appeal only to Geneva. The reply, he remarked, had put him "personally in the greatest difficulty

[100] Montagna (Athens) to Mussolini, September 3, 1923. *Ibid.*, p. 175. The phrase that Montagna objected to in his cable to Rome, read: "in conformità al contenuto della nota rimessa in suo nome" [in compliance with the contents of the note submitted in its name]. The corrected version replaced this with the phrase *de vouloir bien*; the corrected paragraph finally read: "En conséquence, le Gouvernement Hellénique a l'honneur de prier la Conférence des Ambassadeurs de vouloir bien user de toute son influence auprès de Gouvernement Italien, afin que les lourdes conditions de son ultimatum soient retirées et qu'il soit mis fin à l'occupation de l'île de Corfou."

Mussolini versus the League

vis-à-vis the Council," since he had stated before that body that though Greece accepted in advance any decision arrived at by the Council, she had strong reservations in accepting any eventual decision by the Conference of Ambassadors. Responsibility for this mistake, he noted, had to be assumed and the best made of a bad situation. New measures therefore had to be devised to handle this difficulty.

Hence he informed the Foreign Ministry of the new line he was going to take at the next meeting of the Council in order to avoid "new complications." Greece, he intended to state, was obliged to reply to the Conference's "pressing note." In her desire to be "conciliatory vis-à-vis all the Powers" she had to distinguish between two obligations. The first was towards the Conference, whose agents the murdered officers had been, and the second was towards Italy. The latter's actions, however, isolated her from the Conference. Greece had therefore asked the Conference to make an inquiry on the responsibilities arising from the murder and to fix the reparations "to which she has a right." As to Italy, Greece would still conform to any decision of the League of Nations, which would have the right to exercise judicial action against the murderers, fix an indemnity to the families of the murdered victims, and guarantee the evacuation of Corfu. "To this effect" he was going to propose that the Council appoint a special neutral delegate in order to follow an inquiry in Greece. Secondly, a commission would be appointed, to be composed of high magistrates from Italy and Greece and one named by the President of the Swiss Federal Tribunal. This commission would meet as soon as possible at Geneva in order to fix an indemnity, the money for the indemnity being guaranteed by an immediate deposit in a Swiss bank. After these actions had been completed Italy would be invited by the League to evacuate Corfu. Politis ended by pleading that "no act of the Government" diplomatic or other, should compromise this plan.[101]

Alexandris replied that he was surprised that Politis agreed

[101] Politis (Geneva), No. 1146 to the Foreign Ministry, September 4, 1923. French text. Greek Archives.

Mussolini versus the League

that the Conference had competence in the matter. The Ambassadors' Conference had "by no means asked such competence," much less was it acknowledged by the Athens government, he cabled. The Conference, he agreed, had asked the Greek Government to open an inquiry in order to discover the culprits. If any liability was thus uncovered, Greece was to pay reparations. The Greek reply, however, had made the point that there was grave suspicion that the murderers had escaped to Albania, or had come from there. Therefore, it proposed an international committee of inquiry which could work on both sides of the border. Later a second note was transmitted to the Conference informing them that the Greek representative in Geneva would propose that the international committee be instituted by the League. This second note was also in order, inasmuch as the League had already been invested with the dispute by Greece's appeal. Since the first note to the Conference was quickly followed by the second, Alexandris felt that it was not possible for the Conference to judge the proposal for the committee of inquiry until it had received the proposal in the form to be submitted by the Greek representative in Geneva. It would have been entirely different, he observed, had the Conference already undertaken to form such a committee, asserting that it had not understood the Greek answer correctly. On the other hand, it would have been odd not to channel through the League the answer imparted to the Conference on its proposals. This was especially true, since the Greek delegate would ask to have the neutral judge of the commission of inquiry appointed by the League of Nations.[102]

In the long run Politis' initial reaction proved to be right, and Alexandris' subtleties were subsequently disregarded. The Greek decision to submit unreservedly to both the League and the Conference of Ambassadors as to the payment of money was the crucial point.

It is a decision that has been severely criticized. It divided

[102] A[lexandris] No. 8512 to the Délégation Hellénique, Geneva, August 5, 1923 [sic]. Greek Archives.

Mussolini versus the League

the Greek appeal between two jurisdictions and made it easier for France and Italy to take the case from the friendlier atmosphere of Geneva to the secret meetings of the Ambassadorial Conference in Paris.[103] According to the British Ambassador in Paris, Lord Crewe, it was a decision which did not make a defense of the Greek case "easier."[104]

THE ANGLO-FRENCH DILEMMA

As this exchange was going on between Politis and Alexandris, Giuriati was speeding northwards towards Geneva, with instructions for Salandra. From Rome, the Duce was frantically cabling Salandra to obtain a further adjournment of the Council proceedings in order to give Giuriati time to reach Geneva with his "precise instructions."[105] The problem that London and Paris faced was extremely difficult. Though the Italian Government had legal rights to reparations for the harm done to its citizens, its actions at Corfu could not be condoned by the Great Powers who after the Versailles settlement were the preservers of the newly established status quo. The problem that posed itself to both England and France was how to solve the dispute in a way that would serve their best interests, re-establish the Adriatic equilibrium, and reaffirm the cornerstones of the postwar settlement—the Versailles Treaty and the Covenant of the League of Nations. The conflicting policies that they followed in the Corfu dispute to attain these ends illustrate the conflict in policies followed by both nations throughout the interwar years. Their policies

[103] Παναγιώτης Πιπινέλης, Ἱστορία τῆς Ἐξωτερικῆς Πολιτικῆς τῆς Ἑλλάδος, *1923-1941* ('Αθῆναι, 1948) [Panayiotis Pipinelis, *History of Greek Foreign Policy, 1923-1941* (Athens, 1948)], p. 121.

[104] Lord Crewe (Paris) to Lord Curzon, September 8, 1923. Folder marked "Correspondence with Lord Crewe, Ambassador to Paris, 1922-24," Box 22, Curzon Papers. After the incident was closed Lord Crewe was to complain to Lord Curzon that the "Greeks have surely conducted their side of the business with great stupidity, quite otherwise as Venizelos would have managed it." Lord Crewe (Paris) to Lord Curzon, September 26, 1923. Folder marked "Correspondence with Lord Crewe, Ambassador to Paris, 1922-1924," Box 22, Curzon Papers.

[105] Mussolini to Salandra (Geneva), September 3, 1923. *DDI*, p. 169.

Mussolini versus the League

during the interwar period, as in the Corfu dispute, worked at cross purposes and defeated, rather than assisted, each other.[106]

Poincaré's decision to seek a comprehensive solution within the Conference of Ambassadors was in line with the French view that the League was only a *"garantie supplémentaire"* to France's other postwar security arrangements against Germany. To France, the League was to be manipulated against a "specific country" (i.e. Germany), and when attempts were made to use the League machinery against any country other than Germany, France's interests invariably "ceased to exist."[107] The events that were to unfold as August gave way to September would see the establishment of a British position supporting the League and a French attempt to circumscribe it and keep matters within the Conference of Ambassadors. French policies would win in the end. But Britain's defeat and France's Pyrrhic victory undermined the very settlement they were committed to uphold; this was the beginning of that long road that fifteen years later ended at Munich.

[106] Wolfers, passim.
[107] *Ibid.*, p. 175. The League of Nations was to the French "an incomplete project of a superstate." Zimmern, p. 346.

CHAPTER V

THE LEAGUE OF NATIONS AND THE CONFERENCE OF AMBASSADORS

AVEZZANA'S ADVICE

SEPTEMBER 4 was a busy day for Mussolini. At a cabinet meeting that morning he made his attitude towards any possible intervention by the League perfectly clear. The Council, he commented, had "shown a disposition to assume the task of settling the matter." This he found "absolutely inadmissible." Therefore, the Italian delegation at the next meeting of the Council would maintain that that body is definitely not competent to judge the question, "which is altogether outside the scope of the Covenant invoked by Greece." If, however, the Council asserted its competence, the question that would arise for Italy would be "of remaining in the League of Nations or leaving it." His own decision was for the latter alternative.[1]

Later that same day in an interview with G. Ward Price, of the *Daily Mail*, the Duce drew an analogy between his actions and those of Lord Palmerston almost seventy years before in the Don Pacifico affair. The fleet had been ordered to Corfu, he told Price, because he knew the Greeks and was aware that if no pledge were taken for the payment of the reparations requested, Italy would "get nothing out of them." The pledge

[1] *Daily Mail*, September 5, 1923, p. 9. Salandra felt that the declaration was "hard and curt . . . [and] was not made in order to facilitate" his task in the League, nor to minimize the feelings that had arisen over the dispute either in Geneva or in the foreign press. At the same time, however, he had to admit that the threat to leave the League, which at first sight appeared "excessive and imprudent," helped "to moderate the zeal of the most ardent supporters of the League of Nations." His own recommendation to Rome would have been to adopt a "tone of reserve rather than of threats." Antonio Salandra, *Memorie Politiche, 1916-1925* (Milano: Garzanti, 1951), p. 106.

The League and the Conference

had been taken and would be retained until the Greeks had made "a complete and literal fulfilment of the conditions" of the Italian ultimatum. Greek fulfillment would mean Italian withdrawal from Corfu. Mussolini cautioned, however, that the Greeks had "better pay soon, for next week the price will be higher. These naval operations are expensive. Battleships will not steam on songs." The Duce then ominously added that if Greece did not pay, Italy would "remain in possession of Corfu indefinitely." Anyway, he remarked to Price, four centuries before, Corfu had been "Venetian territory."[2]

Though Mussolini appears to have made up his mind, his ambassador in Paris did not hold to the same view. The Duce, Ambassador Avezzana cabled, was quite aware of his "sentiments relative to the League of Nations." Even prior to the Italo-Greek dispute, he had displayed "doubts on the utility of Italy's" remaining at Geneva. The present moment, Avezzana felt, "would not be opportunely chosen" to leave the League of Nations advantageously, either in relation to the solution of the Greek dispute, or to the general situation of Italy in the world. Salandra, at Geneva, he felt, could rely on the support of France and perhaps some of the Latin American states, like Brazil. Together they could attempt to find a solution which having regard for the League would still ensure to Italy the Council's exclusion from any decision in the matter. On the other hand, Italy should make it clear to the Council that without going into the judicial motives declared by Rome it could not intervene in the dispute "by the simple fact" that there did not exist a danger of war. Italy was also to add that since the Conference of Ambassadors was already invested with the question there was no need for the Council to intervene. Avezzana then disclosed that at the Quai d'Orsay there was no attempt to conceal from him the embarrassment that Italian withdrawal from the League would cause France at the present time. He was asked in what way this Italian move could be of use to Italy since under the terms of the Covenant she would be obligated to remain at Geneva for two years

[2] *Ibid.*

The League and the Conference

after her notice of withdrawal. Avezzana replied that with French support a transformation of the League could take place, so that it would function better, and do away with the possibility of overriding "with prearranged combinations the legitimate interests of individual states."[3]

Avezzana then followed with a second cable outlining what the Italian position should be at the Ambassadorial Conference expected to meet the next day [September 5], with respect to the Greek note of September 2. The Conference, he cabled, having regard for its note of August 31 and the Greek reply of September 2, should note the following: that the responsibility of the Greek Government for the murder of General Tellini and his staff existed by the fact that the murders were committed on Greek territory. Other factors that would be held against the Athens government were that the delegation was fulfilling an international mandate in Greek territory with the consent of the Greek Government, and that the assassination was "evidently political," demonstrated by the fact that only the Italian delegation was attacked. Further responsibility was also found in the guarantee of personal safety that the

[3] Avezzana (Paris) to Mussolini, September 4, 1923. *DDI*, pp. 179-180. On September 3, the Brazilian delegate at Geneva was instructed to "support unconditionally" the Italian point of view. Cobianchi (Rio de Janeiro) to Mussolini, September 3, 1923. *Ibid.*, p. 175.

These instructions to Dr. Alfranio de Mello Franco were to the effect that he should support the Italian position in the Italo-Greek dispute "because it was at the suggestion of Italy that Dr. Epitacio Pessoa was proposed for the vacant judgeship in the Permanent Court of International Justice" at The Hague, to which he was subsequently appointed. Morgan (Rio de Janeiro) to the Department of State, September 13, 1923. File 500.0001/223, Record Group 59, NA. It should be kept in mind that at this time Brazil was actively campaigning to secure permanent representation on the League Council, and Italy as a permanent member could have supported her claim. Another consideration that should not be lost sight of is the large Italian community living in Brazil and Chile. It was the presence of this community which probably explains the pro-Italian activities of the Chilean delegate at Geneva, which Mussolini greatly appreciated. Mussolini to Castoldi (Santiago), September 19, 1923. *DDI*, p. 253 and footnote. For the pro-Italian position of the South American press see *Bulletin Périodique de la Presse Sud-Américaine*, No. 98, pp. 5-6.

The League and the Conference

Greek Government had to "give to all legally accredited missions in its territory." This responsibility, Avezzana added, remained in force regardless of who perpetrated the crime. Since Tellini and his staff were part of an international commission on which England and France were also represented, the sanctions demanded by Italy, he noted, could be extended to cover also England and France. Consequently, an apology by the Greek Government should also take place at the British and French Legations. Point three in the Italian ultimatum dealing with honors to the Italian flag by units of the Greek fleet should be extended to include British and French warships.

The investigation demanded under point four of the Italian note would include, besides the Italian military attaché at Athens, two other individuals representing the Conference of Ambassadors. In this investigation as to the assassins the Albanian Government would be asked by the Conference to help in case the culprits had taken refuge in Albanian territory. The British and French representatives should also be present when honors were given by the Greeks at the funeral ceremony and on the embarkation of the corpses at Preveza. As to the Italian request for an indemnity, a demand that the Greeks had found especially humiliating, Avezzana stipulated that this would "be discussed only between Italy and Greece." A time limit, he concluded, had been omitted from the above proposals in view of Rome's decision that the Corfu occupation would "last until Italy declares herself satisfied."[4] Avezzana's last two points, that the request for an indemnity would be discussed only between the two countries and his exclusion of a time limit for the evacuation of Corfu, would prove to be the two major stumbling blocks in the forthcoming negotiations at Paris. His suggested formula for solving the dispute coincided closely, however, with the proposals that would be subsequently proffered by the Quai d'Orsay. The coincidence appears to have been accidental.

[4] Avezzana (Paris) to Mussolini, September 4, 1923. *DDI*, pp. 180-181.

The League and the Conference

GREEK, BRITISH, AND FRENCH PROPOSALS
FOR A SOLUTION

In Geneva, on the afternoon of September 4, the League Council again convened after its adjournment of several days. Salandra, in line with instructions from Mussolini, asked that the discussions be postponed one more day until Giuriati could arrive with his instructions from Rome. This proposal was consented to by Lord Cecil, but it was agreed that all future discussions would be held in public.

The Council meeting was then opened to the public for the first time. At Cecil's suggestion Politis was invited to furnish any further information that might "throw fresh light on the situation." Politis merely repeated the declaration made at the last meeting, namely, that his government was ready to accept any suggestion the Council might make with a view to giving the satisfaction deemed necessary to the Italian Government. He added that his government, "in its desire to achieve as prompt a settlement as possible in the interests of all parties," was ready to go "as far as justice will allow it to go in this matter." His government was willing to accept any conditions "except those which would amount to mere humiliation." Politis then attempted a dissection of the Italian ultimatum, the Greek reply, and the Ambassadorial note of protest, but was interrupted by Salandra, who protested that Politis "was entering into a discussion of the question." Salandra moved for an immediate adjournment. He claimed that Politis by giving reasons and explanations for the attitude of his government was "unavoidably beginning a discussion." He felt that he would be forced to reply and a discussion would inevitably commence. After further exchanges on this point, it was agreed that Politis could "draft any proposals which he might have to communicate to the Council."

In line with his previous communication to Athens, Politis made three suggestions: first, that the Council appoint one or more neutral representatives to supervise in Greece the judicial investigation already instituted by the Greek authorities, as

The League and the Conference

well as the judgment of those found guilty of the murder of the Italian officers; these neutral representatives would also participate in the work of the commission whose appointment had been proposed by Athens to the Ambassadorial Conference in order to carry out both in Albania and Greece an investigation for the purpose of establishing the circumstances that preceded and accompanied the assassination.

The second suggestion was that the Council charge a commission composed of three high judicial authorities—a Greek, an Italian, and a neutral (the President of the Swiss Tribunal, for example)—to be convened as quickly as possible at Geneva, to determine the amount of indemnities which it was equitable for Greece to pay to the families of the slain officers.

The third and last suggestion was that the Council should agree that the Greek Government would deposit immediately in a Swiss bank the sum of 50 million Italian lire, so as to guarantee immediate payment of whatever indemnities the above-named commission should decide.[5]

The "moderation and the conciliatory spirit," Politis observed to Athens, let alone the practicality of the Greek proposals, had made an excellent impression in comparison with Mussolini's intransigeant declarations to the correspondent of the *Daily Mail*.

The "immense majority" of the smaller states in the Assembly were following the development of the dispute "with passionate interest" he disclosed, and were determined, if the Council failed in its task, to open a discussion of the matter before the Assembly. If Greece, Politis concluded, could maintain "until [the] end [the] calm and dignity necessary" in order to avoid any new complications he had the "hope that our cause will have [the] immense support [of the] Assembly and [of] universal public opinion."[6]

---

[5] L.N., *Official Journal*, 4th year, 1923, pp. 1283-1285.

[6] Politis (Geneva) to the Foreign Ministry, September 5, 1923. French text. Greek Archives. The American Minister at Berne, Joseph C. Grew, reported to Washington on September 3, that the Council would not meet until Wednesday, September 5. Grew (Berne) to the Department of State, September 3, 1923. File 765.68/24, Record Group 59,

The League and the Conference

In Rome, that same night, Sir Howard W. Kennard, the British chargé d'affaires, had an hour's talk with Mussolini. His main purpose, cabled the American Ambassador Washburn Child, was to persuade the Duce "to recognize the competence of the League of Nations." Instead Kennard "found Mussolini immovable chiefly because he could see no way to withdraw from his position." Kennard's own impression after the interview was that "if a way could be found, Mussolini might take it."[7]

However, Kennard's interview with Mussolini does not appear to have had the slightest influence on the latter. For the next day in a talk to the cabinet the Duce made it clear that the situation had not changed during the preceding twenty-four hours. Italy, he declared, would await "with firm quietness of conscience, secure in our rights, the decision which will be taken by the Council of the League."[8]

Poincaré, in his desire to assist Italy out of this difficult situation and by so doing to protect French interests, proposed to Mussolini a compromise formula. As the French chargé d'affaires, Charles-Roux, explained to the Duce, it was France's desire to assist Italy in the Corfu dispute, and he admitted to him that "precise instructions in such [a] sense" had been dispatched to Hanotaux at Geneva. The latter was to keep these instructions in mind especially if he became engaged in any negotiations in the coulisses. Poincaré, the chargé added, was interested in reaching with Italy some sort of agreement that would not appear to others as French mediation and thus be interpreted as a limitation on Italy's freedom of action. Secondly, it had to be a solution that would satisfy fully Italy's self-respect by maintaining in substance Rome's position. Yet at

---

NA. This was subsequently followed by another cable that a meeting of the League Council, "was held unexpectedly last evening [Sept. 4]." Grew (Berne) to the Department of State, September 5, 1923. File 765.68/38, Record Group 59, NA.

[7] Child (Rome) to the Department of State, September 5, 1923. File 765.68/34, Record Group 59, NA.

[8] Muriel Currey, *Italian Foreign Policy, 1918-1932* (London: I. Nicholson and Watson, Ltd., 1932), p. 108.

The League and the Conference

the same time it would have to be a solution that would turn the question of the Council's non-competence in such a way that the Council itself would not be compelled to proclaim its non-competence. In line with this French desire, Charles-Roux brought to Mussolini's attention Poincaré's suggested proposals.

According to the latter, the League Council would establish that the Tellini murder had occurred in Greek territory; that both Italy and the Ambassadors' Conference had desired sanctions; and that the former, not having gained the satisfaction that it requested from Athens, had occupied the island of Corfu. It would also note Rome's declaration that it occupied Corfu only in order to obtain satisfaction from the Greek authorities. The Council would then recognize the affirmation of the Italian Government that it had no intention to make war on Greece and that there was no danger of war. By these actions the Council would not pronounce on the important question of competence and "would postpone [the] examination of the admissibility" of Greece's appeal. Lastly, it would express the hope that the question be regulated as quickly as possible "through direct agreement between the interested Powers under the auspices of the Conference of Ambassadors."

Questioned by the Duce, Charles-Roux made it clear that the phrase "under the auspices" could not be interpreted in the literal sense. It would not be a deferment of the question to the Ambassadors' Conference, he explained, but would be a question that would be examined with the assistance of the Conference. After a thorough examination of the proposed French formula, the Duce thought deliberation by the Council on the above points could not be objected to. They corresponded to the facts and to the declarations of the Italian Government. On the last point, however, he had several observations. First, the phrase "to put off" [soprassedere] discussion in the Council of the admissibility of the Greek appeal, in order that the question be regulated through the Conference, was not acceptable. It would allow, Mussolini observed, the possibility of fresh discussions in the Council in the case the

The League and the Conference

Greek Government did not wish to acknowledge the decision of the Conference of Ambassadors. A more acceptable formula, he noted, would be one similar to Avezzana's proposal from Paris whereby the Council would decide not to proceed to any examination of the Italo-Greek dispute. Secondly, he felt a more convenient phrase should be substituted for the expression "under the auspices." It had to be an expression that would make it clear that two rights coexisted side by side—the right of Italy to direct reparations for the harm done to its citizens and the analogous right of the Conference for the harm done to its agents. Mussolini explained to Charles-Roux that, provided these points were taken into consideration, he had no objections to Salandra's keeping in touch with Hanotaux in order to devise a formula that would cover the reservations made. Once a suitable formula had been worked out it would be submitted to both governments for approval. The Duce's last observation to the chargé was that it would not be proper for Italy to show its intentions of withdrawing from its previous position. Every initiative in this regard would be given to others and especially to Hanotaux, who would set about to secure a further adjournment of the Council discussions. Charles-Roux, in concluding the interview, made it clear that Poincaré's proposals were still "indefinite," and that they were to be treated in such a manner, especially in front of third parties, that they would not appear as essentially French proposals.[9]

No sooner had the interview with Charles-Roux ended than a cable was dispatched to Salandra to make no move to leave the League of Nations before receiving further instructions from Rome.[10]

ACTIVITIES IN GENEVA

In Geneva, at the same time that Charles-Roux was having his interview with Mussolini, Salandra, before a crowded

[9] Mussolini to Salandra (Geneva) and Avezzana (Paris), September 6, 1923. *DDI*, pp. 189-190.
[10] Mussolini to Salandra (Geneva), September 5, 1923. *Ibid.*, p. 182.

The League and the Conference

chamber, was presenting to the League Council the official Italian point of view. Reading from a prepared script, he pointed out that the Tellini murder was "not only a flagrant violation of the laws of humanity and of the fundamental rules of international law," but it was also an offense against the Conference of Ambassadors. He made it very clear that Italy's right to compensation was entirely independent of the right of the Ambassadorial Conference. This connection was so obvious that even Greece had not denied its existence. He felt the assassins chose the victims "because they were Italians." The duty of Italy to protect her citizens and the injury to Italian honor and dignity had to be added to the violations of international law. Tellini's murder could not go unpunished, and even Greece had recognized its responsibility by submitting herself to the decisions of the Conference. Salandra observed that Italy's rights had been even more grievously injured than those of the Conference. Therefore, she was entitled to "moral and material compensation." To ensure that Athens would fulfill her obligations, Italy had felt the necessity for some sort of guarantee. This was indispensable, "as the instability and inferior moral position of the Greek Government"—not recognized by many States—did "not inspire that confidence which alone would have rendered such guarantees superfluous." Greece, he noted, had attempted with "great skill" to escape its responsibility by turning the attention of the League and of the public away from the crime committed and toward the seizure of Corfu. The Council, Salandra warned, was being "confronted with a bold attempt to transpose the terms of the question." Italy refused to be designated the accused party. It was Italy who had been attacked in a barbarous act and it was Italy who had the right to institute an accusation and demand punishment for the crime.

In line with Mussolini's orders Salandra then turned to the Conference of Ambassadors, which he termed the "living organ of the Peace Conference for the execution of the treaties." Because of its nature it had the "right to prevent and, therefore, to punish, if need be, violations of its orders and

The League and the Conference

opposition to the execution of its instructions." Until the Conference had spoken, any steps instituted by the League "would be out of place" owing to its clear non-competence. Salandra also dismissed the argument that Greece, not having a representative on the Conference of Ambassadors, could "not be subject to its decisions." Postwar Europe, he noted, had accepted the Conference's competence in all matters that involved the execution of the peace treaties. Numerous states who adhered to the treaties and were subject to their execution had from the beginning recognized that they were answerable to the decisions of the Conference, in which they were not represented. The League, he cautioned, could intervene in questions relating to the execution of the treaties only "if all the interested parties asked for such intervention." It had been previously recognized that the League created by the postwar treaties had "no competence as regards the treaties themselves except, under special provisions or subject to an agreement of the parties."

What was Greece contending, Salandra asked? That the occupation of Corfu was a hostile act which could lead to a rupture dangerous for world peace? His country, however, had solemnly stated that the Corfu occupation had no hostile character, that it had been committed merely to ensure execution of the obligations arising out of the responsibility for the Tellini assassination. There was not the slightest danger of war or even suspension of diplomatic relations. Because of this where could adequate reason be found to justify the application of Articles 12 and 15 of the Covenant founded on the presumption of the danger of war? The creation of the League of Nations did not envisage State renunciation of "all rights to act for the defense and safety of their rights and of their dignity." If this were the case no State would desire to be connected with the League. The authority of the League of Nations and organs of public international law—which Rome had no intention of ignoring—had to be maintained and respected; "but the first condition is that the organ itself should recognize and observe the limits of its authority." World peace would more likely be threatened, he observed, if States thought they could escape their obligations "by complaining of sanctions and endeavouring to ensure that the causes which rendered these sanctions necessary should be forgotten." Concluding, Salandra warned that it was the irrevocable opinion of the Italian Government that the League Council could "not proceed to take action on the request of Greece." Mussolini's instructions to threaten Italian withdrawal from Geneva were ignored in Salandra's statement to the Council.

Politis felt it was difficult to reply immediately after merely hearing a document of so serious a nature. However, he observed that during the reading of the Italian note it was stated that by applying to the League of Nations, Greece was "attempting to evade her responsibilities" and was thus endeavoring "to reverse the position of the two countries." Politis protested strongly against this suggestion. He pointed out that Greece had submitted the dispute without any reservation for the full consideration of the League Council, which was an international body. His government was fully aware that reparations were due to the Italian Government for the crime unfortunately perpetrated on Greek soil. To conclude from that fact that the Greek Government was "morally and materially responsible for the crime" was to judge "without evidence." In his own opinion it was even "presumptuous to assert" as formally as Salandra had done, that Athens was "responsible" and had "even admitted its responsibility." Since Salandra was only the advocate of the Italian case, Politis felt he had no right to say that the Italian representative was expressing his personal opinion. He was merely expressing an official opinion.

At this point Salandra interrupted to inform all present that it was also his personal opinion. There could be, he added, "no difference between the two opinions."

Salandra's declaration to the Council, Politis noted, may have been drafted while the Greek reply was being transmitted to the Ambassadors' Conference. In that reply Athens had protested against the suggestion that it was "morally and ma-

The League and the Conference

terially responsible" for the Tellini murder which had occurred on Greek territory. The law makes it very clear, he continued, that once a crime is committed within a country "the only duty of that country is faithfully to enforce the law of the country for the punishment of the crime." If a State subsequently alleges that the government failed to enforce the laws of the country, "a question of international responsibility then arises." In the present dispute, however, it must be proved that Greek responsibility exists. The proof of this responsibility had not been produced. The Greek reply to the Italian ultimatum had stated that Greece would submit the issue to Geneva if Rome found its reply inadequate. The same day that Athens was drafting its Geneva appeal, the Ambassadorial note of protest was received. The Conference of Ambassadors, which felt itself "to be an international body," presented several demands. As previously agreed with Athens, Politis then attempted to explain Greece's acceptance of the Ambassadorial note, a decision which he had protested. Athens, he informed the Council, though it had appealed to Geneva, also felt itself bound "at least in courtesy" to reply to the Ambassadorial note. Furthermore, it was also "a question of international legality." The Conference felt that it had been injured by the Tellini murder and consequently the Greek Government hastened to give the Conference explanations in its note of September 2.

The Greek note protested acceptance of responsibility for the murder. At the same time, not satisfied by an inquiry already instituted by its own authorities, it had also requested the Conference of Ambassadors to appoint a three-man committee, composed of British, French, and Italian representatives, for the purpose of conducting in Greek and Albanian territory an investigation of the Tellini murder. The Greek note added that it would accept the conclusions reached by the inquiry. The Conference, Politis observed, was not the only party involved in the case. Italy was also involved, but her attitude had separated her from the Conference of Ambassadors and a separate conflict had therefore arisen between Greece and Italy; this conflict Greece had submitted to the Council of the

The League and the Conference

League. As a "logical consequence" of the Greek request for an inquiry by the Ambassadors' Conference, he proposed, as he had the previous day, that the Council also appoint neutral delegates to take part in the inquiry. His government had no desire to escape the obligations that might arise as a consequence of the inquiry and declared in advance that it was "ready to accept them." No country could fear the accusation that it was failing in its duties if it agreed to an inquiry and appealed to the League of Nations.

Politis then turned to the point in Salandra's address that the seizure of Corfu was the taking of a pledge which was neither a hostile act nor involved a risk of war. He repeated to the Council his prior observation, "that acts are characterized more by their essential quality than by the intentions of their authors." He asked if the seizure of a pledge in order to secure the execution of reparations was not a useless act in view of the guarantees offered by several international organs, such as the Conference of Ambassadors and the League of Nations.

The Italian note, Politis observed, also contended that the League was "not competent to examine" the question because no government would accept a solution by the League. The articles of the Covenant, he remarked, which were originally read when the Council first discussed the matter were so clear as to render this argument superfluous. Article 15 of the Covenant, for example, made no reference to "whether the conflict which arises between two countries relates to the execution of a treaty, or as to whether it involves some particular consideration to which a country attaches special importance." It merely stipulates that when a dispute which could constitute a danger to peace arises between two Members of the League, either one of the two parties has the right to appeal to the League. It was not necessary, as Salandra had stated, that there should be agreement between the two parties before the matter could be delegated to the League. In the present crisis Greece exercised a right and had fulfilled an obligation. Articles 12 and 15 not only established the right to submit a dispute to the League, but created the obligation for League Members to

The League and the Conference

appeal to it and desist from all acts of violence "calculated to disturb international peace." It was for the League Council to decide whether it was disqualified "by the fact that one of the interested parties states that it does not recognize its competence." Concluding, Politis observed that if such a contention were to be admitted, "it would be the final ruin of the League of Nations." It would open a Pandora's box, making it possible for any nation to assert for one reason or another that the Covenant did not apply.

Under these conditions the League of Nations "would cease to be what it was certainly intended to be, an organization able to intervene, even on its own initiative, to ensure the maintenance of peace." It would instead evolve into an organization of political arbitration which would function only when disputing parties agreed to its procedures. Politis' rebuttal had ended.

At this point, Lord Cecil proposed that Articles 10, 12, and 15 of the "Treaty of Versailles" be read. This request was obviously aimed at Poincaré and the French delegation, who, while condoning Italy's violation of one section of the Treaty, were simultaneously attempting to force Germany to the strict application of another with their occupation of the Ruhr. As the interpreter finished reading the English and French texts, Cecil remarked that these articles were not only to be found in the Treaty of Versailles but also in the Treaties of St. Germain, Neuilly, and Trianon. Any disregard for these treaties, he warned, would shake the whole postwar European settlement.

Hanotaux, speaking for the first time in the debate and obviously wishing to delay the proceedings, observed that if the next Council meeting were fixed for the following day [September 6] it would perhaps not leave sufficient time for reflection. Undoubtedly aware of French aims, Cecil pressed for a meeting the following day, arguing that the League Assembly would wish to be informed of the decision taken by the Council in a question of such importance.

Viscount Ishii brought the day's discussion to a close, stating

The League and the Conference

he would consult with other delegates and arrange for the next meeting of the Council to take place as quickly as possible.[11]

As soon as the session was over Politis informed Athens that a solution envisaged at Geneva was to ask the Permanent Court of International Justice at The Hague its opinion on the whole question of the Council's competence. It was hoped that the opinion of the Court could be given in three or four days' time. If Italy refused this procedure, "its offenses vis-à-vis the League of Nations would be further revealed."[12]

Salandra in Geneva was equally busy cabling Rome his observations on the day's events. First, he brought to Mussolini's attention that the statement read to the Council, which he had drawn up with Giuriati and Scialoja's assistance, did not contain any threat of Italian withdrawal from the League. This was because everyone considered Italian withdrawal as highly probable after the Duce's statements of the previous day. Salandra felt it was possible for the meeting of the Conference of Ambassadors to be postponed, but without the Council admitting its own non-competence. He therefore inquired exactly what should be his line of approach if this situation should arise. The problem, he warned Mussolini, was further exacerbated by the anti-Italian atmosphere that pervaded the League. This hostility could manifest itself during the general discussions of the League Assembly scheduled to commence the following day. The President of the Assembly, he further cautioned, did not have any authority nor was there any way

[11] L.N., *Official Journal*, 4th year, 1923, pp. 1287-1290. As early as September 3, the American Minister in Berne, Joseph C. Grew, cabled the Department of State the substance of Salandra's instructions. How Grew acquired this information at a time Giuriati was still in Rome, he did not disclose. Grew (Berne) to the Department of State, September 3, 1923. File 765.68/24, Record Group 59, NA.

After the Council session of September 5, Grew reported to Washington that "optimism prevails at Geneva that a favorable result will be reached." Grew (Berne) to the Department of State, September 5, 1923. File 765.68/38, Record Group 59, NA.

[12] Politis (Geneva) to the Foreign Ministry, No. 1168, September 5, 1923. French text. Greek Archives.

The League and the Conference

to obstruct in the Assembly a hostile speech by a delegate of an excited small State or by a delegate used as an "agent provocateur."[13]

Mussolini's immediate response was that the only formula acceptable to Rome would be a decision by the League Council "not to proceed" to an examination of the dispute except on the basis of the first four points indicated in the French formula communicated to him by Charles-Roux. On the other hand, if the Council were to take a different tack Salandra was to abstain from voting and was to declare to the Council that he had to refer to Rome for instructions. As to the Assembly, the Italian delegation was to avoid any impression that Italy desired to "escape from [the] debate." They were, if necessary, to refer to Salandra's declarations in the Council, repeating without enlarging upon them in any way. Any marked show of hostility was to be answered by protests and withdrawal from the Assembly chamber.[14]

Salandra's second cable brought to the attention of the Duce, Nansen's anti-Italian activities in the Assembly.[15] During the crisis, the latter's actions against Italy were to reach dietetic proportions.[16] Nansen's activities, however, do not appear to have been an isolated Norwegian reaction, but rather a concentrated attempt on the part of the Scandinavian representatives at Geneva to support the thesis of the Council's competence and the Greek position.[17]

---

[13] Salandra (Geneva) to Mussolini, September 5, 1923. *DDI*, p. 184. The statement which Salandra read to the Council was also drawn up with the assistance of Italy's former Ambassador to Paris, Count Lelio Bonin Longare. Salandra, p. 111.

[14] Mussolini to Salandra (Geneva), September 6, 1923. *DDI*, pp. 191-192.

[15] Salandra (Geneva) to Mussolini, September 5, 1923. *Ibid.*, p. 183.

[16] In a story that is perhaps apocryphal, it appears that Nansen, while dining with some friends, ordered chicken rather than spaghetti and picked a fine Bordeaux over Chianti in order to show his displeasure with Italy's actions. Liv Nansen Høyer, *Nansen og Verden* (Oslo: J. W. Cappelens Forlag, 1955), p. 175.

[17] Mussolini's threat of September 4, to leave the League, had greatly irritated the Scandinavian representatives. The Danish delegate, Herluf Zahle, along with Nansen and Branting, strongly supported

The League and the Conference

How effective their actions were behind the scenes or in the Council discussions is difficult to say. In Rome, their activities did not go unnoticed, nor were they appreciated, and protests were lodged in Oslo and Stockholm over the actions of Nansen and Branting.[18]

---

the actions of Lord Robert Cecil. Zahle, in common with Nansen and Branting, contemplated leaving Geneva unless the Italo-Greek dispute was adjudicated by the League. The Scandinavian representatives held meetings and engaged in feverish activity, with a view to ascertaining the feelings of the smaller states, in order to induce them to insist on the Council's competence in the dispute. Prince (Copenhagen) to the Department of State, September 10, 1923. File 500.C1a/28, Record Group 59, NA; Prince (Copenhagen) to the Department of State, September 10, 1923. File 765.68/87, Record Group 59, NA.

It appears that the Scandinavian representatives in their desire to withdraw from Geneva, in case the League failed to intervene, recommended to their respective governments that they be given authorization in this sense. The American Legation in Stockholm was informed, however, that the Swedish representatives at Geneva were directed to take no such action without prior instructions. Stockholm to the Department of State, September 6, 1923. File 500.C001/221, Record Group 59, NA.

For the anti-Italian attitude of the Danish and Swedish press see *Bulletin Périodique de la Presse Scandinave*, No. 147, p. 4; No. 149, pp. 3-4.

[18] Mussolini to Franklin (Stockholm), September 16, 1923. *DDI*, p. 240. When presented with Rome's protest the Swedish Prime Minister, Ernst Trygger, pleaded that Sweden had nothing but sympathy for Italy, and none for the Athens government. His government, he explained, condemned the horrible murder of General Tellini and his staff; but at the same time Sweden felt that in the interests of peace and for the protection of small States it was necessary to support the Council's competence in all cases that could lead to war. The Corfu occupation was exactly one of these cases. Franklin replied that he could not understand why Branting persisted in League action when the question was for all intents and purposes being resolved, thanks to Rome's moderation. Trygger's immediate retort was that he had been opposed to Sweden's entrance into the League of Nations. He had felt that the Covenant was unclear and that the small States were very dependent on the Great Powers. However, from the moment Sweden adhered to the League Covenant, he wanted to see the League "exert [a] truly beneficent action." Swedish public opinion, he noted, placed great hopes in the League, and it was only for this reason that he had accepted the League's decision to award the Aaland Islands to Finland in 1921. He wished to make it clear, he told Franklin, that Branting's actions were not meant to be unfriendly towards Italy, but only meant

The League and the Conference

THE CONFERENCE OF AMBASSADORS CONVENES

At eleven o'clock on the morning of September 5, at the very hour that the League Council was meeting in Geneva, the two hundred and twenty-fourth meeting of the Conference of Ambassadors was taking place in Paris.[19] It was to be the first of twelve meetings of the Conference dealing with the Italo-Greek dispute. The Conference had been convened to consider two notes from the secretary of the Commission of Delimita-

---

to strengthen the League's authority. Franklin insisted that perhaps instructions could be given to Branting to moderate his actions at Geneva. The Prime Minister replied that once delegates were named to the League they could be considered in a certain way as independent judges and not as political delegates of their governments. If the contrary were true, the League would give up its character as the "supreme petitioner in order to take that of a political conference that would not be any guarantee to small States." Trygger made it clear that because of his prior attitude towards the League, any pressure on Branting would cause Swedish public opinion to accuse him of having "taken advantage of the occasion for internal political purposes." Franklin (Stockholm) to Mussolini, September 20, 1923. *Ibid.*, pp. 255-256.

In Oslo, Rome's protest found a more sympathetic hearing. The Norwegian Prime Minister, Otto Halvorsen, disclosed to the Italian Minister, Silvio Cambiagio, that after his *démarche* instructions had been dispatched to Nansen. Halvorsen felt that with this cable Nansen would know the government's position and could not fail to comply accordingly. His government, the Prime Minister continued, had "unanimously agreed" to do everything possible so as to avoid strain in the good relations between the two countries. He also disclosed to Cambiagio that instructions had been sent to the other Norwegian delegates at Geneva, Blahr, Like, and Storting, in order to make sure that Nansen said nothing which could "jeopardize relations with Italy." Halvorsen assured the Italian Minister that Nansen would be informed of their conversation, with the insistence that he have regard for Italy's sentiments. The Prime Minister, in closing the interview, expressed his sympathy for Italy and for the "Great Minister who governs its destiny." Cambiagio (Christiania [Oslo]) to Mussolini, September 18, 1923. *Ibid.*, p. 252.

In the light of the above conversation it would appear that Italian pressure was not rejected in Oslo, as cited in Liv Nansen Høyer, p. 175.

[19] Unless cited otherwise the material that follows is drawn from the *procès-verbal* of the two hundred and twenty-fourth meeting of the Conference of Ambassadors, September 5, 1923. File 763.72119/12020, Record Group 59, NA.

The League and the Conference

tion of the Albanian borders, dated August 28 and 30, 1923, as well as a note of the Secretariat-General of the Conference dated September 1, 1923 (text of the Ambassadorial note of protest sent to Athens, August 31). It also had before it the Greek reply of September 2, 1923, and a note from the Albanian Legation in Paris, dated September 4 and addressed to the Conference.

Laroche, who had been assigned by Poincaré the task of handling the French case, opened the meeting. He began by bringing to the Conference's attention the different incidents pertinent to the delimitation of the Greek-Albanian frontier that had occurred in the preceding months.

On August 11, 1922, he reminded the Conference, the Greek Government had withdrawn its delegate from the Commission of Delimitation of the Albanian border on the pretext that the Commission refused to recognize the validity of the Protocol signed at Corfu, May 17, 1914, between the head of the autonomous organization of Epirus and the representatives of the International Commission of Control then instituted in Albania.[20] The Conference had protested against this attempted obstruction by the Greek Government on August 24, 1922, and again on October 26, 1922. Satisfaction was only given to the Conference three months later, on November 9, 1922. Seven months later, in June of 1923, the Greek delegate [Colonel Botzaris] withdrew from the Commission of Delimitation, alleging an insult had been made to the Greek flag in an Albanian village during the course of the [Muslim] feast of *Bayram*. This incident had been adjusted by negotiations between General Tellini and the Greek Ministry of Foreign Affairs. The last and perhaps most serious incident had occurred on July 13, only five weeks before. On that occasion the Greek Commissioner [Colonel Botzaris] had protested against the frontier line in the region of the villages of Bobicko and Radoti. General Tellini had rejected the protest on the grounds that the question had already been decided by the Conference

[20] *Documents Officiels Concernant l'Épire du Nord: 1912-1935* (Athènes: Flamma, 1935), pp. 33-38.

The League and the Conference

in its resolution of January 13, 1923. The Greek delegate then declared he would still oppose the construction of the frontier markers. In order to stop this new obstruction to the work of the Commission, the Conference was forced to intervene with a letter to the Greek Government on August 7, 1923.

In his subsequent report to Rome, Avezzana was to observe that in discussing these precedents Laroche had been "objective," but his "intonation [was] clearly favorable to the Italian point of view." The whole episode, he noted, was "evidently inspired by instructions from Poincaré."[21]

Continuing, Laroche then turned to an examination of the Greek note of September 2, paragraph by paragraph.[22] It seemed, he observed, that the Greeks did everything possible with a view to the organization of an inquiry. On the other hand, it was impossible to accept the affirmations of the Greek Government that the assassination of General Tellini could be an act of criminal folly for which it was impossible to impute responsibility to any nationality. It appeared that the assassination of General Tellini was, on the contrary, a nationalist crime, the reasons for which could be sought in the overexcitement of nationalist passions. The state of mind that the declarations of the Greek Government revealed in this matter was not of a nature to reassure the Conference of Ambassadors. It was to be feared, he concluded, that the men responsible for the assassination of General Tellini might find aid in Greece. Therefore, it was indispensable to control the inquiry of the Greek authorities.

Following Laroche's opening comments, Avezzana maintained that the attitude of the Greek Government justified the proposal made by Rome that the inquiry be carried out with the help of the Italian military attaché in Athens [Colonel Perrone]. He brought to the attention of his colleagues the aid that the assassins of General Tellini would naturally find in the Epirus region. There existed in this region leaders of bands whose identities were as well known to the Greek au-

[21] Avezzana (Paris) to Mussolini, September 5, 1923. *DDI*, p. 185.
[22] *DDDIG*, pp. 21-22.

The League and the Conference

thorities as to the inhabitants of the area. These bands appeared openly in the city of Janina. It was these same bands that had, in 1914, provoked the incidents in Epirus which forced the Great Powers to protest to the Greek Government. From the point of view of both the Italian Government and the Conference, it was indispensable that the representatives of the Conference participate in the inquiry.

He also associated himself with Laroche's declarations concerning the nature of the motives that lay back of the crime. The populations of Epirus were animated by a very ardent national sentiment, which expressed itself in desires for vengeance and outbreaks of hatred like those which provoked the assassination of the members of the Italian delegation. As his government's representative he could only protest against the observations of the Greek Government on this subject, which did not appear to him to be lacking in a certain irony and the opportuneness of which was at least questionable.

Lord Crewe, the British Ambassador, who was to prove Avezzana's chief protagonist, observed that the Ambassadors' Conference had neither to praise nor to blame the methods by which the inquiry of the Greek Government was being pursued. The Conference had simply to decide the nature and the modalities of the inquiry it must institute.

Continuing his reading of the Greek note, Laroche brought to the notice of his colleagues two distinct suggestions, the proposal for the institution of a special Commission of Inquiry and the proposal that the powers of the Commission extend to both Greek and Albanian territory. Concerning the second proposal, Laroche was of the opinion that the Albanians would undoubtedly agree to an extension of the Commission's powers. In their note which was before the Conference, they had made it clear that Albanian responsibility was in no way involved.[23] Until it was proven to the contrary it was the Greek Government, upon whose territory the crime had been com-

[23] Note of the Albanian Government to the Conference of Ambassadors, September 4, 1923. Text. File 763.72119/12020, Annex E, Record Group 59, NA.

The League and the Conference

mitted, that was fully responsible. The Conference should therefore find a formula that, while releasing the Albanian Government of responsibility, would at the same time impose on it the obligation to facilitate whatever work the Commission might wish to undertake in its territory.

Taking a stronger position, Lord Crewe believed that the Conference did not have to ask the authorization of the Albanian Government. It could simply declare that the powers of the Commission extended into Albanian territory.[24]

In the conversation that followed it was not disputed by Avezzana that if the murderers were refugees in Albanian territory they were to be pursued in that territory. However, even if the Greek Government appeared as the most pure and peaceful of governments and the authors of the crime were found to be Albanians, the fact that the crime had been committed on Greek territory would still involve the responsibility of the Greek Government.

Laroche and Avezzana agreed that the responsibility was territorial. However, Lord Crewe and Laroche felt that if it were proven that the crime had been prepared and organized in Albanian territory, the degree of responsibility that would be incumbent upon the Greek Government would obviously be lessened.

Laroche and Avezzana's main contention, according to the American observer, Sheldon Whitehouse, was that the Greek reply of September 2 rested on the premise that Greek responsibility was a "matter to be proven." Both argued, however, that "under unquestionable principles of international law," Greek responsibility was already established by the fact that the crime had been committed on Greek territory.[25]

To support this point of view Laroche brought to the atten-

[24] On the question of Albanian authorization, the American observer could not help reporting cynically that Albania would "be informed (due regard being had to the requirements of diplomatic phraseology) that the Commission of Inquiry is to operate [in] her territory, if and when necessary." Whitehouse (Paris) to the Department of State, September 5, 1923. File 765.68/40 Section I, Record Group 59, NA.

[25] Whitehouse (Paris) to the Department of State, September 5, 1923. File 765.68/40 Section I, Record Group 59, NA.

The League and the Conference

tion of the Conference the Nancy incident of 1913, which had involved Germans and French. Although the French Government had not been in any way responsible for the incident it had not hesitated to withdraw the Prefect of Meurthe-et-Moselle.

Avezzana recalled the example of Passau-Ingolstadt. Although the incidents had occurred in Bavarian territory, it was the German Government that had claimed responsibility. This same government had not only presented apologies, but had assumed payment of the indemnity imposed by the Conference. This example was all the more convincing in that it concerned a federal state and it would have been possible for the German Government, because of this constitutional fact, to decline all responsibility.

The Conference was then pressed by Laroche on the composition of the Commission of Inquiry to be established. Disregarding Avezzana's pleas for a postponement to allow him to consult Rome, Laroche suggested that the Presidency of the Commission be entrusted to an Italian delegate.

It was Lord Crewe's personal opinion that the best solution would be to entrust the inquiry to the delegates of Powers represented on the Conference but not directly interested in the incident: a Belgian, an American, or a Japanese, for example. The Japanese delegate, Mr. Sato, believed that his government would prefer not to participate in the inquiry unless its participation appeared absolutely necessary. Avezzana maintained that the Italian Government had insisted from the beginning upon the participation of the Italian military attaché [Colonel Perrone] in the investigation organized by the Greek Government. There was no doubt that his government would wish to be represented on the contemplated Commission of Inquiry. His government acknowledged that although the question interested the Conference, it interested even more the Italian Government, which found itself particularly affected. Laroche explained it was because of this conviction that he had proposed to entrust the Presidency of the Commission of Inquiry to an Italian delegate.

The League and the Conference

Continuing his exegesis of the Greek note, Laroche thought that from the inter-allied point of view there were no remarks he could make upon the observations regarding the attitude of the Italian Government. Laroche also set aside the observations of the Greek note concerning the occupation of Corfu, stating that this was a distinct question. Lastly, he pointed out the mistake which had inspired the wording of the last paragraph of the Greek note. In this paragraph Athens had declared that if it were demonstrated that the responsibility of Greece was involved in the matter, it would pay all the reparations that the Conference would judge just. This reply Laroche felt was dilatory. The responsibility of the Greek Government was already involved. The intended inquiry did not have as its object the establishment of this responsibility. Its object was simply the pursuit of the culprits and the determination of the extent of the responsibility of the Greek Government.

At this point Jules Cambon, who presided as President of the Conference of Ambassadors during the meetings, intervened. He associated himself completely with Laroche's remarks. He pointed out that Laroche's observations applied equally to the passage in the Greek note reading: "If it came to be established that a share of any responsibility" is incumbent upon the Greek Government for the crimes committed, Greece "will grant all the reparations that the Conference of Ambassadors will indicate to it as opportune." Cambon considered that the responsibility of the Greek Government was from this moment established. He opposed the qualification given by the Greek Government to the reparations that the Conference would have the right to exact. The Ambassadorial Conference did not have the intention to exact reparations it would judge opportune, but rather reparations it would regard as just.

Laroche then turned the attention of his colleagues to the contradictory steps that had been undertaken by the Greek Government. The latter, not content with bringing the issue before the Conference, had also brought it before the League

The League and the Conference

of Nations. The day before in fact [September 4] M. Politis had formulated a new proposal; he had suggested that the League entrust to an arbitral tribunal, composed of a Greek, an Italian, and a neutral, the task of examining the amount of indemnity to be paid by the Greek Government. Leaving aside all reservations that could be made on the substance of the proposal, Laroche thought it was appropriate to remark that the indemnity anticipated was not to be imposed merely as a compensation for the families of the victims, but also as a penalty. He felt that the Greek State could not shirk the payment of an indemnity penalty.

In support of Laroche, Avezzana pointed out that though Greece had also addressed herself to another organization, it was the Conference of Ambassadors that was first of all competent. The Conference should therefore consider itself as called upon to handle the whole of the question. The League of Nations under these circumstances could not ignore the Conference of Ambassadors.

Cambon, in summing up, added that since the Commission of Delimitation held its powers from the Conference, there was therefore no doubt as to the competence of the Ambassadors' Conference. He believed it would be useful for the Conference to make known, as quickly as possible, that it had decided to organize the inquiry proposed by the Greek Government. Avezzana, who in principle was prepared to accept the inquiry, desired, however, to solicit instructions from Rome concerning the modalities by which the inquiry should be conducted.

While the meeting was suspended Laroche drafted a cable to be dispatched to Geneva. The note which Laroche drew up and the Conference approved merely complicated the situation and led to further difficulties.

The cable noted Greece's willingness, if her responsibility were proven, to agree to any reparations which the Conference deemed just. It also noted Athens' suggestion for the institution of a Commission of Inquiry consisting of the three Powers represented on the Delimitation Commission. Concluding, the

The League and the Conference

note declared that the Conference, "recognizing that it is a *principle of international law* that States are responsible for political crimes and outrages committed within their territory," had at once considered how the proposed inquiry was to be conducted.[26]

The note which Laroche had drafted mirrored the conversation which had taken place in the Conference. It reflected the Laroche-Avezzana contention that States were responsible for crimes against foreign nationals committed within their territory. Under international law, however, it is firmly established that no State is required "to guarantee the lives and property of resident aliens."[27] State responsibility for crimes against foreign nationals arises only when it can be proven that the State or its officials failed to exercise "due diligence," or if the State organs and officials failed to apprehend, prosecute, or punish the guilty. In this respect the Greek reply of September 2, which Laroche and Avezzana had dismissed, stating that Greek responsibility had to be proven, was based on firm legal principles. The Ambassadorial representatives unfortunately failed to see the error in their contention. This error, however, was to cause Laroche, Hanotaux, and a number of Geneva delegates, as well as the League Secretariat, some anxious moments.[28]

REACTION TO THE CONFERENCE OF AMBASSADORS' MEETING

"The atmosphere of the meeting," cabled the American observer to Washington, "was marked by the absence of any

[26] Italics added. L.N., *Official Journal*, 4th year, 1923, p. 1294. See Appendix A.

[27] Herbert W. Briggs, *The Law of Nations* (2nd ed.; New York: Appleton-Century-Crofts, Inc., 1952), p. 615.

[28] For a full examination of State responsibility for damages to aliens and the law of international claims see *ibid.*, pp. 601-747. The problems that followed because of the way in which the Conference's message to the Council was drafted and the actions that were taken by Hanotaux, Viscount Ishii, Sir Eric Drummond, the League Secretariat, and Laroche, to readjust the matter are discussed later in this chapter and in Chapter VI.

The League and the Conference

acerbity or even apparent tension." Whitehouse then reported that some of the more interesting comments were made "off the record." During the discussions, he disclosed, the French and Italians made a number of remarks, "to the effect that a restricted and quiet body such as the Conference of Ambassadors" could do a much better job of handling a question of this nature. They felt that the Conference could do more than "the comparatively public and tumultuous League of Nations, where conditions were such that members spoke and acted for publication and to the gallery." While Laroche was busy drafting the cable to Geneva, Avezzana had given his colleagues "a completely informal [and] colloquial exposition of [the] Italian position." The Greeks, Avezzana had observed, "both individually and collectively" had engaged in anti-Italian activities for a considerable period of time, and specifically with respect to the Delimitation Commission.

As to Italy's demand for 50 million Italian lire, Avezzana declared that his government had considered the sum of one million gold marks, the sum that had been imposed on Germany for the incident of Passau-Ingolstadt, and felt that since in the present case five deaths were involved the sum of 50 million lire was not only strictly in proportion, but also moderate. One factor, he admitted, greatly irritated Italy and that was that though the victims were Italians, Greece was striving in every way possible to invoke international considerations so as to avoid making direct reparations and apologies to Italy. He felt it was a great pity from the Italian point of view that before the attitude of his government "was known or considered an appeal was made to the League of Nations," which aroused passions, including those of the parties concerned. Anything that gained time and allowed passions to cool was desirable.

Whitehouse's own opinion was that there was some hope that decisive action on the part of the Conference of Ambassadors might "save the face (and the existence) of the League of Nations." Any predictions, he felt, would be absolutely superfluous since events would probably move very rapidly before the next meeting of the Conference, scheduled for September 7.

Before closing his report, Whitehouse brought to Washington's attention that during the "nebulous discussions" as to the formation of the proposed Commission of Inquiry, Lord Crewe had suggested the appointment of an American. Whitehouse thought that neither the French nor the Italians "approved the idea." He presumed that Washington would also be opposed to any American participation, but at the same time requested definite instructions.[29]

Whitehouse's presumption was correct. In the atmosphere of 1923 Washington, any American involvement in the Balkans was unthinkable. "Discreetly discourage the proposal," cabled Secretary of State Charles Evans Hughes.[30]

During this period other views and reports were being dispatched from Paris. After a visit to the British Embassy the Greek Minister, Athos Romanos, reported to Athens that Lord Crewe had assured him that neither the French nor the British Governments wished to proceed in the Italo-Greek dispute in a manner that would damage the prestige of the League. Lord Crewe had explained that since the Council and the Conference happened to be meeting simultaneously, the latter had also assumed the question. By intervening, the Conference was to share in finding a solution to the question and thus allow collaboration between the Conference and the League. To Romanos' question as to how long the Italian occupation of Corfu would continue, Crewe had replied that this was impossible to answer. His own personal opinion was that Corfu would be evacuated as soon as the League and the Conference had found a solution that would also be acceptable to Rome.[31]

Romanos followed this cable with a report to the Foreign Ministry that he had learned of the Conference's decision to

[29] Whitehouse (Paris) to the Department of State, September 5, 1923. File 765.68/40 Section II, Record Group 59, NA.

[30] Hughes to Whitehouse (Paris), September 6, 1923. File 765.68/40, Record Group 59, NA.

[31] Romanos (Paris), No. 4639 to the Foreign Ministry, September 6, 1923. Greek Archives.

The League and the Conference

disregard Albanian objections to having the inquiry take place on Greek and Albanian territory. As regards the Greek proposition that neutral observers also participate in the proposed inquiry, the Conference had replied that in the Italo-Greek dispute France and Britain were also neutral, so that other countries were not chosen. It appeared, Romanos observed, that Avezzana had directed the Conference's attention to the Greek reply of September 2. Athens, he contended, had not limited itself to recognizing the need to institute a Commission of Inquiry, but had also drawn in the question of the Corfu occupation. He had then demanded that the latter question be maintained strictly within the Conference. This point, however, was not discussed, Romanos concluded, since France and England were interested in avoiding any conflict with the League.[32]

Across the city of Paris, the Italian Ambassador was also busy. Avezzana, in reporting the Conference's proceedings, assured Mussolini that he had affirmed that, for Italy, the actions of the Ambassadors' Conference could in no way substitute for "the direct action of the [Italian] Royal Government towards Greece." He recommended to the Duce that Laroche's proposal for a Commission of Inquiry, presided over by an Italian President and containing a French and British member, be accepted. On the other hand, he pointed out that this committee would be opposed by the British unless a fourth member were also added. Avezzana's own feelings were that a Japanese member would be preferable to an American, since the former "would give us assurances of justice." The selection of a Japanese, he observed, would be logical since Japan was officially represented in the Conference. The creation of a Commission of Inquiry would satisfy the fourth condition of the Italian ultimatum and at the same time help Italy attain her aims. The ambassador felt that a Greek inquiry with Italian participation, and an inquiry by the Conference without Italian participation, "would run the risk of leading

[32] Romanos (Paris), No. 4645 to the Foreign Ministry, September 6, 1923. French text. Greek Archives.

to a conflict that would not resolve itself in a manner advantageous" to Italy. Avezzana then disclosed to the Duce that after the meeting had ended a cable had reached Lord Crewe containing the purported text of a resolution passed by the League Council. The purported resolution was merely Politis' proposals of the previous day, which the Council's President, Viscount Ishii, had requested to have forwarded to the interested governments, but unaware of this fact, and before the text of the resolution had been confirmed by the League Secretariat, Avezzana discussed it with Jules Cambon. After an exchange of views they agreed that the competence of the Conference was implicitly recognized. The decision of the Council, he noted nervously, impelled him all the more to ask Mussolini "to consider with greater attention" the Conference's proposal to establish a Commission of Inquiry. In closing Avezzana again repeated that the proposed Commission of Inquiry would be a fulfillment of the fourth condition of the Italian ultimatum, and warned the Duce that though France was giving Italy "loyal support" it would at the same time be useful for Italy "to facilitate her task."[33]

No sooner had this cable been cleared than a second cable was dispatched to Rome. The resolution taken by the Council, Avezzana informed Mussolini, did not correspond to that telegraphed by Lord Robert Cecil. The latter's communication could, therefore, only be regarded as "tendentious and directed to make [an] impression [on] the Conference of Ambassadors." According to a cable from Hanotaux, a proposal by Cecil that it was "desirable that the efforts of the Council and those of the League of Nations . . . occur in harmony" was rejected. Hanotaux in his cable also disclosed that at Geneva it was thought the question could be submitted to the Permanent Court of International Justice at The Hague. When questioned by Poincaré on this contemplated solution, Avezzana had replied that in his opinion Italy would refuse to go to The Hague, and that it was convenient neither to Greece

[33] Avezzana (Paris) to Mussolini, September 5, 1923. *DDI*, pp. 185-187.

The League and the Conference

nor to England "to prolong [this] Byzantine question" if they intended to obtain the evacuation of Corfu. Poincaré then requested his opinion on Italy's likely reaction to the proposals Politis had made in the League Council. Avezzana retorted that he would pass them on to Mussolini, but added that it appeared to him that Rome would not wish to separate herself from the decision taken that same day at the Ambassadors' Conference relative to the Commission of Inquiry. As for the sum of 50 million Italian lire, he felt the Conference would have to ensure the deposit of the money in Switzerland or elsewhere, but reserved further comment until he knew the Duce's views. Before ending their conversation Avezzana made it clear to Poincaré that Italy would continue to occupy Corfu and would not evacuate it until satisfaction had been received.[34]

Mussolini approved fully Avezzana's performance at the first meeting of the Conference. He was especially pleased, he cabled, with the distinction he made in saying that Conference action could not substitute in any way "the direct action of Italy toward Greece." As to the contemplated Commission of Inquiry, Avezzana was instructed to insist on a "triumvirate" presided over by an Italian. He was also to make it clear that the commission "absorbed" Italy's fourth demand in its ultimatum to Greece. If the British objected to the proposed three-man commission, he was to accept the participation of a Japanese member.[35] Avezzana's recommendations to accept and participate in the proposed Commission of Inquiry had therefore been endorsed.

Not only did the Duce approve Avezzana's performance in the Conference, but he also approved his negative reaction to Poincaré's query on the possibility of submitting the dispute to the World Court at The Hague. As to Politis' proposal before the League Council for a deposit by Greece of 50 million Italian lire in a Swiss bank, the Duce felt it would not be

[34] Avezzana (Paris) to Mussolini, September 5, 1923. *Ibid.*, pp. 187-188.
[35] Mussolini to Avezzana (Paris), September 6, 1923. *Ibid.*, pp. 196-197.

The League and the Conference

compatible with Italy's assumed position. He observed that it could not be taken into consideration unless its interdependence with the remaining portion of Politis' proposals was made perfectly clear. Another problem that posed itself was whether Politis' proposals were to be presented to Italy directly or through the Conference of Ambassadors. For guidance during his conversations, Avezzana was asked to keep in mind the immense costs for Italy of the Corfu occupation, which were accumulating with each passing day because of Greece's nonexecution of its obligations. This situation he had drawn to the attention of the British and French chargés d'affaires.[36] The whole question of occupation costs was to assume greater importance in the days to come.

In London, Lord Crewe's performance at the Ambassadors' Conference was viewed far differently. "I confess," Sir William Tyrrell wrote to Lord Curzon, "I am not happy about the part played by Crewe at the Conference yesterday." It appeared to Tyrrell that "at this stage of the negotiations the main burden" was going to fall on the Conference of Ambassadors. Because of this he was "not at all sure" that Crewe was strong enough to carry the burden. He therefore asked Curzon to "consider the desirability" of either substituting for Lord Crewe the Permanent Under-Secretary of the Foreign Office, Sir Eyre Crowe, or associating the latter as an "assistant adviser" to Lord Crewe. Tyrrell was aware that though greater value would be had by the substitution of Crowe for Crewe, it would also "look like a slap" to the latter. If Crowe were a mere assistant adviser, they would have to be content with getting less value out of him, but they would save the ambassador's face. Sir Eyre Crowe, he informed Curzon, was vacationing near Tours and could easily reach Paris. He felt that the Permanent Under-Secretary "would very soon pick up the threads" and he personally would "feel happier."[37] Tyrrell's recommendation fortunately did not bear fruit. Lord Crewe

[36] Mussolini to Avezzana (Paris), September 6, 1923. *Ibid.*, p. 197.
[37] Sir William Tyrrell to Lord Curzon, September 6, 1923. Folder marked "Letters to Curzon, M-Y, 1923," Box 65, Curzon Papers.

The League and the Conference

continued sitting in the meetings of the Conference, where in the days to come his tenacity, good sense, and tact proved invaluable in what was to become a demanding and trying situation.

The day's events had ended in London, Paris, Geneva, and Rome. The following day, everyone's attention was again drawn to the League Council, where attempts to find some sort of compromise solution monopolized the attention of the delegates.

THE COUNCIL'S OVERTURES TO THE CONFERENCE

Prior to the meeting of the League Council on September 6, "unofficial meetings" from which the Greeks and Italians had been excluded had taken place among the delegates.[38] These meetings produced proposals which were prepared "by [a] majority [of the] members of the Council under the inspiration [of the] British representatives with a view to [a] collaboration [of the] League and [the] Conference for [a] prompt settlement" of the dispute.[39] After discussions among the delegates, José Maria Quiñones de León, Spain's Ambassador to Paris and League delegate, was authorized by his colleagues to propose the points "covering the actions which Greece should be required to take."[40] The selection of Quiñones de León was undoubtedly based on his "acute and conciliatory mind" and his "sincere devotion to the League."[41]

---

[38] F. P. Walters, *A History of the League of Nations* (London: Oxford University Press, 1960), p. 249.

[39] Politis (Geneva), No. 1180 to the Foreign Ministry, September 7, 1923. French text. Greek Archives. According to the President of the League Council, Japan's Viscount Ishii, unproductive Council meetings prompted him to "invite the Council members other than the Italian and Greek to his hotel to deliberate on the case over a cup of tea." As Ishii anticipated, Italian protests "against this procedure" were lodged. Ishii replied "he was not holding unlawful meetings of the Council" nor were his tea parties being given in his capacity as President of the League Council. Viscount Kikujiro Ishii, *Diplomatic Commentaries*, trans. and ed. by William R. Langdon (Baltimore: The Johns Hopkins Press, 1936), p. 168.

[40] Walters, p. 249.   [41] *Ibid.*, p. 453.

The League and the Conference

These "unofficial meetings" were unquestionably inspired by Cecil and Branting, who had strongly desired that the Conference defer the whole question to the Council of the League. Faced, however, by Salandra's uncompromising attitude and by France's undisguised support of Italy, they believed it would be "wiser to attempt to secure common action by the two bodies rather than risk aggravating the crisis by insisting upon the special rights and duties of the Covenant."[42]

The Council meeting commenced, at 5:30 in the afternoon, with a reading of the Ambassadorial note drafted by Laroche the previous day. The President of the Council, Viscount Ishii, felt that a reply should be sent to the Conference. Quiñones de León interjected that his colleagues had discussed the Italo-Greek dispute and had requested him "to submit to the Council a text which might serve as a basis for a discussion of the reply" to be sent to the Conference.

The text Quiñones de León proposed took heed of the Ambassadorial note and recognized the "principle of international law" that all States were responsible for "political crimes and outrages committed within their territory." It declared the Council's intention of "investigating, in conjunction with the Conference," the manner in which the inquiry was to be carried out. The note also expressed the desire of the Council to be kept informed of the Conference's deliberations, scheduled to reopen the following day. Lastly, the Council was to submit for consideration by the Conference certain suggestions as to possible means of giving satisfaction to the demands of the latter, as a consequence of the Tellini murder. The eight suggestions were as follows: (1) the presentation of apologies by the highest Greek authorities to the Ministers of the three Powers represented on the Delimitation Commission; (2) the celebration of a funeral service at Athens in honor of the victims in the presence of all the members of the Greek Government; (3) the giving of a salute by the Greek fleet in accordance with conditions to be later determined; (4) the rendering of military honors when the bodies of the victims

[42] *Ibid.*, p. 249.

The League and the Conference

are embarked at Preveza; (5) the appointment by the Greek Government of a Commission of Inquiry to investigate on the spot the circumstances preceding and accompanying the crime and the supplementing of this Commission by representatives of the three Powers concerned, as mentioned in the Conference's note of September 5; (6) the appointment of representatives of the League of Nations to supervise in Greece the judicial inquiry already ordered by the Greek authorities and the trial of the guilty parties; (7) the immediate deposit by Greece in a Swiss bank of a sum of 50 million Italian lire as security for the immediate payment of any indemnity that might be fixed; (8) the submission to the Permanent Court of International Justice, for decision under the rules of summary procedure, of the question of the indemnity to be paid by Greece.

A careful reading of Quiñones de León's proposed suggestions shows that the more unpalatable of the Italian demands had been dropped and others modified, while some of Politis' recommendations made the day before had been included.

Salandra, who was grateful for the attempt to find a compromise formula, regretted however that he was "quite unable to consent even to discuss one portion" of the text. This was only logical after his previous statement in the Council—that the Italian Government could not "admit that the Council enter into a discussion on the substance of the question." He felt that any Council proposals to the Ambassadors' Conference fixing Greek reparations, as projected in the note read by Quiñones de León, would be tantamount to the League Council's stating its opinion on the extent of the reparations. Has Italy, he asked, "nothing to say on the question of reparations?" It could be argued that Italy was a Member of the League Council and represented on it, just as she was represented on the Conference of Ambassadors. Italy, however, insisted on her right to discuss the question of reparations that were due her for the crime perpetrated upon Italian officers.

Salandra's fundamental observation was that the Italian Government could not "admit that the question of the amount of reparations should be determined by the Conference of Ambassadors and the Council of the League of Nations without the intervention of the Italian Government." He therefore objected to the whole second part of the proposed text. He could see no objection to the Council's declaring that it would be glad to receive information on the deliberations of the Conference of Ambassadors. On the other hand, he feared that the words in the proposed text, "The Council . . . declares its intention of investigating in conjunction with the Conference, the manner in which the enquiry should be carried out," might be dangerous, for they perhaps implied "a declaration of competence, or, at least, an indirect assertion or presumption of competence." He had to insist that the whole question of the Council's competence be reserved. If only a request for information were being addressed to the Conference, he had no reason for objecting to the proposed text. But, if the proposed text as drafted was put to a vote, he would abstain from voting for the reasons he had already enumerated.

Invited by the President of the Council to state his opinion on the question, Politis thought it would be better if he said nothing. It appeared to him preferable to wait until the Council had made a decision. Politis did repeat, however, that as far as his government was concerned the question of the Council's competence was not involved and that his government "was prepared to accept in advance the decisions of the Council."

At this point Gabriel Hanotaux, the French representative, was called upon. In line with his instructions from Paris his approach was one of conciliation. Hanotaux was pleased that the Council had obtained Salandra's "adhesion in principle" to the first part of the proposed text submitted by Quiñones de León. This meant that the Council was continuing its conversation with the Ambassadors' Conference and that everyone was attempting to ensure the continuation of the liaison among all the interested parties.

After these opening remarks Hanotaux was now forced to expose to the Council the mistake of Laroche and the Conference. He revealed that the text received from the Conference

The League and the Conference

of Ambassadors was probably incomplete and that two words of great importance were missing from it. According to Hanotaux the text communicated by the Conference lacked the words, "for the repression" of the crime, or similar words. He felt they must have been omitted. This disclosure produced a sensation in the crowded Council chamber. Hanotaux was quick to point out that he was merely mentioning the opinion expressed in the note handed to him by his secretary. There was no suggestion that the Ambassadorial text, read to the Council, was any other than the text received from Geneva. But it would appear, he observed, that the text was "quite contrary to the opinion of the jurists." He merely wished to prove that the Council should not take action on questions of this type in "too great haste." He cited precedents to prove his point. The attempt in 1862 on the life of Emperor Alexander II, "did not give rise to 'responsibility for the crime' but to 'responsibility for the repression of the crime,'" which legally was not the same thing. In the assassination of the Empress of Austria, and in other cases as well, "responsibility for the repression of the crime" was the issue, not "the responsibility for the crime." It was likely that the salient words had been omitted in the copy, or in the transmission of the note, which often happened. Because of this he felt "the text should be altered to some extent." He concluded with the observation that the Council should "proceed in everything and always with cautious deliberation."

Hanotaux's disclosure prompted Salandra to ask how the Council was to proceed. The Council possessed a text communicated to it by the Conference of Ambassadors. He had the greatest respect for jurists, being one himself, however jurists did not have the right "to reconstitute an existing text in the light of their own arguments." Texts had to be taken as they stood.

Obviously in a difficult position, Hanotaux retorted that he merely desired to mention the point. He was himself prepared to accept the text as transmitted. He felt, however, that he ought to warn the Council and Salandra that the question had

The League and the Conference

been raised "in various quarters." According to opinion which he had just mentioned, the Council was in possession of an incomplete text. It had to be remembered that the Council was working on texts transmitted either by telephone or telegraph, which could be erroneous.

Pressing his point, Salandra asked what Hanotaux proposed. The latter answered that he proposed nothing. He merely wished to say that States were responsible for the repression of crime. He did not "for the moment ask for the modification of the text." Salandra, however, was obviously unsatisfied with Hanotaux's replies. He felt that a change in the text was being proposed and he was "entirely opposed to such an alteration." The Council possessed only the text which had been read to it.

Hanotaux agreed with Salandra and noted that he accepted the text subject to the remarks he had made. He observed that there was therefore, "agreement with regard to the first part of the proposal" before the Council. He was "glad of it" and for his part, he adhered to the text. There remained, Hanotaux noted, the second part of the text proposed by Quiñones de León. Salandra had stated that no agreement on this section was possible. Hanotaux regretted that it was not possible to make the agreement complete. This did not mean it could not be achieved. In the light of the opinions that had been expressed he felt that "the draft proposal constituted a basis for discussion," which would be advantageously employed either by the Council or by the Conference of Ambassadors, to whom the text should eventually be communicated.

The presence of Salandra in the Council chamber, Hanotaux noted, was the best proof of the "spirit of conciliation" that animated the Council. "Let us advance gradually," he added, "along the path of conciliation towards the pacific object which we all seek to attain." This was to be done all the more in view of the fact that the Council had received from Rome declarations justifying the hope that acceptance of sanctions by Athens would hasten the solution of the problem, which was everyone's desire.

Had not the Italian Government declared that in its opinion

The League and the Conference

there was no risk of war with Greece? Therefore, it appeared that this danger, which was the greatest danger of all, was removed. Under these circumstances Hanotaux adhered to the first part of the proposed text which had been submitted to the Council by Quiñones de León. As to the second part of the proposed text, he thought that it should be reserved "for careful consideration and for submission to our governments, with a view to its being examined with the greatest care, in that spirit of agreement and conciliation" that had marked the discussion of the first part of the proposed text.

Cecil agreed "heartily" with Hanotaux's desire that the matter should be brought to a peaceful settlement at the earliest possible moment. The League of Nations existed primarily to promote peaceful international settlements, and every attempt was to be made, whatever the means offered, to accomplish that aim. The Council had before it a proposal by Quiñones de León made "after consultations with some of his colleagues." The proposal first acknowledged the communication sent by the Conference of Ambassadors and expressed the hope that the Council would hear again from the Conference with regard to the matter. Secondly, it made certain suggestions to the Ambassadors' Conference as to a possible settlement of the latter's claims with Greece. It was to be kept in mind, Lord Cecil warned, that there were three parties to the dispute: the Conference, Italy, and Greece. The proposal, he felt, seemed to be a good one, worthy of consideration by the Conference, and one which he thought worthy of being transmitted immediately by the Council for the Conference's consideration and observation. He did not think it would be useful to enter into a discussion with regard to several points raised by Salandra. Nevertheless, he agreed with Salandra's feelings that it was not good to suggest estimates of damages until the degree of culpability had been established; however, he could find no such suggestion in the proposals submitted. He noted that machinery to estimate the damages and the degree of culpability was provided for in the proposals. But there was nothing to show that these estimates necessarily were

The League and the Conference

to proceed simultaneously. Holding these views, Cecil was quite disposed to accept totally and unreservedly the proposals put forth by Quiñones de León. It was a great thing that on the first part—the less important part—there was agreement and that it would be sent as an answer to the Conference. He recognized, however, Hanotaux's argument that this was a matter of the greatest possible importance that had to be handled with the greatest caution. If Hanotaux wished to consult his government before he assented to any action by the Council, he thought that he was fully entitled to do so. As far as he himself was concerned, Cecil said, Whitehall has "given me sufficient instructions to enable me to approve this proposal as it stands."

At this point Lord Cecil very cleverly suggested that the *procès-verbal* of the Council's proceedings be forwarded to the Conference of Ambassadors, since it would be "only courteous" to keep the latter "fully informed." He could visualize no objections to this procedure. Even the full adoption of Quiñones de León's proposals would leave the proceedings incomplete. Many more things would have to be said before the matter could be terminated. Cecil thought, however, that he could best serve the cause of peace by remaining silent "on the other aspects of this question at present."

Closing, Cecil turned once again to the question of the Council's competence. He thought that the President of the Council would inform them when it would be more convenient to discuss this question. Nevertheless, he was "perfectly ready to have it thrashed out and discussed." Unless contrary arguments were developed—which he could not in the least imagine—he was unable to bring himself "to believe that there is the very slightest doubt as to the competence of the League of Nations to deal with all matters which have been submitted to it by the Greek Government, acting, as it tells us, and I think rightly tells us, under the terms of Article 15 of the Covenant." Cecil expressed the desire not to speak further on this point until discussions had taken place, but he did not wish to have it thought that his government questioned, or

The League and the Conference

doubted "the full competence of the League of Nations in this matter."

The discussions were continued by the Belgian delegate, Paul Hymans, who described Quiñones de León's proposal as "a happy one." He felt that the proposal expressed the feelings of a great many members of the Council. Agreement, he noted, had been reached on the first part of the proposal, though Salandra had made it clear that he would abstain from voting on the second part. Nevertheless, Hymans had the impression that the second part of the proposal contained suggestions that were "both just and practicable." Those who had drafted the second part of the proposal had been "animated with the sincerest desire to be conciliatory." There was no question then that the Council would reserve for more careful examination the second part of the proposal as suggested by Hanotaux and agreed to by Lord Robert Cecil. Commenting on Cecil's suggestion to send to the Conference the Council's *procès-verbal*, Hymans thought it was perfectly natural. The communication of the Council's minutes to all governments was done almost as a matter of course. In this case, however, the communication would have to be more rapid.

Like Lord Robert Cecil, Hymans also turned to the question of the Council's competence. He felt that this was an extremely grave problem, "both legally and from the standpoint of the future of the League of Nations." Any immediate and full discussion of "so delicate a question" seemed to him an imprudence that no one was interested in committing. Though he felt a sympathy "for the glorious Italian nation," admired it, and believed in its destiny, he had to make it clear, to his great regret, that he was unable to accept the case developed by Salandra regarding the non-competence of the Council in this matter. In Hymans' opinion Articles 12 and 15 of the League Covenant were "clear and precise" and applied in the Italo-Greek dispute. He saw in these articles "the most valuable guarantee for small countries"—guarantees which appeared to him to constitute the very foundation of the League Covenant. The interests of small Powers as well as respect for the principles upon which the League was based, demanded an untiring application of the Covenant, which was the foundation stone of the "new international order" in which everyone had placed great hopes.

Hymans' words were echoed by Branting of Sweden, who felt that by adoption of the proposed text the Council would be giving "formal and definite expression of its anxiety" to settle the dispute which threatened the peace and could undermine the foundations of the League. It was his opinion that Quiñones de León's proposals associating the Conference of Ambassadors with the League Council "in its work of pacification" were of a nature "to strengthen the position of the Council in any action which it may later deem necessary to take." Branting emphasized how important it was for the Council that a solution be found which, resulting in the immediate evacuation of Corfu, would at the same time guarantee that reparations be forthcoming for the Tellini murder. As to the Council's competence, he was "in entire agreement with the views so eloquently expressed" by Hymans.

Salandra again took the floor and thanked Hymans for his kind words about Italy. These sentiments were also felt by Italy for Belgium. There were many who loved Italy, Salandra observed, the Italy of perpetual sunlight, beautiful scenery, art, museums and churches. This Italy, however, was not the Italy he was here to represent. He represented "new Italy"—the country that had shared in the Allied victory and had sacrificed the lives of six hundred thousand men, the Italy that cared above all else "for her prestige and national dignity." Because of "this reason and, for this reason alone," he had to uphold his "view that, in a question of prestige and national dignity," Italy could not leave the decision to the League Council. Salandra reiterated that personally he had the greatest respect for the League's authority. He felt that such a dispute as the Italo-Greek one was not contemplated by Article 15 of the League Covenant, to which references had been made. "A political crime," he observed, had "been committed against Italy as a political entity," and for that crime Italy demanded reparations and punishment. As to the question of the Council's competence, he thought the time was ill-opportune and that the question would be discussed when the Council saw fit.

Turning to Hymans' comment about small nations, Salandra protested that the case in question was not an issue between a great Power, as such, and a small Power. Hymans and Branting, he caustically remarked, were fortunate in that they represented countries where assassination was not a political instrument. Their countries were therefore not concerned as small Powers, they had no interest in the question. He repeated that he would abstain from voting and would not oppose the communication of the first part of the proposed text to the Ambassadors' Conference. He would follow this course in order to avoid the suggestion that he had allowed his point of view, "on the question of competence to be in the least affected."

As to the proposal by Lord Robert Cecil that the *procès-verbal* of the meeting be forwarded to the Conference, Salandra had no objection. He felt that such a procedure was an act of courtesy towards the Conference of Ambassadors, especially since the meeting of the Council was public and the *procès-verbal* could be given all the publicity desired. His only qualification was that the minutes not be telegraphed until the speakers who had taken part in the debate had approved them. Salandra pointed out that minutes of a meeting had no legal value until they had been approved by the body engaged in the discussion.

The conclusion of Salandra's address to the Council prompted Politis to request the floor. He noted that Salandra had made certain remarks which he was "unable to leave unnoticed." He was referring to Salandra's comment to Hymans and Branting that they did not belong to countries in which political assassination was the order of the day. Politis could not admit that this allusion could in any way apply to Greece. History recorded numerous political crimes in the most civilized nations. Hanotaux had in the discussions recalled to the Council's attention two crimes committed against political personages

The League and the Conference

who also happened to be crowned heads. The commission of these crimes in no way impaired the reputation of the countries involved. He was willing to admit that an "abominable crime" had unfortunately been committed in Greek territory against distinguished foreigners. Greece regretted it and admitted that reparations were in order, and would give them "in all good faith."

Politis was immediately followed by Alberto Guani, the delegate from Uruguay, who supported Hymans' "eloquent speech" on the question of the Council's competence. Guani maintained that the Council's competence in international questions, such as the Italo-Greek dispute which could affect or actually did affect the peace of the world, was "unquestionable."

Guani's short speech over, Ishii observed that the first part of the draft reply submitted by Quiñones de León had met with the general approval of the Council since Salandra had no objections to its wording. Because the second part of the proposed draft met with Salandra's formal opposition, he thought Quiñones de León would be good enough to withdraw it.

The Council's decision to send the first part of the draft reply to the Conference of Ambassadors prompted Salandra to request that it be clearly stated in the record that he had abstained from voting. Lord Cecil assured him that the verbatim report would mention that fact. As to the verbatim report, Salandra personally wished to be allowed to examine it before giving his approval. Cecil replied that to avoid misunderstandings, it was to be made clear that the second part of the draft reply had been discussed and a decision postponed. The verbatim report was to be sent, he continued, in order to show the Conference exactly what had happened.

Cecil's proposal that the Council should decide whether or not the verbatim report of the Council's discussions be sent to the Conference was put to a vote by Ishii and passed. The only point that remained, Ishii remarked, was how the verbatim report would be sent.

The League and the Conference

This point was solved when the Secretary-General of the League, Sir Eric Drummond, disclosed that a stenographic report would be ready in half an hour and could be distributed to the delegates at their hotels. If they could return the stenographic minutes without delay to the League Secretariat, they could be communicated to the Ambassadors' Conference in time for its meeting scheduled the following day. Ishii added that the entire text of the draft reply originally proposed by Quiñones de León would of course appear in the verbatim report.

Before closing the day's session, Viscount Ishii reminded his colleagues that the question of the Council's competence was still unresolved. He felt that this was "a grave juridical question" and proposed, therefore, to postpone its discussion to a subsequent meeting.[43] The day's events at the Palais des Nations had ended. Cecil and his supporters, though unsuccessful in having Salandra accept the draft reply submitted by Quiñones de León, had, nevertheless, cleverly managed to have its contents forwarded to Paris. It was the Conference which now held the spotlight and the responsibility of achieving some sort of solution to the Italo-Greek dispute.

THE CONFERENCE'S COMMUNICATION CAUSES
DISQUIET IN GENEVA

Though the Council had adjourned, its actions still reverberated in Geneva the following day. Viscount Ishii, disturbed by reports that various delegations, particularly Switzerland's, had been aroused by the Council's agreement with the Conference's resolution, "that States are responsible for crimes and political outrages committed within their territory," called on the Secretary-General of the League, Sir Eric Drummond. He disclosed to Sir Eric that he had heard that certain South American delegations intended to bring up the matter before the League Assembly on the grounds that the doctrine as laid down was inconsistent with accepted practice under international law. Ishii's own view was that much depended on the

[43] L.N., *Official Journal*, 4th year, 1923, pp. 1294-1301.

The League and the Conference

definition given to the word, "political." Sir Eric replied that in his estimation perhaps more depended on the meaning placed on the word, "responsible." In order to clear up the confusion Ishii requested that the Legal Section of the Secretariat, "prepare, if possible, some interpretation consonant with accepted practice," which could then be given to him and to Quiñones de León, who was the original draftsman. The Secretary-General agreed and expressed to Dr. Joost-Adrian van Hamel, the Director of the Legal Section, the desire to see if the proposal were "really practicable."[44]

In his reply the following day, Dr. van Hamel thought that the explanation of the Legal Section contained "the proper interpretation of the sentence in the Council's decision on the Greek-Italian note." He felt that the explanation made it clear that, "if read with good will," the expressions used by the Council were acceptable. However, he could not help admitting to the Secretary-General that he found many lawyers upset by the somewhat general terms of the Council's resolution. Viscount Ishii, he also disclosed to Sir Eric, had spoken to him on his own initiative and asked him "to think over what he [Ishii] could do to set things right." Dr. van Hamel did not know whether anything could or should be done. He thought that the explanation of the Legal Section might be forwarded to Ishii. His own advice to Ishii would be to do nothing. Dr. van Hamel thought that the explanation of the Legal Section "might be kept *in petto* in case the matter should arise." "It seems an admirable statement," Sir Eric scribbled in the margin, and asked that private copies be forwarded to Ishii and Quiñones de León.[45]

The memorandum of explanation from Dr. van Hamel's Legal Section made it clear that the responsibility referred to

[44] E[ric] D[rummond] to Dr. van Hamel, September 7, 1923. Political 1923: 11/30650/30508, League of Nations Archives. Undoubtedly, Swiss apprehensions over the Council's resolution can be traced to the assassination at Lausanne, on May 10, 1923, of the Russian envoy, V. V. Vorovsky. Walters, p. 232.

[45] Dr. van Hamel to the Secretary-General, September 7, 1923. Political 1923; 11/30650/30508, League of Nations Archives.

The League and the Conference

in the Council's resolution was "international responsibility, that is to say, that vis-à-vis other governments." However, international law, it noted, did not impose "in a general fashion on governments an international responsibility for acts committed by individuals on their territory." Avoiding the whole problem of "due diligence," the memorandum approached the problem of State responsibility from an entirely different direction. According to the Legal Section, criminal actions directed "against a friendly State and acts of violence or injurious acts committed towards representatives or officials of a friendly State exercising their functions on the territory of another State with the consent of this latter and having there the right to a special protection" involved the responsibility of the latter State vis-à-vis the former. It was in this sense, it observed, that the Council had expressed itself in its resolution of September 6, 1923. On the other hand, the above doctrine did not apply "to acts of a political nature which were not crimes and political outrages." The memorandum added that the responsibilities in question would always be dependent on two criteria: the circumstances of the case and the attitude adopted by the government involved. The memorandum concluded with the observation that this thesis of governmental responsibility for acts of violence committed towards representatives of other States possessed with the right to special protection had been recognized by innumerable authorities in the field of international law.[46]

REPORTS FROM GENEVA TO ATHENS AND ROME

While Ishii was listening to the murmurs of discontent having to do with the problem of State responsibility, the two

---

[46] Dr. van Hamel, Directeur de la Section Juridique, Note Juridique sur la responsabilité des états des crimes et attentats politiques commis sur leur territoire, September 8, 1923. Political 1923: 11/30650/30508, League of Nations Archives. The authorities that Dr. van Hamel cited were: Borchard, *Diplomatic Protection of Citizens Abroad*, pp. 216-217; Moore, *International Law Digest*, v, paragraph 704; vi, paragraph 791; Oppenheim, *International Law*, i, p. 258; Bonfils, *Droit International Public*, No. 332; Liszt, *Das Völkerrecht*, p. 179.

The League and the Conference

delegates directly affected were busy cabling their impressions of the day's events to their respective governments.

Politis observed to Athens that if Italy were in the end to accept the procedure offered, everything would be quickly settled. He disclosed that a "great majority [of the] Council has decided to proceed to take [a] decision, and to seek to impose it," if Rome persisted in its uncompromising attitude. He also reported that things would develop slowly, since it was everyone's wish to gain time "in [a] desire to cause [the] French Government to abandon [the] support given to [the] Italian thesis." Turning to an examination of the suggestions in the second part of the draft resolution submitted by Quiñones de León, Politis felt it contained those demands that Greece had already accepted in the Italian ultimatum and included the proposals he had conveyed to the Council several days before. The only suggestion that he scrutinized was the one dealing with a salute to the fleet. He thought an advantage had been gained in that honors were to be given to the three Powers collectively rather than to Italy alone. Even if the final condition had been harder, Politis continued, Greece could not have withdrawn, since it had already accepted in advance the decisions of the League Council and the Conference of Ambassadors—her only means of having Corfu evacuated. He observed that public opinion in Greece should not lose sight of this fact and cautioned that the press should do everything possible to bring these "inevitable obligations" to the attention of the public.[47]

Salandra in his report to Rome could not help observing that the day's proceedings were evidence that the position of the British Government was contrary to that of Lord Robert Cecil, who twice before had declared the competence of the League Council. He warned that the whole question of the Council's competence was avoided only "with difficulty" and would be re-examined at the next meeting of the Council, primarily because of the pressure of Cecil and the representa-

[47] Politis (Geneva), No. 1180 to the Foreign Ministry, September 7, 1923. French text. Greek Archives.

The League and the Conference

tives of the smaller states. The declarations by Cecil, Hymans, and Guani made it almost certain that the Council would be opposed to Italy's thesis as to the League's non-competence. Italy's only hope, Salandra felt, was if France supported the Italian thesis, or if she found some "way of evading the question." He noted that the conduct of France's Hanotaux and Spain's Quiñones de León, "his tool," had been "friendly but feeble." This was demonstrated, he continued, by the fact that both had hastily decided to support the draft formula for which Quiñones de León had been "made [the] mouthpiece," though both delegates had admitted to him confidentially that the draft formula was "unacceptable." Nevertheless, Salandra warned, Rome had to be prepared at the next meeting of the League Council for a vote affirming the latter's competence, though the affirmation might be "founded [on] kindly sentences." Foreseeing a diplomatic debacle, Salandra cautioned that any further attempt to postpone the question would only be "humiliating and useless," since Geneva was evidently resolved "to carry [the] matter to the extreme." He reiterated that the question of the Council's competence could be avoided, or at the very least postponed, "only by France's resolute support." Therefore, he requested that the Duce "define exactly" Italy's eventual attitude if the Council declared itself competent in the dispute. His own feelings were that he should propose to the Council, immediately after the vote was taken, that he would report the results to Rome, which would examine the situation and make its decision. In closing, he disclosed that the feeling in Geneva was that Italy's withdrawal from the League was "unavoidable" after the publication of the cabinet's statements.[48]

In anticipation of eventual Italian withdrawal from Geneva,

[48] Salandra (Geneva) to Mussolini, September 7, 1923. *DDI*, pp. 199-200. Disclosure of Hymans' anti-Italian attitude quickly swung the Duce into action. A cable was immediately dispatched to the King, asking him to bring "discreetly" to King Albert's attention that Hymans' attitude at Geneva had been a "surprise [for] Italian public opinion." Mussolini to Vittorio Emanuele III (Racconigi), September 7, 1923. *Ibid.*, p. 200.

The League and the Conference

Giuriati cabled Mussolini and reiterated his previous recommendation to leave the League as soon as the Council announced its competence. However, to Giuriati, Italy's withdrawal was to be immediate and without the two years' notice required under the last paragraph of the first article of the Covenant. It was possible, he admitted to the Duce, that subsequent events unknown to him at the present time might make this action "impossible or extremely dangerous." Mussolini alone would have to be the judge of what action was to be taken. In case immediate withdrawal proved impossible, Giuriati envisaged withdrawal as stipulated under the Covenant. The action appeared to him to be the very "minimum" after the cabinet's statements of the previous days. He admitted that withdrawal from the League by the second method gravely limited Italy's "liberty of action" during the required waiting period. Yet it would put Italy in a "morally strong situation" and would avoid the greater danger that would eventually develop by not executing Rome's threat to leave the League.[49]

Faced with a dangerous situation and well aware that Italy's only hope lay in Paris, Mussolini almost instinctively turned to Poincaré. Salandra was informed that Avezzana in Paris had been instructed to bring to Poincaré's attention, "with all the necessary efficacy," Italy's position. He was to be told that Italy, in spite of its keen desires to conform in a most friendly and conciliatory spirit toward the Allied Powers and other friendly States, found it impossible to "withdraw from the fundamental position that it has after reflection and with perfect conscience of equity assumed in defense of its honor and its rights." Because of this position and given the opposition manifested against it at Geneva, Italy's withdrawal from the League could be avoided only by Poincaré. This could be done if "explicit instructions" were sent to Hanotaux to "sustain resolutely and firmly" the application of a formula which, while excluding the Council's competence, would accept the project communicated by the French chargé d'affaires several

[49] Giuriati (Geneva) to Mussolini, September 7, 1923. *Ibid.*, p. 201.

The League and the Conference

days before. As to Geneva, the Duce approved Salandra's recommendation that once the vote confirming the Council's competence had been taken, he was merely to confine himself to declaring that he would refer the results to Rome, which would examine the matter and make its decision.[50]

This information, however, crossed with a cable from Salandra, who had discussed with Hanotaux, Poincaré's formula for settlement, conveyed to Mussolini several days before by the French chargé d'affaires. Hanotaux, Salandra noted, had been quick to study the Duce's proposed modification on the fifth point and agreed with him that any proposed solution should be offered directly or through Quiñones de León. Salandra also revealed that he had been informed that Lord Robert Cecil, who had intended pressing the question of the Council's competence and the evacuation of Corfu, had been calmed and dissuaded from doing so by the British Ambassador in Paris, Lord Crewe. He warned, however, that these good intentions might be frustrated by pressure on Cecil from Norway's "Nansen and other agents provocateurs," who hoped to send the British fleet to Corfu.[51]

By the time Salandra's cable arrived in Rome, Mussolini had already departed for Milan. Mario Arlotta, the Director-General of Political Affairs, immediately forwarded it, with some added observations, to the Duce's *chef de cabinet*, Baron Russo (Giacomo Paulucci de Calboli). Arlotta noted to Baron Russo that since it appeared from Salandra's cable that Hanotaux might use Quiñones de León to propose a compromise formula, it did not appear to him to be the opportune moment to risk straining relations with Spain. Therefore, he had on his own initiative cancelled the Duce's orders to the Italian Ambassador at Madrid requesting that a protest be lodged with the Spanish Government over the attitude assumed by Quiñones de León at Geneva. If Mussolini still desired to execute his original instructions to Madrid, Arlotta asked that urgent orders should

[50] Mussolini to Avezzana (Paris) and Salandra (Geneva), September 7, 1923. *Ibid.*, pp. 200-201.
[51] Salandra (Geneva) to Mussolini, September 7, 1923. *Ibid.*, pp. 201-202.

The League and the Conference

be communicated to the Italian Ambassador directly from Milan.[52]

BRITISH MILITARY WEAKNESS

While these exchanges were going on between Geneva, Rome, and Milan, other important events were taking place in London and Paris. At 5 o'clock on the afternoon of September 7, some hours before Mussolini departed for Milan, a secret cable was dispatched by the Minister of Marine, Thaon di Revel, to all authorities of the maritime periphery. Di Revel informed these authorities that the political situation with England was "very delicate" and could lead to "complications." It ended with the erroneous comment that Yugoslavia had started mobilization.[53]

The dispatch of this cable had been preceded by a report, the previous day, from the Italian naval attaché in Paris, Captain Giovan B. Gabetti, saying that the English and French press reported that if the League of Nations decided that Italy must evacuate Corfu, England would "willingly put its fleet at [the] disposition [of the] League," in order to execute the Geneva decision. In an operation of this type, Gabetti disclosed, it would be clearly understood "that the British fleet would act in [the] name [of the] League and not of Great Britain."[54]

However, Di Revel's and Gabetti's cables were at variance with a report filed from the Italian Embassy at London on the evening of September 6, which reached Rome in the early morning hours of September 7. From information that had come to Della Torretta's attention it appeared that the Foreign Office "should have transmitted to [Lord Robert] Cecil instructions to moderate his action and his language," at

---

[52] Arlotta to Baron Russo (Milan), September 8, 1923. *Ibid.*, pp. 205-206. For Mussolini's instructions to the Italian Ambassador at Madrid to protest Quiñones de León's actions at Geneva, see Mussolini to Paulucci de Calboli (Madrid), September 7, 1923. *Ibid.*, p. 202.

[53] Thaon di Revel to all authorities of the maritime periphery, September 7, 1923. *Ibid.*, p. 202.

[54] Gabetti (Paris) to Thaon di Revel, September 6, 1923. *Ibid.*, footnote p. 202.

The League and the Conference

Geneva.[55] Lord Curzon's retreat from his original strong position to support the League, assumed on September 2, had begun. It was a decision the antecedents of which could be traced back to consultations among different departments of the British Government, as well as to French rejections of certain British overtures.

On September 5, a report was forwarded by Curzon to the British Consul at Geneva, explaining the Treasury's opinion on the application of sanctions under Article 16 of the League Covenant.[56] According to Vice-Admiral Sir Roger Keyes, Deputy Chief of Naval Operations, "the Treasury were very alarmed at the idea of exercising economic pressure under Article 16 of the League." They felt that economic sanctions "could not be put into force without adopting war-time measures and could not be effective unless it was equally strongly enforced in all countries. Honest traders and countries would suffer, dishonest flourish."[57]

In a discussion by the Treasury, however, of sanctions against Italy, certain important trade patterns would have had to be pointed out. During the previous year, Britain, British India, Ceylon, and Australia had supplied Italy with 23 per cent of its imports, while Britain took 12 per cent of Italy's exports. At the same time the United States had supplied Italy with almost 28 per cent of its imports, which made the United States Italy's largest supplier of imported materials. In turn, about 11 per cent of Italy's overseas exports went to the United States. France on the other hand, supplied Italy with 7.3 per cent of its imports and took 14.7 per cent of its exports.[58]

[55] Della Torretta (London) to Mussolini, September 6, 1923. *Ibid.*, p. 194; Della Torretta (London) to Mussolini, September 11, 1923. *Ibid.*, p. 218.
[56] Lord Crewe (Paris) to Lord Curzon, October 15, 1923. Folder marked "Correspondence with Lord Crewe, Ambassador to Paris, 1922-1924," Box 22, Curzon Papers.
[57] Carbon copy of a letter from Vice-Admiral Sir Roger Keyes, to another admiral, September 7, 1923. Unfortunately, the name of the addressee is illegible. Keyes Papers.
[58] United States Tariff Commission, *Italian Commercial Policy and*

The League and the Conference

With the United States outside the League system, the institution of sanctions against Italy would of necessity have required French cooperation and assistance. This assistance and cooperation, however, as the French made quite clear, would not be forthcoming.

From the beginning Cecil had announced his intentions of invoking Article 16 of the Covenant, and Curzon "was as much inclined as his representative at Geneva to see the matter through to the end." Queried about the possibility of British naval intervention, "the English delegates [at Geneva] showed that they were giving the matter the most serious consideration."[59] However, instead of a unilateral British naval action, Cecil proposed to the French delegation at Geneva the possibility of a joint Anglo-French "naval demonstration" at Corfu in order to force Italian evacuation of the island. This proposal by Cecil was "received coldly" by the French.[60] It was a decision in keeping with their short-term policy of trying to settle the matter within the Conference and outside the League. It was also in keeping with their general policy of viewing the League as merely "another instrument to keep Germany in her place, and to deter or defeat *'une agression de l'Allemagne.'*" To Paris, sanctions proposed against any country other than

---

Foreign Trade 1922-1940, Report No. 142, Second Series (Washington: Government Printing Office, 1941), p. 78.

During 1923, the percentage of imports supplied by the United States to Italy jumped to almost 43 per cent, while Italian exports to the United States rose to 21 per cent. Imports from Britain were 20 per cent, a drop of 3 per cent, while Italian exports to Britain rose to 17 per cent, an increase of 5 per cent. In the case of France, Italian imports rose to 12 per cent, while Italy's exports to France were 23 per cent, nearly double. *The Statesman's Year Book, 1925* (London: Macmillan Co., 1925), p. 1046.

[59] Henry de Jouvenel, "France and Italy," *Foreign Affairs*, v, No. 4 (1927), p. 538.

[60] Salandra, p. 104. Salandra felt that Lord Robert Cecil may have acted without orders. The French reason for refusing Cecil's offer was that they did not want to see the English return to the Ionian Islands.

The League and the Conference

Germany were frowned upon.[61] As Henry de Jouvenel, Hanotaux's fellow delegate, admitted after the incident was closed, France had opposed the application of sanctions which some delegations had proposed. "Between the prestige of the League of Nations and the interests of peace," he wrote, there was "no hesitation possible: peace first."[62] Nevertheless, the French rejection of Cecil's overtures only weakened the British position, a situation Cecil had foreseen earlier.[63]

Cecil's request for French support is undoubtedly traceable to the fact that the British fleet was thought to be in no position to challenge the Italians, therefore incapable of participating at Corfu in a unilateral naval demonstration. As Vice-

[61] Arnold Wolfers, *Britain and France between Two Wars* (New York: Harcourt Brace and Co., 1940), pp. 155, 193.

[62] *Le Matin*, October 1, 1923, p. 1.

[63] Lord Robert Cecil (Geneva) to Lord Curzon, September 4, 1923. Folder marked "Letters to Curzon A-F, 1923," Box 65, Curzon Papers.

The letter cited is interesting for the light it throws on the behind-the-scenes pressures and attitudes of a number of delegations. As Lord Cecil saw the situation on September 4, there was "a great hardening of opinion in favour of the League, and consequently against the Italian action. The one weak spot is the French who are unfortunately not behaving quite straightly. Their Delegation are allowed to say very friendly things to me and profess a great desire to support the League, but I am afraid that M. Poincaré is using very different language in Paris. I was told on very good authority yesterday that he was encouraging the Italians to resist, and today I hear that he saw the American journalists and spoke to them in a very pro-Italian sense. It is really criminal, and exceedingly foolish from a French point of view, and it may cause the League great difficulties. It is becoming known that the difficulty in the way of firm League action, is France and all the small Powers are becoming very indignant. The Serbian whom I saw told me that he had said to Hanotaux that the French were pursuing a very foolish policy; that they were making the same mistake at Lausanne when they backed the Turks, and that they were seriously injuring their international position. Even the Poles and the Bulgarians are entirely against them on this point. Nevertheless, I do not conceal from myself that if it came to strong action the absence of French support would be a serious matter. . . . De Jouvenel I have seen two or three times. He professes I think honestly to be quite of my view about the Italo-Greek question, though they are anxious to find some way of saving the Italian face. That also I am quite ready to do provided we really secure what seems to me the essential thing, namely the evacuation of Corfu and the limitation of the indemnity to something reasonable."

The League and the Conference

Admiral Sir Roger Keyes, Deputy Chief of Naval Operations, admitted: "From a Naval point of view [the situation] was even more serious than the economic."[64]

Because of this, "ships were not rushed to the Adriatic nor did they 'stand by' at Malta for immediate action." This lack of naval initiative was due to the fact that the Mediterranean fleet was, "almost to a keel, still holding a watching brief in the Near East." The Turkish coast—Constantinople (Istanbul), Smyrna (İzmir), and Chanak—claimed almost every ship except two battleships and five destroyers. One of the two battleships, the *H.M.S. Benbow*, was docked and being fitted and was not due back until October, while the *H.M.S. Ajax* had been ordered to leave for recommission. Of the five destroyers, only four were available for immediate duty, since the *H.M.S. Sportive* was in dockyard. Assistance from the Atlantic fleet was also difficult since the concentration of its vessels in the eastern Mediterranean "had already been dispersed." The only ship of the line from the Atlantic fleet remaining in Mediterranean waters was the battleship *H.M.S. Royal Sovereign*, but she was due to leave for Sheerness. This Italian action at Corfu demonstrated "that the British Fleet normally in the Mediterranean was not of sufficient strength to deal with two simultaneous and separate crises."[65] Nevertheless, on the morn-

[64] Carbon copy of a letter from Vice-Admiral Sir Roger Keyes, to another admiral, September 7, 1923. Unfortunately, the name of the addressee is illegible. Keyes Papers.

[65] Kenneth Edwards, *The Grey Diplomatists* (London: Rich and Cowan, Ltd., 1938), pp. 86-87.

It appears that the Admiralty in London was not prepared when the crisis broke. When Captain Luigi Bianchi, the Italian naval attaché, appeared at the Admiralty on September 2, he found it deserted of almost all important officials. The First Lord of the Admiralty, Mr. Leopold S. Amery, was cruising in the Mediterranean; the First Sea Lord, Admiral David Beatty, was also absent, as was the Permanent Under-Secretary, Sir Oswyn Murray. The only responsible officer that Bianchi found was Vice-Admiral Sir Roger Keyes, Deputy Chief of Naval Operations, who had been naval attaché in Rome from 1907 to 1908. Bianchi, however, found it impossible to talk even to Keyes. Bianchi (London) to Thaon di Revel, October 4, 1923. *DDI*, pp. 276-277.

The lack of officials in the Admiralty did not upset King George V

The League and the Conference

ing of September 7, Lord Robert Cecil ventured to suggest to Lord Curzon that aircraft concentrations should be made at Malta. In particular, Lord Robert thought that the aircraft carrier *H.M.S. Ark Royal* should be retained at the island and that the Admiralty should "also be asked to consider concentrating the Fleet at Malta." Cecil "believed that if such steps could be taken they would become known through the Italian Secret Service and would produce an excellent effect in Rome." Vice-Admiral Keyes observed that though Cecil belonged to the "Air Party," the *H.M.S. Ark Royal* was in no position to help. That ship carried only seaplanes "which would be at the mercy of small [Italian] fighters." However, the whole suggestion, Sir Harold Nicolson hastened to assure the Vice-Admiral, had been "scotched" by Lord Curzon. Irritated, Keyes found Cecil's entire plan "intolerable." He felt that "there would be something in all these threats if we really meant to fight, but it can only end in our climbing down and trying to save face in the humiliating way we did at Lausanne" if Mussolini held out, which he was likely to do since he had all Italians solidly behind him.[66]

ITALIAN MILITARY WEAKNESSES

Though unaware of England's fear that she was navally weak and unprepared, the Italian General Staff in Rome under-

---

as much as the absence of his Prime Minister from 10 Downing Street during a time of crisis. As Lord Stamfordham, the King's private secretary, wrote to Lord Curzon on September 5, "His Majesty says, he is the last person to wish to curtail the holiday of any of his hard-worked Ministers. But he cannot help feeling that, though you yourself are quite capable of dealing with the Italian-Greek situation, serious though it may be, public opinion, which cannot be entirely disregarded, may be inclined to criticize Baldwin's being absent from the Seat of Government and in a Foreign Country [France], while Poincaré is in Paris, Mussolini in Rome and the Greek Premier in Athens—especially as Baldwin is the Prime Minister of, a comparatively newly formed Government." Lord Stamfordham to Lord Curzon, September 5, 1923. Folder marked "Letters to Curzon M-Y, 1923," Box 65, Curzon Papers.

[66] Carbon copy of a letter from Vice-Admiral Sir Roger Keyes, to another admiral, September 7, 1923. Unfortunately, the name of the addressee is illegible. Keyes Papers.

The League and the Conference

took studies of the whole situation. As the Minister of Marine, Thaon di Revel, pointed out to Mussolini in a memorandum on September 13, the General Staff during the preceding days had studied the problem of possible Italian involvement against a Yugoslav-Greek coalition supported by the British Empire. The Minister of Marine made it clear that though the General Staff had no anxieties over a Yugoslav-Greek coalition, it did feel that grave difficulties would be presented if these nations should form a coalition with Great Britain. Even this situation would not be desperate, a priori, if the General Commissariat of Air could assemble in Sicily a force of not less than 200 planes, provided the necessary fuel and other supplies from Germany and France were assured. To supplement the concentration of planes in Sicily, an invasion of Egypt could be initiated from Cyrenaica, assisted by an Italian-led insurrection in Egypt itself. Continuing his memorandum, Di Revel noted that though the British might develop bases in the Aegean, their main dependence would be on their established bases at Malta, Gibraltar, and Alexandria. The latter two bases of course would be immune from naval and air attack because of their distance from Italy and also because Italy lacked aircraft carriers and suitable submarines. This was not true, however, in the case of Malta, which was close to Sicily. If the Italian air force could make Malta inoperable as a naval base, Italy would be able to view "with greater tranquillity" a Yugoslav-Greek-British coalition. It was true, Di Revel observed, that it would be necessary to consider the British aircraft carrier force, two units of which were included in the Mediterranean fleet. These units in turn could be supplemented by five more units, now stationed in the North Sea, capable of launching 120 planes. This threat by aircraft carriers, he noted, could be neutralized by the navy through the use of quick attack ships and by seaplanes provided by the General Commissariat of Air.

The minister, therefore, reiterated the navy's previous request that the principal air base in Sicily be at Trapani. He also thought indispensable the creation of a large air force center in the southern part of Sicily. This center would serve not only

The League and the Conference

to defend the southern coast of Italy, but would also be aimed at the destruction of the British naval base at Malta. In order to offset any British naval bases that might be established in Greece, Di Revel recommended that Italian air power be increased in the Salentina peninsula. Before closing his report he turned Mussolini's attention to Sardinia. The General Staff, he noted, felt that on this island there was need for strong airplane groupings in the southwestern parts of the island. These groupings would be primarily defensive in character. Their main purpose would be to prevent seizure by the British Navy of the island's principal anchorages, which could then be transformed into naval bases in spite of any Italian naval attacks.[67]

This somewhat optimistic memorandum by Di Revel was followed, on the same day, by a second report dealing with defensive conditions along Italy's maritime periphery in the eventuality of future "political complications" with Britain. The report made sad reading. After an eighteen-point description of Italy's naval weakness and unpreparedness, the minister recommended that there would have to be an evacuation of the ports of Genoa, Livorno, Civitavecchia, Cagliari, Trapani, and perhaps Palermo. This evacuation, he observed, would necessitate that maritime commerce be redirected to the ports of southern Italy and eastern Sicily. Because of its "insufficient means" the Italian Navy would not be in a position to defend merchant ships while they were on the high seas.[68]

The British, however, made no naval demonstration which "might well have made matters worse by accenting any cleavage with Italy."[69] Whitehall heeded the advice of Ken-

[67] Memorandum of Minister of Marine Thaon di Revel to Mussolini, September 13, 1923. *DDI*, pp. 229-230.

[68] Thaon di Revel to Mussolini, September 13, 1923. *Ibid.*, pp. 230-231. Though Admiral Thaon di Revel's report sounds gloomy, active naval preparations were made at the time to defend Italy against British attack. Antonio Foschini, *La Verità sulle Cannonate di Corfù* (Roma: Giacomaniello, 1953), pp. 58-59.

[69] Edwards, p. 86. As early as August 31, the Italian Embassy in Paris was reporting British naval concentrations at Malta, aimed at limiting "Italian action towards Greece." The embassy frankly admitted it could not vouch for the accuracy of this information. Vannutelli (Paris) to Mussolini, August 31, 1923. *DDI*, p. 148.

The League and the Conference

nard, the chargé d'affaires at Rome, who warned "what the results of any drastic pressures here" might be.[70]

The French by rejecting Cecil's overtures for collective action had narrowed Curzon's field of choice. Like all British Foreign Secretaries he was fully aware that a war between England and Italy would work to the disadvantage of both; an Anglo-Italian conflict would sacrifice interests that both deemed vital. To the British it would mean an interruption in their communications across the Mediterranean, their "life-line" of Empire. Secondly, it would expose their Mediterranean possessions to Italian attacks. To the Italians it would mean denial of entry into and exit from the Mediterranean, and would make them, for the duration of the war, a prisoner of Great Britain.[71]

WHITEHALL RETREATS

In the Palazzo Chigi, Guariglia and his colleagues were well aware that England might ask for the application of sanctions under Article 16 of the Covenant. They felt, however, that Whitehall would be unwilling to go to war and lose the friendship of Italy.[72] In Rome, their own efforts were geared to keeping Italy at Geneva, and to discovering "a solution outside the League with tangible satisfaction for the crime perpetrated against [the] Tellini Mission."[73]

Unknown to them, Whitehall and Lord Curzon were willing to meet the Italians halfway. The British, finding them-

[70] Sir Howard W. Kennard (Rome) to Lord Curzon, September 7, 1923. Folder marked "Letters to Curzon G-L, 1923," Box 65, Curzon Papers.

[71] Wolfers, p. 312.

[72] Raffaele Guariglia in an interview with the writer in Rome, August 1961.

Within the Foreign Office there was talk of sending the fleet to Corfu. Sir Harold Nicolson has no recollection that any discussions on this point took place with the Admiralty. He does remember that at one point the situation had become so dangerous that Sir Ronald Lindsay asked him to sleep in the Foreign Office, which he did. Sir Harold Nicolson in an interview with the writer in London, July 1961.

[73] Raffaele Guariglia, *Ricordi 1922-1946* (Napoli: Scientifiche Italiane, 1950), p. 29.

The League and the Conference

selves too weak and unwilling to go it alone, especially after their collective approach had been stymied by the French, reverted to the traditionalist policy.

In a letter of September 6 to Lord Crewe, Sir William Tyrrell spelled out in clear terms the position that was to be maintained at the meeting of the Conference of Ambassadors scheduled for the following day. Sir William observed that Poincaré found himself "in an extremely difficult position as between the League and Italy." Therefore, he was concentrating all "his efforts upon finding a solution" that would "save the face of both." Because of this possible solution Poincaré would "spare no efforts to reach some settlement in the Ambassadors' Conference" before they had been able "to come to grips with the question in Geneva." To accomplish this, he would probably propose a formula for settlement "which by establishing the principles and methods" by which Greek reparations would be assured, would in turn enable Avezzana to give an assurance that Corfu would be evacuated.

At this point, Tyrrell felt, Poincaré would proclaim the incident closed. He would argue that any attempt to reopen the question of Italy's defiance of the League Covenant would be tantamount to "flogging a dead horse." Sir William, however, believed that British policy should "be one of avoiding on the one hand a complete deadlock at the Ambassadors' Conference and on the other a moral defeat for the League." Britain was perfectly willing, since it would ease tension, that the Conference deal with the murder of Tellini and his staff. It did not desire that Poincaré should so maneuver things as to be able to represent the whole dispute as having been settled and claim there was no further need for discussion. "The Covenant has been challenged," Tyrrell observed, "and it is a cardinal point in our policy that the Covenant should be upheld." He pointed out to Lord Crewe that it would "damage the prestige of the League" if the question were settled by the Conference before the League had the opportunity seriously to examine it "or manifest to Italy that such defiance will incur for her the reprobation of the world." He therefore instructed

The League and the Conference

Lord Crewe that during the meeting scheduled for the following day, if it became apparent that Poincaré and the French were attempting to rush a settlement, he was to "ask for an adjournment," in order to receive further instructions. In closing, Sir William reassured Lord Crewe that no criticism of the Conference, as one of the instruments for settling the Italo-Greek dispute, was intended. Essentially Whitehall wished to prevent Poincaré "in his passion for saving faces, from doing so at the expense of the League."[74]

In a covering note to Lord Curzon, Tyrrell enclosed a copy of his letter. He reiterated his main reason for writing it: his "fear lest Poincaré rush our Ambassador [Lord Crewe] into a solution entirely at the expense of the League." This situation he felt might in turn "create a position of intolerable difficulty for you after the stand we have taken on the subject of the competency of the League." Sir William believed that though the League's competency had to be safeguarded, in the business of settling the question it became "a matter of expediency rather than principle as to what methods are employed to obtain a peaceful solution."[75]

---

[74] Sir William Tyrrell to Lord Crewe (Paris), September 6, 1923. Folder marked "Letters to Curzon M-Y, 1923," Box 65, Curzon Papers.

Sir William's letter divided the legal aspects of the question along two lines. First, the Conference was competent *ratione personae* for the murder of General Tellini and his staff. As regards Italy's action at Corfu the Conference was in no way competent *ratione materiae*. See Charles Rousseau, *La Compétence de la Société des Nations* (Paris: Imprimerie Administrative Centrale, 1927), p. 291. Whether the Conference was even competent *ratione personae* is questioned.

According to Stéphan Ph. Nicoglou, *L'Affaire de Corfou et la Société des Nations* (Dijon: Librairie Generale Felix Rey, 1925), p. 82, the Conference did not have the quality of an injured party. Under international law only a subject of international law can "incur international responsibilities or obtain reparations for damages." In the case of the Conference of Ambassadors Nicoglou feels this was impossible for it was "un organe diplomatique temporaire, et rien de plus au point de vue juridique."

[75] Sir William Tyrrell to Lord Curzon, September 6, 1923. Folder marked "Letters to Curzon M-Y, 1923," Box 65, Curzon Papers.

On September 5, the American Embassy in London reported that it had been "reliably informed" that while the Conference would deal with the investigation of the Tellini murder, France would support

The League and the Conference

In an attempt to safeguard the delicate negotiations at Paris, the Foreign Office, on September 7, instructed Leopold S. Amery, the First Lord of the Admiralty, who was cruising in the Mediterranean, not to visit Athens. Whitehall felt "that any visit by a British Minister would be taken as a gesture of sympathy and evoke public demonstrations."[76]

London had established its policy, but it was in Paris, and with Poincaré, that the main burden of finding some sort of a compromise solution lay. All eyes now turned from the Palais des Nations in Geneva to the Quai d'Orsay where the Ambassadors' Conference always convened.

Great Britain in insisting that the Corfu question be submitted to the League. The French action according to the embassy was due to "representations made by the Little Entente, [and] Jugoslavia in particular which for strategic reasons dreads the retention of Corfu by Italy." Wheeler (London) to the Department of State, September 5, 1923. File 765.68/39, Record Group 59, NA.

[76] Leopold S. Amery, *My Political Life* (London: Hutchinson and Co. Ltd., 1953), II, p. 269.

CHAPTER VI

SETTLEMENT BY NEGOTIATION AND COMPROMISE

A COMPROMISE FORMULA DEVISED

THE two hundred and twenty-fifth meeting of the Conference of Ambassadors, the second dealing with the Italo-Greek dispute, met at 11:00 A.M. on September 7.[1] The Conference was to sit for almost eight hours. For consideration by the Conference was a telegram from the Secretary-General of the League of Nations, Sir Eric Drummond, dated September 6;[2] the *procès-verbal* of the Council meeting held the previous day, September 6;[3] and a letter from the Albanian Legation in Paris also dated September 6.[4]

As in the previous meeting, Laroche was the first to speak; he began by asking his colleagues the sense to be attached to the expression: "to follow . . . the study" which was used in the telegram sent by the Council to the Conference. The sentence read: "The Council manifests the intention to follow in agreement with the Conference, the study of the modalities of the inquiry."[5] Avezzana and Cambon were of the opinion that the Council would wish to be kept informed of the inquiry.

The Council's work of the previous day was next discussed.

[1] Unless cited otherwise the material that follows is drawn from the *procès-verbal* of the two hundred and twenty-fifth meeting of the Conference of Ambassadors, September 7, 1923. File 763.72119/12023, Record Group 59, NA.
[2] File 763.72119/12023, Annex A, Record Group 59, NA.
[3] File 763.72119/12023, Annex B, Record Group 59, NA.
[4] File 763.72119/12023, Annex C, Record Group 59, NA.
[5] The *procès-verbal* of the Conference is probably somewhat inexact. The note from the Council actually read: "The Council . . . declares its intention of investigating, in conjunction with the Conference, the manner in which the enquiry should be carried out."

Negotiation and Compromise

On Laroche's initiative the Council's *procès-verbal* was read to the Conference. Laroche correctly pointed out to his colleagues that the Council had examined a draft communication more broad than that which had been transmitted to the Conference. This draft had not been adopted because of the opposition of the Italian representative, Salandra, who contested the Council's competence. The Conference would be obligated during the current meeting to agree on the terms of a reply to be addressed to the Greek Government, and on the grounds under which the Conference would be "obligated to back up this reply." During this meeting, Laroche continued, the Conference must attempt to make the demands of the Conference coincide with those of the Italian Government. If the Ambassadors' Conference succeeded in this endeavor the Italo-Greek dispute could be considered settled. In Laroche's opinion the Conference "by reason of the strictly confidential character of its debates" was better suited than all other assemblies to arrive at an agreement. Cambon seconded Laroche by declaring that the French Government shared this view. It was the view of Avezzana and Laroche that the Conference would even be rendering a great service to the League of Nations if it brought about a settlement acceptable to all, so permitting the League not to declare itself on the question at issue. To Avezzana, the Conference was undoubtedly the organization whose intervention would be most capable of giving satisfaction to the League.

At this point Laroche began to read to his colleagues the *procès-verbal* of the Council meeting of the previous day. He explained to the Conference the incident raised by Hanotaux's declaration to the League Council concerning the accuracy of the telegram transmitting the Conference's decision of September 2. The incident was the result of a misunderstanding. It began after the last meeting of the Conference when, on reflection, he wondered if the Ambassadors' Conference had not adopted a position a little broad in defending as it did the thesis that according to international law "every State is responsible for crimes and political outrages committed on its territory." In this general form the formula was inexact. If it

Negotiation and Compromise

were applied strictly it could give rise to great difficulties. Could one for example, say that Switzerland was not within her rights when she declined all responsibility for the assassination of the Russian diplomat V. V. Vorovsky?[6] Laroche then disclosed that he had telephoned Hanotaux in order to acquaint him personally with the problem. He assured his colleagues, however, that he had not asked Hanotaux to rectify the terms of the communication sent in the name of the Ambassadors' Conference. Because of this episode he asked the Conference to examine the question carefully. He wished the Conference not to repeat a thoughtless reservation in the preamble of the reply to be addressed to Greece. Lord Crewe and Avezzana agreed entirely with Laroche on this point. Avezzana in particular added that it might be stated precisely in the reply that the Conference, in speaking of territorial responsibility, was to be understood to have in mind only the Tellini case. This proposal was approved unanimously.

The composition and the powers of the Commission of Inquiry to be sent to Epirus were next discussed. Having thoroughly examined the proposal made to entrust the Presidency of the Commission to an Italian, Cambon declared that in his opinion it would not be wise to do so. He did not doubt that the Italian delegate would execute his task with great impartiality, but he thought that public opinion would not be favorably impressed by such a choice. Since neither the British nor the French Government wished a national to assume the Presidency of the Commission, the possibility had to be considered of entrusting the presidency to a delegate of an Allied Power not directly interested in the conflict, for example, a Japanese or a Belgian. He thought that the choice of a Belgian would present numerous advantages. The Conference could

[6] On May 10, 1923, the Russian diplomat V. V. Vorovsky was murdered in Lausanne. The murderers were subsequently acquitted "after an unjustly conducted trial." Vorovsky's murder broke the connection between the League and the Soviet Union at this time. Moscow refused to take part in any League meetings on Swiss territory. F. P. Walters, *A History of the League of Nations* (London: Oxford University Press, 1960), p. 232.

Negotiation and Compromise

not ignore the sensitivities that the Italo-Greek incident had stirred up at Geneva among the delegates of the small Powers. Belgium, though not officially represented on the Conference, was very often brought in to take part in its discussions.[7] She was an Allied Power. Most important, she was not directly interested in the conflict and could be considered as the most distinguished of the small Powers.

His statement made it obvious that the French had shifted their position since the previous meeting of the Conference at which Laroche had suggested an Italian as President of the Commission of Inquiry. Undoubtedly wishing to avoid the unenviable position of president, the Japanese delegate Sato asked that the Conference ascertain the opinion of the Belgian Government before turning to his own.

In line with Mussolini's instructions that the President of the Commission of Inquiry must be an Italian, Avezzana opened his attack. He agreed with Cambon that the Conference could not deny the necessity of taking into account the sensitivities of the small Powers as well as the sensitivities of the League of Nations. He asked, however, that the Conference think equally of the just sensitivities of Italy. If the Conference entrusted to an Italian the Presidency of the Commission, Italian public opinion would surely receive this designation with satisfaction, and the task of the Italian Government would be greatly facilitated. He wished to refrain from closing the door to an agreement, but he asked his colleagues to take into account the following consideration. When the Conference has constituted its Commission of Inquiry, will not the League of Nations also claim the right to send an observer to Epirus? In this case the Commission would be composed of a Belgian President, an observer from the League of Nations, and finally the Italian delegate. Italy, the principal interested power, would be in a minority on the Commission.

This opinion was not shared by Cambon. The question that was before the Conference was of particular interest not only to Italy, but also to the "general peace." He believed that it

[7] *Supra*, Chapter I.

Negotiation and Compromise

would weaken the authority of the Commission of Inquiry, as well as the authority of the Conference of Ambassadors, to entrust the Presidency of the Commission to an Italian representative: the Conference would no longer have the approval of universal public opinion.

As was to be expected Lord Crewe added his voice to that of Cambon. He had full confidence in the impartiality of the delegate Italy would entrust to represent it on the Commission of Inquiry. However, he asked the Conference to be good enough to take into account the impression its decision would produce upon "world public opinion." Faced by an Anglo-French desire to have the Presidency of the Commission in the hands of a delegate other than an Italian, Avezzana succumbed. In a "spirit of conciliation," he agreed that he would not insist on an Italian President but would accept a Japanese.

Regretfully the Japanese delegate, Sato, was unable to designate a representative to the Commission of Inquiry. First, he knew of no person competent enough for the position. Second, it was necessary that he solicit the express authorization of his government. Given the difficulties of communication with Japan, he thought it would be difficult to obtain an immediate reply.[8] At any rate, Sato felt he could not accept responsibilities for his government without first consulting his ambassador.

Desiring to close this question, Cambon urged Sato to communicate with Viscount Ishii[9] as quickly as possible, as only the appointment of a Japanese President had unanimous approval, and this was one of the essential points of the scheme considered by the Conference.

Regarding the Commission of Inquiry, Laroche asked his colleagues if special powers should not be given to it so that it could pursue its inquiry in Albanian territory, if this were deemed necessary. On this point Avezzana asked that the Con-

---

[8] In September of 1923, the home islands of Japan were laid waste by severe earthquakes that caused heavy property damage and took the lives of thousands. These earthquakes had also disrupted cable communications with the outside world.

[9] Viscount Kikujiro Ishii was not only the President of the Council of the League of Nations, but also Japan's Ambassador at Paris.

Negotiation and Compromise

ference use a certain amount of discretion with regard to the Albanian Government. The chargé d'affaires of Albania, he disclosed, had manifested the desire that the Conference make a preliminary overture to the Albanian Legation. He had even expressed the wish to make the first approach if this were possible. A preliminary overture made to the Albanian Government, Laroche agreed, would be better. The President of the Conference would do this by addressing a letter to the Albanian Legation in Paris. In the communication that would be addressed to the Greek Government, the Conference would make it known that it reserved the right, should the occasion arise, to address itself to the Albanian Government in order to facilitate the investigation of the Commission in Albanian territory.

By now it was 1:00 P.M. and the Conference suspended its sitting until 4:00 P.M. The first three hours of discussion had been fairly friendly, the next five hours would prove arduous for all concerned.

At the opening of the afternoon session Mr. Sato, the Japanese delegate, informed his colleagues that he was authorized by Viscount Ishii to designate the Japanese military attaché in Paris, Colonel Shibouya, as Japan's delegate and President of the Commission of Inquiry. With an undoubted sigh of relief, Cambon thanked Sato for the quickness with which he had acted and for the satisfying news that he had given them.

The Conference then began an examination of the conditions that were to be imposed on Greece. Discussed was the matter of naval honors, funeral services for the dead officers at Athens, and the honors to be paid them upon their embarkation at Preveza.

Attention was then turned to the proposed Commission of Inquiry by Laroche, who pointed out the concern that should be felt about the number of commissions of inquiry: a Greek Commission was functioning at the moment. The Conference envisaged sending an Allied Commission. The League of Nations considered the institution of a third Commission. He thought that he could not discuss the Conference's Commis-

Negotiation and Compromise

sion, except to fix the date by which its inquiry should be terminated. Avezzana proposed the date September 27, exactly one month from the day of the assassination of Tellini and the members of his mission.

The object of the Commission of Inquiry, warned Henri Fromageot, Laroche's assistant, was the determination of the degree of culpability of the Greek Government. The amount of the indemnity to be paid by Greece would be fixed after an examination of the Commission's report. It was to be well understood that only the report of the Commission should be binding.

Lord Crewe felt that the amount of indemnity to be deposited by the Greek Government should constitute the maximum amount. Avezzana said he feared that if the amount of the indemnity were fixed at a maximum of 50 million Italian lire, the Greek authorities might no longer have an interest in pursuing the culprits and punishing them.

Punishing the culprits in an exemplary manner, Laroche replied, would have to be pledged by the Greek Government. If it did not pledge to do it the Conference would have to intervene; the Italian Government had nothing to fear on this point. Since the Conference anticipated that the amount of the indemnity would be fixed by the Permanent Court of International Justice it would be preferable not to speak of a maximum, and to leave, in this matter, all liberty to the Court. The deposit by Greece of 50 million Italian lire, Cambon made clear to his colleagues, would be considered merely a surety.

The conversation was then turned by Lord Crewe to another point, perhaps the most important. He asked whether Italy would await the results of the Ambassadorial Commission of Inquiry before evacuating Corfu. To calm Lord Crewe's fears Laroche proposed that the following preamble be included in the note to be sent to Greece: "The Conference taking note of the fact that Italy promises to evacuate Corfu as soon as the demands of the Conference of Ambassadors shall have been satisfied, invites the Greek Government, etc. . . ."

For the moment discussion on this point was allowed to

Negotiation and Compromise

lapse. The meeting, which had been in session exactly one hour, was suspended at 5:00 P.M. in order to permit Laroche and his assistants to draw up the contemplated reply to the League of Nations and the Ambassadorial note to Greece.

When the session resumed, Laroche read to the Conference the reply that would be sent to the League Council[10] communicating to it the text concerning the reparations that the Conference would ask the Greek Government to execute. This reply to the Council containing the seven following demands was immediately approved by the Conference. (1) Apologies would be presented by the highest Greek military authority to the diplomatic representatives at Athens of the three Allied Powers whose delegates had been members of the Conference's Delimitation Commission. (2) A funeral service in honor of the victims would be celebrated in the Roman Catholic Cathedral at Athens in the presence of all members of the Greek Government. (3) Vessels belonging to the fleets of the three Allied Powers, the Italian naval division leading, would arrive in the roadstead of Phalerum after 8:00 A.M. on the day of the funeral service, and after the vessels of the three Powers had anchored in the roadstead the Greek fleet would honor the Italian, British, and French flags with a salute of 21 guns for each flag; the salute would be returned gun for gun by the Allied vessels immediately after the funeral service; during the service the flags of the Greek fleet and of the vessels of the three Allied Powers would be flown at half-mast. (4) Military honors would be rendered by a Greek unit carrying its colors, when the bodies of the victims were embarked at Preveza. (5) The Greek Government would give an undertaking to ensure the discovery and exemplary punishment of the guilty parties at the earliest possible moment. (6) A special Commission consisting of delegates of France, Great Britain, Italy, and Japan, and presided over by the Japanese delegate, would supervise the preliminary investigation and inquiry undertaken by the Greek Government; this work was to be completed by September 27, 1923.

[10] *The Times* (London), September 8, 1923, p. 12.

Negotiation and Compromise

The Commission appointed by the Conference would have full powers to take part in the execution of these measures and to require the Greek authorities to take all requisite steps for the preliminary investigation, examination of the accused, and inquiry. The Commission of Inquiry would submit its report and conclusions to the Conference of Ambassadors, while the Greek Government would afford the Commission all facilities in carrying out its work and would defray all expenditure thereby incurred.

The Conference would also invite the Albanian Government to take all measures necessary to ensure that the Commission, duly accredited for this purpose, would be able, should it consider such action necessary, to proceed to Albanian territory, and in agreement with Albanian authorities, to conduct there any investigations likely to assist in the discovery and punishment of the guilty persons.

Lastly, (7) the Greek Government would undertake to pay to the Italian Government, in respect for the murder of its delegates, an indemnity of which the total amount would be determined by the Permanent Court of International Justice at The Hague, acting by summary procedure. The Court would give judgment on consideration of the report of the Commission of Inquiry as specified in point 6. This report would be transmitted by the Conference, with its comments, to the Court of Justice.

The Greek Government would deposit without delay, as security, at the Swiss National Bank, a sum of 50 million Italian lire, this deposit to be accompanied by the following instructions: "to be paid, in whole or in part, to the Italian Government, upon the decision of the Permanent Court of International Justice at The Hague." During the final days of the crisis, this last stipulation created unexpected problems which caused some anxious moments for all concerned.

The Conference then approved the preamble to the note to the Greek Government containing the seven demands enumerated above. The preamble declared that Greece had undertaken "to accept, if her responsibility" were proven, "all

Negotiation and Compromise

reparations which the Conference may deem just." It noted that the murder of Tellini and his staff, "was of a clearly political character ... committed on Greek territory." In an attempt to repair the damage that the Conference had wrought several days before, the preamble added that the Delimitation Commission had been entrusted with an official mission by the Conference "in agreement with the Greek Government, which [had] had to ensure its security." Considering, however, that the murder of Tellini and his staff directly entailed the responsibility of the State on whose territory the crime had taken place, the Conference had decided to ask for the seven sanctions and reparations, which were then stipulated.

With the preamble out of the way, Laroche proposed to his colleagues to come to an agreement on the concluding portion of the note to Greece. He suggested that the note invite the Greek Government to make known without delay, simultaneously and separately to each of the diplomatic representatives of the three Powers in Athens, its acceptance of the conditions enumerated in the note. The note was to add that the Italian Government had renewed its assurances that the occupation of Corfu and the adjacent islands had no other object than to obtain satisfaction for the demands which it had presented to the Greek Government. The acceptance by Greece of the Conference's demands would be considered by Italy as giving satisfaction to its own demands.

Before he could accept this proposed formula, Avezzana desired to consult with Rome. In the discussion that followed, Lord Crewe declared that if the Conference could not include this passage in the text of the note to be addressed to the Greek Government, it would have to put off sending the note. Modification of the proposed text would no longer require on Italy's part any kind of formal agreement. Desiring no delay, Laroche sharply insisted to his colleagues that the discussion must be finished that same night. If the Conference could not adjust the dispute which had been submitted to it that same day, the situation would become "very grave."

He had no doubts that his government would evacuate

Negotiation and Compromise

Corfu, Avezzana retorted, as soon as it had obtained satisfaction. On the other hand, he was authorized to declare that the reparations demanded by the Conference from Greece would "cover" [couvrent] the demands for reparations made by Italy to Greece. He did not believe that his government would refuse to accept the formula proposed by the Conference. Yet, he felt that the question was so important that he desired to leave this point to the decision of his government. Avezzana was reminded by Laroche how much the Conference had endeavored to make its reparations coincide with those of the Italian Government. The Conference had manifested the greatest desire for conciliation.

To placate all concerned, Cambon proposed that the following formula be adopted: "The Italian Government confirms that the occupation of Corfu and the adjacent islands has no other object than to obtain the just satisfaction to which it has a right. Accordingly the Conference taking note of this declaration, invites the Greek Government to make known its acceptance."

Laroche subsequently revealed his own feelings about the problem and his approach to a solution. He felt that if the demands of the Conference could coincide with those of Italy, be accepted by Greece, and be joined with Mussolini's assurances that the Corfu occupation was only the taking of a pledge, the evacuation of Corfu would be accomplished and the whole incident closed. Lord Crewe was willing to accept this approach, "but expressed the fear that Italy nevertheless would persist in occupying Corfu."

To assuage Crewe's fears, Laroche's proposed solution was "to connect by a 'preamble' the end of this occupation [Corfu] to the acceptance by Greece of the demands of the Conference." The contradictory demands of Crewe and Avezzana made agreement on any proposed "preamble" difficult. Lord Crewe, as the minutes show, wished to secure from Avezzana a clear admission that the demands of the Conference would be considered by Italy as giving satisfaction to its own demands. Avezzana, on the other hand, desired to consult Rome. He

Negotiation and Compromise

tried to assure the Conference that Italy would evacuate Corfu as soon as satisfaction was obtained from Greece. The only commitment he was willing to make was his oral declaration that the Conference's demands to Greece would "cover" [couvrent] the Italian demands to Greece for sanctions and reparations.

Jules Cambon was in despair. At this point Laroche requested a break in the discussions. He suggested to Cambon that tea be served to the ambassadors, while he "would try to clarify with their assistants a formula acceptable to all." These proceedings do not appear in the minutes of the meeting. As Laroche admitted, he felt "that an agreement would be easier outside the meeting, by an exchange of proposals that would not appear in the *procès-verbal*." As the ambassadors and Jules Cambon sipped tea in the garden of the Quai d'Orsay, Laroche, aided by his French assistants, Henri Fromageot and René Massigli, hammered out a compromise "preamble" to be included in the concluding paragraph of the Conference's note to Greece.

When the tea break was over the Conference reassembled to hear Laroche's new compromise formula read. Lord Crewe hesitated to accept it. Avezzana repeated his desire to consult Rome. Jules Cambon recalled to his colleagues the urgent need of making a decision that same night.[11]

Finally Laroche's proposal to add a paragraph stating that the demands of the Italian Government had been *covered* by the demands of the Conference was accepted. His new compromise formula cleverly integrated Avezzana's verbal declaration to the Conference that the latter's demands would "cover" [couvrent] the demands made by his government to Greece. The concluding paragraph agreed upon by the Conference read as follows: "The Conference taking note of the fact that the Italian Government confirms that the occupation of Corfu and the adjacent islands has no other purpose than that of

[11] Jules Laroche, *Au Quai d'Orsay avec Briand et Poincaré, 1913-1926* (Paris: Librairie Hachette, 1957), pp. 175-176.

Negotiation and Compromise

obtaining fulfillment of the demands which it has submitted to the Greek Government, and that these demands are found *covered* by the aforesaid conditions formulated by the Conference, invites the Greek Government to make known without delay, simultaneously and separately, to each of the diplomatic representatives of the three aforesaid Powers at Athens, its entire acceptance of the conditions that precede."[12]

With this immense hurdle out of the way, Lord Crewe asked who would pay the costs of the the Corfu occupation. In no position to answer this question, Avezzana asked his colleagues what precedents existed. In its occupation of the island of Mytilene, Henri Fromageot recalled, France had paid the occupation costs. The settlement of the dispute would be greatly facilitated, Cambon observed to Avezzana, if the Italian Government assumed the occupation costs. He therefore asked him to be so good as to draw this point to the attention of his government. Adding his voice to that of Cambon, Laroche declared that it was of the greatest importance that the Allied Governments be able to obtain the assurance that the question which was in sight of settlement not be reopened on the subject of the occupation costs. He asked Avezzana to consider the very great sacrifices which had been consented to by the British and French delegations. Public opinion, as well as all the governments involved, would conclude from the terms of the note addressed to Greece, that Corfu would be evacuated as soon as Greece had replied that it would give satisfaction to the demands requested. If this hope were to be disappointed, the situation would become extremely grave and the Conference of Ambassadors, instead of improving it, would only have made it worse.

Feeling that Rome would declare itself satisfied, Avezzana promised to telegraph in this sense to his government. He then expressed appreciation to all concerned for the spirit of conciliation shown during the course of the discussions. He was

[12] The concluding paragraph of the note actually sent to Greece varies in certain small details with the above cited text, but is in substance almost identical. *DDDIG*, pp. 36-39.

Negotiation and Compromise

certain that the Italian Government would be profoundly touched by this attitude.

These same sentiments were echoed by Cambon, who expressed his appreciation to Lord Crewe, especially, for the spirit of conciliation he had displayed throughout the course of the debates and to Mr. Sato, who by his alacrity had helped the Conference in a difficult situation; lastly he expressed "all the gratitude of the Conference for their very active collaboration" to his French colleagues, M. Laroche and M. Fromageot. The last comment was obviously made in appreciation of their delicate work in arranging a compromise formula during the tea break suggested by Laroche.

The day's work was over; the "Italian ultimatum had been gently but efficiently side-tracked," by the Conference of Ambassadors.[13]

MUSSOLINI'S QUALIFIED ACCEPTANCE OF THE CONFERENCE'S NOTE

Whitehouse, the American observer, considered that the success of the meeting "was largely due to the ability and the conciliatory spirit" shown by the delegates, though he was forced to admit that there "were many moments when it seemed" that the Conference would "inevitably fail in its efforts to save the situation." Lord Crewe, he reported to Washington, had been unsuccessful in securing a "categorical Italian assurance of [an] immediate evacuation" of Corfu upon Greece's acceptance of the Conference's note. Since it had been imperative to reach some sort of a decision on this point that same day, Crewe, strongly supported by the French, contented himself with placing Italy "under a very strong obligation" to evacuate Corfu. This obligation, according to Whitehouse, was "evidenced partly by [the] unusually solemn statements spread on [the] record—which . . . will be most difficult for [the] Italian Government to evade."[14]

---

[13] Walters, p. 250.
[14] Whitehouse (Paris) to the Department of State, September 7, 1923. File 765.68/48, Record Group 59, NA.

Negotiation and Compromise

As for Lord Crewe, he found the whole business "very awkward." "I have done my best," he wrote to Lord Curzon, "to carry out your instructions and to play up to Geneva as far as possible." At the same time the Greeks had not made the situation easier by placing themselves unreservedly, as far as the payment of an indemnity was concerned, in the hands of both the League and the Conference. He thought that under these circumstances it was something of a victory that the French had agreed that the final fixation of the indemnity should be in the hands of The Hague Court, after the figure had been examined by the Ambassadors' Conference. He only hoped that Geneva would regard this procedure "as reasonable."

Crewe also felt he had to tackle the question of Italy's claim, "so monstrously made by Mussolini," for reimbursement of the Corfu occupation costs. Though the Conference had not been "officially seized by this claim" the French agreed that it was a dangerous one, lest it be used as an excuse by Rome for remaining at Corfu even after the 50 million Italian lire had been deposited to cover the possible indemnity. During discussions on this point, Avezzana had made it clear that he was not in a position to drop the claim offhand. Therefore, Rome was being told that the Conference expected this "unprecedented claim" would not be pursued. Crewe observed to Curzon that Avezzana had been on the whole "not unreasonable," but in conversation with him *a deux* he assumed much the same line that Della Torretta in London had taken —of complaining that England was no longer friendly to Italy and was taking the side of Greece in the dispute. This charge Crewe had "indignantly repudiated." He also disclosed to Lord Curzon an interesting comment dropped by Avezzana on the nature of the new government at Rome. Avezzana, in speaking of his government, had used a rather curious phrase describing it as "in reality a military Government," meaning, Lord Crewe supposed, "a Government of the Napoleonic type." Though he had not replied to Avezzana, he thought it was

Negotiation and Compromise

"almost as much a revolutionary Government as that of Athens."

Turning his attention to the League, Lord Crewe hoped that it would be able to accept the Conference's "answer to Greece as relieving them from the necessity of further action," provided Athens accepted the terms submitted and that the evacuation of Corfu was announced. As to the latter problem, Avezzana had expressed the hope that Italy would not be expected to leave Corfu as though it were being turned out. To which Lord Crewe had replied that such an impression depended entirely on the way Italy took the solution offered by the Conference. Rome had only to say it was perfectly satisfied with the proposed Commission of Inquiry and with the arrangements for the indemnity; having obtained all they desired, they could "depart with flying colours." Lord Crewe felt that the whole question of censuring Italy for its "indefensible action" was still open to the League. However, if the League were to take action before the evacuation of Corfu, he would "expect Mussolini to proceed according to . . . [the] frank estimate of his character" made by Kennard, the chargé d'affaires at Rome, "with consequences which nobody can calculate."[15]

The same day that he wrote this letter to Curzon, Lord Crewe visited the Quai d'Orsay. It appeared that Laroche's behavior of the previous day was still on Crewe's mind. He complained to Jules Cambon of the "excessive role" that he felt Laroche had played in the discussions. Cambon retorted that since his own actions were limited by the fact that he was president of the Conference, it was only natural that Laroche should be the "spokesman for the Quai d'Orsay."[16]

In Rome, thinking that the Council would make a decision the following day [September 8], and acting without instructions, the British chargé d'affaires, Sir Howard W. Kennard, called on the Duce in order to "see how far he would go to

[15] Lord Crewe (Paris) to Lord Curzon, September 8, 1923. Folder marked "Correspondence with Lord Crewe, Ambassador to Paris, 1922-1924," Box 22, Curzon Papers.
[16] Laroche, pp. 176-177.

203

Negotiation and Compromise

wiggle out of the attitude he had taken up." He emphasized to Mussolini that the compromise he suggested was to be treated "as a purely private one," which would probably not even receive any consideration by his government.[17] His overtures, however, met with no success; he admitted after the interview to his Greek colleague, Constantinos Psaroudas, that he considered the question "very serious." Mussolini, Kennard disclosed, "insisted on his point of view and given the character of the man and his internal situation," which would be weakened, it was possible that new and even more daring decisions might be made in Rome. Kennard thought it was indispensable to find some sort of compromise solution which would save Mussolini's prestige, without proving a burden to Greece. The Duce, he admitted to Psaroudas, had no objection to interference by the Conference of Ambassadors, provided it did not deal with the question of the Corfu occupation. Even when his attention had been turned to the solidarity of feeling expressed in the Council against the Italian thesis, Mussolini had "insisted on his resolve." Kennard observed to Psaroudas that Mussolini's decision on the whole question was personal, since Contarini, the Secretary-General of the Palazzo Chigi, was still absent. In closing the interview he repeated to Psaroudas that the question was not between Italy and Greece, but between Italy and the League of Nations.[18] Summing up his interview to Lord Curzon, Kennard had almost the impression that Mussolini was "anxious to bring the whole world about his ears and go up, as he thinks, in a blaze of glory."[19]

[17] Sir Howard W. Kennard (Rome) to Lord Curzon, September 7, 1923. Folder marked "Letters to Curzon, G-L, 1923," Box 65, Curzon Papers. So well did Mussolini understand that Kennard was acting on his own, that his suggestion was not even cabled to Della Torretta in London.

[18] Psaroudas (Rome), No. 1551 to the Foreign Ministry, September 7, 1923. Greek Archives.

[19] Sir Howard W. Kennard (Rome) to Lord Curzon, September 7, 1923. Folder marked "Letters to Curzon, G-L, 1923," Box 65, Curzon Papers. In the above letter to Lord Curzon, Kennard describes in a most striking manner the problem of trying to negotiate with the Duce. "Mussolini has," he wrote, "as a matter of fact, been quite friendly and calm in our conversations, and has not even shown any

Negotiation and Compromise

Like their American and British colleagues, the Greek diplomats were also busy during this period. In Geneva, Politis was cabling Athens that the Conference's note should be accepted "without delay." He also recommended that the Greek Government in its reply make the following points: (1) that with its acceptance of the Conference's note the affair be terminated; (2) that it express the confident hope that Italy would put an end to the occupation of Corfu. His final observation was that the British and French representatives at Athens should be thanked for the part their governments had played in arranging a "rapid settlement of the conflict." This gesture he felt should also be repeated at London and Paris by the Greek Legations.[20]

To make sure that no hasty decision was taken which might lead to a rejection of the Conference's note, Politis sent Athens another cable dealing with the proposed Commission of Inquiry. Like Athos Romanos, his counterpart in Paris, he wished to dissuade the government from rejecting the proposed Commission of Inquiry if it did not include neutral representatives, as originally requested by Greece. Politis agreed with Romanos that any further discussion of the question would be dangerous for Greece and would have as a logical consequence the loss of whatever support they now possessed in the League and the Ambassadors' Conference.[21]

---

resentment at remarks which might be calculated to cause an outburst such as that Italy would not dare to treat a powerful nation in the manner she has Greece. His arguments frequently show childish ignorance and while he has the Covenant of the League at his elbow, he invariably shows that he has in no way grasped, or does not wish to grasp its contents. He occasionally enlivens our discussions by amusing sidelights. When I asked him how he could defy the League on which over fifty nations were represented he turned up the list and religiously counted them. He then remarked with a smile that the number was even greater, and his face lit up as if he were enchanted with the idea that the son of a blacksmith should challenge the whole world."

[20] Politis (Geneva), No. 1182 to the Foreign Ministry, September 8, 1923. French text. Greek Archives.
[21] Politis (Geneva), No. 1189 to the Foreign Ministry, September 8, 1923. Greek Archives.

Negotiation and Compromise

Though the Greek Legation in London viewed the Conference's decision on the evacuation of Corfu as "indefinite and irresolute,"[22] Romanos in Paris recommended its acceptance. The "evacuation of Corfu being implied [in the note]," he cabled Athens, "the slightest hesitation on our part even on [a] point of detail serves [as a] pretext for Italy, to escape from this obligation."[23] Advice along this same line was also communicated to the Greek Government from one of its most vociferous and sincere foreign supporters. From Geneva, Politis reported that Lord Robert Cecil had recommended to him that Greece accept "quickly and without any reservations" the Conference's note. If this were not done, Cecil felt that the evacuation of Corfu would then be accomplished only with the "greatest difficulties."[24]

Athens, heeding the advice of Politis, Romanos, and Cecil, accepted the Conference's note without the slightest reservation. The Greeks in their reply, however, felt the necessity of pointing out that the Conference of Ambassadors in its first note had merely confined itself to requesting that an inquiry be instituted into the murder of General Tellini and his staff, with a view to determining the responsibility for the crime. On the basis of the results of this inquiry the Conference would submit any eventual demands for reparations and sanctions. With its second note, the Greeks observed, the Conference was modifying the basis of its intervention and was accepting "independently of any inquiry, the civil responsibility of the State on whose territory the crime was committed." By so doing it was formulating demands for sanctions and reparations. The Greek reply noted that Italy confirmed the Corfu occupation as having no other object than the obtainment of satisfaction for the demands which it had presented to the Greek Government, and that these demands were covered by

[22] London, No. 3147 to the Foreign Ministry, September 8, 1923. Greek Archives.

[23] Romanos (Paris), No. 4664 to the Foreign Ministry, September 8, 1923. French text. Greek Archives.

[24] Politis (Geneva), No. 1203 to the Foreign Ministry, September 8, 1923. Greek Archives.

Negotiation and Compromise

the conditions stipulated in the Conference's note. Since these conditions were being accepted in their entirety, Greece wanted to reiterate its previous requests to the Conference, that the evacuation of Corfu take place at the earliest possible moment.[25]

In their reports to Rome, Avezzana and Salandra recommended acceptance of the Conference's note, as their Greek counterparts had done in their cables to Athens. Avezzana felt that the Conference's note had "almost word for word underwritten" the Italian demands to Greece and was in accord with the plan he had submitted to Mussolini on September 4.[26] He disclosed to the Duce that because of the dangerous situation that was developing at Geneva, he had agreed to the last paragraph of the Conference's note to Greece. He assumed responsibility for the decision which the Conference "had urgently taken" with the wish to forestall any hostile action by the League Council. His act of acceptance, he added, would not compromise any future actions which Mussolini might desire to take. Avezzana warned, however, that French circles expected Italy to accept the Conference's decision with a declaration that would not only satisfy British and French public opinion but also the small States at Geneva, who had stirred up a violent attitude relative to the Corfu evacuation.

The Quai d'Orsay also feared that, under the influence of Lord Robert Cecil, Geneva might again raise the whole Italo-Greek question. The French feared this move, since they might not be in a position to support Italy as in the past, burdened as they were with the Ruhr controversy and their strained relations with England and Germany. Avezzana believed that it was his duty to bring these dangers to the Duce's attention so that in case they appeared "worthy of consideration," he could direct the Italian press and public opinion to look upon the Conference's note as satisfactory to Italy. Naturally, he cautioned, everything depended upon Athens' acceptance of the Conference's note and on the Council's deci-

[25] *DDDIG*, pp. 38-39.   [26] *Supra*, Chapter V.

Negotiation and Compromise

sion to desist from any further intervention in the dispute.[27]

As to the latter problem, reports from Geneva appeared quite encouraging for Italy. According to Salandra, the impressions in Geneva of the Conference's note were "excellent," in the sense that it was thought of as the "beginning [of the] solution [of the] incident." That was not to say that there were not "fanatics" who took every opportunity to assert the League's competence. However, he revealed, more temperate elements, who could have voted against the Italian thesis of non-competence, recognized that, with the question of substance solved, it would be absurd to allow the question of the League's competence to remain standing. At any rate, Salandra observed, in any future debate Italy could validly hold that the Council in its desire to affirm its competence was only exciting international discords already solved. Everything, he warned, depended on the behavior of the Italian Government towards the Conference's decision. If Rome accepted it, the question would be considered closed and the solution looked upon as an Italian victory. On the other hand, if the Italian Government did not demonstrate its complete satisfaction and left the question open, Italy's "opponents would profit from it by insisting [on the] affirmation [of the] competence [of the] League of Nations."

From Salandra's own impressions and from "authoritative information" that had come to his notice, Italian failure to accept the Conference's note "would cause disappointments [in] French circles." His own personal opinion was that this would be a "favorable moment to close [the] dispute" and by so doing to achieve success over Greece, whose responsibility had been solemnly recognized, and over the League, which would be blocked from further interference. Salandra felt that there were no important differences in form between the reparations ordered by the Conference and those demanded by Italy from Greece. Any failure by Rome, he warned, to accept

[27] Avezzana (Paris) to Mussolini, September 8, 1923. *DDI*, pp. 207-209.

Negotiation and Compromise

the Conference's note would inevitably lead to Italy's withdrawal from the League and to its diplomatic isolation. Italy's recent experience at Geneva necessitated a serious re-examination of its position in the League, but it would be preferable that any decision made not be violent thus antagonizing universal public opinion. Salandra also described as "vain" the hopes manifested in the press that there was support for the Italian thesis. In the atmosphere of Geneva no one would "dare support us," he warned. Even France would not go "beyond certain limits." Besides, as Mussolini well knew, excessive protection by others was not "without danger." In expectation of further orders Salandra promised to maintain the greatest reserve, but requested immediate guidance so he could be prepared for the Council meeting scheduled for Monday, September 10.[28]

Avezzana's statement that the Conference's note had underwritten Italy's demands to Greece was no more correct than Salandra's statement that there were no important differences between the Conference's demands and those of Italy. The Conference in its meeting of September 7 had rejected the more unpalatable of Mussolini's original seven demands. Its note to Greece contained five revisions. Greece was to make excuses not to Italy but to the three diplomatic representatives of the Allied Powers at Athens. A salute was to be made not to Italian ships but to an Allied squadron, and was to be returned gun for gun. An inquiry was to be conducted not with the assistance of the Italian military attaché at Athens, but by a Commission of Inquiry composed of Italian, French, and English representatives and a Japanese President. Instead of an unconditional indemnity of 50 million Italian lire, the amount of indemnity would be fixed by The Hague Court. Finally, the Italian demand for a death penalty was suppressed altogether. Only two of the Duce's original demands were accepted in full, namely, a funeral service in honor of the

[28] Salandra (Geneva) to Mussolini, September 8, 1923. *Ibid.*, pp. 209-210.

Negotiation and Compromise

victims at the Roman Catholic Cathedral at Athens, in the presence of all the members of the Greek Government, and military honors to be rendered when the bodies of the victims were embarked at the Greek port of Preveza. The only major difference between the Conference's demands and Quiñones de León's proposals was that the judicial inquiry would not be conducted by the League. The Conference's adoption of certain features of Quiñones de León's scheme was tempered by "just enough changes to mark its independence."[29]

Mussolini's initial reaction from Milan, on the evening of September 8, to the Conference's decision appeared to be one of approval. The Italian Government, he cabled Avezzana, intended the evacuation of Corfu and the adjacent islands as soon as Greece "will have given full and definite execution to all the reparations requested."[30] In London, what appeared to be the Duce's acceptance was greeted with enthusiasm. Tyrrell was happy, he wrote to Della Torretta, "that we have arrived at a solution that bestows credit to all sides."[31] Tyrrell's expressions of joy, however, were premature. The Duce had no sooner sent Avezzana the cable cited above than he followed it with another, more detailed statement of Italy's intentions. Acceptance of the Conference's demands by Greece does not "mean simultaneous evacuation of Corfu" by Italy, since "acceptance does not mean execution," he cabled Avezzana. Only the indemnity clause was guaranteed by Greece's deposit of 50 million Italian lire. All the other demands were still to be executed, especially the fifth demand concerning the investigation and punishment of the assassins. The latter point, he stressed, would require time, but its execution was for Italy a sine qua non before the evacuation of Corfu could proceed. Avezzana was therefore instructed to pick the right moment

---

[29] Walters, p. 249.

[30] Mussolini (Milan) to Avezzana (Paris), September 8, 1923. *DDI*, p. 210. This cable was transmitted in a modified form as a Stefani Agency release. Giannini to Diplomatic Representatives abroad, September 9, 1923. *Ibid.*, pp. 210-211.

[31] Della Torretta (London) to Mussolini, September 9, 1923. *Ibid.*, p. 215.

Negotiation and Compromise

to make this known to the Conference, in order to "avoid [a] deplorable misunderstanding."[32]

Not fully aware that Mussolini's qualified acceptance had opened a Pandora's box, Avezzana replied that he would communicate the Duce's approval to the Conference. He disclosed that the British and French, and especially Laroche, who was speaking for Poincaré, had manifested to him during the last meeting of the Ambassadors' Conference their anxieties concerning the occupation of Corfu. They felt anxious not because they distrusted Italian assurances that the only aim of the Corfu occupation was the attainment of the reparations requested from Greece, but because any uncertainty as to the date of the evacuation of the island, after the Conference's reception of the Italian demands, would give the Council and the Assembly of the League an opportunity to reopen the question from which they felt they had been excluded.

Avezzana had retorted that they could not expect Italy to evacuate Corfu quickly, inasmuch as the occupation was made primarily to protect the prestige of Italy, "before Greek insolence." He privately asked Lord Crewe to call Curzon's attention to this point and to the fact that the sole object of the Corfu occupation was to enforce acceptance of the Italian demands. Therefore, termination of the island's occupation could not take place in such a way that it would be unsatisfactory to Italian honor. Avezzana thought that the principal pressure from the Conference would be on the issue of the occupation of Corfu. It would be pointed out to him that an Anglo-French guarantee affirmed by the Council would be equivalent to any territorial occupation of the island. To show the Duce how sensitive the continued occupation of Corfu would be, he recounted how the Conference had pressed him not to propose as a condition for the evacuation of the island, the payment of the occupation costs. The fear was that such a demand could be used as a pretext for an indefinite occupation of Corfu. It had even been suggested during the Conference discussions

[32] Mussolini (Milan) to Avezzana (Paris), September 9, 1923. *Ibid.*, p. 211.

Negotiation and Compromise

that the occupation costs be assumed by Italy; supporting precedents had been cited. Avezzana thought he should be authorized to declare that though Italy would not renounce the question of the occupation costs, Rome would be willing to have the Conference refer the question to The Hague Court for a decision. As to the occupation of Corfu he would declare that Italy would evacuate the island immediately after the execution by Greece of the Conference's demands. The execution of these demands would occur within a few days, since the Greek inquiry, opened immediately after the Tellini murder, was nearly finished.[33] On the following day, September 10, Avezzana communicated Mussolini's qualified acceptance to the Conference of Ambassadors.

INSTRUCTIONS TO LORD ROBERT CECIL

While the above cables were being exchanged between Mussolini and Salandra and Avezzana, the Conference of Ambassadors had convened its two hundred and twenty-sixth meeting on the morning of September 8. This unusual Saturday session was called to iron out certain details dealing with the proposed Commission of Inquiry.[34] At the beginning of the proceedings Cambon submitted the text of a letter to be addressed to the Albanian Government. The letter invited the Albanian Government to give every assistance possible to the Commission of Inquiry to allow it to pursue its investigations in Albanian territory. The letter was approved without discussion.[35]

With this piece of business out of the way, the Conference turned to a discussion of the instructions to be given to the Commission of Inquiry. Colonel Shibouya was warned by Cambon of the difficulties that the Commission would have to overcome. It would work in a part of the world which was

[33] Avezzana (Paris) to Mussolini, September 9, 1923. *Ibid.*, pp. 212-214.

[34] Unless cited otherwise the material that follows is drawn from the *procès-verbal* of the two hundred and twenty-sixth meeting of the Conference of Ambassadors, September 8, 1923. File 763.72119/12024, Record Group 59, NA.

[35] File 763.72119/12024, Annex A, Record Group 59, NA.

Negotiation and Compromise

not civilized, where diverse elements of a very mixed population were in continual struggle. He thought it would be proper to receive with the greatest reserve the testimony of these people, who in general were no great lovers of the truth. He knew from personal experience certain parts of Algeria where the customs and habits were similar. In order to triumph over these obstacles a mixture of firmness and suppleness would be necessary. As to the rest of its work in Epirus, the Conference entrusted itself in this respect to Colonel Shibouya and to the wisdom of the Commission.

In the discussions that followed it was agreed by the Conference that the Commission of Inquiry would have a completely free hand in the conduct of the investigation. It was also decided that the Commission would operate as a body in both Albania and Greece, and that it would never be separated. It was the feeling of M. Fromageot of the French delegation, that it would enhance the prestige of the Commission if it moved as a bloc. Unity was to be maintained even if there were a momentary divergency of views among the Commissioners. The Conference stipulated that all actions by the Commission would have to be in the name of the Commission.

Upon arrival in Greece the Commission was to maintain contact with the Allied Ministers in Athens. During its stay in Greece, however, it was to be entirely independent of the Conference's Commission of Delimitation. Should it prove useful the Commission could, if it wished, convoke the Commission of Delimitation. While in Greece, the Commission would have the power to take part in the operations of the inquiry pursued by the Greek authorities and to request the latter to proceed to all cross-examinations and supplementary inquiries that the Commission desired. Its most essential task at the beginning would be to examine as many witnesses as possible.

Closing the meeting, Cambon proposed that all the Conference's observations be summed up in the instructions which would be addressed to Colonel Shibouya as President of the Commission of Inquiry. These instructions, it was agreed by

Negotiation and Compromise

the Conference, would be presented by the Secretary-General, M. Cambon, and the Secretariat of the Ambassadors' Conference.[36]

With the Council of the League scheduled to reconvene on Monday, September 10, the problem of supporting and pressing the issue of the Council's competence had to be squarely faced by Lord Curzon and the Foreign Office in London. A preview of the policy Curzon would follow can be seen as early as September 8, in a report from the American chargé d'affaires in London. The Foreign Office anticipated that the Greeks would acquiesce in the Conference's demands and that the League would accept this solution since it practically embodied the points brought out by its meeting of September 6, cabled Wheeler to Washington. Whitehall, he disclosed, also emphasized that the method devised for solving the dispute did not "weaken the prestige or [the] authority of the League." They did admit, however, that the violent opposition of Rome had made it "impossible without grave consequences," for the League to have "sole and direct jurisdiction" in the dispute. This tight corner, according to the Foreign Office, was only turned when the League invited the cooperation of the Ambassadors' Conference and made suggestions to the latter on September 6. The subsequent adoption by the Conference of the League's suggestions placed the former "under the aegis of the League and left its authority unimpaired."[37]

With a solution within sight, after Greece's acceptance of the Conference's demands on September 9, the only outstanding problem that remained was whether or not to press the issue of the Council's competence. To have pressed the issue would have been tempting fate and assuming unnecessary risks. Mussolini's character, as Kennard at Rome[38] and Lord Crewe at Paris warned,[39] was of such a nature that one could not be sure what his reaction would be to a declaration of the

---

[36] Cambon's letter of instructions to Colonel Shibouya, September 17, 1923. File 765.68/94, Record Group 59, NA.

[37] Wheeler (London) to the Department of State, September 8, 1923. File 765.68/53, Record Group 59, NA.

[38] *Supra,* footnote 19.   [39] *Supra.*

Negotiation and Compromise

Council's competence. Therefore, on September 10, the very day the Council was scheduled to reconvene, Lord Curzon "withdrew his support" from Lord Robert Cecil and the League. Simultaneously, Lord Crewe at Paris "was instructed to accept the compromise scheme elaborated by the Ambassadors."[40]

On instructions from Curzon, Tyrrell communicated to Cecil at Geneva the pertinent orders. "I believe that the Paris solution is most likely to succeed," Tyrrell wrote to Lord Curzon, "if Mussolini is fairly honest and Geneva does not play the fool." He thought that the orders he had dispatched to Cecil would "help to prevent the latter." Tyrrell then revealed that the Paris Embassy had telephoned to say that the Conference of Ambassadors would meet at 3:00 P.M. that same afternoon [September 10]. According to the embassy, "Laroche intended to tackle the Italians at the Conference with regard to the breach of the understanding arrived at on Friday [September 7] for the evacuation of Corfu." This understanding was that Italy's acceptance of the Conference's note to Greece would also establish the moment at which the Italian occupation of the island would cease. The embassy gave the Foreign Office to understand that Laroche "was going to bargain with the Italians on the subject." At the same time it appeared that Poincaré was absent from Paris and would not return till the following day [September 11]. Tyrrell had replied to the embassy that he thought the French move ill-advised and suggested that sooner than proceed the meeting should be adjourned until the next day when Poincaré would return to Paris. He was convinced that the Italians should be made "to stick to their understanding, which amounted to an honourable understanding." On the other hand, he wrote, "as the French no doubt negotiated it with the Italians I think we should concentrate on forcing the French to put pressure on the Italians, while we take the line of gingering up the French." Tyrrell thought that this approach would be even more suc-

[40] Sir Harold Nicolson, *Curzon: the Last Phase, 1919-1925* (New York: Harcourt, Brace and Co., 1939), p. 371.

Negotiation and Compromise

cessful with Poincaré in Paris. Though he was not sure of success, he was very anxious that the Foreign Office "should stick to the principle of the evacuation of Corfu as *the* essential part of the compromise" to which the British had assented. It was also to be made clear to Poincaré that England, having taken its stand on the League Covenant—the vindication of the Public Law of Europe—was determined that Italy would have to give satisfaction at some time or other. Tyrrell hoped that this would "ginger up Poincaré in his dealing with the Italians and safeguard" the British position.[41]

In a conversation with Della Torretta that same day, Tyrrell admitted that Curzon and Prime Minister Baldwin had instructed Cecil during the preceding days "to act at Geneva with great moderation." Similar orders had been repeated to Cecil that same day, instructing him on the position he should assume in case some delegates raised the Italo-Greek question at the Council. Tyrrell also drew Della Torretta's attention to the "misunderstanding" which appeared to have occurred at the Ambassadors' Conference relative to the date on which the evacuation of Corfu would take place. He pointed out that the Foreign Office desired that the situation "return to normal as soon as possible." It thought that a settlement of the "misunderstanding" could be achieved "exclusively between [the] Conference of Ambassadors and the Italian Government." The Foreign Office, Tyrrell remarked in passing, had no desire to intervene since it was merely "a question of fact."

Della Torretta correctly surmised that the Foreign Office under Lord Curzon's direction had used all its influence in order to resolve the dispute in a manner which would avoid controversy with the League. From his own conversation with Tyrrell and from other information gathered at the Foreign Office, it appeared that while Great Britain formally supported the League, the Foreign Office's diplomatic moves had in fact

[41] Sir William Tyrrell to Lord Curzon, September 10, 1923. Folder marked "Letters to Curzon, M-Y, 1923," Box 65, Curzon Papers.

Negotiation and Compromise

been geared for a solution through the Conference, which would better satisfy the Italian point of view.[42]

While Della Torretta was visiting the Foreign Office in London, at Geneva that same morning the Council again met to discuss the Italo-Greek dispute. This private session was conspicuous by its brevity and by the sphinx-like silence of Lord Robert Cecil, who in previous meetings had energetically supported the League's competence.

After an exchange of views, Viscount Ishii was asked by the Council members to appeal to the Assembly not to discuss for the time being the Italo-Greek dispute. He was to justify this request on the grounds that the dispute was still under the Council's consideration and that "important negotiations were proceeding, which the Council hoped would have a satisfactory conclusion." With this point out of the way, Politis then read to the Council a telegram from the Greek Foreign Minister, Apostolos Alexandris, which disclosed that Greece accepted the Conference's demands and that it insisted upon the evacuation of Corfu. It also revealed that arrangements had been made for the stipulated 50 million Italian lire to be transferred to the Swiss National Bank, as requested by the Conference's note. Politis added that his government was doing everything possible to "reach a rapid settlement of the dispute," and that Athens sincerely desired that there should not be the "least trace of this affair" in its relations with Italy. The only memory he hoped would be preserved would be the recognition of the goodwill shown at the League and at the Ambassadors' Conference in trying to safeguard the peace, which was the "supreme interest of humanity."

Like Politis, Salandra also desired that no traces of the dispute remain in the relationship between the two countries, especially since the Greek Government had decided to do everything possible to reach a rapid settlement of the conflict. The meeting had ended.[43] The only comment Ishii could

[42] Della Torretta (London) to Mussolini, September 11, 1923. *DDI*, p. 218.
[43] L.N., *Official Journal*, 4th year, 1923, pp. 1304-1305. Viscount Ishii's

Negotiation and Compromise

muster in his reply to the Conference was the hope that the Council would be kept *au courant* on all subsequent deliberations of the dispute.[44] Faced with the withdrawal of London's support, the Council members were obliged "to renounce their own authority."[45]

In his report to Rome, Salandra tried to explain the nonintervention "of fanatics like Lord Cecil and Branting." He theorized that perhaps Italy's communication to the Conference may not have been repeated to the Council. Salandra then revealed that the previous evening (Sunday, September 9) an unofficial and private meeting was held by the Council members, without his participation. This meeting decided that it was impossible to drop the Italo-Greek question without first finding some way of affirming the competence of the League of Nations. The members thought that this move was indispensable in order to give satisfaction to the Assembly of the League before it adjourned at the end of the month. In closing he warned Mussolini that the issue might still be transferred to the Assembly, but he felt that at this point Italy's "position [was] much better."[46]

The reasons behind the Council's request to Ishii to appeal to the Assembly not to discuss the dispute, were fully explained by Politis. There was a "desire [to] avoid in [the] Assembly [any] premature discussion" of the dispute, he cabled Athens, which would "poison affairs and delay [the] Corfu evacuation." It was the impression in Geneva that Italy would wish to avoid the Assembly as long as possible, so that it would not have to make any decision on the evacuation date. On the other hand, other League members held that Assembly discussion was inevitable, and would act as a "Sword of Damocles" suspended over Italy's head in order to force "her

---

communication to the League Assembly asking them to desist from any discussion of the dispute as requested by the Council was made several days later, on September 12.

[44] *The Times* (London), September 11, 1923, p. 10.
[45] Nicolson, *Curzon . . .*, p. 371.
[46] Salandra (Geneva) to Mussolini, September 10, 1923. *DDI*, p. 215.

Negotiation and Compromise

to give as quickly as possible [a] formal assurance on [the] evacuation date."

As to the Greek press, Politis recommended that it avoid "carefully all polemics on [the] date of the evacuation," and limit itself to saying that Greece had every confidence in Italy, convinced that Rome would evacuate the island as quickly as possible. He also recommended that the Conference's conditions be executed with dispatch so that Greece would be in a position to say that it had fulfilled all the conditions without delay. By rapidly complying with the Conference's demands, Greece would be in a better position to maintain that any possible delay in the arrest and punishment of the assassins could not be used as a motive to delay the evacuation of Corfu.[47]

In Paris, stories appearing in the French press that no evacuation of Corfu would occur until the culprits had been arrested and punished,[48] propelled the Greek Minister, Athos Romanos, into action. He immediately called on Jules Cambon, at the Quai d'Orsay. The latter informed Romanos that at the Friday meeting of the Conference [September 7], it had proved impossible to fix an exact date for the evacuation of the island. Avezzana lacked the necessary instructions and in order to avoid a quarrel a decision was postponed until he would receive word from Rome.

Today's meeting [Monday, September 10], Cambon disclosed, would examine the question, and he assured Romanos that Greece's rights would not be disregarded by the Conference. In passing, Cambon asked whether September 27, the day the Commission of Inquiry would terminate its work, would be acceptable as an evacuation date. Romanos replied that he did not think so. The evacuation, he felt, should take place a few days after Greece fulfilled the Conference's de-

[47] Politis (Geneva), No. 1205 to the Foreign Ministry, September 11, 1923. French text. Greek Archives.

[48] An interview with Mussolini in which the Duce made it quite clear that until the culprits were arrested and punished Italy would not evacuate the island had been printed by the Paris press. *Le Matin*, September 10, 1923, p. 1.

Negotiation and Compromise

mands. Cambon said his own feelings were that the occupation could end when the Commission of Inquiry assured the Conference that the Greek officials had done everything possible to discover the culprits. Romanos insisted that all indications showed that Italy wished to prolong the occupation. Cambon then requested Romanos, since Poincaré was absent, to relate his apprehensions to Laroche, who would represent France at the afternoon meeting of the Ambassadors' Conference.[49]

In a letter to Laroche at his residence, Romanos observed that the Italian thesis that it would evacuate Corfu only after the arrest and punishment of the culprits, presented the "greatest danger." There was not the smallest doubt that the assassins were hiding in Albanian territory. Their discovery in Albania would prove difficult because of the nature of the terrain and the unfriendly attitude of the Albanian Government. The fear expressed in the Paris press that the Greek authorities might not do everything possible to facilitate the work of the Commission of Inquiry was without foundation. Greece had the greatest interest in discovering and punishing the culprits. If Greece were to fail in its duty, the Great Powers could easily seize some of the Greek islands as a pledge or even blockade its ports. Was it really necessary, he queried, that the island be occupied after Greece's execution of the Conference's demands.

This could not be the "spirit of the decision" taken by the Conference of Ambassadors in its session of September 7. The prolongation of the occupation, he continued, would be "contrary to equity" and would "prolong, in the island, a state of things prejudicial to the material and moral interests of Greece." Stories in the French press made this last point obvious. Italian officials had been dispatched from Rome and had replaced the Greek officials in all the island's public services. Would it be just to allow this state of affairs to persist even after Greece had accepted and executed all the conditions stipulated by the Conference? He was sure, Romanos con-

[49] Romanos (Paris), No. 4738 to the Foreign Ministry, September 10, 1923. Greek Archives.

Negotiation and Compromise

cluded, that the French Government recognized that the island's occupation "must cease as quickly as possible."[50]

MUSSOLINI'S QUALIFIED ACCEPTANCE ANNOUNCED TO CONFERENCE

Some hours after the delivery of Romanos' letter, the Conference of Ambassadors convened for its two hundred and twenty-seventh meeting.[51] The session lasted two hours.

The Conference quickly moved to a reading by Avezzana of Mussolini's communication that Italy would evacuate Corfu and the adjacent islands immediately when Greece had "given full and definitive execution to all the reparations demanded." Aware of the significance of Mussolini's qualified acceptance, Cambon asked Avezzana if he could give to the Conference more details on the precise meaning that the Italian Government attached to the expression, "full and definitive execution." His own interpretation of Mussolini's communication, Avezzana replied, was that the Italian Government would only evacuate Corfu when all the conditions posed by the Conference, including the punishment and execution of the culprits, had been fulfilled. Most of the conditions posed by the Conference, he felt, would present no problem. In certain cases it would be possible to anticipate the actual date of their execution, as for example the naval ceremony at Phalerum and the embarkation of the bodies of the victims at Preveza. The delicate point was the punishment and the execution of the culprits. It raised grave questions. To justify Mussolini's position Avezzana noted that in Italy sentiment was strong that Greece had no desire to fulfill this condition. The fact that after twelve days they had not yet succeeded in arresting the culprits was a good indication of this. Avezzana's comments,

[50] Copy of a letter from Athos Romanos to Jules Laroche, September 10, 1923, under cover of a dispatch Romanos (Paris), No. 4738 to the Minister of Foreign Affairs. Greek Archives.

[51] Unless cited otherwise the material that follows is drawn from the *procès-verbal* of the two hundred and twenty-seventh meeting of the Conference of Ambassadors, September 10, 1923. File 763.72119/12029, Record Group 59, NA.

Negotiation and Compromise

however, were unfair. Indeed, from the very beginning all the forces of the Greek State had been mobilized to apprehend the assassins. The delay which Avezzana had exposed was only natural if one kept in mind the nature of the terrain, the primitiveness of the communication system, the semi-anarchy of the area, the inability of the police to operate beyond their own borders, and the reticence in assisting officials that one encounters in an attempt to investigate crimes of this nature. Though the Greek authorities and police officials could perhaps be charged with inefficiency, it was unfair to cast doubts on the good faith of the Athens government, which had been genuinely shocked by the murder and considered it a disaster for Greece. Nevertheless, Avezzana refused to reply with greater precision to the question posed by M. Cambon and desired an adjournment of the Conference in order to communicate with Rome. As soon as he received a reply he would inform the Conference.

His government, Lord Crewe declared, would be greatly disappointed by these latest developments. The British Government had always considered that the evacuation of Corfu would take place immediately after the deposit of the security and the funeral ceremony. Avezzana's assertion that his government desired very much to leave Corfu, but that only Greece had the power to hasten this evacuation by swiftly arresting the culprits, placed him in an "absolutely new situation," which obligated him to consult again with London.

The decision of the Conference on September 7, Cambon remarked, had brought about a great relaxation in the international situation. Today, however, his British and Italian colleagues desired again to consult their governments. He believed it pressing that they obtain precise instructions which would permit the Conference to calm the anxieties being manifested this very moment at Geneva. As for himself, Cambon thought that the Commission of Inquiry would be in a position to see what the Greek Government had done and to give information on this subject to the Conference. If the Commission of Inquiry should inform the Conference that the

Negotiation and Compromise

Greek Government had acted with diligence and honesty, the Conference would be in a position to intercede with the Italian Government and would notify it that since satisfaction had been obtained, the Conference could see no objection to the evacuation of Corfu.

The intention of the Conference, Laroche pointed out, in making its demands coincide with those of Italy, was to bring about a relaxation in the international situation from the instant Greece made known its acceptance. The communication from his government that Avezzana had read put the Conference in a difficult situation. He wondered if it would not be possible to discover a field of agreement. It would be easy to specify the date by which most of the conditions set forth by the Conference could be fulfilled: apologies, funeral service, salute, embarkation of the victims at Preveza. He desired similarly to find a date to tie together as closely as possible the execution of points five and six: the Greek promise to ensure the discovery and exemplary punishment of the guilty parties at the earliest possible moment, and the work of the Commission of Inquiry. The Conference could, for example, hasten the departure of the Commission of Inquiry and invite the latter to send the Conference its report as quickly as possible. The Conference would thus be in a position to know rapidly whether points five and six had been carried out. Acting on this suggestion the Conference decided that the Commission should depart for Epirus on Thursday, September 13.

To assist the departure of the Commission of Inquiry, Avezzana offered to put at its disposal an Italian destroyer to transport the Commission from Brindisi to Santi Quaranta in Albania. To hasten the work of the Commission, Laroche suggested that it be instructed to make known its impressions to the Conference as quickly as possible after its arrival in Greece. The essential thing for the Commission to ascertain was whether the Greek Government had seriously pursued its investigations. It was quite possible that after its arrival in Greece the Commission would be unable to discover the cul-

Negotiation and Compromise

prits and would find that the Greek Government had found out nothing.

Continuing the discussion, Cambon added that it would be possible to disclose to the Greek Government that the Commission of Inquiry would be charged with the task of informing the Conference whether the execution of its conditions had been performed. Avezzana interjected that he completely understood the desires of his colleagues. He of course realized, as they did, that there was some concern to reassure the League of Nations. However, at the same time, he asked his colleagues to take into consideration what would occur if Greece were given the impression that Italy would immediately evacuate Corfu. Laroche's reply was that it would be possible to draw the attention of the Greek Government to this point, by making it clear that the Conference depended on it to hasten the evacuation of Corfu by actively searching for the culprits. He felt it would be desirable to find a formula which would reassure the League of Nations on the one hand, and quicken the zeal of the Greek Government on the other.

Lord Crewe then reverted to the question he considered to be of capital importance: Mussolini's qualified acceptance, read to the Conference by Avezzana at the beginning of the meeting. He requested that the meaning of the expression, "full and definitive execution of the reparations demanded" be specified exactly by Avezzana at the next meeting of the Conference.

Revealing French uneasiness over the latest developments, Laroche declared that it would be repugnant to him if it appeared as if he were applying pressure on the Italian Government. He did not desire to come to the assistance of the Greek Government in any way. However, he thought it would be in the interests of the Conference to send without delay a further communication to the Greek Government which would be of a nature to reassure the League of Nations.

As to Greece's acceptance of the conditions of the Conference, Laroche and Lord Crewe, before closing the meeting, agreed it would be solely with the Conference that she would have to deal. Reservations would be accepted from the Italian

Negotiation and Compromise

Government and these would be conveyed through its representative at the Ambassadors' Conference.

REPORTS TO ATHENS AND ROME

After the Conference had ended, Laroche, who had probably been impressed by Avezzana's comments on the Greeks, asked Romanos to recommend to his government that strict orders be given to end the inquiry quickly and apprehend the culprits. Without hesitation and undoubtedly in an attempt to show his government's good faith, Romanos replied that his government had hastened from the first day to search for the guilty persons and had even offered a reward of one million drachmas for information leading to their discovery. The fact that they had not been found up to this point meant that they were hiding in Albanian territory. Seemingly unimpressed by Romanos' remarks, Laroche was of the opinion that by the application of exceptional measures, like martial law and other forms of coercion, the villages in the region where the murder was committed could be induced to denounce the culprits. There was no doubt in his mind about the sincere desire of the Greek Government to discover the culprits. However, local authorities, he felt, were another matter and they could apply "with more or less zeal [the] orders received."[52]

The issue of arresting and punishing the culprits also monopolized Avezzana's report to Mussolini. According to Avezzana, Italy's acceptance of the Conference's note to Greece had moved Lord Crewe to ask whether "following such acceptance Italy intended to evacuate Corfu." Furthermore, Crewe revealed to his colleagues that the British Government had adhered to the Conference's note inasmuch as the guarantee given by the Great Powers for the integral execution of the demands removed every reason for the continuation of the island's occupation. Rome's qualified acceptance, however, put the whole issue in doubt. It made it clear that Italy would evacuate Corfu only when Greece had given full and definitive execution to all of

[52] Romanos (Paris), No. 4740 to the Foreign Ministry, September 11, 1923. French text. Greek Archives.

Negotiation and Compromise

the Conference's demands. Lord Crewe pointed out the impression that this would produce not only in the League of Nations, but also on English public opinion and the British Government. It would be interpreted to mean that points five and six of the Conference's note dealing with the arrest and punishment of the culprits would have to be executed. In fact certain conditions might make it impossible to proceed to the arrest of the culprits. They might, for example, have succeeded in escaping to America. In this case the occupation of the island would last indefinitely. For these reasons, Crewe asked that the thoughts of the Italian Government be stated precisely.

Avezzana made it clear to Lord Crewe that the Conference, in its decision, had spoken of the "satisfaction of the demands and not acceptance of the same." The Conference could not request that Italy be satisfied by Greece's simple acceptance. The pressure exerted by the occupation of the island would make Greece conscious of the necessity of arresting and punishing the culprits. This was in reality the major part of the reparations requested by the Conference. The Italian Government, he added, had no intention of modifying the object of its landing at Corfu, nor of the occupation. Therefore, he was not in a position to give any other interpretation to Mussolini's communication, except that which could be derived from its terms.

Avezzana observed to the Duce that varying interpretations could be applied to the terms, "full and definitive execution of the reparations." He thought Lord Crewe's formula—simple acceptance by Greece as sufficient—could not be accepted. It "was contrary to the spirit that had led the Italian Government to occupy Corfu." Secondly, it was a formula that would damage Italy's prestige. He warned Mussolini, however, that the controversy was fast changing and that the Italo-Greek conflict could be replaced by an Italo-British one. This was especially true because Greece at this point was out of the picture and only England continued to be concerned at seeing Italy remain on Corfu. Since this condition appeared to be developing, Avezzana offered to the Duce a compromise

Negotiation and Compromise

formula which was essentially the Cambon-Laroche scheme propounded during the meeting of the Conference. This scheme was offered in case Mussolini did not wish to prolong the dispute or remain at Corfu because of the "effect that it could have on our general policy, and our relations with England."

According to Avezzana, the position taken by Italy in claiming full execution of the Conference's demands before evacuating Corfu, would be maintained. The first four demands presented no problem and would be easily executed by the Greeks. As to points five and six, the Italian Government would wait for confirmation from the Commission of Inquiry that the investigation of the assassins had been vigorously pressed. The seventh demand was of course covered by the sum deposited by the Greek Government in the Swiss National Bank. The taking of this line would assure Italy of French support. It would also free Mussolini from the incident and regain for him that "liberty of action that is necessary in order to contribute authoritatively to the more grave problems that present themselves": the question of reparations and the problem of inter-allied debts. Knowing how important the problem of prestige was considered in Rome, Avezzana added that Italy's prestige would not be damaged by this action. His last request was for immediate orders.[53]

Mussolini, however, was in no mood for compromise formulas concocted either by Avezzana or by the French. Yet at the same time he probably understood the seriousness of the situation and the warnings Avezzana had sent. He probably also realized the necessity of shifting his position to make it more reasonable. He therefore again confirmed, as he had done in the past, that the occupation of Corfu was of a temporary character, subordinated to the full execution of Italy's "just requests for sanctions." This was the only significance that could be logically attached to the expression, "obtenir satisfaction aux demands qu'il a présentées." This phrase the Con-

[53] Avezzana (Paris) to Mussolini, September 11, 1923. *DDI*, pp. 216-217.

Negotiation and Compromise

ference had used in its note to Greece in describing the object of the Italian occupation of Corfu. Mussolini noted that doubts had arisen on the part of the British about the full execution of point five of the Conference's note because of certain conditions which might not permit the arrest and punishment of the assassins. Nevertheless, nonexecution of point five would be contrary to the categorical obligations placed on Greece and the guarantee given by the Great Powers for the integral execution of all the demands. It would amount to a failure to give satisfaction to "our prestige and our national honor." It was perfectly clear that Italy had to maintain the Corfu occupation as an "indispensable guarantee" to obtain the satisfaction which a "unanimous Italian Nation insists upon with [an] unquestionable right." The Duce had no doubts that Avezzana's colleagues at the Conference would recognize "all the fairness of such [a] point of view." However, he was disposed to relax his position so as to dispel any notion provoked by the "indeterminateness of the date" for Italy's evacuation of Corfu and also to give proof of Rome's honest intentions. Italy would agree to examine the possibilities of subordinating the evacuation to other reparations in case the inquiry could not lead to the immediate arrest and punishment of the culprits. If the inquiry did not succeed in identifying the culprits and declared that they could not be discovered, Italy would find herself in a position of not having had its just requests satisfied. In such a situation, before the evacuation of the island could occur, it would be necessary to provide Italy with other reparations. This could be the full payment of the 50 million Italian lire deposited by the Greek Government. The Duce's final point was that it would be necessary to resolve differently the whole question of the expenses of the occupation.[54]

[54] Mussolini to Avezzana (Paris), Salandra (Geneva), and Della Torretta (London), September 12, 1923. *Ibid.*, pp. 222-223. The Foreign Ministry in Athens was informed from London that during this period Poincaré had been under heavy pressure by the Little Entente. This forced him to notify Rome that if Italy persisted on the conditions of her ultimatum to Greece, France would be forced to cooperate with England on the whole question of the Council's competence. London

Negotiation and Compromise

This reply by Mussolini was not sent until the early morning hours of September 12. Since Avezzana was still without orders on September 11, the meeting of the Conference scheduled for that day was cancelled. The sessions of September 12 and 13, in which a compromise solution was finally hammered out, would prove to be the most difficult and trying for all concerned.

---

noted, however, that Italy's acceptance of the Conference's note to Greece had been framed in such a way as to "save its internal prestige" and to "prolong the occupation of Corfu." London, No. 3197 to the Foreign Ministry, September 10, 1923. Greek Archives.

CHAPTER VII

CRUCIAL DAYS: SEPTEMBER 12-13

STRUGGLING FOR A FORMULA

WITH Mussolini's new instructions in hand, Avezzana and his colleagues convened on the morning of September 12 in the two hundred and twenty-eighth meeting of the Conference of Ambassadors.[1] The opening exchanges dealt quickly with the logistics of transporting the Commission of Inquiry from Brindisi to Santi Quaranta and to the Greek border. When these details had been worked out, Cambon read to the Conference Greece's reply of September 9, accepting the demands of the Conference.[2]

The discussions which followed the reading of the note decided the following points: the type and number of Allied ships which would take part in the naval ceremony, though the details of the ceremony were delegated to the officers of the three admiralties; the hour of the funeral ceremony in Athens and the embarkation of the bodies of the Italian officers at Preveza; the apologies that were to be presented by the highest Greek military authority to the diplomatic representatives of the three Allied Powers at Athens.

With these details out of the way Avezzana then informed the Conference that he was in a position to reply to the question which had been previously posed by Lord Crewe on the subject of the payment of the Corfu occupation costs. His government did not believe it could renounce its requests to the Greek Government for reimbursement of the occupation costs. At the same time, the Italian Government declared that the settlement of these costs would not, in any manner, have the

[1] Unless cited otherwise the material that follows is drawn from the *procès-verbal* of the two hundred and twenty-eighth meeting of the Conference of Ambassadors, September 12, 1923. File 763.72119/12029, Record Group 59, NA.
[2] *DDDIG*, pp. 38-39.

Crucial Days: September 12-13

result of prolonging the occupation of Corfu. His government had decided to entrust to the World Court at The Hague the settlement of the question as to who must bear the expenses of the occupation.

At this juncture, Cambon turned to the crucial issue: Italy's evacuation of Corfu. He asked Avezzana if he could furnish to the Conference some particulars concerning the information that had been transmitted to it by the Greek Minister in Paris concerning the character of the Italian occupation of Corfu.[3] It appeared from this information that the Italian authorities in Corfu acted as if they wished to remain there permanently. The channel of Corfu had been mined.[4] Trenches had been dug. The town administrations had been dissolved and had been replaced by Italian military authorities.[5] Cambon admitted that he had no information concerning the veracity of this information, but he believed that similar information had reached the notice of Lord Crewe. He would be happy if Avezzana could furnish the Conference some particulars on this point.

He had no information on this subject, was Avezzana's response. However, the instructions that he had received from Rome concerning the character of the occupation of the island were so clear, so precise, that he could only contest the accuracy of the facts which had just been stated by Cambon. His government had no other desire than to be able to leave Corfu

[3] Undoubtedly Cambon was referring to his conversation with Athos Romanos on September 10, and Romanos' letter to Jules Laroche, later that same day. *Supra*, Chapter VI.

[4] Leopold S. Amery, the First Lord of the Admiralty, cruising near the Corfu channel on September 14, 1923, was met by an Italian naval launch and told the channel waters were mined. He was asked to follow closely behind the launch—"a bit of pure make-believe, as we discovered afterwards," he wrote in his diary. Leopold S. Amery, *My Political Life* (London: Hutchinson and Co., Ltd., 1953), II, p. 271.

[5] Intensification of the Italian occupation undoubtedly took place during this period. The island was fortified, ships could pass through the channel only after sunset, and all public services were in Italian hands. All public buildings were occupied, the customs houses included. *The Times* (London), September 11, 1923, p. 10; September 14, 1923, p. 10.

Crucial Days: September 12-13

under conditions calculated to safeguard its own dignity. He was indignant that anyone could put in doubt the declarations of his government and desired that this protest be formally inscribed in the *procès-verbal*.

This statement prompted Cambon to point out that the delicate point was really the declaration. The situation could arise where the punishment of the culprits would be delayed without the Greek Government's being responsible. He asked what would be Rome's attitude in that case.

Avezzana admitted that his government contemplated the possibility of evacuating Corfu before the complete fulfillment of the Conference's demands. Nevertheless, he could not agree to fix in the Conference a precise date for the evacuation of the island. By doing so, the Conference would run the risk of allowing the Greek Government to hope that the impunity of the culprits could be assumed without danger. This was denied by Lord Crewe who felt that the occupation of Corfu had nothing to do with the search for the culprits.

Trying to find an acceptable solution, Laroche believed that the Commission of Inquiry would very quickly be in a position to make known to the Conference its findings. Because of this, he proposed the following compromise formula. The Conference would inform Athens that it noted Italy's desire not to prolong the occupation of Corfu, and would examine and see whether the conditions of the Greek investigation for the culprits were such that the Italian Government could proceed without delay to the evacuation of the island. It would be understood that the Italian Government reserved the possibility to turn to new sanctions if it considered that justice had not been completely rendered by the Greek Government.

That the Italian Government might be sincerely disposed to evacuate Corfu was not contested by Lord Crewe. At the same time, it was possible that its occupation could be indefinitely prolonged. In such a case the situation "would be grave." He knew very well what difficulties a government could go through in evacuating under these circumstances. He cited, as an example, England's occupation of Egypt in 1882. Certainly

Crucial Days: September 12-13

Prime Minister Gladstone and subsequently Lord Salisbury, the Foreign Secretary, seriously intended to evacuate Egypt. Yet British troops were still in Egypt.

In line with Mussolini's instructions Avezzana replied that if it transpired from the report of the Commission of Inquiry that the culprits could not be arrested, or that the inquiry was destined to drag on, the Italian Government would still leave Corfu. His government would then act in concert with the Conference on other pledges to be substituted for the occupation of Corfu in order to bring the Greek Government to respect its promises. He thought that the payment of a certain sum would be in order. His request was that the tenor of the note addressed to Athens by the Conference be only that Greece make every effort to arrest the assassins.

Examining the proposal carefully, Lord Crewe thought that there were several very different questions involved: the Commission of Inquiry would have to inform the Conference of what had been done and state whether the Greek Government had acted "fair and square"; secondly, if, after some weeks, they did not find the culprits, the Commission would inform the Conference of its thoughts on the matter. These, he felt, were two very distinct questions. It was possible for a long time to elapse before the Conference would know whether it was actually possible to find the culprits.

Avezzana did not agree; he felt that either the Commission of Inquiry would inform the Conference that the culprits had been arrested, in which case the Italian Government would withdraw immediately from Corfu, or, on the other hand, it was possible that the Commission would not find the culprits immediately. In the latter situation Italy declared that it would still consent to evacuate Corfu, reserving only the right to concur with the other governments represented at the Conference on the measures which should be substituted for the occupation of the island.

All this would depend, Cambon remarked, on the report of the Commission of Inquiry, which would inform the Conference whether the Greek police had or had not "acted with honesty." Wishing to reassure his colleagues, Avezzana again repeated his government's intentions. If it was reported by the Commission that the investigation had been conducted by the Greek authorities in an "insufficient manner," the Italian Government would evacuate Corfu from that moment. In that event the Italian Government would examine together with the Conference what inter-allied measures could be substituted for the occupation of the island. He was ready to pledge his government on this point but admitted that this declaration could be overruled, and asked his colleagues to keep it strictly confidential.

Wishing to tie the Italians down, Lord Crewe desired that the promise taken by Avezzana bind the entire Italian Government, but he did not insist that it be made public. Undoubtedly in an attempt to reassure public opinion and the League, Cambon thought it could be made public that the Conference would occupy itself with bringing about the evacuation of Corfu upon reception of the report of the Commission of Inquiry.

The Conference, Avezzana felt, could restrict its reply to the League to the statement that it was in the process of solving in a satisfactory manner the question of the evacuation of Corfu. Simultaneously, they could make it understood that League intervention would only succeed in spoiling things. Fully aware of London's obligations toward Geneva, Lord Crewe thought it was indispensable that the League Assembly be reassured. At the same time, he desired to indicate to the Foreign Office that Avezzana had made a formal promise. To speed things up, Cambon then turned and asked Colonel Shibouya if the Commission of Inquiry would be able to report to the Conference in five days. Shibouya replied affirmatively. The morning session had ended.

IMPRESSIONS OF THE MEETING

The American observer believed that the British would be satisfied by Avezzana's declarations which "were very definite and quite clear." The difficulty, he reported to the Department

Crucial Days: September 12-13

of State, had been to embody in a note to Athens "sufficient assurances as to the evacuation of Corfu [so as] to satisfy the League of Nations, and general public [opinion] and yet . . . make [the] evacuation seem dependent on [the] carrying out of the conditions formulated by the Conference of Ambassadors."[6]

In a letter to Lord Curzon, Lord Crewe admitted that the whole business had been "an exceedingly troublesome job." He had no complaint to make against Avezzana's personal part in the meetings except insofar as he had tried to get the Conference to act "on the strength of assurances of which he was not able to say that they represented the final judgment of his government." More than once Avezzana had warned his colleagues that he ran the "risk of being *dégommé* from Rome." Crewe felt that the real risk that Avezzana ran "was that after engaging his government, they might refuse to be engaged." This would have placed the Conference "in the humiliating position of having solemnly insisted" upon Greece's execution of the Conference's demands, "without securing to that unlucky country its *quid pro quo* in the shape of a certain evacuation of Corfu in the course of this month." He found it impossible to say whether the problem would be settled after the second meeting scheduled for that day. Lord Crewe acknowledged receipt of Curzon's instructions to secure a further adjournment if Avezzana's instructions did not enable him to accept the Conference's formula.

As to the French, he felt they had "played up very fairly." "Jules Cambon, like an old diplomat," he observed to Lord Curzon, "has no love for the League of Nations, tolerating the Council almost with friendliness, but disliking and despising the Assembly." Laroche, he found, had been "very ready and helpful," and noted that several times he had "stood up manfully to the mandates from Rome." Crewe also thought the latter realized the necessity of working with Geneva. He believed that it had been "reasonable enough" for the Confer-

[6] Whitehouse (Paris) to the Department of State, September 12, 1923. File 765.68/61, Record Group 59, NA.

Crucial Days: September 12-13

ence to examine the circumstances of the Tellini murder. And, had it not been for Italy's "mad act" of occupying the island, the whole question would have been settled even if the assassins had not been discovered.[7]

Avezzana reported to the Duce that the Italian position during the morning session had been maintained only "with great difficulty." He admitted that he had assumed responsibility by attempting to define more precisely for the Conference Mussolini's concessions. He thought that "even at [the] price of some trifling sacrifice" it was necessary to consolidate the successes Mussolini had won and which were still endangered from many sides.[8]

PRESSURE FOR AN EVACUATION DATE

The afternoon session of the two hundred and twenty-ninth meeting of the Conference of Ambassadors started at 3:00 P.M.[9] The Conference's first decision upon convening was to approve a plan, prepared by the naval experts, dealing with the ceremony at Phalerum Bay to take place on September 19.[10] With this minor problem out of the way, the Conference once again turned to the crucial issue: the Italian evacuation of Corfu.

The conditions that the Conference would address to the Greek Government clearly depended on the assurances Avezzana would be able to give to his colleagues on the date for the evacuation of Corfu. At this point, therefore, Laroche read to the Conference, from the *procès-verbal* of the morning session, the text of Avezzana's statement: "Baron Avezzana desires to reassure the Conference on the intentions of the Italian Government. Even in the case where it would result from the report of the Commission [of Inquiry] that the investigation

[7] Lord Crewe to Lord Curzon, September 13, 1923. Folder marked "Correspondence with Lord Crewe, Ambassador to Paris, 1922-1924," Box 22, Curzon Papers.

[8] Avezzana (Paris) to Mussolini, September 12, 1923. *DDI*, p. 223.

[9] Unless cited otherwise the material that follows is drawn from the *procès-verbal* of the two hundred and twenty-ninth meeting of the Conference of Ambassadors, September 12, 1923. File 763.72119/12029, Record Group 59, NA.

[10] File 72119/12029, Annex A, Record Group 59, NA.

Crucial Days: September 12-13

has been conducted by the Greek authorities in an insufficient manner, Baron Avezzana declares that the Italian Government will evacuate Corfu from that moment. In that case, however, the Italian Government will examine together with the Conference, what inter-allied measures will be substituted for the occupation of Corfu. Baron Avezzana is ready to commit his government on this point. He admitted that this statement can be overruled, but he asks his colleagues to keep it absolutely confidential."

The accuracy of the statement read by Laroche was not contested by Avezzana. He proposed, therefore, that the Conference sum up its essential features formally confirming the intention manifested by his government to evacuate Corfu and the adjacent islands. The evacuation would take place immediately after Greece would have satisfied points one through four of the Conference's note of September 8. Concerning the seventh condition, relative to the indemnity, Italy considered the pledge deposited by Greece as a sufficient security. Thus there would be no need to prolong the occupation on this point, even if The Hague Tribunal were to delay its decision with regard to the payment of the indemnity. At the same time the Italian Government, with the object of facilitating the task of the Conference, had declared that it would also entrust to The Hague Tribunal, and under the same conditions, the question of the occupation costs. Italy felt that these costs were due to it. As for point five, he had declared that in case the investigation by the Commission of Inquiry made it appear that no immediate fulfillment could be expected on this point, the Italian Government would be ready to examine the conditions under which the Corfu pledge could be replaced by other sanctions. This would be necessary so that all the conditions of the Conference's note of September 8 could be fulfilled.

It was realized by Laroche that the Italian Government did not want to appear to be submitting to an ultimatum, and that it also did not wish to be obliged to evacuate Corfu on the very day the Commission of Inquiry's report was received. On the other hand, it was only natural that the English and

Crucial Days: September 12-13

French Governments desired to avoid a new crisis. They wished to be able to give to the League of Nations assurances that the Italian Government would evacuate the island. He noted that the Commission of Inquiry would be ready to present its report on September 22, and that the Conference had fixed September 27 for the conclusion of the inquiry. Would it be possible, Laroche queried, for Italy to evacuate Corfu on September 27, at the latest? If so, he suggested the adoption by the Conference of the following formula: "Even in the case where it would result from the report of the Commission [of Inquiry] that the investigation has not been conducted by the Greek authorities in a satisfactory manner, Baron Avezzana declares spontaneously that Italy will evacuate Corfu at the latest September 27, a date fixed by the Conference for the end of the Greek Inquiry. In this case, on the request of the Italian Government the Conference will examine, what inter-allied measures of *another kind* will be substituted for the occupation of Corfu either as a means of coercion, or by right of penalty. He admits that this declaration, that he is making in the name of his government can be overruled, but he asks his colleagues to keep it absolutely confidential." He drew the attention of his colleagues to the additional phrase proposed by the French delegation: "what inter-allied measures of *another kind*." The French Government judged it opportune to state that the Conference did not consider that any other territorial occupation should be substituted for that of Corfu.

He had made his declaration in a spirit of honesty, Avezzana exclaimed. He regretted that he could not approve the form that the Conference intended to give it, since it implied a spirit of mistrust. He had already gone very far in the way of concessions. If the formula presented by his British and French colleagues represented the last word from these delegations he would be obliged to refer the matter to Rome for instructions. In an attempt to assuage Avezzana's feelings, Cambon recalled to him that he had accepted that the date be fixed confidentially. It was not the intention of the French delegation, interjected Laroche, and certainly not the intention of the

Crucial Days: September 12-13

British delegation, to pester the Italian Government on the matter of a day. What was necessary was a firm date.

His instructions did not permit him to accept an agreement in this form, appealed Avezzana. If the investigation were unsatisfactory and Italy had to evacuate the island *before having obtained assurances*, it would find itself in an inadmissible situation.[11] In order for the evacuation to take place, it was necessary that the Conference be able to consider what other sanctions would be substituted for the occupation of Corfu.

Closing the meeting, Lord Crewe reiterated that his government wished a precise and formal promise from the Italian Government as to the date of the evacuation of Corfu. In order to consult his government Avezzana proposed an adjournment of the session. The meeting ended at 7:30 P.M. after four hours of discussion.

BRITISH PRESSURE AND MUSSOLINI'S DECISION

According to the American observer the atmosphere during this meeting "was at times rather tense." Whitehouse noted to the Department of State that during the afternoon recess, the secretaries of the different embassies had attempted "to make a draft of the declaration of the Italian Ambassador to place on the minutes, but the difficulties turned out to be very great, and even the ingenuity of M. Laroche was unable to overcome them." Finally, however, a draft was drawn up which could serve as a basis for discussion. When the Conference reconvened Avezzana "was depressed." During the discussion as to the manner of the Greek salute, he remarked with bitterness that his colleagues appeared "disposed to deliver him an ultimatum on the question of Corfu." Avezzana thought the least they could do was to yield to his government on a minor point.

During the discussions Mr. Hudson of the British Embassy, who was in consultation with the Foreign Office over the proposed declaration, entered the room. He informed Lord Crewe that while Whitehall "did not like the text proposed,

[11] Italics added.

it was willing to accept it if an agreement could be reached that evening." Avezzana, however, desired "certain modifications" of the declaration, to which Lord Crewe would not agree. After some discussion, a formula was finally drawn up "which seemed to cover all the points raised." Avezzana, who throughout the discussions had been "most conciliatory," thought it would be acceptable to Rome. However, before making any decision, he desired to consult his government. Crewe, who had been to the races, "did not know his government's instructions except as whispered to him by his secretary [Hudson], who was intransigeant." The British attempted to have Avezzana accept the new draft formula immediately. When Avezzana replied that he could not, "the British retorted that their consent was only good for that evening and they would in turn demand modifications the following day." The French throughout the discussions had also been anxious to settle the matter in order to send some sort of communication to Geneva.[12]

In his report to Rome, Avezzana related for Mussolini the day's discussions and the declaration which had been proposed by the Conference. Regarding the Conference's note to Greece, he observed that execution of the fifth condition would be handled in the following manner. Greece would be informed that the Commission of Inquiry would begin its work on September 17 at Janina. Five days after its arrival it would submit telegraphically to the Conference its first observations. On receipt of this report the Conference would establish whether the fifth condition of its note of September 8 to Greece could be considered as executed. If the report proved this condition had been satisfactorily executed Italy would

---

[12] Whitehouse (Paris) to the Department of State, September 21, 1923. File 765.68/95, Record Group 59, NA. In his first report after the afternoon session had ended, Whitehouse informed the State Department that the "difficulty was that the French and British wished to make [the] evacuation definite, while the Italians wanted, for face saving purposes a loophole, although they promised not to use it." Whitehouse (Paris), to the Department of State, September 13, 1923. File 765.68/62, Record Group 59, NA.

Crucial Days: September 12-13

be asked to act in conformity with the declaration it had made relative to the evacuation of Corfu. In the case the culprits could not be discovered and should the inquiry made by the Greek Government be considered to be insufficient, the Conference would examine collective measures of another nature that could be taken by the Allied Powers in place of the Corfu occupation.

Avezzana revealed that it had proved impossible to extract from the French and the British greater concessions. On the contrary, both delegations maintained that they had given Italy all the satisfaction which it demanded from Greece. They felt that the Conference's request could not be received badly by his government if Rome intended to evacuate Corfu. At one point, Avezzana disclosed, Lord Crewe pressed him for an immediate acceptance of the two formulas proposed. He warned the Duce that Crewe had then reserved to take the following day "complete liberty of action" in the Corfu question. Therefore, Avezzana requested immediate instructions. Before ending, he reiterated that Paris would not support Italy "beyond certain limits." He felt that the moment had arrived where Italy could not "rely [any] more on [France's] unconditional support." As in his previous reports he drew the Duce's attention to the dangerous situation that would arise should the Italo-Greek dispute turn into an Anglo-Italian conflict.[13]

The fear of an Anglo-Italian conflict prompted Avezzana to send Mussolini a second cable the following day. He disclosed that information reaching him as to England's attitude caused him to repeat that Italy's gains could be cancelled.

[13] Avezzana (Paris) to Mussolini, September 12, 1923. *DDI*, pp. 225-226. On the following day, September 13, Pertinax (Henri Géraud), the political commentator for the *Écho de Paris*, quoted Lord Crewe as saying that "England would assume liberty of action," if the Conference did not arrive at a decision. Della Torretta (London) to Mussolini, September 14, 1923. *Ibid.*, p. 231.

That same day the *Petit Parisien* made it quite clear that if no agreement could be reached "England would take up immediately her liberty of action." Gabetti (Paris) to Thaon di Revel, September 13, 1923. *Ibid.*, footnote p. 226.

Crucial Days: September 12-13

He therefore urgently requested instructions before 5 o'clock that afternoon. To accentuate that time was of the essence the hour was repeated twice at the end of the cable.[14]

The danger that the dispute could turn into an Anglo-Italian conflict was also touched upon in a cable to the Minister of Marine sent by the naval attaché in Paris. According to the latter, sources close to Lord Crewe considered that "the situation would become most grave" if Italy did not accept the declaration proposed by the Conference.[15]

From London, Della Torretta cabled that Tyrrell had indicated that any settlement had "to occur between [the] Conference of Ambassadors and the Italian Government without [the] Foreign Office expressing any opinion" on the question. Tyrrell felt that the whole question was a "misunderstanding." The Conference, he thought, had been under the impression that Italy's acceptance of its note of September 8 had also fixed the moment at which the island would be evacuated. This likewise had been the impression of Sir Eric Phipps, the Counsellor of the Embassy at Paris, who had been present during the discussions. Tyrrell felt the "misunderstanding" had to be cleared up at the place of origin. Della Torretta's attempt to reply was brushed aside by Tyrrell, who turned to another subject. The Italian Ambassador noted that the question had changed since his last conversation with Tyrrell. He cautioned the Duce that it could no longer be presumed that the Foreign Office, as cited in his last cable, would limit itself to wishing the situation to return to normal as quickly as possible. On the contrary, the Foreign Office would perhaps be willing to display "special action" on this point. In ending, he admitted to Mussolini that his task in London was far from pleasant. British public opinion was unanimous in insisting on an immediate evacuation of Corfu.[16]

Poincaré, in his desire to find some sort of solution to the question that faced the Conference, attempted to approach

[14] Avezzana (Paris) to Mussolini, September 13, 1923. *Ibid*., p. 226.
[15] Gabetti (Paris) to Thaon di Revel. *Ibid*., footnote p. 226.
[16] Della Torretta (London) to Mussolini, September 12, 1923. *Ibid*., p. 224.

Crucial Days: September 12-13

Rome via Geneva. Salandra in a report to Mussolini disclosed that Hanotaux had admitted receiving a letter from Poincaré suggesting that he contact Salandra to discover a formula which would determine the time for the evacuation of Corfu. This was to be done so as to keep the Geneva "atmosphere clear." Salandra had retorted to Hanotaux that a "definitive formula can be sought not at Geneva but at Paris with the Conference of Ambassadors." Hanotaux had agreed but thought that he and Salandra could work out a formula that would not obligate anybody and could be transmitted as a "suggestion to the respective governments." Salandra, unprepared and without instructions, postponed any meeting until the following day.[17]

With these reports from Paris, London, and Geneva in hand, Mussolini's hour of decision had arrived. Fully aware of England's hostility and the limits of French support, the Duce agreed to fix a specific date for the evacuation of Corfu. However, he stipulated that one important qualification be made. Should the fifth condition of the Conference's note of September 8 not be fully executed, Italy was to be paid the 50 million Italian lire deposited by Greece. The question of the occupation costs he consented to have adjudicated by the Permanent Court of International Justice at The Hague.[18]

Mussolini continued his instructions in a second cable to Avezzana. He protested with indignation the phrase in the proposed declaration which read: "in the case in which it results from the report of the Commission that the inquiry may not have been conducted by the Greek authorities *in [a] satisfactory manner*," Italy would still evacuate Corfu by September 27. The Duce found this phrase "contrary to every principle of international morality." He thought it would encourage Greece to evade the execution of the one condition that remained most important to Italian public opinion, namely, the search for and punishment of the assassins. The Conference's note to Greece was, therefore, to be modified in

[17] Salandra (Geneva) to Mussolini, September 12, 1923. *Ibid.*, pp. 223-224.
[18] Mussolini to Avezzana (Paris), September 13, 1923. *Ibid.*, pp. 226-227.

Crucial Days: September 12-13

relation to the solution accepted by Italy. Avezzana was also to make it clear that Italy would have no objection to associating herself with the Conference in any sanctions or conditions that it intended to request from Greece, as collective punishment for the crime committed against General Tellini. If the Conference did not accept Rome's point of view Avezzana was instructed to reserve Italy's "liberty of action."[19] With these instructions, Avezzana prepared for the next meeting of the Conference of Ambassadors.

AVEZZANA'S DECLARATION

The meeting at the Quai d'Orsay on September 13 commenced at 6:30 P.M.[20] It began with Avezzana's disclosing that he had submitted to his government the draft declaration proposed by the British and French delegations the previous day and that his government, in reply, had manifested its dissatisfaction with the mistrust which was shown in the declaration. It had also considered the declaration immoral.

However, Rome wished to be consistent. It intended first of all to remain faithful to its formal agreements. Italy understood that the question constituting the essential point of the negotiations was the evacuation of Corfu. To evacuate the island Italy set only one condition—a penalty to be imposed upon Greece in the event that it would not give satisfaction to the Conference's demands. The penalty would be the 50 million Italian lire deposited by Greece. If the penalty were to be inflicted on Greece, Italy would renounce the indemnity which was to be fixed by The Hague Court, but would allow the occupation costs to be adjudicated by that Court. His government affirmed that in formulating this condition it sought no financial advantage. On the contrary, it felt that

[19] Mussolini to Avezzana (Paris), September 13, 1923. *Ibid.*, pp. 227-228.

[20] Unless cited otherwise the material that follows is drawn from the *procès-verbal* of the two hundred and thirtieth meeting of the Conference of Ambassadors, September 13, 1923. File 765.72119/12029, Record Group 59, NA.

Crucial Days: September 12-13

it was its duty to obtain assurances that Greece would not completely escape the just punishment it deserved.

After an exchange of views between the different delegations it was decided to inscribe in the *procès-verbal* the declaration which Avezzana had been authorized to make in the name of his government. The declaration was as follows:

"I desire to make known to the Conference that, in its desire to show its attachment to peace, the Italian Government, according to its reiterated declarations, is resolved to evacuate Corfu and it has decided to do so September 27, the date fixed by the Conference for the end of the Greek investigation. But, if on this date, the culprits are not discovered, and if it is *not established* that the Greek Government *has not committed* any negligence in their pursuit and their search the Italian Government estimates that it would be contrary to morality and to justice, as well as to the dignity of Italy that the latter renounce the pledges which it seized in order to obtain satisfaction, without satisfaction having been accorded to it. It asks, therefore, that the Conference, taking note of the spontaneous decision of the Italian Government relative to the evacuation of Corfu on September 27, decide from now that, in the aforesaid stated eventuality, the Conference will inflict on Greece, as penalty the payment of a sum of 50 million lire to Italy, who will waive consequently all requests to the Permanent Court [of International] Justice at The Hague, [pursuant] to the terms of paragraph 7 of the note of September 8, excluding recourse of the Italian Government before the Permanent Court [of International Justice] for the costs of the occupation."[21]

The Conference took formal note of Avezzana's declaration and adopted the proposals formulated in his statement. A closer reading of the declaration shows that it was skillfully worded. Greece was assumed to be guilty. The burden would

---

[21] Italics added. French text. Avezzana (Paris) to Mussolini, September 14, 1923. *DDI*, pp. 234-235. A rough translation is found in Whitehouse (Paris) to the Department of State, September 14, 1923. File 765.68/66, Record Group 59, NA. See Appendix B.

Crucial Days: September 12-13

be upon Greece to prove herself innocent. This point would prove to be of paramount importance in the days to come.

The wording of Avezzana's declaration invoked comments from the different delegations. Lord Crewe, who had received a letter from Lord Curzon complaining "that unless we get the Italian out of Corfu pretty quickly a great blow will have been struck at the public law of Europe," was the first to speak.[22] Undoubtedly aware of the implications of the declaration, he attempted to specify exactly the responsibilities of the Greek Government by having the Conference adopt the following formula: "If it is established, without dispute, that the Greek Government has committed a negligence in the pursuit or the investigation of the culprits. . . ."

This proposal by Crewe was energetically resisted by Avezzana, who insisted that the Conference preserve the negative formula proposed. He asked Lord Crewe not to protect the Greeks from a punishment that was on the whole moderate. Avezzana won his point; the original formula was maintained.

With the evacuation date now set, Laroche pointed out that everything depended on the report of the Commission of Inquiry. There were in fact three possibilities: the Commission might consider unanimously that the Greek Government had done everything possible, in which case no difficulty would be anticipated; the Commission might be of the unanimous opinion that Greece had not done its duty, in which case the Conference would impose on the Greek Government a penalty of 50 million Italian lire; thirdly, there was the possibility that the Commission's decision might not be unanimous. The vote might be divided equally or it could be three to one. If the vote were not unanimous, the Conference would have to reconsider whether it was bound by the report of the Commission. The Conference then decided that its decision would vary according to the division and distribution of the votes.

Wishing to close all loopholes, Lord Crewe asked what would

[22] Lord Curzon (Geneva) to Lord Crewe (Paris), September 13, 1923. Text. James Pope-Hennessy, *Lord Crewe, 1858-1948; the Likeness of a Liberal* (London: Constable and Co. Ltd., 1955), p. 166.

Crucial Days: September 12-13

happen if satisfaction were not completely accorded to Italy. Let us say, he theorized, the investigation were to establish that there were four culprits and that the Greek authorities succeeded in arresting only three. In that case, Laroche retorted, he did not think the Italian Government had any intention of making difficulties. This was assented to by Avezzana.

Splitting hairs, Lord Crewe also asked whether Rome would commence the evacuation of Corfu on September 27, or whether it intended to begin it sooner and complete it on September 27. In deference to Avezzana's desire it was agreed by the Conference that the word "complete" would not be inserted in his declaration. The understanding, however, Lord Crewe repeated, was that the Italian evacuation of Corfu would be completed by September 27, at the latest. His government, Avezzana observed, would probably have no objection to beginning the evacuation as soon as the Conference had received the report of the Commission of Inquiry.

The Conference's note to Greece, delivered the following day by the French chargé d'affaires in Athens, spelled out in detail the manner in which the conditions stipulated in the Conference's note of September 8 were to be executed. First, the Allied Ministers in Athens would decide in agreement with the Greek Government the date on which the apologies were to be made. The apologies were to be presented by September 18 at the latest. Second, the funeral service in honor of General Tellini and his staff would take place in Athens on September 19 at 10:30 A.M. Third, the ships of the three Allied Powers would arrive at Phalerum Bay for the rendering of the salute on the day of the funeral. Fourth, military honors would be rendered on the same day to the corpses of the victims on their embarkation at Preveza. Fifth, and most important, the Conference's Commission of Inquiry would commence its work at Janina on September 17. Five days after its arrival it would report its first observations to the Conference. If the culprits had not been discovered it would disclose to the Conference the conditions under which the inquiry was being carried out. On the basis of this report the Conference would ascertain whether the fifth condition of its note of September 8 could be considered as fulfilled. Should the condition not be fulfilled, in view of the Italian statement that it would in any event evacuate Corfu on September 27, the Conference reserved the right to notify Greece of any other measures of a coercive or punitive nature which might be taken against her by the Allied Powers. The particular measure envisaged was the payment of a sum of 50 million Italian lire to Italy. In this case, the Conference would request the Permanent Court of International Justice at The Hague to restore to Greece the security deposited by her. Lastly, no further application would be made to The Hague Court as stated in paragraph 7 of the note of September 8 unless special recourse were made to the court by Italy for the charges entailed by the occupation.[23]

The Conference's note was also forwarded to the Council of the League of Nations. In its covering letter of explanation the Conference expressed the conviction that the steps taken would lead to a satisfactory settlement of the dispute.[24]

MUSSOLINI'S REACTION

The American observer, in his report to Washington, made it clear that Avezzana's statement was not adopted "without long discussion." Lord Crewe's comments had put in doubt the good faith of the Italian Government. The declaration which promised Italian evacuation of the island on September 27, provoked the British delegation to ask if that meant every Italian would be out of Corfu by this date. Avezzana answered that he did not know. After consulting with his military and naval attachés, he replied that it might take two or three days. At this point the British wished to insert a definite statement in the declaration ensuring that every Italian would be out of the island by September 27. Avezzana interrupted, saying "he was at the Conference in a political capacity and giving his government's word and he was not there to draw up a watertight legal document." To satisfy British apprehensions, how-

[23] *DDDIG*, pp. 39-40.
[24] L.N., *Official Journal*, 4th year, 1923, pp. 1305-1306.

Crucial Days: September 12-13

ever, he was willing to fix September 25 as the beginning of the evacuation to ensure complete evacuation by September 27. The French delegation at this point intervened and after "some argument" induced the British to accept. Whitehouse felt that if Lord Crewe and the British desired to antagonize Rome, they certainly had succeeded. Cambon had remarked to him afterwards that he was shocked at the way the British delegation had spoken to Avezzana, who Cambon "thought had behaved admirably under such provocation."

Judging by Avezzana's attitude, Whitehouse observed, "whatever may have been the original intentions of Mr. Mussolini, when he found he had stirred up a hornets' nest by the occupation of Corfu, he became really desirous of settling the affair if it could be done, without loss of prestige." Credit for the settlement of the dispute, he noted, was being attributed to the Conference. Though the Conference had undoubtedly done "good work," Whitehouse felt "it was apparent at every moment that fear of something occurring at Geneva was the driving power."[25]

The Greek Minister was also busy during this period. In a series of talks with Cambon and Laroche about the fifth condition of the Conference's note, Romanos made it clear that punishment of the culprits could not depend on Greece alone. He pointed out that the culprits might be refugees in Albania. Cambon and Laroche replied that the competent Greek authorities would have to make the most severe and intensive efforts to find the culprits. The authorities were also to lend all their support to the Conference's Commission of Inquiry. If the assassins crossed the border into Albania and if the Greek authorities could not apprehend them, they were to identify them and give their names to the Commission of Inquiry. Lack of such action, they noted to Romanos, would make it "hard for the Conference to prove that [the] fifth condition of its note has been fulfilled."[26]

[25] Whitehouse (Paris) to the Department of State, September 21, 1923. File 765.68/95, Record Group 59, NA.
[26] Romanos (Paris), No. 4828 to the Foreign Ministry, September 14, 1923. French text. Greek Archives.

Crucial Days: September 12-13

In a report to Mussolini of the day's meeting, Avezzana disclosed that the Italian declaration had provoked a "lively discussion with [the] English delegation." However, with French support assured to him in advance by the Quai d'Orsay, the Conference was able "to accept substantially" the proposals Mussolini had authorized Avezzana to make. Avezzana felt that the Conference's note to Greece could be considered a "satisfactory document" for Italy since he could remember no similar situation followed by "political sanctions as solemn." He thought that Italy could be proud and grateful to the Duce for having "so efficaciously protected its prestige." On the other hand, the concessions made to the Conference, fixing the evacuation date, would be "judged an act of high wisdom." Avezzana believed it would not have corresponded either to Mussolini's intentions or to the interests of Italy "to convert a moral punitive action into a question of Mediterranean equilibrium."[27]

Mussolini's initial reaction to Avezzana's declaration before the Conference was one of reserve.[28] A deeper examination of the declaration, however, prompted him to cable Avezzana that he found it "satisfactory."[29]

Avezzana in reply assured the Duce that a better solution could not have been hoped for by Italy. In the long run it "avoided complications," while the continuation of the problem would have agitated European public opinion, creating a very unfavorable atmosphere for the attainment of Italy's foreign policy aims. He felt that in the solution the British had been forced to ratify and execute the Italian ultimatum, which they had at first thought excessive. Victory had also been achieved over the League of Nations, which had been prevented from taking any part in the solution of the dispute. Well aware of Italy's great debt to France, Avezzana recommended that the Italian press emphasize "the cordial and

[27] Avezzana (Paris) to Mussolini, September 14, 1923. *DDI*, p. 233.
[28] Mussolini's first reaction to Avezzana's declaration was made clear in the course of a telephone conversation. See *ibid.*, p. 235, footnote 2.
[29] Mussolini to Avezzana (Paris), September 14, 1923. *Ibid.*, p. 235.

Crucial Days: September 12-13

friendly attitude displayed by France" throughout the dispute. He had reasons to believe, he concluded to Mussolini, that this action would be especially welcome to Poincaré and to French public opinion.[30]

The subsequent arrival in Rome of a copy of the Conference's actual note to Greece provoked a violent reaction from Mussolini. The results of the Conference, he cabled Avezzana, were not in tune with his instructions. He reminded his ambassador of what his precise conditions had been—identification of the culprits or immediate payment by Greece of the 50 million Italian lire already deposited. It appeared from the Conference's note that payment was subordinate to proof of the negligence of the Greek Government. A simple majority vote by the Commission of Inquiry, he observed, rejecting the thesis of Greek negligence, would deny to Italy the 50 million lire. The Duce felt that this condition would not produce execution of clause six of the Conference's note of September 8. It would be a "monstrous hoax" that had to be prevented at any price. It would be "monstrous," he pointed out to Avezzana, if on September 27 the following sequence should occur: (1) the Greek Government is found to have been diligent; (2) that in spite of this diligence the Greek authorities have not been able to discover the culprits; (3) that therefore Italy has no right to the entire indemnity; (4) that Italy nevertheless has to evacuate Corfu, on the basis of its declaration to the Conference of Ambassadors.[31]

Avezzana in reply pointed out that he could not ask the Conference to exclude the case in which the innocence and diligence of the Greek Government were proven. In the formula that had been adopted it was necessary that Greek diligence be "unanimously established" by the Commission of Inquiry. The Conference was already pledged to inflict a penalty of 50 million lire if this evidence was not forthcoming. The Conference, he observed to the Duce, was a *corpo politico* suitable for determining any violation of the pledge taken.

[30] Avezzana (Paris) to Mussolini, September 14, 1923. *Ibid.*, p. 238.
[31] Mussolini to Avezzana (Paris), September 14, 1923. *Ibid.*, p. 237.

Crucial Days: September 12-13

Avezzana felt that the three-day interval between the reconvening of the Conference on September 24 to examine the report of the Commission of Inquiry and Italy's promised evacuation of Corfu on September 27 gave Rome time to judge whether or not the Conference had failed in its pledge. If Rome should feel it had failed, Italy could resume "liberty of action towards [the] Conference."[32]

A report from Athens that the Conference's note was viewed as a victory for Greece was forwarded by Mussolini to Paris. He maintained in his cable to Avezzana that Italy's "diplomatic success" at the Conference which Avezzana continued "to exalt" was merely "a charming and shameful hoax injurious to Italy."[33]

Relations between Mussolini and Avezzana were obviously strained. In a secret cable Salvatore Contarini, the Secretary-General of the Palazzo Chigi, warned the ambassador that the Duce was not convinced by his explanation of the reservation contained in the Conference's note concerning Greece's negligence. The Duce thought, Contarini revealed, that only the end result would prove whether Avezzana was right or wrong. It was therefore "absolutely indispensable," the Secretary-General observed, to obtain immediate payment of the 50 million Italian lire should it prove impossible to punish the culprits before September 27.[34] Avezzana immediately retorted to Contarini, I have "always seen the problem in the precise terms [in] which you have placed it."[35]

At Whitehall the Paris settlement was viewed far differently. The Prime Minister, Mr. Baldwin, felt that if Lord Curzon could get Mussolini out of Corfu by the end of the month he would have done a "great thing." "I am delighted with your general direction of affairs in a most difficult situation," he

---

[32] Avezzana (Paris) to Mussolini, September 15, 1923. *Ibid.*, p. 239.
[33] Mussolini to Avezzana (Paris), September 18, 1923. *Ibid.*, p. 250. The cable from Athens that Mussolini forwarded to Avezzana was Montagna (Athens) to Mussolini, September 18, 1923. *Ibid.*, pp. 248-249.
[34] Contarini to Avezzana (Paris) September 18, 1923. *Ibid.*, p. 250.
[35] Avezzana (Paris) to Contarini, September 19, 1923. *Ibid.*, p. 254.

Crucial Days: September 12-13

wrote to Curzon, "and I hope the country will realize what an awkward corner you have got them round."[36]

In Geneva, another Englishman had an entirely different attitude. In a long memorandum on the repercussions of the Italo-Greek dispute in the League of Nations, Sir Eric Drummond, the Secretary-General of the League, wrote:

[36] Stanley Baldwin to Lord Curzon, September 14, 1923. Folder marked "Letters to Curzon A-F, 1923," Box 65, Curzon Papers. On the morning of September 14, at a time when the Paris settlement was probably not yet known in London, the Italian Ambassador, Della Torretta, had an interview at the Foreign Office with Sir William Tyrrell. The latter tried to explain to the Italian Ambassador the Conference's actions. He pointed out that the Conference desired a formula which, guaranteeing Italy's reparations from Greece, permitted at the same time an end to the Italian occupation of Corfu. Tyrrell in referring to the Paris talks appeared optimistic. Della Torretta retorted that he had no recent news from Paris, but if the discussions proceeded in the same way as in the previous days he could not share his optimism. He thought that his government could not be induced to evacuate the island before the essential part of the Italian ultimatum had been executed: the investigation and punishment of the culprits. Tyrrell replied that Franco-British solidarity with Rome towards Greece and the inter-allied composition of the Commission of Inquiry constituted the best pledge for getting complete satisfaction from the Greeks. The ambassador insisted that the dispute was predominantly Italo-Greek in character. Tyrrell disagreed. He noted that from the moment the Conference of Ambassadors was invested with the problem, Italy's reasons for unilateral action had come to an end. Sir William thought Della Torretta would agree that the Conference was trying to "safeguard Italian sentiment and prestige." Della Torretta lamented that it was Britain who had insisted on the evacuation of the island, though the Duce had declared that Corfu would be returned to Greece as soon as Italy had obtained the reparations requested. Tyrrell answered that England had no particular point of view and that at the Conference the French delegation had acted in the same sense as the British. He regretted that the French and other persons concerned had permitted the notion to arise in Italy that France had held a friendlier attitude towards Italy than had England. Sir William pointed out that Whitehall's main concern "was not to establish a precise date for the evacuation but only the indication of a determined moment," in the case the culprits were not identified. Della Torretta was convinced that this latter consideration was what had inspired the British Government, and according to Tyrrell this point of view was also fully shared by the French. Della Torretta (London) to Mussolini, September 14, 1923. *DDI*, pp. 235-236.

Crucial Days: September 12-13

"It cannot be doubted that, for the moment at least, the events of the last two weeks have done much to weaken both the moral authority of the Council and the general confidence that the precise obligations of the Covenant will be universally accepted and carried out.

. . . .

"It is no doubt very generally believed, both in Government circles and by the public at large, that a powerful member of the League has refused to carry out its treaty obligations under the Covenant, and has succeeded in doing so with impunity, some might even say, with an increase of prestige. It is generally held that the authority of the League has been challenged in a sphere which is precisely that for which it was created, and that this challenge has brought in question the fundamental principles which lie at the root of the public law of the new world order established by the League."[37]

Though the Secretary-General looked upon the events of the previous weeks in despair, the Greeks on receipt of the Conference's note undoubtedly felt a sense of relief. The Greek Foreign Minister, Apostolos Alexandris, promised the Italian Minister, Montagna, that the Greek Government would execute all the conditions of the Conference's note "with [the] greatest carefulness" and to Italy's satisfaction.[38]

THE LEAGUE WITHDRAWS FROM THE DISPUTE

During this period Mussolini had other fears. He was stirred by a report from Salandra that advantage would be taken of the Conference's reply to the League to reopen the dispute either in the Council or the Assembly. The embassies in London and Paris were requested by the Duce to make the necessary overtures in order that the French and British representatives at Geneva receive instructions to support Salandra in

[37] Memorandum by Sir E[ric] D[rummond], September 14, 1923, entitled "Corfu Incident." Political 1923: 11/30889/30508, League of Nations Archives. See Appendix C.
[38] Montagna (Athens) to Mussolini, September 15, 1923. *DDI*, pp. 239-240.

Crucial Days: September 12-13

his attempt to resist a reopening of the question. They were to make it clear to the host government that a reopening of the question at Geneva, after it had been transferred with the agreement of all concerned to Paris, would only provoke Italy to claim "liberty of action vis-à-vis [the] Allied Governments concerning the Italo-Greek dispute." Simultaneously, another cable was dispatched to Salandra asking that similar pressures be applied to his French, English, and Japanese colleagues at Geneva.[39]

Two days later Salandra reported to Mussolini that the previous evening [September 15] the members of the Council, at a private meeting, had produced a reply to the Conference's note. The reply contained nothing new except congratulations to the Conference for bringing the dispute to a successful conclusion. The vote of the League Council, he noted, was judged to be "anodyne and insignificant." Salandra felt that the question would not be exhausted with the Council's acceptance of the proposed reply to the Conference. The question inevitably to be faced was the Council's communication to the Assembly. A hostile debate would doubtlessly ensue. Salandra believed that in the Council he could obtain communication to the Assembly of a booklet of the documents compiled during the dispute. However, even the communication of the booklet would be enough to provoke Assembly discussion. His own opinion was that any communication by the Council to the Assembly should be opposed on the basis that the question was exhausted. If in spite of this argument a communication was sent to the Assembly he would maintain that Italy would abstain from any Assembly discussion. By this action Rome could declare valueless any discussion and deliberations by the Assembly in which Italy did not participate.[40]

Mussolini consented to Salandra's approving the Council's reply to the Conference of Ambassadors on the following conditions: the question was to be understood as ended; the Coun-

[39] Mussolini to Avezzana (Paris), and Della Torretta (London), September 14, 1923. *Ibid.*, p. 231 and footnote.
[40] Salandra (Geneva) to Mussolini, September 16, 1923. *Ibid.*, p. 241.

Crucial Days: September 12-13

cil would not pass it on to the Assembly. He reiterated that a reopening of the dispute at Geneva would move Rome to assume its "liberty of action vis-à-vis the Allied Governments." Salandra was therefore instructed to approach his French and Japanese colleagues asking them to oppose any communication from the Council to the League Assembly.[41]

The Duce's threats proved effective. The debates in the League Council on September 17 and 18 were an anticlimax after the previous days' hectic discussions in the Conference. The proposed reply to the Conference by the Council's President, Viscount Ishii, was accepted. It took note of the Conference's communication and welcomed its efforts to put an end to a situation which had "aroused intense anxiety."

Branting had no comments to make about the Council's reply. He could not help noting, however, that Italy's actions in denying the League's competence were "in clear contravention of the principles laid down in the Covenant." This "might set up dangerous precedents" for the future.

Lord Robert Cecil's words were far different from his previous talks before the Council. He felt that the function of the League was "not to impose any particular settlement in a dispute," but to promote agreement between the disputing parties. Certainly the League was in no way a "super-State." It was "more nearly a forum for the discussion of international questions," which could lead to agreement in regard to them. The object of the Covenant was "to promote peaceful settlement and not to promote a victory of one side or the other, or even a victory of the Council or the League over both." He thought that the Council had done its duty in acting as it had. To have entered into a discussion of the Council's competence when the real problem was to bring the disputing parties together would have been contrary to the great task with which the Council had been entrusted.[42]

Salandra's recapitulation of Italy's position during the dis-

[41] Mussolini to Salandra (Geneva), September 16, 1923. *Ibid.*, pp. 243-244.
[42] L.N., *Official Journal*, 4th year, 1923, pp. 1305-1310.

Crucial Days: September 12-13

pute was made the following day. It provoked Branting to reply that Salandra's arguments had not convinced him in any way. He maintained that there was a difference "between what was permissible to States before the signature of the Covenant, and what was permissible now that the majority of States had adhered to that Covenant." Branting felt that world public opinion would have difficulty in understanding how Italy's so-called pacific actions could be innocent and in conformity "with the spirit of the Covenant." The Council's part in the whole dispute had come to an end.[43]

[43] *Ibid.*, pp. 1313-1316. As Appendix C shows, the events of the previous weeks had raised in Sir Eric Drummond's mind a number of questions. Drummond's memorandum therefore helps to explain the action of Viscount Ishii on September 20, when he announced to the Council that the interpretation of certain articles of the Covenant dealing with the Council's powers and other questions of international law had received the attention of some of his colleagues. Ishii thought they should be studied and settled in order to avoid any future differences of opinion and also to facilitate the work of the League. Therefore, he proposed to the Council that it undertake with the help of legal experts a studied and thorough examination of these questions. After a series of meetings in which Salandra fought a skillful rear guard action, the Council succeeded in posing five questions which were submitted to a special committee of jurists nominated by members of the Council. The first three questions dealt with the right and duty of the Council to act under Article 15 of the Covenant when one of the parties to the dispute claimed that the procedure of Article 15 was for some reason inapplicable. Question four asked whether measures of coercion which were not intended as acts of war were consistent with the obligations of the Covenant. The last question related to the responsibilities of States for crimes committed on their territory.

The reply of the Commission of Jurists was forwarded to the Council in March of 1924. Its reply to the first three questions was a vindication of the Covenant. In question five it rejected the Conference's thesis on state responsibility for crimes committed on their territory. To question four, which was perhaps the most crucial, the Commission gave an ambiguous answer which failed to satisfy many members of the League. *Ibid.*, pp. 1317; 1320-1325; 1328-1332; 1338-1348; 1349-1352; Antonio Salandra, *Memorie Politiche, 1916-1925* (Milano: Garzanti, 1951), pp. 115-117; F. P. Walters, *A History of the League of Nations* (London: Oxford University Press, 1960), pp. 251-253; Konstantin von Neurath, *Der italienisch-griechische Konflikt von Jahre 1923 und seine völkerrechtliche Bedeutung* (Berlin: Dümmler, 1929); Quincy Wright, "Opinion of the Commission of Jurists in the Janina-Corfu Affair," *American Journal of International Law*, 18, No. 3 (1924), pp. 536-544.

Crucial Days: September 12-13

The importance of these deliberations, however, was overshadowed by events unfolding in northwest Greece. On September 17, the Conference's Commission of Inquiry arrived in Epirus. Attention shifted from Geneva to the rugged mountain country bordering the Albanian-Greek frontier and to the officers that composed the Commission.

THE COMMISSION OF INQUIRY IN EPIRUS

The Commission of Inquiry had its first meeting almost immediately after its arrival at Janina on the afternoon of September 17. It was essentially an organizational meeting.[44] The first impressions of Major R. E. Harenc, the British delegate, were that Colonel Shibouya, the Japanese delegate and President of the Commission, "had been well propaganded on his way here," while Colonel Lacombe, the French delegate, "had a perfectly open mind."

The following day at the invitation of the Italian delegate, Colonel Eugenio Beaud, the Commission attended the funeral service held for the victims in Janina. After the service, the Greek Procureur General read to the Commission a summary of the actions that had been taken by the Greek authorities to apprehend the assassins. Unfortunately, Major Harenc wrote, he "completely wrecked the Greek case which is quite a good one, by making stupid and quite incorrect answers to questions put by [Colonel]Beaud." Harenc felt the latter had come, "with instructions to justify the occupation of Corfu" and would "stick at nothing to do so." When Colonel Beaud attempted to take complete charge of the proceedings, Colonel Shibouya appeared "quite helpless to stem the tide of his eloquence." Though stunned by Beaud's actions, Harenc recovered enough to suggest an adjournment of the meeting until the necessary translations of the pertinent documents could be made.

The meeting that afternoon attempted to discuss the order

---

[44] Unless cited otherwise the material that follows is drawn from a carbon copy of a letter written by Major Harenc to Mr. Hartopp of the British Legation in Athens, September 23, 1923. Attached to file 765.68/125, Record Group 59, NA.

Crucial Days: September 12-13

in which evidence was to be taken. The discussion got nowhere "chiefly owing to the fact that B[eaud] was continually interrupting to put his side of the case, and reading quite irrelevant reports which as he said were of enormous importance." At these meetings, Baron Modica, the Italian Consul at Janina, was present. It appeared to Harenc that the latter "was largely instrumental in working up the Italian case." Though these meetings were to be confined to the four officers, Colonel Beaud justified Baron Modica's presence on the grounds that he knew all about the crime and could help the Commission form an opinion. Since the other delegates did not object neither did Major Harenc. At another meeting later that day, translated copies of the Greek résumé were handed to the Commission. Colonel Beaud paid no attention to the documents, "but insisted on going on with his reading of extracts from various documents produced by his government." These documents, Harenc noted, were depositions by Italians and Albanians and had no bearing whatever on the actions of the Greek authorities after the murder of Tellini and his staff. At this point Harenc suggested that the Commission ought to proceed with its examination of the actual steps taken by the Greek Government following the murder. He felt if this were not done the Commission would never be able to send its first report to the Conference of Ambassadors by Saturday, September 22. The major's suggestion, which infuriated Colonel Beaud, was seconded by Colonels Shibouya and Lacombe. After the Greek résumé was read it was decided to examine on the following day Colonel Botzaris, the Greek representative to the Delimitation Commission and the first person to find the bodies of General Tellini and his staff. It was also decided to question other police and army officials and to visit the scene of the crime.

At this point in the proceedings it became apparent to Major Harenc that Colonel Shibouya "was quite incapable of dealing with B[eaud]." He felt that the latter had probably received instructions from Rome "to carry the Commission with him to give a verdict throwing all blame on the Greek Government, and if possible to prove that Botzaris had actually engineered the crime." If this proved impossible Beaud was to prevent the Commission from "taking really relevant evidence as to the neglect on the part of the Greek authorities." The course of events prompted the major to intervene. He decided to have "a long talk" with Colonel Lacombe, inasmuch as he was the "strongest character," and the only one of the three officers who was "impartial." Lastly, Lacombe was "furious at the way B[eaud] had taken charge" of the investigation. While Harenc was speaking to Lacombe, one of his assistants talked to Colonel Shibouya. The result of these conversations was that the three officers decided "to join forces in order to allow Shibouya to take charge." They also decided to be always ready with questions which would be put to the witnesses by Colonel Shibouya. The latter step appeared necessary since Shibouya "had no idea how an inquiry of this kind should be carried out."

The next morning, September 19, was taken up with an examination of Colonel Botzaris. Major Harenc observed that throughout the examination "Beaud behaved as if he was the prosecuting counsel in a murder case, and Botzaris was the prisoner, and from Beaud's point of view this was actually the case." The whole Botzaris examination he characterized as an "unpleasant business." In the Beaud-Botzaris encounter he felt the former "came out badly for Botzaris is a devilish clever man, and from what I've seen of him Beaud isn't." During the examination Beaud lost his temper with Botzaris. Attempts by Harenc and Lacombe to induce Shibouya to intervene proved unsuccessful. The entire proceedings caused Botzaris after the examination to exclaim to the waiting correspondents: "The Italians are demanding my head."[45]

During the afternoon session the Commission examined the Director-General of the Gendarmerie, Colonel Florias. Colonel Florias proved unproductive as a witness chiefly due to the irrelevant questions posed by Beaud. At the end of this examination Major Harenc and Colonel Lacombe agreed that

[45] *The Times* (London), September 21, 1923, p. 10.

Crucial Days: September 12-13

the "Greek authorities had done all that they could" to find the culprits. Even Colonel Beaud was forced to admit: "If I had not been sure that Botzaris had been instrumental in organizing the crime, really I should have been persuaded also."

The next day the Commission proceeded to the scene of the crime. As previously arranged, all officers and men were in the positions that they had occupied at the time of the murder. Major Harenc, with the approval of the Commission, had prepared a questionnaire which was to be submitted to everyone by Colonel Shibouya. The Commission was especially interested in finding out if telephone messages by Colonel Botzaris on the day of the murder ordering precautions to be taken against the escape of the assassins had been received and what action, if any, had been taken. This field trip proved a failure. Colonel Beaud continually interrupted and insisted on reading statements made by various individuals "which had nothing to do with the matter in hand." His tactics thus restricted the Commission's interrogation to the "lieutenant in command of the post [Kakavia] and telephonist, one shepherd and a couple of goatherds." Harenc and Lacombe agreed that all the witnesses interviewed "were reliable." Beaud, as was to be expected, disagreed. "His method of argument," Major Harenc wrote, "being first to shout one down, and then without drawing breath to start a perfectly good fresh hare." Colonel Botzaris, who accompanied the Commission of Inquiry, attempted to show what actions he had taken when he found the car of the Italian officers and saw the bodies lying on the road. Beaud's behavior during this testimony, the major observed, "was simply disgraceful, it absolutely sickened me."

Friday, September 21, the Commission examined more witnesses, who testified on the various orders given to carry out the arrest of the assassins. Also examined was the examining magistrate, Mr. Constantinidis, whom Colonel Beaud "treated in his best (or rather worst) manner." Major Harenc believed that the Commission might have accumulated more important evidence and interrogated more people if it had not been for Beaud's "interruptions, and irrelevant questions." At about

Crucial Days: September 12-13

5:00 P.M. the Commission stopped its work for the day in order to take stock of the situation. It also wished to allow the individual members of the Commission time to prepare their opinions for the telegram scheduled to be sent to the Conference of Ambassadors the following day. Beaud opposed the sending of any telegram to the Conference. He felt that nothing had been produced by the Commission. Besides, he added, he had a lot more statements to read which proved that Athens "had done the whole thing." Ultimately he was persuaded to accept the need to send the preliminary report to Paris.

Major Harenc failed to mention in his letter to Athens that Beaud had almost caused a serious incident with the Greek authorities. During the Commission's stay at the scene of the crime it was protected by fifty Greek soldiers. Beaud, however, was dissatisfied with this guard. The arrival at the frontier of Italian *carabinieri* in response to his request provoked a vehement Greek protest. Beaud declared that he desired them to accompany him on Greek territory so he could establish a "courier service to and from Italy." He insisted that the troops be allowed to cross the border. The Greek border troops were ordered to resist if the *carabinieri* attempted to cross the frontier. Colonel Shibouya intervened and advised Beaud not to create a "grave incident." The latter declared that his life was in danger. The rest of the Commissioners failed to agree with this statement. After further discussion the Italians withdrew from the Greek-Albanian frontier.[46]

The crucial meeting to draw up the telegram that was to be dispatched to the Conference was convened the next morning. Beaud's view, as was to be expected, was that the "Greek authorities had been guilty of culpable neglect both as regards the measures taken on the spot, and the subsequent inquiry." Harenc was willing to admit that in both cases "there were instances in which their action might be criticized." But he felt it was easy to criticize, and he believed that the Commission had to keep in mind certain factors: "the well-known inefficiency" of Greek police methods and "the almost insuperable

[46] *Ibid.*, September 24, 1923, p. 12.

Crucial Days: September 12-13

difficulties" involved in capturing persons who committed crimes of this type. Even if witnesses existed, they would not give evidence in "fear of reprisals." Because of these reasons he thought that the Greek Government could not be held guilty by the Commission. Colonels Shibouya and Lacombe "held the same view . . . more or less." The conflicting views of Beaud and the three other officers produced a "stormy meeting." Beaud wanted to dissociate himself from the Commission and "to retire from the unequal contest." However, by "toning down" their opinions the officers were able to arrive at a text to which Beaud agreed.[47] The compromise text was then wired to Paris.[48] The whole episode, Harenc reported to Athens, made him appreciate what "searching for a formula means."

The report sent to the Conference of Ambassadors by the Commission of Inquiry was short. The Commission believed that its investigation up to that point and the complexity of the problem to be solved made it impossible for the Commission to formulate a "firm opinion, definitive and unanimous on the responsibilities incurred during the crime of August 27." However, from the inquiries made and the testimony gathered by the Commission the following had emerged: first, the murder of General Tellini and his staff was so carefully prepared and executed that it was either a "political crime" or a vendetta against General Tellini; second, the investigation following the crime by the Greek authorities revealed several shortcomings, but the evidence gathered on this point was incomplete and

[47] The British chargé d'affaires, Sir Charles Bentinck, informed the American Legation that the British and French representatives on the Commission were inclined to believe that the Greek authorities had acted in "good faith." This view was opposed by the Italian representative, while the Japanese representative was "wavering." Atherton (Athens) to the Department of State, September 23, 1923. File 765.68/83, Record Group 59, NA.

[48] The American Legation reported that it had been "reliably informed that it appeared from the beginning that neither the British nor French delegates felt permitted to hold out against the Italian member of the Commission to such an extent as to cause him to withdraw or announce that Italy was not receiving sympathetic treatment." Atherton (Athens) to the Department of State, October 1923. File 765.68/125, Record Group 59, NA.

Crucial Days: September 12-13

did not permit the Commission to judge if the Greek Government was to be rendered responsible. There was a possibility that these shortcomings resulted from defective police organization and administration. On this point the Italian Commissioner, Colonel Beaud, for reasons of a moral order [*d'ordre moral*], inclined rather towards the former hypothesis, while Colonels Shibouya and Lacombe and Major Harenc inclined towards the latter. The third point was that the Commission had discovered several Greek negligences in the search for the culprits, but noted that the "atmosphere of silence and of fear" which surrounded the crime made the search extremely difficult. Lastly, it assured the Conference that it would actively pursue its investigations and that it was pressuring the Greek authorities to hasten the search for the assassins.[49]

Later that evening the Commission again convened to decide what further measures should be taken to discover the assassins. This meeting like the morning one was "stormy." Since the atmosphere at the morning session had been "overcharged with electricity" Major Harenc had not gotten any definition from Beaud as to what was meant by the phrase "moral order" [*d'ordre moral*]. During this meeting, however, he asked Beaud for a clear definition. The definition given "after much argument was something between suspicion and intuition." In what Harenc admitted was a "tactless" question he asked Beaud, "if people could be condemned on an intuition." This query propelled the Italian Commissioner into explaining why he held the view he did. The end result of this harangue, Harenc observed, was a virtual admission by Beaud that for "all intents and purposes he had been given instructions by his government to prove Botzaris guilty of organizing the crime."

---

[49] Report of the Commission of Inquiry, September 22, 1923. File 768.7515/66, Record Group 59, NA; George Glasgow, *The Janina Murders and the Occupation of Corfu* (London: The Anglo-Hellenic League, 1923), pp. 18-19; partial text in Pierre Lasturel, *L'Affaire Gréco-Italienne de 1923* (Paris: L'Ile de France, 1925), pp. 146-147.

Crucial Days: September 12-13

MUSSOLINI'S INSTRUCTIONS

Beaud's reports of the Commission's work moved Mussolini to cable the Italian Embassies in London and Paris. There was no doubt, he informed them, that the results achieved by the Commission were inconclusive on two points: (1) the identification of the culprits; (2) the possibility of their punishment. Therefore, sufficient grounds existed for awarding Italy the 50 million Italian lire as previously arranged. He wanted to warn that the facts as related by Beaud "about the attitude and the behavior of his colleagues," and especially that of Major Harenc were grave. Even the payment of the 50 million lire would make it hard for Italy to assist in this "cynical action," intended "to give just reparations for a ghastly crime of exceptional gravity." The Duce pointed out that during the Conference discussions, in an attempt to induce Rome to decide on a specific date for the evacuation of Corfu, repeated assurances had been given that the execution of the Conference's demands by Greece would be guaranteed by the Allied Powers. He felt that the Janina investigations demonstrated that this guarantee was being undermined by the Commission of Inquiry. The Commission was impeding and not assisting in the identification and punishment of the assassins. If this situation were to persist Mussolini threatened that Rome "would find itself forced to re-examine if it may not be rightful for it to maintain the pledge of Corfu notwithstanding the payment of the 50 million." This would be done to thwart what appeared to be a "contemptible oppression of international justice." Avezzana in Paris was therefore directed to bring to the attention of the Quai d'Orsay and his colleagues at the Conference "this grave situation which, exasperating the [Italian] Government and [Italian] public opinion" could force it to "run any risk." Della Torretta was requested to take somewhat similar action at the Foreign Office in London.[50]

Avezzana was fully aware of the seriousness of this proposal.

[50] Mussolini to Avezzana (Paris), and Della Torretta (London), September 23, 1923. *DDI*, pp. 259-260.

Crucial Days: September 12-13

Therefore he requested that the Duce give him "precise instructions" on this point. The ambassador noted that at the Conference meeting scheduled for the following day the award of the 50 million lire to Italy would be subordinated, as agreed, to the evacuation of Corfu on September 27. If Mussolini felt this evacuation could not take place for the reasons stipulated in his cable, Avezzana proposed to declare to the Conference that the manner in which the Commission of Inquiry had executed the mandate entrusted to it had impeded rather than assisted the investigation concerning the arrest and punishment of the culprits. Italy could not be satisfied by the penalty offered, which for the moment Rome renounced, keeping instead Corfu, until the arrest and exemplary punishment of the culprits had been realized. He warned, however, that this declaration would provoke all the other members of the Conference, who would never concede that their own officials could be "doubted and disavowed."[51]

With the responsibility for so important a decision squarely in his own hands the Duce struck a quick retreat. If Italian public opinion, he cabled Avezzana, came to know what had occurred at Janina, it would demand the continued occupation of Corfu until the discovery and punishment of the culprits. He felt that he could evade this demand only with difficulty. However, realizing the "gravity of the situation" that could be created, he was "disposed to proceed to the evacuation of Corfu upon the terms decided." His one condition was that the 50 million lire be awarded to Italy by the Conference as quickly as possible. In the case where the Conference failed to assign the 50 million to Italy Avezzana was to claim Italy's "liberty [of] action."[52]

In line with Mussolini's instructions, Della Torretta in London hurried to the Foreign Office. In a long conversation with the Assistant Under-Secretary of State for Foreign Affairs, Sir Ronald Lindsay, he made it clear that a very "grave situa-

[51] Avezzana (Paris) to Mussolini, September 24, 1923. *Ibid.*, pp. 261-262.

[52] Mussolini to Avezzana (Paris), repeated to Della Torretta (London), September 24, 1923. *Ibid.*, p. 262.

Crucial Days: September 12-13

tion" could develop if the Janina inquiry continued to develop in the same manner. Della Torretta repeated the Duce's threat that the Italian Government might have to "re-examine the entire situation especially in respect [to the] Corfu pledge." The ambassador noted that his government wanted to warn London of the dangers that lay ahead because of the attitude of the Allied Commissioners at Janina. He added that the time had arrived to avoid such dangers by calling the attention of Major Harenc to a "more strict observance of his task." Sir Ronald "remained very much impressed" by Della Torretta's remarks, but protested against allegations having to do with the behavior of Major Harenc. He confirmed that it was the desire of his government to see justice done. Della Torretta retorted that the British Commissioner at Janina had not given proof of his correct behavior. However, Della Torretta himself had no distrust of the British Government. At the conclusion of the interview Lindsay informed the ambassador that "opportune instructions would be sent to Janina" after he had consulted with Lord Curzon.[53]

Any instructions subsequently sent, however, were to be of no importance. The Conference in its meeting the following day, September 25, acted on the strength of the Commission of Inquiry's ambiguous report of September 22.

[53] Della Torretta (London) to Mussolini, September 24, 1923. *Ibid.*, pp. 262-263. Receipt of the Commission of Inquiry's report in Paris prompted Avezzana to write to Della Torretta. He felt that the wording of the report justified that the 50 million Italian lire be awarded to Italy under the terms of his September 13 declaration to the Conference. Avezzana "had reason to believe" that the French delegation at the Ambassadors' Conference would support this point of view. Therefore, he requested that Della Torretta bring the whole question to Tyrrell's attention as a "precaution." The latter, he explained, on a recent trip to Paris had been warned that the result of a "contrary decision would be to defer" the whole question of the Corfu evacuation. Avezzana (Paris) to Della Torretta (London), September 23, 1923. Italian Archives. Della Torretta replied two days later that he had brought the whole matter to the attention of Sir Ronald Lindsay. His impression, however, was that the Foreign Office doubted the report sent by the Commission of Inquiry on September 22 would be sufficient to warrant a "definite decision" at this time. Della Torretta (London) to Avezzana (Paris), September 25, 1923. Italian Archives.

CHAPTER VIII

SURRENDER

THE CONFERENCE'S DECISION: GREECE MUST PAY

THE two hundred and thirty-first meeting of the Conference of Ambassadors, called to consider the Commission of Inquiry's report of September 22, convened on the afternoon of September 25. It was in session for almost three hours.[1]

The discussion was begun by Lord Crewe, who declared that in the opinion of his government the report did not justify a penalty of 50 million lire. The British Government considered this report a preliminary report, and not a final one. He was willing to admit it indicated that the Greek authorities had not arrived at any results, but it did not prove that the Greek Government had been guilty of negligence. It was possible that after further investigation the Commission of Inquiry would succeed in establishing in a more precise manner the responsibility of the Greek Government. At the moment, however, this responsibility was not clearly established. Crewe, therefore, thought that the Greek Government and public opinion had good grounds for believing that the amount of the penalty would not be immediately determined, but that the Conference would have to leave it to the Permanent Court of International Justice at The Hague for final settlement.

As expected, Avezzana's opinion was exactly contrary to that of Lord Crewe. He called his colleagues' attention to the terms of his declaration of September 13. In this declaration each ex-

---

[1] Unless cited otherwise the material that follows is drawn from the *procès-verbal* of the two hundred and thirty-first meeting of the Conference of Ambassadors, September 25, 1923. File 763.72119/12033, Record Group 59, NA.

For an excellent synopsis of the meeting see Whitehouse (Paris) to the Department of State, September 26, 1923. File 765.68/86, Record Group 59, NA.

Surrender

pression had been carefully formulated and had been accepted and recorded as a decision of the Conference of Ambassadors. The declaration did not allow very much latitude to the Conference. During the discussions of September 12 and 13 he had been pressed to fix a specific date for the evacuation of Corfu. Ultimately he had come to an agreement with the Conference on a proviso that would operate automatically.

The Conference had considered that if the Italian Government would evacuate Corfu before September 27, it would be equitable that before this date a final decision be taken on the matter of the arrest and punishment of the culprits. This decision conformed to the promises made by the Conference, and it commanded the attention of Italian public opinion. The latter was more directly interested in the regulation of the affair than British public opinion, since the victims of the outrage were Italian. For reasons of self-respect, of prestige and of public opinion, it was therefore indispensable that September 27, the date of the conclusion of the investigation, also marked the conclusion of the incident. Avezzana observed that in the note addressed to Greece, the Conference had written as follows: "the Commission of Inquiry ... five days after its arrival, will communicate ... its first impressions. On the basis of this report, the Conference will decide."[2] He therefore felt that the Conference had to take an immediate decision.

He then turned the attention of his colleagues to an examination of his declaration of September 13, in which he had stated the following: "if on this date [September 27], the culprits are not discovered, and if it is not established that the Greek Government has not committed any negligence ... the Conference will inflict on Greece as penalty, the payment of a sum of 50 million lire to Italy."[3] The Conference, he noted, certainly could not have forgotten the discussion of this text. In particular it could not have forgotten his insistence, in spite of the objections of Lord Crewe, that the Conference maintain the following negative formula: "if it is not established that the Greek Government has not committed any negligence."[4]

[2] *DDDIG*, p. 40. [3] *Supra*, Chapter VII. [4] *Ibid*.

Surrender

Avezzana understood this phrase to indicate, and the Conference had agreed with him, that it laid upon the Greek Government a presumption of culpability. Thus it put the burden of proof on the shoulders of the Greek Government. In order for the Greek Government to be acknowledged culpable it was only necessary to show that it had been unsuccessful in establishing that it had not committed any negligence.

Turning to the report of the Commission of Inquiry, Avezzana next attempted to establish that the terms of this report permitted the Conference to inflict on the Greek Government the penalty provided for. First, he recounted to his colleagues all the details of the crime: the breakdown of the automobile of Colonel Botzaris, which providentially permitted him to escape the massacre, and the trees thrown across the road in order to retard the progress of Tellini's automobile. He asked his colleagues the following questions. Could one admit that no clues were left from a crime so minutely prepared? Had the Greek Government done anything in order to attempt to hasten the investigations? Had it dispatched to Epirus officials other than those who were present on the spot? His answers were no. On the contrary, the Greek Government had not even hesitated to confide the direction of the inquiry to a personality as implicated as Colonel Botzaris. None of these statements by Avezzana and particularly the latter was challenged.[5]

Second, the report of the Commission of Inquiry pointed out that certain shortcomings had been revealed in the conduct of the investigation. This, he admitted, was qualified by the second paragraph in which the Commission attempted to attenuate the responsibilities of the Greek Government by attributing these shortcomings to the defective organization of the

[5] Colonel Botzaris was not in charge of the investigation. When word of the murder reached Janina, Colonel Platis, the commander of the Epirus gendarmerie immediately took charge of the investigation, supported by other police and judicial officials. He was subsequently assisted by Colonel Florias, the Director-General of the Greek gendarmerie as well as other police and judicial officials who had been dispatched from Athens by the government. *Supra*, Chapter II.

Surrender

Greek police.[6] Avezzana could not admit these attenuations. Statistics showed that Athens did not have more unpunished crime than either London or Paris. The Greek Government had at its command an excellent police. The Greek criminal code of instruction was perfected and patterned on the German criminal code of instruction.

Third, the report of the Commission also established that negligences had been revealed in the search for the culprits. These admissions alone, Avezzana declared, were enough to set in motion the clause provided for in his declaration of September 13, which read: "if it is not established that the Greek Government has not committed any negligence." He was willing to admit that in this case also the Commission believed it had found an excuse for the Greek Government in calling attention to the atmosphere of fear that surrounded the crime.[7] He personally was not convinced by this argument, but saw rather aggravating circumstances.

Lastly, the Commission's cable pointed out that it was acting energetically in order to bring about the discovery of the culprits. He concluded from this expression that the Commission had brought pressure on the Greek authorities and surmised that the latter had not done their duty.[8] For all these reasons he considered that he had the right to insist on the penalty provided. If Italy were to evacuate Corfu without the 50 million lire being awarded to her, and without the culprits having been discovered, she would consider herself deceived.

Taking somewhat the same line as Lord Crewe, Mr. Sato, the Japanese delegate, declared that in his opinion the report of the Commission was perhaps not conclusive enough. He appreciated the difficulties of the Italian Government with respect to internal public opinion, but wondered if out of regard for the sensitivities of the small Powers, it would not be possible to wait for the end of the Greek investigation and

[6] George Glasgow, *The Janina Murders and the Occupation of Corfu* (London: The Anglo-Hellenic League, 1923), p. 18.
[7] *Ibid.*, p. 19.   [8] *Ibid.*

Surrender

the second report of the Commission before determining the penalty to be inflicted.

This would be too late, Avezzana replied. He had presented a bill of exchange on the date of expiration. He had a right to demand that his request be acceded to. The penalty provided for had to be applied. Avezzana reaffirmed all the terms of his September 13 declaration. If Italy had to evacuate Corfu on September 27, it was necessary to obtain the satisfaction demanded. The report of the Commission of Inquiry was conclusive; the culprits had not been arrested nor was it foreseen that the situation would change within the next two days. Negligences for which the Greek Government was responsible had also been cited. The decision of the Conference had to be executed.

What did the report of the Commission of Inquiry in fact say, Lord Crewe queried? That the Greek police are not as well organized as the Prefecture of Police of Paris or that of Scotland Yard? This was very obvious. Had not England undergone in Ireland great difficulties in discovering similar persons of the type who had murdered the Tellini Mission and had not the Italian Government run up against the same difficulties in Sicily?

At this point, according to the American observer, Whitehouse, "matters became rather strained and the Italian Ambassador remarked that the evacuation of Corfu was dependent [up]on the Conference['s] carrying out [the] terms of his declaration."[9]

That Greece must be held to the payment was not contested by Lord Crewe, but he regretted that the Italian Government did not believe it could wait for the definitive report of the Commission. This report would permit perhaps the infliction of a less rigorous penalty on the Greek Government.

Here Jules Cambon intervened and "made a long and masterly exposition of the whole case."[10] He considered that

---

[9] Whitehouse (Paris) to the Department of State, September 26, 1923. File 765.68/86, Record Group 59, NA.

[10] Whitehouse (Paris) to the Department of State, September 26, 1923. File 765.68/86, Record Group 59, NA.

Surrender

the Conference was bound; it had taken a decision, it had to execute it. The pledge deposited by the Greek Government had to be converted into a penalty. There really was nothing more to discuss concerning the penalty. Though the Commission's report revealed certain differences among the Commissioners it had been unanimous on the following points: no culprits had been discovered, and there had been negligences on the part of the Greek Government. These two statements were enough to set in motion the proviso of September 13. Cambon was also struck by two other points. First, though there was nothing to incriminate the Greek Government directly, it appeared that the same did not hold true for Greek officials and army officers. This fact in itself was sufficient to involve indirectly the responsibility of the Greek Government. What had the latter done to clear itself? What had it done in order to dissipate the presumptions that resulted from the conduct of its agents? Had it removed from office, or at least suspended, a single local official? Had it sent from Athens a single higher official, foreign to the local passions, in order to affirm its impartiality? Cambon's reply to these questions was negative. On the contrary, the Greek Government had excused all its agents, and the investigation had been entrusted precisely to those officials and army officers who were in Epirus. As was the case with Avezzana, no one at the Conference contested his statements and conclusions.[11] There was no need to assume, Cambon observed, that these officials had themselves participated in the crime, in order to explain the laxity with which they had pursued the investigation. If their negligence had permitted the crime, their negligence in searching for the culprits explained itself perfectly. Second, he raised another question that seemed to call for the Conference's attention. This was the breakdown of the automobile of Colonel Botzaris who was accompanying General Tellini. The breakdown of Botzaris' automobile permitted him to escape the outrage. Was it not strange, he asked, that it took Botzaris one hour to repair his vehicle. Why hadn't he tried to take another automo-

[11] *Supra*, this chapter, footnote 5.

Surrender

bile?[12] Avezzana interrupted to state that when General Tellini encountered Colonel Botzaris on the road he offered to take him in his vehicle and the latter refused.[13] Continuing, Cambon found equally peculiar Colonel Botzaris' attitude after the murder. The latter had merely gazed at the corpses and left the scene of the crime. He felt that this was a peculiar reaction on the part of a colonel.[14] Because of these facts, why hadn't the Greek Government hesitated before entrusting to Colonel Botzaris the direction of the investigation?

Finally, Cambon desired to submit to his colleagues one last observation. There was no doubt the Janina affair was entering into the judicial phase of its investigation. This, however, did not change the character of the Conference. The Conference should remember that it was not a tribunal but a diplomatic body. Consequently, it had to take into account certain considerations. The Conference knew the sentiments that animated the statesman who was the chief of the Italian Government. If this statesman had occupied Corfu it was because he wished to give satisfaction to his country's public opinion, satisfaction that would perhaps calm this over-excited opinion. Cambon admitted that he was struck by Avezzana's declaration that in Italy they would think themselves deceived if the Italian Government evacuated Corfu without the culprits having been discovered or a penalty inflicted on the Greek Gov-

---

[12] Cambon's statement was incorrect. Colonel Botzaris had attempted to switch vehicles with the nephew of the Archbishop of Janina. Colonel Botzaris' Report, September 5, 1923. Pierre Lasturel, *L'Affaire Gréco-Italienne de 1923* (Paris: L'Ile de France, 1925), p. 43.

[13] Avezzana's statement would appear incorrect. According to Colonel Botzaris, General Tellini had only dispatched his aide-de-camp, Lt. Bonaccini, to ask if their chauffeur could assist in the repair of the Greek vehicle. *Ibid.*, p. 43.

[14] Colonel Botzaris had spotted only four bodies when he arrived at the scene of the crime. He believed that Lt. Bonaccini might have been taken captive. Therefore, he quickly retraced his steps to alert the army troops stationed in the area in order to save Bonaccini. *Ibid.*, pp. 44-45.

The inference in Cambon's statement was regrettable. Colonel Botzaris had served in the Greek Army with great distinction, especially in the Greek campaign in Anatolia. The sight of a human corpse was thus not new to him.

Surrender

ernment. If Italian public opinion were thus to interpret the decision of the Conference the consequences could be "grave." Would not the Italian Government be tempted to say: "We have promised to evacuate Corfu, we will evacuate it, but we do not wish to appear to have let ourselves be taken advantage of by the Conference of Ambassadors, which takes decisions without having the courage to execute them"? Would not the Italian Government under these conditions be brought to consider measures similar to those of the Corfu occupation? Perhaps they might even maintain the occupation of Corfu. These measures might have the effect of reopening difficulties that the Conference wished permanently to put aside. Cambon did not contest that 50 million lire represented a considerable sum of money; but appeasement of public opinion in Italy, satisfaction given to the League for the evacuation of Corfu, complete recovery by Greece of its sovereign authority in the Ionian Islands, the peace of Europe, and the peace of the world would not be very dearly bought at this price. One fact was certain: the Greek Government was responsible for its agents. The conditions laid down in Avezzana's declaration of September 13 had not been satisfied. Under these conditions the Conference had the right to say, "if [by] September 27, the date fixed for the end of the Greek investigation, the Conference is not advised that the culprits have been arrested a penalty of 50 million lire will be inflicted on Greece."

Striving to reply, Lord Crewe pointed out to Cambon that it was not absolutely exact to say that the Greek Government had never thought of entrusting the investigation to other than local officials. The Greek Government had sent to Janina, on the very first day, an English police official who had been charged with the reorganization of the Greek police. If the latter did not actually proceed to Janina it was on the formal instructions of the British Government, which feared that such a mission would produce a bad effect.[15]

He was not convinced by Lord Crewe's observations, Cam-

[15] In an obvious error, the *procès-verbal* states that it was the Greek Government which ordered him not to proceed to Janina.

Surrender

bon retorted. He recalled, as an example, an incident between France and Germany in 1913 when he was ambassador to Berlin. In Nancy, four or five Germans in a café had been insulted by some students. The French Government under M. Poincaré did not hesitate in the least. It was certainly not a criminal matter, but simply a quarrel in a café; the Prefect was innocent. The French Government, however, had considered that the Prefect was, in any case, responsible for the good order in his Department. It had had him immediately removed. The investigation pursued by his successor had demonstrated the correct behavior of the Prefect and the French authorities. Thus Cambon had been able to bring simultaneously to the attention of the German Government the news of the Prefect's removal and the results of the investigation which had been carried out by the Prefect's successor. This had established officially that the public authority had had nothing to do with the incident.

The Greek Government, Cambon believed, could have at the very least given similar satisfaction to the Italian Government. Satisfaction of this type might have dispelled all suspicion of Greek indifference. In consideration of the gravity of the matter, it could have sent from Athens a personage more important than a chief of police. It could have sent a member of the government, or some other official, who could have taken the principal direction of the investigation. Instead, the Greek Government had done nothing. The Conference was therefore in the presence of a situation which permitted it to penalize the Athens government if, by September 27, it had not succeeded in discovering the culprits. In taking such a decision the Conference would only be remaining faithful to its obligations.

This penalty was not without precedent, Avezzana recalled. The American Government had only recently demanded a penalty of $25,000 for the murder of one of its nationals in China. He also recalled the lynchings of Italian citizens in New Orleans. In that incident it had been impossible for the American Government to find the culprits because of the com-

Surrender

plicity of the local authorities. But the Federal Government, prevented by the American Constitution from intervening in the investigation conducted by the authorities of New Orleans, had offered spontaneously to pay an indemnity. The doubts, Avezzana believed, of his colleague from England concerning the amount of the indemnity would not be insurmountable. On the other hand, he regretted that he found himself unable to accept the suggestion made by Cambon. It was impossible for the Italian Government to wait until September 27 to fix the penalty.

The report of the Commission, Avezzana maintained, established the negligence of the Greek Government. The proviso in his declaration of September 13 had to be executed. This was a moral question. It would be difficult to postpone a decision. What will the Conference do, he queried, if it is advised on September 27 that the Greek Government has arrested a rural policeman. If the Conference had not insisted that the Italian Government fix a specific date for the evacuation of Corfu, it would perhaps have been possible for him to lend himself to concessions. But the Conference had pressed him and the Italian Government had not hesitated to comply with these pressures, despite the reluctance it felt in consenting to such a sacrifice. Therefore, his government had the right to demand today that an obvious penalty be inflicted on the Greek Government. This penalty was the only reparation that Rome could still hope to obtain for the horrible massacre of its officers. Conforming to Mussolini's instructions, Avezzana made it clear to the Conference what Italy's future position might be if no penalty were inflicted on Greece. Rome had given great publicity to the promise made by the Conference. If the latter were not in a position to keep its promise, Italian public opinion would be disappointed and his government "would no longer be able to give assurances that it will be in a position to keep its promises with regard to the date of the evacuation of Corfu."

In an attempt to stop the Franco-Italian steamroller, Lord Crewe commented that if the Greek Government had not yet

Surrender

removed the officials it would perhaps do so after the end of the investigation. Such a gesture would be tardy, Cambon declared. It was no longer a question today of the dismissal of an official. In any case, none of the local officials had been the object of a disciplinary measure and this was enough to involve the responsibility of the Greek Government. "Obviously impressed" by Cambon's statement, Lord Crewe, in a "conciliatory way,"[16] replied that his instructions did not permit him to accept the proposal of the Italian Ambassador. He suggested that the Conference reassemble the following day. Cambon, however, insisted that in the interests of peace of mind the Conference had to make a decision that same day. At this point, Crewe was deserted by Sato, the Japanese delegate, who declared that he adhered entirely to the formula proposed by M. Cambon.

Referring to Avezzana's declaration of September 13, Laroche now called to the attention of his colleagues that in the opinion of M. Fromageot the burden of proof was upon the Greek Government. He feared that some confusion in this regard might have been created in the minds of the Allied Commissioners at Janina. There existed not only a general presumption against the Greek Government, but also a particular presumption. It was enough that omissions and negligences on the part of the Greek authorities had been discovered in order that the decision of September 13 be applied. Lastly, he wished to make known to the Conference, in all confidence, that he had received information from M. Henri de Marcilly, the French Minister in Athens, to the effect that there was reason to assume that the Greek Government had attempted to cover up the trail of the assassins.

Insistent, Avezzana regretted that he was unable to accept the compromise proposal suggested by M. Cambon. He asked that the penalty of 50 million lire be immediately imposed on the Greek Government. At Avezzana's insistence, Cambon succumbed and recognized that the interpretation given by his

[16] Whitehouse (Paris) to the Department of State, September 26, 1923. File 765.68/86, Record Group 59, NA.

Surrender

Italian colleague to the decision of September 13 was absolutely exact. Under these conditions, he did not insist on his compromise proposal, especially since September 27 was so close that tomorrow [September 26] the investigation would be virtually finished.

Refusing to be pressured, Lord Crewe reiterated that he would have to refer the matter to his government. Though Avezzana understood perfectly the qualms of the English Government, he wondered if the latter understood the "gravity of the situation." He assured Lord Crewe that if he were also compromising it was because of his love of peace. He repeated the desire that Corfu be evacuated by September 27. He then added that his government was in possession of a report from its delegate, Colonel Beaud, on the Commission of Inquiry. He had not wished before now to make an issue of this report, but if it were published in Italy it could create a very serious situation and provoke a general swelling of indignation which would be difficult for his government to resist. Lord Crewe retorted sharply that he would regret such publication, because the question would then be posed whether or not to publish the reports that certain governments had received from their Commissioners on the conduct of the Italian delegate.

Closing the meeting, Laroche declared that the French Government considered itself bound by the Conference's decision of September 13. If the Conference decided this very day to inflict on Greece a penalty of 50 million lire, it would only be adhering strictly to the letter of its decision. With these words the Conference adjourned. As on other occasions during the preceding weeks it was in London and with Lord Curzon that the fateful decision lay.

CURZON AGREES TO THE CONFERENCE'S DECISION

Avezzana immediately informed Mussolini that the Conference's inability to come to a decision was the result of England's opposition. Lord Crewe had "made use of every sort of argument in order to demonstrate [the] innocence [of the] Greek Government." However, on the basis of his declaration

Surrender

of September 13 and the report of the Commission of Inquiry he had requested the transferral to Italy of the 50 million lire deposited by Greece. Avezzana felt the French had loyally supported him throughout the discussions. He also disclosed that in conformity with the Duce's instructions he had warned Lord Crewe that if the Italian request were turned down Rome would consider that the Conference had not executed its pledge because of British opposition. This situation would give to his government "liberty of action relative to the evacuation of Corfu."[17]

From London, the Greek Legation reported to Athens that the "general impression" was that the question of the indemnity had to be referred to The Hague Court. It cautioned, however, that information arriving from Paris indicated that the French Government wanted to deliver immediately the 50 million lire to Italy in order to "avoid new difficulties."[18]

No sooner had this cable been sent than a second one was flashed to Athens. According to the legation, the French Government had received a "very alarming telegram" from M. Camille Barrère, its ambassador in Rome, dealing with Italy's attitude and its continuing military preparations. Receipt of this report, it informed the Foreign Ministry, had prompted the Quai d'Orsay to consider it preferable to award Italy the 50 million lire in order to hasten the evacuation of Corfu.[19] Somewhat similar reports by the Greek Minister in Paris, after interviews with Jules Laroche[20] and Jules Cambon,[21] must have spread gloom throughout the Greek Ministry of Foreign Affairs.

Any hope in the Greek Foreign Ministry that England

[17] Avezzana (Paris) to Mussolini, September 25, 1923. *DDI*, pp. 263-264.
[18] London, No. 3386 to the Foreign Ministry, September 25, 1923. French text. Greek Archives.
[19] London, 3388 to the Foreign Ministry, September 25, 1923. Greek Archives.
[20] Romanos (Paris) to the Foreign Ministry, September 25, 1923. Greek Archives.
[21] Romanos (Paris), No. 5046 to the Foreign Ministry, September 26, 1923. Greek Archives.

Surrender

might save the situation was futile. Lord Crewe, in a dispatch and telegram to Lord Curzon, pointed out that the decision of his colleagues at the Conference to award Italy the 50 million lire, "left no alternative solution."[22] As Crewe revealed years afterwards, it was understood that if the matter reverted to the League and Italy's action was condemned, "Italy would at once have retired from the League." This threat was not surprising, for Italy had never been one of its most enthusiastic members and the League ideals were in direct opposition to the Duce's conception of "what was due to the Roman Empire." However, collective security by a combination repudiated by the United States, Germany, and Russia, as well as Italy, "did not sound genuine, so that the French and British Governments did not relish the prospect of becoming solely responsible for the peace of the world. So it was thought wise not to haggle, but to admit the excessive indemnity."[23] Curzon, explaining his decision to award Italy the 50 million lire, wrote to Lord Crewe that after a careful reading of Avezzana's declaration of September 13, he found that Crewe's colleagues "had apparently given the case away, whether consciously or not," he could not say. He found it difficult to believe that the Conference had meant to compel the Greeks to pay the full fine and to drop the reference to The Hague Court. Yet this appeared to be what the Conference had done by agreeing to Avezzana's declaration. The only consolation was that the Greeks would rather pay than see the Italians "remain in Corfu."[24]

[22] James Pope-Hennessy, *Lord Crewe, 1858-1948; the Likeness of a Liberal* (London: Constable and Co. Ltd., 1955), p. 166.
[23] The Marquess of Crewe, "Lord Cecil and the League," *The Fortnightly*, CXLIX, New Series (March 1941), p. 214.
[24] Lord Curzon to Lord Crewe, September 26, 1923. Pope-Hennessy, pp. 166-167.
The text of Lord Curzon's letter is as follows: "that the attitude of the French was all wrong, and that the Ambassadors were about to condemn Greece in the face of the evidence to pay the full penalty for an offence which there was no proof that she had ever committed—and all this to prevent a fresh display of lawless bravado and duplicity on the part of Mussolini. But when I began to look carefully into the text of your note of September 13—and of Avezzana's declaration of the

Surrender

Curzon reiterated this point at the Imperial Conference two weeks later—that the Ambassadors had given "away the case by the language they had accepted." Thus England found that it "had no alternative" but to instruct Lord Crewe to agree to the award of the 50 million to Italy. England, he admitted to the Prime Ministers, "felt very greatly the responsibility" that might devolve upon her if any action on her part, "however justifiable, were responsible for a great European conflagration which really was on the verge of bursting out." The attitude assumed, or as Curzon called it, this "sacrifice," was taken in order to maintain what he "held to be the cardinal principle of European policy at this moment, namely, the entente between ourselves and our allies." He thought that the Conference's decision "was unjustified by the evidence, that it was a political and not a judicial decision." Its sole "justification . . . was that it saved . . . Europe from the chances of very grave complications."[25]

---

same date, I found (I wish I hadn't) that your colleagues had apparently given the case away, whether consciously or not I cannot say. . . . That you can ever have meant to compel the Greeks to pay the full fine—even increased—and to drop the reference to the Hague (except on the point of costs of occupation) I can hardly believe. But that seemed to me the actual result of what the Ambassadors had done, tho', being no lawyer, I have no authority in interpreting texts. . . . It is rather a humiliating finale (if indeed it is that) of the episode. But I daresay even the Greeks would sooner pay than see the Italians remain in Corfu."

[25] Imperial Conference 1923. Stenographic notes of the Sixth Meeting, held at 10 Downing Street, S.W., on Thursday, October 11, 1923, at 11:00 A.M., pp. 5-6. Folder marked "Imperial Conferences, 1921, 1923," Box 22, Curzon Papers.

Lord Curzon also revealed to the Imperial Conference the actions of the Commission of Inquiry. "The Italian representative on this Commission," according to Lord Curzon, "conducted his case with shameless partiality. He announced that he was not only a member of the Commission, but that he had come with a special mission from Signor Mussolini—which was only too true; he assumed throughout the guilt of the Greeks; he acted upon the hypothesis that a Greek Colonel, Colonel Botzaris, was the person responsible; he threw every possible obstacle in the way of his colleagues who were united on the other side. The Commission sent a preliminary report that they could not fix the responsibility for the murder, that there had been some negligence

Surrender

Curzon's decision not to oppose the award of the 50 million lire to Italy was taken without consultation with Lord Robert Cecil at Geneva. As the latter complained years later, the whole episode was "an excellent example of the evil of treating our League policy as something apart from the general foreign policy of the country."[26]

The explanation by Curzon to the cabinet, on the morning of September 26, as to why Lord Crewe had been instructed to support the award to Italy of the 50 million lire provoked a sharp reply from the First Lord of the Admiralty, Leopold S. Amery. He declared that the decision "was a really bad blow to the League of Nations." Amery felt that the League "might have survived the reference to the Ambassadors' Conference with credit if the decision had been a just one." However, the present decision "was bound to shake the faith of all the small Powers."[27]

THE CONFERENCE'S NOTE TO GREECE

In Paris, Lord Crewe hurried to relay to the Conference Curzon's message agreeing to award to Italy the 50 million lire. The Conference reconvened on September 26 at 11:15 A.M. for its two hundred and thirty-second meeting.[28] The session was very short.

---

on the part of the Greek local authorities in conducting the enquiry and making the necessary search for the criminals, but whether the Greek Government had any responsibility for this they were not agreed. It now transpires that the three of them were agreed that no responsibility was attached to the Greek Government at all, but that in order to get the unanimous consent of all parties on the Commission, they put the thing in that negative and ambiguous way, not knowing what had happened at Paris and not realizing for a moment that this ambiguity would be taken advantage of there, in view of the words that had been accepted at Paris, to afford the excuse to the Italian Government to escape from their obligation with regard to the evacuation [of Corfu]."

[26] Lord Robert Cecil, *A Great Experiment* (New York: Oxford University Press, 1941), pp. 150-151.

[27] Diary of L[eopold] S. A[mery] 1923. Entry [September] 26, 1923. Amery Papers.

[28] *Procès-verbal* of the two hundred and thirty-second meeting of the Conference of Ambassadors, September 26, 1923. File 763.72119/12033, Record Group 59, NA.

Surrender

Lord Crewe was thanked by Avezzana and Cambon for his message permitting the successful adjustment of an incident whose consequences could have been disagreeable. The decision, Cambon felt, would bring a great relaxation of tension in the Adriatic and would contribute to the general peace. Crewe observed crisply that his government believed it was important to adjust the incident as quickly as possible and this was the reason it had decided to make known its acceptance.

The Conference then drew up the note which was to be forwarded to the Greek Government informing them of the Conference's decision. The Conference's communication to Athens took note of the fact that Greece had executed reparations 1, 2, 3, and 4, required by its note of September 8, in addition to the subsequent conditions set forth in its note of September 13. It also took note of the report of the Commission of Inquiry dated September 22. In conformity with paragraph 5 of its note of September 13, it examined this report in respect to the execution of paragraph 5 of its earlier note of September 8. The note went on to state that on the day the Commission's report had been issued, the culprits had not been found. It observed that the report of the Commission had pointed out failures concerning the conduct of the inquiry by the Greek authorities, as well as negligences concerning the search for the culprits. Consequently, the Conference had decided that the fifth condition of its note of September 8 had not been fulfilled. By way of penalty it directed the Greek Government to pay to the Italian Government a sum of 50 million Italian lire.

The Conference and the Italian Government at the same time renounced any recourse to The Hague Court as contemplated by paragraph 7 of its note of September 8, as well as any other penalty. The question as far as the Conference and Italy were concerned was settled. The only "particular recourse" to The Hague Court that the note envisaged was "by Italy . . . on the question of the costs of the occupation." The note specified that the money was to be paid to the Italian Government by transferring the 50 million lire deposited by

Surrender

the Greek Government on September 10 in the Swiss National Bank. Therefore, The Hague Court was to be requested to order the transfer of the said sum by the Swiss National Bank to the Bank of Italy in Rome to the account of the Italian Government. The note observed that the Italian Government would carry out on September 27 its previously announced decision to evacuate Corfu on that date. It ended by asking the Greek Government to execute all the necessary measures as quickly as possible.[29]

While the note to Athens was being drafted by his colleagues, Cambon left the room to speak to the First Secretary of the Greek Legation, Léon Melas, who was waiting outside. He explained to Melas that though it might appear strange, he felt that Greece should congratulate herself on the decision taken by the Conference. In reality, he observed, Greece would have had to pay in any event an equivalent sum to the slain victims' families and for the occupation costs. The Conference's decision, however, excluded all arbitration payments. In ending the conversation, he added "that if [the] decision ratified [by the Conference] had been different Italy would have taken against . . . [Greece] measures which would have rendered [the] situation extremely grave."[30]

The communication of the Conference's note the following day to the Greek Legation in Paris moved its minister to write immediately to Jules Cambon. Romanos inquired what was meant in the Conference's note by the statement that Italy could have "particular recourse" before The Hague Court "for the costs of the occupation." He desired Cambon to renew the assurances he had given Melas the previous day that the decision taken by the Conference "excluded all other payments." The minister informed Athens it was not certain that Italy would address herself to the International Court of Justice at The Hague. However, he believed that in such an eventuality Greece would in turn be able to "demand intervention for

---

[29] *DDDIG*, pp. 40-41. *Infra*, Appendix D.
[30] Romanos (Paris), No. 5057 to the Foreign Ministry, September 26, 1923. French text. Greek Archives.

Surrender

damages sustained by fact of the occupation and for [the] victims [of the] bombardment."[31] Romanos' suggestion had already been anticipated by Politis ten days before when he had sent the Foreign Ministry a detailed plan.[32]

Cambon in reply to Romanos' letter feared that some sort of a misunderstanding may have occurred between himself and M. Melas. He believed that he had told Melas that the capital point was the Italian evacuation of Corfu which was tied to a specific date.[33] Romanos' anxieties, however, proved unfounded. Rome never appealed to The Hague Court for the costs of the occupation.

ATHENS CONCEDES

Lord Crewe observed in a letter to Lord Curzon that the Corfu business had ended in a way that was inevitable when "the burden of proving no negligence had been shown by the Greeks was placed upon *them*, and not, as it should have been, upon the Commission to prove positively." He agreed with Curzon that the 50 million lire would be regarded simply as a payment for the evacuation of the island. He had stressed this during the Conference discussions. Avezzana, as was to be expected, had contradicted him and, though Jules Cambon had said nothing on this point, he did admit "privately that it was impossible to regard the payment in any other light." Crewe reported that Avezzana's contention was that his government simply could not evacuate Corfu "without having something to show in order to satisfy public opinion." He felt

---

[31] Romanos (Paris), No. 5076 to the Foreign Ministry, September 27, 1923. French text. Greek Archives; Copy of a letter Romanos (Paris) to Jules Cambon, September 27, 1923. Greek Archives.

[32] Politis (Geneva), No. 1252 to the Foreign Ministry, September 18, 1923. French text. Greek Archives.

Politis proposed that in any adjudication before the Permanent Court of International Justice at The Hague, Greece could claim damages for the following: (1) the bombardment of Corfu; (2) taxes gathered by the Italian authorities; (3) reduction in customs caused at Corfu during the Italian occupation.

[33] Copy of a letter by Cambon (Aix-les-Bains) to Romanos (Paris), October 1, 1923. Greek Archives.

Surrender

this was true in a sense, but that this often followed "when public opinion is deliberately excited, as it was in this instance." Lord Crewe believed that under the circumstances it was the "best conclusion that could have been reached," and he certainly did his "utmost to make it a better one." The major achievement was to have "secured a definite promise of the immediate evacuation of Corfu," but since the occupation was "an invasion of public right," one could not "regard the outcome as a triumph." On the other hand, since "nobody was prepared to take stronger measures, there may have been no other way." He revealed that he told Avezzana that the Foreign Office had not altered its opinion that Italy had been wrong in occupying Corfu. Avezzana admitted that the "action was unwarranted," but pointed out that in the past England had taken similar steps in order to achieve redress. Crewe acknowledged that this had been true in the past, but added that after the war everyone had hoped "a new era was beginning, in which reparation for injury done would be secured by combined action, and not through the use of force by any one nation." Avezzana agreed that England had reformed and was ahead of Italy in this respect. He hoped that in time Italy would also reform. "He spoke almost laughingly," Crewe noted to Curzon, "but I am pretty sure that he feels that his government made a gross blunder, and that, they are lucky to escape from it so easily."[34]

This letter by Lord Crewe was followed by another letter to Lord Curzon the following day [September 27]. The whole business still bothered him and he observed that it was a "sorry instance of the low level which postwar morality had reached," in every European state without exception. Therefore, it was only natural that the United States "enveloped in her white robe of virtue does not wish to soil it by rubbing shoulder with such an unclean crowd."[35] Words in a similar vein were

[34] Lord Crewe (Paris) to Lord Curzon, September 26, 1923. Folder marked "Correspondence with Lord Crewe, Ambassador to Paris 1922-1924," Box 22, Curzon Papers.

[35] Lord Crewe (Paris) to Lord Curzon, September 27, 1923. Folder

Surrender

repeated in a third letter dealing with the affair. What Lord Palmerston or Napoleon III did, he noted, had no more bearing on current events than the acts of men like Oliver Cromwell or Cardinal Richelieu. He believed, he wrote to Curzon, that "all these controversies are barren if since the war, the nations are going to attempt to move on a higher plane of conduct."[36]

In Janina, word of the Conference's decision provoked a sharp reaction from the Allied Commissioners. Colonel Lacombe, the French delegate, felt the Commission of Inquiry had been "duped." According to Lord Curzon, Colonel Shibouya declared that the Commission's work had been futile from the start "since a decision was evidently taken in advance."[37] Similar sentiments were held by Major Harenc, who stated that too much importance had been given to the "unconclusive impressions of [the Commission's report] and the intent and content of the telegram obviously 'twisted' to enable the Conference of Ambassadors to arrive at any such conclusion."[38] The decision of the Conference moved Harenc to protest to London and to the British Legation in Athens. He felt that the Conference had given the Italians a promise in advance; that the Commission had been sent on a wild goose chase and its report purposely misinterpreted.[39]

In Athens, advice to adhere quickly to the Conference's decision was received by the Foreign Ministry from two of its most respected officers. From London, the Greek Minister,

---

marked "Correspondence with Lord Crewe, Ambassador to Paris 1922-1924," Box 22, Curzon Papers.

[36] Lord Crewe (Paris) to Lord Curzon, September 30, 1923. Folder marked "Correspondence with Lord Crewe, Ambassador to Paris 1922-1924," Box 22, Curzon Papers.

[37] Imperial Conference 1923. Stenographic notes of the Sixth Meeting, held at 10 Downing Street, S.W., on Thursday, October 11, 1923, at 11:00 A.M., p. 6. Folder marked "Imperial Conferences, 1921, 1923," Box 22, Curzon Papers.

[38] Atherton (Athens) to the Department of State, October 1923. File 765.68/125, Record Group 59, NA.

[39] Dendramis (Janina), No. 2064 to the Foreign Ministry, September 28, 1923. Greek Archives.

Surrender

Dimitrios Caclamanos, cabled that he did not believe Greece would be able to oppose the decision of the Conference "in spite of its innocence." He recommended that Athens submit to the verdict of the Conference with a "dignified protest," declaring that it was submitting only to the "tyranny [of] *force majeure*."[40] Similar advice against this "crying injustice" was tendered by Politis in a long and very detailed cable from Geneva. Politis felt that the Conference's decision should not move the Greek nation and government from the "calm and dignity displayed till now." Since Greece had "no direct means" to redress the Conference's injustice she had to "bow before the calamity." Like his colleague in London, Politis recommended a "very measured and very objective note to the Conference in order to point out [the] injustice committed."[41] Faced by a joint note of the Great Powers, Greece was in no position to resist.

The Greek reply on September 29, accepting the decision of the Conference, was extremely long and closely followed Politis' recommendations. It began by assuring the Conference that the necessary orders had been transmitted to the Swiss National Bank to transfer to the account of the Italian Government in the Bank of Italy at Rome the 50 million lire demanded. Athens protested "with all its force" against the Conference's decision which considered unfulfilled the fifth condition of its note of September 8, relative to the promise of the Greek Government to ensure the investigation and exemplary punishment of the culprits as quickly as possible. The note pointed out the various police, military, and judicial measures undertaken by the Greek authorities in an attempt to apprehend the culprits. It would not admit that these authorities could have neglected to take the slightest measure that would have aided the inquiry and contributed to the discovery of the culprits. It observed that although the preliminary report of the Commission of Inquiry had not been communicated to the

[40] Caclamanos (London), No. 3409 to the Foreign Ministry, September 26, 1923. French text. Greek Archives.
[41] Politis (Geneva), No. 1295 to the Foreign Ministry, September 27, 1923. French text. Greek Archives.

Surrender

Greek Government, the latter had "deep faith" that this document did not contain any assertion that the Greek authorities had "failed in their duty." The general conviction, it noted, was that the assassins came from Albania and that they had taken shelter there immediately after the crime. Since the Albanian border was very close to the scene of the crime no action could have stopped the assassins. Pursuit by the Greek authorities into Albanian territory was impossible. Because of this the Greek Government had requested the Conference and the League for the formation of an International Commission of Inquiry. The investigation by the Commission of Inquiry as well as by the Greek authorities had produced "the most serious signs that the crime was devised in Argyrocastro in Albania and perpetrated by agents commissioned . . . from Albania." Given these facts the imposition on Greece by the Conference of a penalty of 50 million lire only produced the most painful impression and stirred the mistrust of the Greek people and government, "that they had placed all their confidence in the spirit of justice of the Great Powers."

Punishment, the note continued, was the result of a wrong committed, but the wrong could not be attributed to Greece, not even in the way in which the inquiry was conducted. The Commission of Inquiry in its report to the Conference had by a vote of 3 to 1 excluded all responsibility of the Greek Government and stated the good faith and good will of the Greek authorities. The penalty, the note complained, was excessive since it was without example in diplomatic history that a country be condemned to pay so many millions for a crime committed on its territory. This penalty was particularly hard on Greece, which had only recently borrowed from the Bank of England in order to settle the Greek refugees on its territory. In ending, the Greek Government futilely asked for a revision of the Conference's decision. In order that the decision not be suspected, it asked that the Greek protest be accepted by the Conference and submitted for examination by the Permanent Court of International Justice at The Hague.[42]

---

[42] *DDDIG*, pp. 42-44. For the police and judicial measures taken by

Surrender

While the Greek Government was submitting to the dictates of the Conference, the Duce was carrying out his last act of bravado at Corfu. On September 26, the Minister of Marine, Thaon di Revel, had ordered suspension of the Corfu evacuation order as a consequence of Lord Crewe's opposition at the Conference to the payment of the 50 million lire to Italy. The award of the money rescinded this order. The evacuation commenced the following morning, September 27, as scheduled. The Italian squadron left the surrounding waters a few hours later. No sooner were the Italian ships out to sea than at 1:30 P.M. an order was received to return immediately to Corfu.[43]

The return of the squadron had been prompted by the delay of the Greek Government in transferring the 50 million lire to the account of the Italian Government in the Bank of Italy at Rome.[44] An order by the National Bank of Greece to the Swiss National Bank to release the money moved the latter to ask the Conference on September 28 if this met with its approval. The Conference answered affirmatively that same night. Further delay, however, was caused when the Swiss National Bank again cabled the Conference to know if it were also necessary to receive the approval of The Hague Court. Immediate assurances by the Conference that this was not necessary finally induced the Swiss National Bank to transfer the 50 million lire.[45] On September 29, after a two-day wait, the Italian squadron again set sail and returned to Italy.[46] Corfu was once more firmly in Greek hands.

ROME THWARTS CONTINUATION OF INVESTIGATION

Although the Italo-Greek dispute was to all intents and

---

the Greek authorities, at least during the first days after the murder of General Tellini, see *supra*, Chapter II.

[43] *DDI*, p. 266, footnote 2.
[44] Mussolini to Avezzana (Paris), September 27, 1923. *Ibid.*, pp. 265-266.
[45] Avezzana (Paris) to Mussolini, September 29, 1923. *Ibid.*, p. 268.
[46] *Ibid.*, p. 266, footnote 2.

Surrender

purposes settled, events dealing with the affair were still unfolding behind the scenes. On October 30, the Conference of Ambassadors convened its two hundred and thirty-third meeting.[47] Up for the Conference's consideration was the second and final report of the Commission of Inquiry, dated September 30, 1923.[48]

The conclusions of the Commission of Inquiry were repeated by Colonel Shibouya, who also described to the Conference the difficulties encountered by the Commission during its stay in Epirus. He discussed the suggestion of the Commission that a neutral party, namely, a national of a power not interested in the dispute, but expert in matters of criminal investigation, be put at the disposal of the Albanian and Greek Governments with a view to pursuing the unfinished investigation. He believed that Greece would accept the Commission's proposals.

It was pointed out by Laroche, however, that a commission of inquiry as proposed by Colonel Shibouya was not the same thing as the Conference's Commission of Inquiry, which was essentially a commission of control. Nevertheless Avezzana thought it was important to have a judicial continuation of the Conference's Commission of Inquiry, whose work terminated on September 27, a date which closed the political period of the Italo-Greek incident. He felt that the assassination of Tellini had a double aspect: first political and secondly judicial. The second aspect, as far as he was concerned, continued to be important after September 27, when the Conference proved that justice had not been done and that the culprits had not been arrested. The proposal made by the Commission of In-

---

[47] Unless cited otherwise the material that follows is drawn from the *procès-verbal* of the two hundred and thirty-third meeting of the Conference of Ambassadors, October 30, 1923. File 763.72119/12038, Record Group 59, NA.

[48] After its preliminary report of September 22, the Commission continued its work until September 27. During these five days the Commission intensified its investigation for the assassins of General Tellini. Though it came to no definite conclusions, its report to the Conference pointed out possible avenues of investigation on both the Greek and Albanian sides of the frontier that might yield the answer as to who the assassins were. For the text of the report see Glasgow, pp. 16-24.

quiry resulted from the necessity for ensuring the carrying out of justice.

For a moment the Conference turned its attention to the Greek protest appealing the Conference's decision of September 27 adjusting the Italo-Greek dispute.[49] Cambon thought that there was no need to proceed with this protest for several reasons: Greece had promised in advance to submit to the Conference's decisions; and secondly, the Conference was not a tribunal, it acted politically in the name of the governments which it represented and could not allow an appeal of a decision rendered. The Conference was therefore not interested in reopening the political phase of the Italo-Greek dispute. At present it was dealing exclusively with the judicial phase of the dispute and for that reason felt it could accept without difficulties the proposals of the Commission of Inquiry.

However, before accepting the Commission's proposals Avezzana requested a postponement in order to consult with Rome. No objections to a postponement were voiced by Lord Crewe, who found the proposals both just and reasonable and wished that Rome would accept the solution advanced by the Commission. He hoped that at the Conference's next meeting a decision would be made on the proposals, for the Conference could not delay a decision on this matter. On the question of whether a separate report would be filed by the Italian delegate of the Commission of Inquiry, Avezzana declared that he was not in a position to answer. He felt that the attitude of the Italian delegate would depend upon the decision that would be taken by the Conference in the course of its next meeting. Before the meeting ended it was agreed that all delegations would refrain from publishing the report of the Commission of Inquiry and from giving any indication to the press on the subject of the present discussion.

No matter how "just and reasonable" Lord Crewe thought the Commission's proposals were, the reaction in Rome was somewhat different. Mussolini was in principle willing to continue the investigation for the assassins of General Tellini. His

[49] The Greek reply of September 29. *DDDIG*, pp. 42-44.

Surrender

important qualification was that an Italian magistrate had to be included in any such investigation. Lord Curzon, however, after Colonel Beaud's memorable performance on the Commission of Inquiry, had no desire to be bitten twice. As the Permanent Under-Secretary of the Foreign Office, Sir Eyre Crowe, explained to the Counsellor of the Italian Embassy, Gabriele Preziosi, Lord Curzon wished "to avoid every friction" with Italy. He therefore thought it desirable to drop the Commission's proposal for the appointment of a neutral expert who would assist in the investigation to be continued by the Greek and Albanian authorities. Preziosi noted in his cable to the Duce that Crowe had accentuated the pronunciation of the word "neutral" in order to draw his attention to it. Instructions in line with Lord Curzon's belief, Crowe informed Preziosi, had been sent to the British Embassy in Paris.[50]

The next meeting convened by the Conference to deal with the Commission's proposal was held November 30. It was the Conference's two hundred and fortieth meeting since its inception.[51]

The discussions were begun by Avezzana, who made it clear that his government could not accept the proposals tendered by the Commission of Inquiry. He explained to his colleagues that Rome considered these proposals insufficient to ensure that justice would be done. The state of disorder existing at the Greek-Albanian border would make difficult the attainment of the kind of results which the fulfillment of justice required. Therefore, he explained, the Italian Government consequently thought that any new commission of inquiry sent to Epirus should be composed of a Greek and an Albanian representative, a neutral delegate, and an Italian representative. The president of the commission could if the Con-

---

[50] Preziosi (London) to Mussolini and Avezzana (Paris), November 6, 1923. *DDI*, pp. 310-311; Mussolini to Avezzana (Paris), and Preziosi (London), November 7, 1923. *Ibid.*, pp. 312-313.

[51] Unless cited otherwise the material that follows is drawn from the *procès-verbal* of the two hundred and fortieth meeting of the Conference of Ambassadors, November 30, 1923. File 763.72119/12055, Record Group 59, NA.

Surrender

ference deemed it necessary be a representative from the Conference of Ambassadors.

True to his instructions, Lord Crewe replied that the British Government had the feeling that the Italo-Greek affair had been in suspense for such a long time that it would not[52] be useful to return to the idea of sending a neutral commissioner or of setting up some sort of investigation at the scene of the crime. In his opinion it was better to abstain from any decision of this kind and to leave to the Greek and Albanian Governments the task of doing their duty concerning the search for the assassins of General Tellini. This view was also shared by the French Government, declared Cambon.

That the Conference could not accept the Italian proposals, Avezzana regretted, and he reserved for his country all liberty of action for the realization of Italy's desires. Speaking for his colleagues, Cambon acknowledged Avezzana's declaration made in the name of his government.

The discussion of the Conference then turned to the request of the Greek Government that it be given the reports of the Commission of Inquiry.[53] Numerous passages from these reports, Cambon pointed out to the ambassadors, had already appeared in the press.[54] He thought no problem would arise in giving satisfaction to the request of the Greek Government. In forwarding the reports to Greece, the Conference would be able to indicate to Athens the desire to see that it seriously pursue the investigation and the punishment of the culprits. It could also ask what results had been achieved by the Greek investigation. Agreeing, Avezzana recommended that the last paragraph of the note which the Conference would address

---

[52] The *procès-verbal* at this point is obviously incorrect for the negative, "not," is missing from the record.

[53] On November 4, the chargé d'affaires of the Greek Legation, Léon Melas, had addressed a note to the Conference of Ambassadors asking for a copy of the Commission of Inquiry's report of September 22 and its final report of September 30. *DDDIG*, p. 44.

[54] An excellent summary of the Commission of Inquiry's report of September 30 had been filed by the diplomatic correspondent of the *London Daily Telegraph* as early as November 9, 1923. *The Daily Telegraph*, November 9, 1923, p. 12.

Surrender

to Greece contain the following: "The Conference considers that the search and punishment of the culprits is still incumbent on Greece, but it has not believed it necessary to enter into the examination of the modalities proposed to this end by the Commission of Inquiry." In order, however, that there be no misunderstanding, Cambon and Lord Crewe reiterated that in spite of the prior declaration made by Avezzana the Conference still considered the affair as definitely closed.

The last point was made by Lord Crewe, who thought that the postscript in the Commission's report of September 30 should be omitted when communicated to Greece. This postscript provided for a special report[55] by the Italian delegate. He also observed that the Commission's reports should be communicated to the Albanian Government. Avezzana agreed, and informed Lord Crewe that he had already advised the Italian delegate to renounce the sending of a special report to the Conference. At its next, and last, meeting dealing with the incident, on December 6, the Conference also decided to transmit the Commission's reports to the League of Nations.[56]

The reports were communicated by the Conference to Greece and Albania on December 12, and to the Secretary-General of the League on December 13.[57] The Corfu incident was ended. The Powers had made the first in a series of retreats which culminated with the German annexation of the Sudetenland, fifteen years later.

---

[55] The *procès-verbal* at this point is obviously incorrect. Lord Crewe is quoted as saying that a postscript in the report of September 30 stated that each delegate was to file a separate report.

[56] *Procès-verbal* of the two hundred and forty-first meeting of the Conference of Ambassadors, December 6, 1923. File 763.72119/12062, Record Group 59, NA.

[57] Though the reports were communicated by the Conference to the League and to the two governments involved, questions persisted in the House of Commons and in the French Chamber of Deputies, asking that the reports be released publicly. Great Britain, *Parliamentary Debates*, Fifth Series, House of Commons, *Official Report*, Vol. 168. November 15, 1923, cols. 359-361, 397-398; *ibid.*, Vol. 169, February 20, 1924, col. 1803; *ibid.*, Vol. 172, April 16, 1924, col. 1385. France, *Journal Officiel de la République Française*, Chambre des Députés, *Débats Parlementaires*, December 7, 1923, p. 3985.

CONCLUSION

WITH his assumption of power in late 1922, Mussolini sought a philosophic basis for Fascism designed to solve the age's great problems. But his theory of the transcendental state with its motto: "Everything for the state; nothing against the state; nothing outside the state," was not enough to buttress his shaky government. Therefore, he feverishly strove to consolidate power. To assist him in this task he endeavored in the realm of foreign affairs to achieve some sort of diplomatic success. His first two ventures ended as failures: his abortive attempt during the Lausanne Conference to reopen the question of mandates and, secondly, his attempt to act as a mediator between the French and British Governments over the issue of German reparations at the London and Paris Conferences (December 1922 through January 1923).[1]

These failures at London and Paris necessitated a "success" in the diplomatic field. By the early summer of 1923, this necessity was paramount in the Duce's mind.[2] The fortuitous murder of General Tellini and his staff provided the incident and the excuse needed for the Italian action—the occupation of Corfu—which prior naval arrangements had made possible.

Mussolini launched an adventurous foreign policy designed to consolidate his position and assert Italy's place in world affairs. It was a policy repugnant to the more cautious officials of the Palazzo Chigi, who continually tried to adjust the Duce's Fascist desires to Italian national interests.[3] It was this policy which put Italy into conflict with the League of Nations and the world order that the League desired to establish.

Though the episode was only a minor fracas in the history

[1] Ettore Anchieri, "L'Esordio della Politica Estera Fascista," *Il Politico*, Anno xx, No. 2 (1955), pp. 211-231.
[2] Raffaele Guariglia, in an interview with the writer in Rome, August 1961.
[3] *Ibid.*

Conclusion

of the interwar years, there can be gleaned from an examination of the incident certain patterns of behavior which would repeat themselves with increasing intensity during the years that followed. Of particular interest are the relations between Mussolini and the career officials of the Palazzo Chigi. The latter were members of the Italian nobility and upper classes. They were trained diplomats having more in common with their English, French, and Greek counterparts than with their own political leader. Avezzana, Contarini, Della Torretta, Sir William Tyrrell, Cambon, Laroche, and Romanos were of a common cultural and social background. They had similar values, wrote and spoke the same language—French. Most important, they viewed the arena of foreign affairs and diplomacy as one in which dangerous issues were never pushed to the fore. They realized that in foreign affairs the conflicting interests and desires of national states placed immense hurdles between what a nation desired and what it could actually achieve in its relations with other national states. As diplomats, they believed that the intricate and delicate task of negotiation and compromise was preferable to the assumption of impossible positions which could only lead to situations where compromise proved impossible and resort to force became a necessity. A similar conflict would arise in Germany a decade later between the elite of the Wilhelmstrasse and the Nazi leadership after Hitler's advent to power in January of 1933.[4] In the Italian case, as in the German, the ability of career officials to operate as a restraining influence upon the political leadership proved to be virtually nil. In Italy, the career officials controlled major posts within the Italian Diplomatic Service until very late in the Fascist regime, but they were able to influence Fascist policy very little. These officials showed scant courage in resisting the political leadership; though some may have disagreed with the policies pursued, few desired to protest. Resignations such as Contarini's in 1925 were rare.

[4] Paul Seabury, *The Wilhelmstrasse; a Study of German Diplomats under the Nazi Regime* (Berkeley: University of California Press, 1954), passim.

Conclusion

How did this situation come about? The answer must be sought not only in the overpowering personality of Italy's political leader, but also in the transformation of the diplomat's role because of changing world conditions. Some of these conditions were political in nature, others were administrative, and still others technical. Most of these conditions had come to the fore prior to the First World War, but their effects were not fully felt until after the war. The industrial revolution, for example, and the corresponding increases in trade multiplied the number of people who could speak with authority on other countries, shattering the diplomat's position as an expert and exposing him to competition and criticism. The function and scope of diplomacy had also expanded and information had to be provided on military, economic, and other highly technical problems. This requirement, in turn, increased the ambassador's staff and divided his mission into functional offices so that he came to depend more and more upon his experts. In the realm of communication, technological advances had removed him from his physical isolation which in the past had made it possible for him to pursue, at times, an almost independent policy; it curtailed his freedom of action and helped to transform his office. In addition, the growth of international organization and the establishment of the League made direct confrontation between foreign ministers and other government leaders easier. Sessions at Geneva provided the meeting place where personal contacts could take place, helping further to develop among these political leaders the custom of personal negotiations. Thus the realm of diplomatic negotiation, once the virtual monopoly of the diplomat, was absorbed by his political superior. This development also led to the increased use of the personal emissary—men like the ubiquitous Giuriati—who, because of their access to men of power, could be relied upon to undertake special missions and speak with greater authority than the accredited career officials. Most important was the postwar belief that there had to be democratic control of foreign policy. This concept challenged the most charac-

Conclusion

teristic feature of the diplomatic profession—its dependence on secrecy.[5]

The onetime power of the career officials was superseded by forces and movements which these officials could neither control nor fully understand and made it possible for the political leadership to bypass or ignore them altogether. Because of these developments Mussolini faced a weakened community of civil servants and, like Hitler a decade later, easily turned aside whatever restraining influence the career officials could muster. The transformation of the diplomat's role helps in part to explain the impotence of Avezzana, Contarini, and Della Torretta and accounts for their difficulties and frustrations in dealing with Mussolini throughout the incident.

In international affairs, Mussolini could not grasp, or did not wish to grasp, the traditional diplomatic approach to foreign affairs, which was one of slow negotiation based on compromise. His own approach was conditioned by the revolutionary character of his government—revolutionary in the sense that it was committed to an expansionist foreign policy. Thus Fascism, like its later German counterpart, was little disposed to accept for long the status quo established by the peace treaties of 1919, and therefore it was almost inevitable that Rome would come into conflict with the two powers that supported the League system: England and France. The Corfu Incident was the first encounter.

Mussolini's attitude toward traditional diplomacy is to be contrasted with the attitude of the Greek Revolutionary Government. The recommendations of Politis, Romanos, and other Greek diplomats were carefully noted by the government in Athens, and often executed. Unlike the Duce's government, the Greek Revolutionary Government was "revolutionary" only in the constitutional sense. Its leaders wished to depose the Greek monarchy but to maintain a democratic and constitutional form of government. As military men, they had little

[5] Gordon A. Craig and Felix Gilbert (eds.), *The Diplomats: 1919-1939* (Princeton: Princeton University Press, 1953), pp. 4-6; Seabury, pp. 149-159.

Conclusion

knowledge of foreign affairs and diplomacy and therefore trusted implicitly the recommendations and suggestions offered by their diplomats.

The Greek career officials, in turn, had no illusions about the effectiveness of the League of Nations should the interests of the Great Powers fail to coincide and should these Powers refuse to support the Greek appeal. On the other hand, since Greece was a small Power and without allies, they also realized that the League was an excellent forum which could be used to arouse the small States and keep the issue before public opinion. To achieve this result, the Greeks, and especially Politis at the Council discussions, used the tools that all small nations invariably invoke in any debate against a greater Power: the appeal to international law and morality and to world public opinion.

In a sense, Politis and the Greeks were more aware of the limitations and weaknesses in the League system than were many of its well-meaning supporters like Lord Robert Cecil. What men like Cecil failed to realize was that the League of Nations was in no way a super-state but only a super-association of states joined together by a multilateral treaty. By joining the League, the signatory states had not surrendered an iota of sovereignty and therefore had reserved their freedom of action.

Nevertheless, the feature in the League structure that was unique and had the greatest appeal for all well-meaning people —and was in a sense its *raison d'être*—was the League's system of collective security established by the Covenant. The attraction of this system, in theory, was that it established a set of universal legal obligations by which all signatories of the Covenant were bound together to act against any aggressor nation. The great innovation that the League system of collective security introduced was that it was directed against no specific state, and was therefore friendly to all. It secured universal advantages rather than advantages to a small number. Conversely, it also established universal responsibilities and obligations. Its underlying assumption was that nations would henceforth follow disinterested foreign policies and would be

Conclusion

motivated only by community interests and community law; that states would abandon the desire to increase their power positions; and that force would only be used to maintain the peace and order of the world community, rather than to further the national interests of one state over another.

However, the rejection by the United States Senate of the Versailles Treaty and with it the League Covenant was an immense setback for the League and its supporters. Senate rejection of the League Covenant prompted England and France, the nations which might have been willing to police the world in conjunction with the United States, to re-examine the League and their position in it. Both decided that in any attempt to use force to maintain peace and order, there had to be an immediate relationship between the aggression being committed, against which collective action was required, and their own national interests. This Anglo-French attitude was a serious blow for the League, which had been molded around the Great Powers. This Great Power monopoly within the League was in keeping with European historical experience; from the Congress of Vienna in 1815 to the beginning of the First World War, the Great Powers had been dominant. Their superior position within the League was codified in the Covenant, which stipulated that the Council, which was to serve as the executive organ of the organization, would contain permanent Great Power representation and that any substantive decision of the Council required unanimous agreement. Thus, unless the interests of the Great Powers coincided in every question of collective security this feature of the League was doomed to failure. To expect from the League decisive action against a major Power when the Great Powers did not wish it, would be the height of self-deception. The League Council could be no more successful than the Great Powers wished to make it. Disagreement among the Great Powers outside the League would of necessity be reflected in disagreement among the Great Powers inside the League. It would be reasonable to say that it was not the League which failed, but rather the Great Powers which failed the League. During the League's lifetime the notion of

Conclusion

an international community was too abstract a concept to compel sacrifices for people about whom one knew nothing, people living in distant lands.

The inability of the Great Powers to act in unison under the aegis of the League during the Corfu Incident in 1923 repeated itself in Manchuria in 1931, and in Ethiopia four years later. In Manchuria, no Great Power was willing to collide with Japan in an area halfway around the globe when the United States and the Soviet Union, states interested in the area but outside the League, were little disposed to interfere or take necessary measures. During the Ethiopian crisis, the conflicting interests of London and Paris with respect to Mussolini were never completely reconciled. In the end, France's desire to continue the Stresa front against Hitler and England's efforts to save the League saved neither the Stresa front nor the League.

The difficulty presenting itself during the Corfu crisis and throughout the interwar years was that the League's two principal supporters approached the problems facing the League, within the context of their own conflicting interests and desires. Though England and France agreed that the Versailles Peace Treaty and the League system were to be maintained, at the same time they disagreed as to the means that were to be employed to do this. The conflict between England and France over the problem of means and ends caused them to work at cross purposes and in so doing weaken and ultimately help to destroy the very system they were pledged to defend.

France's attitude was dictated by her fear of Germany and the knowledge that Germany was potentially a far stronger state. It had to face the inescapable fact that a nation of only forty million faced across the Rhine a nation of seventy million. The belief that Germany was an aggressive and militaristic nation only added to French fears.

Britain, however, having no common frontier with Germany, was not as influenced as France by geographical position and historical experience. The Foreign Office was relatively free from the obsessive fear of another war with Germany that

Conclusion

pervaded the halls of the Quai d'Orsay. To the French, the League was to be used to keep Germany in her place; to the English, it was an institution in which all nations could gather in order to discuss their differences and cooperate in the needs of a peacetime Europe. England was devoted to the League only in so far as it could supplement the older and more traditional forms of diplomatic negotiation.[6]

France's actions throughout the Corfu dispute are therefore understandable. Poincaré saw no advantage to France in supporting the Greek appeal and bringing the Corfu dispute to the League Council. For France, the one great overriding consideration was Germany and the Ruhr occupation. Collective action with England or through the League against Italy was out of the question. Even if collective action had been possible, would the almost certain departure of Italy from the League have been worth it? Could the League have meant anything or operated effectively if of the European Powers only England and France were counted among its members? Was it not better to compromise and attempt to find outside the League some sort of solution which, restoring Corfu to Greece, would at the same time assuage the Duce's feelings and maintain Italy, at least for the moment, within the League and the Versailles Treaty system? This dilemma Whitehall and the Quai d'Orsay faced throughout the crisis. Thus the French policy of trying to find some sort of solution to the dispute within the Conference of Ambassadors and outside the League of Nations becomes understandable. It furnishes the explanation for Hanotaux's comparative silence during the Council discussions and for Laroche's and Cambon's efforts to placate Italy during the meetings of the Conference of Ambassadors.

In the case of England, Lord Curzon's decision to support the League, unusual in the light of British policy towards Geneva, had to be abandoned for several reasons. The feeling that the application of sanctions under Article 16 of the Covenant would be, on the basis of the Treasury's pessimistic re-

---

[6] Arnold Wolfers, *Britain and France between Two Wars* (New York: Harcourt, Brace and Co., 1940), passim.

Conclusion

port, virtually impossible turned attention to other means of coercion. However, military coercion also proved impossible when the Foreign Office and the Admiralty realized that England was militarily overextended in the Mediterranean by its naval patrol of the Turkish coast and that any joint Anglo-French measures against Italy either separately or through the League would never materialize. Thus, Britain's military weakness, the feeling that coercive action through the League was impossible, plus the desire not to go it alone provide the key to why Lord Curzon revoked Cecil's previous instructions to support the Greek appeal. London's decision was to solve the dispute within the Conference. This action was undoubtedly taken to avoid a showdown with Italy in the League, a showdown which would have been to no one's interest. It is likely that a direct confrontation at Geneva would have placed the Baldwin government in the position of choosing either to support the League or to allow Italy to flaunt it, thus undermining the whole postwar settlement. The high regard in which the League was held by British public opinion, a fact Curzon stressed in his conversation with Della Torretta, would in all probability have necessitated a cabinet decision to support the League even though England was in a weakened state in the Mediterranean. In any clash, London was not positive that French support would be forthcoming, and even if the League were victorious they felt an Italian withdrawal from Geneva would be certain. A League minus Italy, Germany, Russia, and the United States was as uninviting a proposition in London as it was in Paris. Most important, as Curzon admitted, a clash between Italy on one side and Britain and the League on the other would have ruptured the coalition which had won the war and which everyone desired to continue in order to guide Europe's postwar adjustment, especially the readmittance of Germany into the family of nations.

For Rome, the decision to allow the Conference's demands to replace her own was also dictated by hard facts. It was better, Rome decided, to have the issue solved at Paris than at Geneva, and so avoid a possible clash with England and the League.

Conclusion

Even her threat to withdraw from the League had its disadvantages, for it would isolate her from the one organization which at that moment appeared to be the hub of European politics. A decision to adhere to the Conference also assured her of French support, not only at Paris but also at Geneva, while any other decision would have alienated that support. Because of common interest, therefore, London and Rome, almost against their wills, but to France's relief, decided to accept the compromise formula devised by the Conference and avoid the pitfalls awaiting each side at Geneva. The desire to avoid Geneva compelled Lord Crewe to accept Avezzana's declaration of September 13, committing Britain to a formula which two weeks later would tie Curzon's hands. Crewe's decision made it almost automatic that England would have to agree to the French-Italian-Japanese decision and, in the light of Avezzana's declaration and of the Commission of Inquiry's ambiguous report of September 22, to have Greece pay Italy the 50 million lire. The national interests of the Great Powers had merged; but to achieve a peaceful settlement of the dispute it was necessary to resolve the issue outside the League, not within it.

Of special interest in an examination of the Corfu Incident is the breakdown in communication or lack of coordination between the Secretariat of the Conference of Ambassadors and the Commission of Inquiry. Why the Secretariat never informed the Commission of Inquiry of the specific nature of Avezzana's declaration of September 13 remains a mystery. It should be noted, however, that the composition of the Conference's Secretariat was French. Therefore, keeping the Commission in the dark over the meaning of Avezzana's declaration would have assisted French policy aims: to solve the dispute within the Conference and in a manner acceptable to Rome. If the Conference's silence is difficult to fathom, especially strange is the silence of the British Foreign Office. There appears to have been a lack of coordination or communication among Lord Crewe, the Foreign Office, and the British Legation in Athens, which kept Major Harenc completely in the dark

Conclusion

over the wording and meaning of Avezzana's declaration. The problem, however, does not appear to have been peculiarly British, for Colonel Shibouya, the Japanese President of the Commission of Inquiry, and Colonel Lacombe, the French representative, also appear to have been kept in the dark over the meaning of Avezzana's declaration.

The Duce's success during the Corfu crisis must therefore be viewed within the context of these conditions. At the same time, the League during the Corfu dispute had merely gone through one ordeal. Whether it is considered to have failed or have succeeded in handling its first important political crisis depends upon the role that one assigns to the League, and to international organization in general. Some view it as a potential Areopagus of the world; others consider it as one instrument among many others perfected by nation states to adjust *peacefully* disputes in the international arena. If one accepts the former concept, then its actions during the Corfu dispute are certainly disappointing. If one takes the latter approach, then its actions during the dispute are something less than disappointing. This is especially true if one recognizes that the League was a realistic institution which attempted to unite in one organization all previous international practices for peaceful settlement of disputes developed by the European state system prior to the First World War.[7]

Though a settlement was found outside the League it should not be thought that the League contributed nothing to bringing the dispute to a peaceful conclusion. By their very presence the League Council and especially the League Assembly acted as catalysts forcing the Conference of Ambassadors to find some sort of reasonable solution to the Italo-Greek dispute. The Assembly in particular acted as the spokesman for an outraged public opinion. Constant threats by the small Powers to have it openly intervene in the dispute created pressures on the Conference of Ambassadors, both diplomatic and psychological, which cannot be accurately measured. Reading over the

[7] Alfred Zimmern, *The League of Nations and the Rule of Law, 1918-1935* (2nd ed. rev.; London: Macmillan Co., 1939), passim.

Conclusion

procès-verbaux of the Conference one is struck by the delegates' constant apprehensions about the omnipresent danger that loomed on the horizon in the direction of Geneva.

Many critics of British and French policy during the Corfu crisis lose sight of the fact that the dispute was peacefully settled. They also fail to see that the League Council and the Conference cooperated closely together, and by doing so helped adjust a very dangerous situation. Final credit for a peaceful settlement must of course be bestowed upon the Conference of Ambassadors. Whether it usurped the League's role is really of secondary importance. Of primary importance is that the Conference was successfully manipulated by the Great Powers to solve peacefully a dispute which could not be solved by the League Council without grave dangers for all concerned.

The factors which made this procedure possible were: Mussolini's admission that the Conference as well as Italy had rights to reparations from Greece since the murdered members of the Tellini Mission were agents of the Conference; the problem of competence as between the Council and the Conference of Ambassadors; and the Duce's contention that Article 12 and Article 15 of the Covenant did not apply to Italy's actions at Corfu.

In a sense, the first two factors were bound together, though during the crisis the first factor was never dealt with or even questioned. There was no doubt in anyone's mind that the Italian Government under established rules of international law had rights to reparations for the harm done to its citizens. The rights of the Conference, however, were another matter. But even if the Conference's rights were established, did they devolve to one of its subsidiary organs, in this case the Commission of Delimitation? Certainly during the postwar years, with the establishment of the League of Nations and after the headquarters agreements with Switzerland, there was a tacit understanding that international personality could no longer be, as it historically had been, confined to states. Did this apply to an organization like the Conference of Ambassadors? The right of the Conference to reparations for the murder of General

Conclusion

Tellini was never questioned during the settlement of the crisis. There appears to have been an implicit acceptance by all concerned that the Conference had the right to press an international claim against a national state for harm done to agents of the Conference. The Conference's position was undoubtedly strengthened by the knowledge that, prior to the Tellini murder, it had successfully pressed claims for acts committed against its agents, especially in Germany. Silence, in a sense, was a type of acquiescence. The fact that the harm was done to the president of a subsidiary organ of the Conference, the Delimitation Commission, appears to have been of no consequence. Subsequent experience in the United Nations following the murder of Count Folke Bernadotte, appears to show that it is quite possible for a claim to be presented simultaneously by an international organization, possessing international personality, and by the nation whose national is injured.

The question of competence as between the League Council and the Conference of Ambassadors further complicated the Corfu Incident. However, there can be no doubt that the League Council was the body competent to handle the Italian action at Corfu. Of the two organizations it was the League which had the broader mandate. The Conference had merely been established to see to the execution of the details of the Versailles Treaty. Even its decision to delimit Albania's borders was a usurpation of power not directly delegated to it at Versailles. It was the League of Nations which had been established by that same treaty to handle political questions, like the Corfu one, which might arise and disrupt relations between states. To accomplish this task it had a world-wide membership, with established organs and procedures, ready and willing to apply itself to the task. Furthermore, all parties to the dispute were members of the League and were duty bound to refer to that organization a question of this type. Assuming that the Conference had the right to press for reparations because of the injury suffered by its agent, it certainly had no competence to settle any further matter. Nevertheless it can be argued that the Conference was competent to extend itself

Conclusion

beyond the question of reparations since the Tellini murder and the occupation of the island was a linked series of events which could not be separated into two distinct questions. Mussolini's cynical insistence that Greek acceptance of the Conference's demands—not those of Italy, technically—would lead to an evacuation of the island appeared to many as a solution that would make it possible to avoid a direct confrontation between Italy and the League and the necessary application of sanctions. Though pro-Leaguers like Branting found no support among the Great Powers, they cogently argued that the Tellini murder did not warrant the occupation of Corfu; that although this might have been a valid procedure before the League was established, it certainly was invalid after the signature of the Covenant. Expediency, not logic or legalisms, motivated Great Power decisions with regard to the role of the League in the Corfu Incident.

The peculiar relation of the League in comparison with that of the Conference throughout the crisis can to some extent be traced to the fact that the establishment of the League was inextricably tied to the Versailles Treaty and to the other peace treaties of 1919. This tie was serious and unfortunate, for those resentful of the Versailles Treaty and the postwar treaty arrangements often made no attempt in their attacks to differentiate between the Treaty and the Covenant. To show their dislike for the former they often attacked the latter. The League became synonymous in certain quarters with the status quo. Its usefulness was therefore curtailed from the beginning, and it was viewed with suspicion and mistrust. This situation explains in part Mussolini's willingness to settle matters in Paris rather than Geneva.

Fortunately, the League experience was not forgotten and the mistake made in incorporating the Covenant into the peace treaties was not repeated after the Second World War. The United Nations, the League's successor, when established at San Francisco in 1945, was organized under a separate multilateral treaty which was in no way connected to the postwar treaties as was the League Covenant.

Conclusion

On the contention that Italy's actions at Corfu were not covered by Articles 12 and 15, the Committee of Jurists, which the Council later appointed to examine the five legal questions arising from the Corfu dispute, never clearly indicated whether coercive measures by one member of the League against another were legitimate. The principal defect of the League Covenant was that though it prohibited resort to war it did not prohibit the use of force. It is true that member states were committed to submitting "any dispute likely to lead to a rupture" to the arbitration, judicial settlement, and conciliation procedures of the Council. Essentially, however, the Covenant was an instrumentality which attempted only to restrict for member states the traditional right of a state to resort to war. Its actions and procedures therefore were in the nature of regulations, not prohibitions. The League tried only to reduce the former right to war by requiring preliminary recourse to the measures of pacific settlement stipulated by the Covenant. The use of force short of war, however, was another matter. Nowhere in the Covenant is it outlawed. Since war and especially the use of force short of war were not outlawed by the Covenant there was a tacit admission in the Covenant that these measures could be used to solve certain international conflicts. In the case of force short of war, there was no obligation even to submit the dispute in question to peaceful settlement under the Council. Some held that measures short of war were outlawed by the Covenant as being at variance with the terms of Article 12, since they were a type of action "likely to lead to a rupture." Thus it was not even necessary to prove that forceful measures short of war constituted a "resort to war."[8] This contention is debatable. In the Corfu Incident, forceful measures were used which did *not* "lead to a rupture," and they were measures which both sides accepted as *not* being a "resort to war." This situation repeated itself in 1925 during the Greco-Bulgarian Incident and in 1931-1932 during the Japanese

---

[8] Charles de Visscher, "L'Interprétation du Pacte au lendemain du différend Italo-Grec," *Revue de Droit International et de Législation Comparée*, 3rd Series, v (1924), pp. 213-230; 377-396.

Conclusion

invasions of Manchuria and Shanghai. In all of these cases diplomatic relations continued uninterrupted.

The Corfu experience was not wasted, and the flaw in the wording of the Covenant was not repeated twenty-two years later in framing the United Nations Charter. Under Article 2 of the Charter it is firmly stipulated that: "All members shall refrain in their international relations from the threat or use of force against the territorial integrity or political independence of any state, or in any other manner inconsistent with the Purposes of the United Nations." The Charter's sweeping provision under Article 2 has gone far beyond anything in the League Covenant and, instead of providing merely for the regulation of resort to war, has made it illegal to threaten or use force contrary to the purposes of the United Nations.

If the League suffered from flaws in the Covenant, of what use was it and in what way could it contribute to world peace? A memorandum by Sir Eric Drummond (see Appendix C) makes it quite clear what the basic purpose in establishing the League was: "the creation of permanent institutions and the building up of a system of international cooperation, permanently to maintain the peace of the world." The underlying assumption, however, was that nations and particularly the Great Powers would desire to solve peacefully through the machinery of the League, disputes in which they were directly involved. If they found it in their interests to do so, then in time it would be possible to establish a tradition and practice of settling peacefully through the League dangerous disputes that might arise. Confidence would have been established that the provisions of the Covenant would be upheld. The League may therefore be looked upon not as an instrumentality intent on changing the world, but as an organ available to help nations toward the peaceful settlement of their disputes. But the decision to use the League and its organs of peaceful settlement rested squarely on the shoulders of the member states.

The settlement of the Corfu Incident, as Drummond's memorandum points out, undermined the League's position in this regard. The Great Powers in finding a solution outside the

Conclusion

League had circumvented the spirit of that organization. It was an action which was to be repeated many times and with increasing frequency in the years to come. Yet the Great Powers in solving the Corfu dispute outside the League were still working in the spirit of international organization by finding through the offices of an established international body a peaceful means of adjusting a dispute likely to disturb the peace.

The tragedy of the Corfu crisis was not that the dispute was solved outside the machinery of the League, but that it in no way denied Mussolini the fruits of his aggression. The Duce retired from this perilous adventure unscathed and with his prestige enhanced. The incident furnished him with his first real success on the international scene. In the Balkans especially, his use of force and his escape from the League's retribution did not go unobserved. It gave Mussolini the reputation of a dangerous international firebrand and strengthened his position in subsequent Balkan negotiations. In a dramatic way it was an announcement that a vigorous Italy under a new and dynamic leadership had begun to play a more important role in world affairs. In Eastern Europe, the impotency of the League when it did not have Great Power backing was exposed, and the desirability, if not necessity, of achieving security through one's own armed strength in alliance with France was heightened.

In London and Paris, Mussolini's actions were considered to be merely a mad adventure from which he was fortunate in having escaped without injury. The belief was still held that the League had a valuable part to play in world affairs within the limitations with which it was viewed by both countries. Simultaneously, in Rome, the Corfu settlement produced the greatest contempt for the League and all that the League system personified, an attitude seen again a decade later in Hitler's Germany.

In retrospect, the Corfu dispute provides the first clear indication of differing Anglo-French interpretations regarding implementation of the League machinery and the maintenance

Conclusion

of the League system, a divergency that would occur with increasing frequency throughout the interwar years. In the end, however, Mussolini, like his future German ally, intoxicated by one success after another, refused to heed the warning, "beware the fury of a patient man."

APPENDIX A

Text of the Conference of Ambassadors' Message to the Council of the League of Nations

At its meeting this morning [September 5] the Conference of Ambassadors adopted the following resolution, which it decided to communicate immediately to the Council of the League of Nations:

The Conference of Ambassadors has considered the reply from Greece to its note regarding the murder of the Chairman of the Inter-Allied Greco-Albanian Delimitation Commission and of the other members of the Italian Military Mission in the Janina district. It has noted, in particular, that Greece declares her willingness, if her responsibility is proved, to agree to make any reparation which the Conference may regard as just and that the Greek Government suggests the appointment of a commission of enquiry, consisting of the delegates of the three Powers represented on the Delimitation Commission, to assist actively in the work of discovering the guilty parties. The Conference of Ambassadors, recognising that it is a principle of international law that States are responsible for political crimes and outrages committed within their territory, at once considered how the enquiry should be conducted. The next meeting of the Conference will be held not later than Friday morning next.

(Signed) Poincaré

APPENDIX B

*Text of Avezzana's Declaration to the
Conference of Ambassadors*

Paris, le 13 Septembre 1923

Je tiens à faire connaître à la Conférence que, dans son désir de témoigner de son attachement à la paix, le gouvernement italien, conformément à ses déclarations réitérées, est résolu à évacuer Corfou et il a décidé de le faire le 27 septembre, date fixée par la conférence des Ambassadeurs pour la fin de l'enquête. Mais, si à cette date, les coupables ne sont pas découverts et s'il n'est pas établi que le Gouvernement grec n'a pas [sic] commis aucune négligence dans leur poursuite et leur recherche le gouvernement italien estime qu'il serait contraire à la morale et à la justice, aussi [sic] qu'à la dignité de l'Italie que celle-ci renonçât aux gages dont elle s'était saisi[e] pour avoir satisfaction, sans que satisfaction lui soit accordée. Il demande donc que la conférence, prenant acte de la décision spontanée du Gouvernement italien relative à la [sic] évacuation de Corfou à la date du 27 septembre, décide à present que, dans l'éventualité ci-dessus visée, la conférence infligera à la Grèce, à titre de pénalité le versement de la somme de cinquante millions de lires italiennes à l'Italie, laquelle se désistera dès lors de toutes requêtes à la Cour permanente et de [sic] Justice de la Haye, aux termes des paragraphes sept de la note du huit septembre, sauf recours du gouvernement italien devant la Cour permanente pour les frais d'occupation.

APPENDIX C

Memorandum by Sir Eric Drummond on the Corfu Incident

September 14, 1923

The fundamental purpose of the League of Nations is, by the creation of permanent institutions and the building up of a system of international cooperation, permanently to maintain the peace of the world. In any work which it may undertake for the settlement of any given international dispute which arises there are, therefore, two different points that must be borne continually in mind: the effects of the action that is taken on the actual dispute in question and its effect on the future efficacy of the League. In other words, in dealing with any given dispute the task of the Council is not merely to secure a pacific settlement, but also to do what lies in its power to build up a tradition and a practice that will prevent dangerous disputes from developing in the future.

In the building up of such a tradition and practice, there are two elements which are of principal importance. The first is the moral authority of the Council and the Assembly of the League, the second is the creation of a general confidence that the clear and precise obligations of the Covenant will be loyally fulfilled by its members.

It cannot be doubted that, for the moment at least, the events of the last two weeks have done much to weaken both the moral authority of the Council and the general confidence that the precise obligations of the Covenant will be universally accepted and carried out.

So far as the first of these two elements is concerned, there can be no doubt that the weakening of the moral authority of the Council which has resulted is due, for the most part, to ignorance, and that when the Governments of the members of the League and the public opinion of their peoples have understood the true course of events and the true nature of the action which the Council has taken, its position should be rather strengthened than otherwise. I am afraid, however, that

Appendices

unless something further is done to restore the general confidence in the sanctity of the obligations of the Covenant, a severe blow will be struck at the future usefulness of the League.

It is no doubt very generally believed, both in Government circles and by the public at large, that a powerful member of the League has refused to carry out its treaty obligations under the Covenant, and has succeeded in doing so with impunity, some might even say, with an increase of prestige. It is generally held that the authority of the League has been challenged in a sphere which is precisely that for which it was created, and that this challenge has brought in question the fundamental principles which lie at the root of the public law of the new world order established by the League.

Everyone who had taken the trouble to read the Covenant, believed it lay upon the members of the League an absolute obligation to submit their disputes to arbitration or to enquiry by the Council, and an absolute obligation not to resort in the conduct of its disputes to methods of coercion until measures of pacific settlement has been tried without success.

These fundamental principles have been called into question, and until they are re-established in the minds of Governments and peoples, there will be a sense of uncertainty which will rapidly disintegrate the power of the League.

There can be no doubt as to what is the opinion of the overwhelming majority of the members of the Assembly on these points. To endeavor to settle them by general discussion of the dispute which has just happily been brought to a conclusion would, however, have a number of disadvantages. It would avoid all possibility of exacerbating the recent quarrel if these same questions could be dealt with, not in relation to the dispute which has taken place, but as abstract questions. This I believe could most satisfactorily be done by referring them in some general form to the Permanent Court of International Justice for an advisory opinion. This procedure would secure the most authoritative possible decision on the questions involved, and would more effectively than could be done in any

Appendices

other way, re-establish general confidence in the meaning and the sanctity of the obligations of the Covenant.

I suggest that the specific questions to which it is important to have an answer are legal in character and three in number:

(1) are there any disputes between members of the League which, either because
- (a) they concern the national honour and dignity of a country;
- (b) fall within the sphere of competence of another international authority;
- (c) they do not threaten the immediate outbreak of war;
- (d) the Government of one of the parties has not been accorded full diplomatic recognition by all the members of the League;

or for any other reason except that provided in paragraph 8 of Article 15 of the Covenant, do not fall within the competence of the League, and in respect of which the members of the League are not bound by the undertakings of Articles 12, 13 and 15? This appears to me a question with which the Permanent Court of International Justice could adequately deal, and upon which its decision would be accepted as conclusive by the world.

(2) Is a resort to methods of coercion, such as the forceable occupation of territory, legitimate under the Covenant before the dispute has been submitted either to arbitration or to enquiry by the Council?

It is of course true that such occupation of territory and other measures short of war were on a number of occasions resorted to before the establishment of the League, and that they were accorded certain recognition in the text books of International Law. It appears at least probable, however, that the provisions of Articles 10 and 12 have made such measures definitely illegal, even if it could have been claimed that they were legal before the League was established. Article 10 appears quite

Appendices

clearly to impose an obligation to respect and preserve as against external aggression the territorial integrity and existing political independence of every member of the League. Article 12 appears to impose an obligation not to resort to war, and therefore to refrain from acts which might be taken by any other State as establishing a state of war, before a dispute has been submitted to the League.

There is no doubt that practically every member of the Assembly, and particularly the representatives of the small States, are exceedingly anxious that this point should be cleared up in order that if the Covenant is not clear the necessary amendment may be made to it; and I suggest that again it is a question which can most suitably be submitted to the Permanent Court of International Justice, and upon which the Permanent Court's decision would be accepted by the world as final.

> (3) A third and less important question refers to the extent and the character of the responsibility which falls upon the Government of a State upon whose territory members of a diplomatic or international mission are murdered. There have been a great many such incidents in the past, but it is doubtful whether there has been any general practice which could be held to lay down clear principles of international law on the subject.

It is no doubt generally agreed that a certain responsibility mu[st] fall on the Government of a State upon whose territory such acts are committed. But the exact character and extent of this responsibility needs careful definition. It may be that the question is rather one of quasi-legislative definition than of strictly legal interpretation, and that therefore it might be more suitable to refer it to a committee of jurists than the Permanent Court. I would be prepared to accept either solution.

E[ric] D[rummond]

APPENDIX D

*Note of the Conference of Ambassadors
to the Greek Government*

Athènes, le 27 Septembre 1923

Le Chargé d'Affaires de France a l'honneur de communiquer ci-après à son Excellence le Ministre des Affaires Étrangères la décision prise par la Conférence des Ambassadeurs dans sa séance du 26 de ce mois:

La Conférence des Ambassadeurs prenant acte de l'exécution par la Grèce des réparations éxigees par la note du 8 Septembre sous le No. 1, 2, 3, et 4 dans les conditions énoncées par la note subséquente du 13 Septembre de la Conférence;

Ayant pris connaissance du rapport que la Commission de contrôle, envoyée par elle à Janina, lui a addressée sous la date du 22 Septembre;

Ayant, conformément au paragraphe 5 de sa note du 13, examiné ce rapport au point de vue de l'exécution du paragraphe 3 de la note du 8 Septembre;

Considérant qu'à la date du dit rapport, les coupables n'étaient pas encore découverts, que d'autre part plusieurs manquements ont été relevés à la charge des autorités grecques en ce qui concerne la conduite de l'enquête, qu'en ce qui concerne la recherche des coupables, plusieurs négligeances ont été constatées;

Estimant que la 5ème condition de la note du 8 Septembre ne peut en conséquence être considérée comme remplie;

Décide qu'à titre de pénalité de ce chef, le Gouvernement Héllénique paiera au Gouvernement Italien une somme de cinquante millions de lires italiennes, la Conférence et le Gouvernement Italien renonçant par ailleurs au recours devant la Cour de Justice Internationale de la Haye prévu par le paragraphe 7 de la note du 8 Septembre, ainsi qu'à toute autre pénalité, et considérant la question comme réglée à leur égard, sauf recours particulier de l'Italie devant la Cour de Justice Internationale pour la question des frais d'occupation.

Appendices

Décide que le paiement de la somme de cinquante millions de lires italiennes ci-dessus visée, sera effectué par le remise au Gouvernement Italien de la somme de cinquante millions de lires italiennes déposées le 10 Septembre 1923 à la Banque Nationale Suisse; qu'en conséquence la Cour de Justice sera priée d'ordonner le transfert de la dite somme de la Banque Nationale Suisse à la Banque d'Italie à Rome, au compte du Gouvernement Italien. La Conférence constate à cette occasion que le Gouvernement Italien déclare qu'il réalisera le 27 Septembre sa décision antérieurement prise d'évacuer Corfou à cette date.

Le Chargé d'Affaires de France prie son Excellence le Ministre des Affaires Étrangères de vouloir bien lui donner acte de cette notification.

Se référant aux engagements antérieurs du Gouvernement Royal Héllénique, notamment à ceux qui résultent des notes du Gouvernement Royal en date du 1 et 9 ce mois, il a également l'instruction de demander, au nom de la Conférence, que les mesures soient prises le plus tôt possible pour effectuer et hâter le transfert au compte du Gouvernement Italien à la Banque d'Italie à Rome de la somme de cinquante millions de lires italiennes déposées le 10 Septembre à la Banque Nationale Suisse.

BIBLIOGRAPHY

THE previously unpublished materials used in the preparation of this study were secured in a number of widely scattered places. Some of the most important materials were found in the Foreign Affairs Division of the National Archives of the United States in Washington, D.C. These materials included the reports of American Diplomatic Missions overseas as well as the *procès-verbaux* of the Conference of Ambassadors' meetings for September through December 1923. All of these materials can be found in the National Archives.

The remaining materials were found in England, Italy, Switzerland, and Greece. In England, the personal papers of Lord Curzon, Mr. Leopold S. Amery, and Admiral Sir Roger Keyes were inspected. All were extremely important for the light they shed on British policy and British attitudes during the course of the crisis. The Curzon, Amery, and Keyes Papers may be examined only with the permission of the families.

The Archives of the League of Nations at the Palais des Nations in Geneva, were also examined. They can be inspected only by permission of the director of the U.N. Library. Unfortunately, a large portion of Sir Eric Drummond's personal papers were burned in 1941 when a German invasion of Switzerland appeared imminent.

The remaining papers examined were found in Rome and Athens. The Archives of the Italian Foreign Ministry are open for inspection up to 1943, but may be seen only after permission has been secured from the director of the archives.

In Athens, the Corfu materials were found in the Archives Division of the Greek Royal Ministry of Foreign Affairs. These materials were examined only after special permission had been secured from the Greek Government, since all papers in the Archives Division of the Foreign Ministry are closed for inspection for fifty years. The Corfu materials would normally not have been opened until 1973.

The only official Greek materials available, prior to the preparation of this study, can be found in the Greek White Book

Bibliography

published by the Athens Government after the crisis had been settled. This publication is cited in the bibliography.

UNPUBLISHED SOURCES

Amery, Leopold S. Personal Papers and Diaries. August through December 1923. London, England.

Curzon, Lord. Personal Papers. August through December 1923. Kedleston, Derby, England.

Italian Ministry of Foreign Affairs. Archives Division. Rome, Italy. Corfu Dossiers.

Keyes, Admiral Sir Roger. Personal Papers and Letters. August through December 1923. Tingewick House, Buckingham, England.

League of Nations. Archives Division. United Nations Library. Palais des Nations, Geneva, Switzerland. Corfu Dossiers.

National Archives of the United States. Foreign Affairs Division. Washington, D.C. *Procès-verbaux* of the Conference of Ambassadors' meetings, September through December 1923. Record Group 59.

——— Foreign Affairs Division. Washington, D.C. Reports of American Diplomatic Missions Overseas, August through December 1923. Record Group 59.

——— Foreign Affairs Division. Washington, D.C. Collected Papers of the American Embassy, London, England, January through December 1923. Record Group 84.

Royal Greek Ministry of Foreign Affairs. Archives Division. Athens, Greece. Corfu Dossiers.

OFFICIAL PUBLICATIONS AND DOCUMENTARY SOURCES

Documents Officiels Concernant l'Épire du Nord: 1912-1935. Athènes: Flamma, 1935.

France. *Journal Officiel de la République Française*, Chambre des Députés, *Débats Parlementaires*.

Great Britain. Foreign Office. *British and Foreign State Papers*.

——— Foreign Office. *Documents on British Foreign Policy 1919-1939*; First Series. London: H.M. Stationary Office, 1947-1960. 9 Vols.

Bibliography

———— *Parliamentary Debates,* Fifth Series. House of Commons. *Official Report.*
Greece. Ministère des Affaires Étrangères. *Documents Diplomatiques. Différend Italo-Grec: Août-Septembre 1923.* Athènes: Macris, 1923.
Italy. Ministero degli Affari Esteri. *I Documenti Diplomatici Italiani.* Settima Serie. Roma: Libreria dello Stato, 1955. 2 Vols.
League of Nations. *Official Journal.*
———— *Treaty Series.*
Permanent Court of International Justice. Series C.
U.S. Department of State. *Foreign Relations of the United States, 1919.* Washington: Government Printing Office, 1934. 2 Vols.
———— *Foreign Relations of the United States, 1919, Paris Peace Conference.* Washington: Government Printing Office, 1942-1947. 13 Vols.

BOOKS

Amery, Leopold S. *My Political Life.* London: Hutchinson and Co. Ltd., 1953-1955. 3 Vols.
Borgese, G. A. *Goliath; the March of Fascism.* New York: The Viking Press, 1937.
Briggs, Herbert W. *The Law of Nations.* 2nd ed. New York: Appleton-Century-Crofts, Inc., 1952.
Caudana, Mino. *Il Figlio del Fabbro.* Roma: Centro Editoriale Nazionale, 1960. 2 Vols.
Cecil, Lord Robert. *A Great Experiment.* New York: Oxford University Press, 1941.
Craig, Gordon A. and Gilbert, Felix (eds.) *The Diplomats: 1919-1939.* Princeton: Princeton University Press, 1953.
Currey, Muriel. *Italian Foreign Policy, 1918-1932.* London: I. Nicholson and Watson, Ltd., 1932.
Edwards, Kenneth. *The Grey Diplomatists.* London: Rich and Cowan, Ltd., 1938.
État Albanais, Bureau de la Presse. *Deux Documents sur la crime de Janina.* Tirana, 1923.
Foschini, Antonio. *La Verità sulle Cannonate di Corfù.* Roma: Giocomaniello, 1953.
Frangulis, A. F. *Mémoire sur l'Albanie et l'Épire du Nord.* Athènes: Imprimerie Nationale, 1921.

Bibliography

Glasgow, George. *The Janina Murders and the Occupation of Corfu*. London: The Anglo-Hellenic League, 1923.

Guariglia, Raffaele. *Ricordi 1922-1946*. Napoli: Scientifiche Italiane, 1950.

Hasluck, Margaret. *The Unwritten Law in Albania*. Edited by J. H. Hutton. Cambridge: The University Press, 1954.

Helmreich, Ernst C. *The Diplomacy of the Balkan Wars, 1912-1913*. Harvard Historical Studies, XLII; Cambridge: Harvard University Press, 1938.

Hertslet, Edward. *The Map of Europe by Treaty*. London: Butterworths, 1875-1891. 4 Vols.

Høyer, Liv Nansen. *Nansen og Verden*. Oslo: J. W. Cappelens Forlag, 1955.

Ishii, Viscount Kikujiro. *Diplomatic Commentaries*. Translated and edited by William R. Langdon. Baltimore: The Johns Hopkins Press, 1936.

Kadragic, Catherine S. *International Delimitation of Albania, 1921-1925*. Unpublished Ph.D. dissertation, Columbia University, 1956.

Kellor, Frances and Hatvany, Antonia. *Security against War*. New York: Macmillan Co., 1924. 2 Vols.

Laroche, Jules. *Au Quai d'Orsay avec Briand et Poincaré, 1913-1926*. Paris: Librairie Hachette, 1957.

Lasturel, Pierre. *L'Affaire Gréco-Italienne de 1923*. Paris: L'Ile de France, 1925.

Legatus. [pseudonym—Roberto Cantalupo?]. *Vita Diplomatica di Salvatore Contarini*. Roma: Sestante, 1947.

Neurath, Konstantin von. *Der italienisch-griechische Konflikt von Jahre 1923 und seine völkerrechtliche Bedeutung*. Berlin: Dümmler, 1929.

Nicoglou, Stéphan Ph. *L'Affaire de Corfou et la Société des Nations*. Dijon: Librairie Generale Felix Rey, 1925.

Nicolson, Sir Harold. *Curzon: the Last Phase, 1919-1925*. New York: Harcourt, Brace and Co., 1939.

——— *Diplomacy*. 2nd ed. London: Oxford University Press, 1950.

Oppenheim, L. *International Law*. Edited by H. Lauterpacht. 7th ed. London: Longman, Green and Co., 1948-1952. 2 Vols.

Ortega y Gasset, José. *The Revolt of the Masses*. New York: W. W. Norton and Co., 1932.

Bibliography

Philippe, Albert. *Le rôle de la Société des Nations dans l'Affaire de Corfou.* Lille: Librairie Robbe, 1924.

Pink, Gerhard P. *The Conference of Ambassadors (1920-1931).* Geneva Studies, Vol. XII, Nos. 4-5, 1942; Geneva: Geneva Research Centre, 1942.

Pope-Hennessy, James. *Lord Crewe, 1858-1948; the Likeness of a Liberal.* London: Constable and Co. Ltd., 1955.

Rousseau, Charles. *La Compétence de la Société des Nations.* Paris: Imprimerie Administrative Centrale, 1927.

Salandra, Antonio. *Memorie Politiche, 1916-1925.* Milano: Garzanti, 1951.

Salvatorelli, Luigi and Mira, Giovanni. *Storia del Fascismo.* Roma: Novissima, 1952.

Satow, Sir Ernest M. *A Guide to Diplomatic Practice.* Edited by Nevile Bland. 4th ed. London: Longman, Green and Co., 1957.

Seabury, Paul. *The Wilhelmstrasse; a Study of German Diplomats under the Nazi Regime.* Berkeley: University of California Press, 1954.

Scritti e Discorsi di Benito Mussolini. Milano: Ulrico Hoepli, 1934-1939. 12 Vols.

Sforza, Count Carlo. *Contemporary Italy.* Translated by Drake and Denise De Kay. New York: E. P. Dutton and Co., 1944.

——— *L'Italia dal 1914 al 1944.* Roma: Mondadori, 1946.

Statesman's Year Book, 1925. London: Macmillan Co., 1925.

Survey of International Affairs, 1920-1923. By Arnold J. Toynbee. London: Oxford University Press, 1925.

United States Tariff Commission. *Italian Commercial Policy and Foreign Trade 1922-1940.* Report No. 142. Second Series. Washington: Government Printing Office, 1941.

Vattel, Emmerich de. *Le Droit des Gens; ou, Principes de la Loi Naturelle.* London, 1758. 2 Vols.

Villari, Luigi. *Italian Foreign Policy under Mussolini.* New York: Devin-Adair Co., 1956.

Walters, F. P. *A History of the League of Nations.* London: Oxford University Press, 1960.

Weissberg, Guenter. *The International Status of the United Nations.* New York: Oceana Publications, 1961.

Bibliography

Wolfers, Arnold. *Britain and France between Two Wars.* New York: Harcourt, Brace and Co., 1940.

Zimmern, Alfred. *The League of Nations and the Rule of Law, 1918-1935.* 2nd ed. revised. London: Macmillan Co., 1939.

BOOKS IN GREEK

Ἀλεξανδρῆς, Ἀπόστολος. Πολιτικαί Ἀναμνήσεις. Πάτραι, 1947. [Alexandris, Apostolos. *Political Recollections.* Patras, 1947.]

Γονατᾶς, Στυλιανός. Ἀπομνημονεύματα 1897-1957. Ἀθῆναι, 1958. [Gonatas, Stylianos. *Memoirs 1897-1957.* Athens, 1958.]

Δαφνῆς, Γρηγόριος. Ἡ Ἑλλάς μεταξύ δύο Πολέμων 1923-1940. Ἀθῆναι: Ἴκαρος, 1955. 2 Vols. [Dafnis, Grigorios, *Greece between Two Wars 1923-1940.* Athens: Ikaros, 1955. 2 Vols.]

Πεπόνης, Ἰωάννης Α. Νικόλαος Πλαστήρας, Στά Γεγονότα, 1909-1945. Ἀθῆναι, 1947. 2 Vols. [Peponis, John A. *Nikolaos Plastiras and the Events of 1909-1945.* Athens, 1947. 2 Vols.]

Πιπινέλης, Παναγιώτης. Ἱστορία τῆς Ἐξωτερικῆς Πολιτικῆς τῆς Ἑλλάδος, 1923-1941. Ἀθῆναι, 1948. [Pipinelis, Panayiotis. *History of Greek Foreign Policy, 1923-1941.* Athens, 1948.]

ARTICLES

Anchieri, Ettore. "L'Esordio della Politica Estera Fascista," *Il Politico,* Anno xx, No. 2 (1955), pp. 211-231.

Crewe, The Marquess of. "Lord Cecil and the League," *The Fortnightly,* CXLIX, New Series (March 1941), pp. 209-218.

Foschini, Antonio. "A trent anni dall' occupazione di Corfu," *Nuova Antologia,* Anno 88, Fasc. 1836 (Dicembre 1948), pp. 401-412.

Hudson, Manley O. "How the League of Nations Met the Corfu Crisis," *World Peace Foundation,* VI, No. 3 (1923), pp. 176-210.

Jouvenel, Henry de. "France and Italy," *Foreign Affairs,* v, No. 4 (1927), pp. 538-552.

Scialoja, Vittorio. "La Società della Nazioni e il conflitto italo-greco," *Rivista di Diritto Pubblico e della Pubblica Amministrazione in Italia,* Serie II, Anno XVI, Fasc. 1 (Gennaio 1924), pp. 69-74.

Visscher, Charles de. "L'Interprétation du Pacte au lendemain du

Bibliography

différend Italo-Grec," *Revue de Droit International et de Législation Comparée*, 3rd Series, v (1924), pp. 213-230; 377-396.

Wright, Quincy. "The Neutralization of Corfu," *American Journal of International Law*, 18, No. 1 (1924), pp. 104-108.

——— "Opinion of the Commission of Jurists in the Janina-Corfu Affair," *American Journal of International Law*, 18, No. 3 (1924), pp. 536-544.

NEWSPAPERS AND JOURNALS

Corriere della Sera.
The Daily Mail.
The Daily Telegraph.
Le Matin.
Le Messager d'Athènes.
Oriento Moderno.
La Semaine Judiciaire, Journal des Tribunaux.
The Times (London).
France. Ministère des Affaires Étrangères. *Bulletin Périodique de la Presse Grecque.*
——— *Bulletin Périodique de la Presse Italienne.*
——— *Bulletin Périodique de la Presse Scandinave.*
——— *Bulletin Périodique de la Presse Sud-Américaine.*
——— *Bulletin Périodique de la Presse Yugoslave.*

INTERVIEWS

Sir Harold Nicolson, London, July 1961.
Raffaele Guariglia, Rome, August 1961.

INDEX

Aaland Islands, 141n
Adriatic Sea, 41-43, 180, 284
Aegean Islands, 102, 182
Aegean Sea, 43, 67, 69-70
Ajax, H.M.S., 180
Albania, 20-21, 23n, 42, 68, 83, 121, 213, 220, 223, 249, 290, 296; delimitation of frontiers, 16-19; Press Bureau, 28n, 29n; Red Book, 28, 28n
Albert, King, 173n
Alexander II, Emperor, 161
Alexandria, 101, 182
Alexandris, Apostolos, 50-52, 58, 71, 80-83, 120-22, 217, 254
Algeria, 213
American Mission at the Paris Peace Conference, 6-7, 8n
Amery, Leopold S., 180n, 187, 231n, 283
Anatolia, 20, 35n, 43, 92, 274n
Anzio, 46
Argyrocastro, 24, 24n, 28, 290
Ark Royal, H.M.S., 181
Arlotta, Mario, 57n, 69, 175
Asia Minor, 24n, 35, 78n, 80
Atherton, Ray, 35-36, 36n, 52, 81, 81n
Attolico, Bernardo, 72, 90
Austria, 44, 45
Austria, Empress of, 161
Austria-Hungary, 41, 43, 102, 102n
Avezzana, Baron Camillo Romano, 46, 61, 113, 132, 144, 146-47, 149, 150-51, 153-56, 174, 189, 210, 212, 221-22, 224-32, 265-66, 267n, 268-81, 284-87, 292-96, 298, 300
    compromise formula, 233-41, 243-52, 281, 306-307; and Conference's second note, 188-202, 207, 211, 219; conversation with Poincaré, 114-15; report to Mussolini, 125-27
Avricourt, Count Balny d', 37n, 58, 82, 83, 118, 119, 247

Baldwin, Stanley, 64n, 107-108, 181n, 216, 305
Balfour, Lord, 3, 6, 6n
Balkan Wars (1912-1913), 16, 103n
Barrère, Camille, 88n, 280
Beatty, Admiral David, 180n
Beaud, Colonel Eugenio, 258-65, 279, 294
Belgium, 13, 88, 104, 166, 191
Bellini, Rear-Admiral, 77n
Benbow, H.M.S., 180
Bentick, Sir Charles, 36, 39n, 58, 60, 64, 82, 118, 263n
Bernadotte, Count Folke, 309
Berthelot, Philippe, 8
Bianchi, Captain Luigi, 180n
Blahr, Mr., 142n
Bonaccini, Lt. Mario, 22, 24, 274n
Botzaris, Colonel Dimitrios, 22, 143, 259-61, 270, 270n, 273-74, 274n, 282n; attempted assassination, 30-31; discovery of crime, 23-25
Branting, Karl Hjalmar, 96, 98, 119, 140n, 141, 141n, 142n, 158, 166-67, 218, 256-57, 310
Brazil, 125, 126n
Brenner Pass, 44
Brindisi, 21, 223, 230
Bulgaria, 42, 43, 45

Caclamanos, Dimitrios, 289
Cagliari, 183
Calboli, Giacomo Paulucci de, *see* Russo, Baron
Cambiagio, Silvio, 142n
Cambon, Jules, 12, 12n, 88, 148-49, 154, 212-14, 220-22, 224, 227, 230-31, 272-78, 280, 284-86, 293, 295-96, 298, 304; compromise formula, 232-35, 238, 249; and Conference's second note, 188-203, 219
Cecil, Lord Robert, 64n, 83, 86, 86n, 91, 141n, 154, 167-69, 172-73, 176, 178, 178n, 179, 179n, 181, 184, 206-207, 214, 216-18, 256, 283, 301, 305; and Greek appeal, 91-97,

331

Index

107-108, 128-29, 138; supports League competence, 94-96, 98, 109, 114, 119, 158, 163-65, 175
Charles-Roux, François, 90, 130-32, 140, 156, 175
Child, Washburn, 130
Chile, 126n
China, 276
Chinda, Viscount, 11
Civitavecchia, 183
Clemenceau, Georges, 3, 4n, 11
Commission of Delimitation, 19, 33, 142-44, 149, 151, 158, 195, 197, 213, 308-309; Albanian delegation, 22, 23n, 24, 24n, 28n; Greek delegation, 22n, 23n, 259; Italian delegation, 23, 23n, 27
Commission of Inquiry, 24, 24n, 25, 25n, 28, 28n, 145-49, 153-55, 159, 203, 205, 209, 219-20, 222-24, 227, 230, 232, 234, 236-38, 240, 246-47, 249, 251-52, 253n, 258, 307; composition and powers, 190-93, 196, 212-13; investigation, 258-67, 263n, 267n, 282n, 286, 290; reports, 268-75, 277-80, 282n, 283n, 284, 288-89, 292-96, 306
Commission of Jurists, 257n, 311
Commissions on Reparations, Military, Naval and Air Control, 5, 8n
Committee on the Execution of the Clauses of the Versailles Treaty, 4, 6
Conference of Ambassadors, 72, 89, 114, 116, 133, 151, 152, 155, 156, 158, 172, 212-13, 220, 227-29, 242-43, 253n, 254-56, 259, 262-67, 267n, 283, 284, 286, 288-91, 304-308, 310
American observer at, 11-12; Belgium's representation at, 13; Commission of Inquiry's reports, 268-75, 277-82, 281n, 282n, 292-96; competence of, 84-85, 94, 96-98, 105, 119, 125-27, 131-32, 133-39, 149, 160-69, 185-87, 186n, 214-18, 309; Council's note, 188-201; Declaration of November 9, 1921, 19; extension of powers, 9-10; fixes Albanian frontiers, 17-19; formally established, 11; Greek replies to, 117-22, 133, 144-48, 153, 202, 206-207, 210, 217, 219, 230, 240, 289-90; inception, 3-6; legal status of, 15, 15n; Limperany's report to, 27, 49; Mussolini's qualified acceptance of Conference's note, 221-26; notes to Greece, 49-50, 60-61, 62-63, 73, 115, 117-22, 128, 195-203, 205-209, 230, 240, 247-48, 283-85; organizational structure of, 13; position of French President at, 12; problem of Greek responsibility, 142-50
Conference of Ambassadors (London, 1913), 16-17
conferences of ambassadors, prior to the First World War, 3; as instruments of diplomacy, 14; compared to Conference of Ambassadors, 14
Congress of Vienna (1815), 302
Constantinidis, Mr., 26, 27, 261
Contarini, Salvatore, 35n, 44, 44n, 46, 46n, 79, 204, 252, 298, 300
Co-ordinating Committee dealing with questions of Interpretation and Execution of the Versailles Treaty, 7-9
Corfu, 10, 13, 45, 69, 70, 70n, 71, 74n, 75, 105, 116n, 122, 123, 124, 130, 178, 179, 180, 187n
bombardment of, 65, 67n, 74, 78n, 79, 81n, 82, 83, 93, 101; evacuation of, 125, 127, 155, 166, 172, 175, 176, 179n, 194, 198, 199, 200, 201, 203, 206, 207, 210, 215-25, 231-48, 251, 252, 265, 266, 267n, 269, 271, 272, 274, 275, 277, 279, 280, 285-87; neutralization of, 102-103, 102n, 103n, 104n; occupation of, 32, 35, 40, 55, 64n, 67, 68n, 72, 73, 78, 81, 84, 85, 86, 88, 90, 94, 108, 113, 114, 117, 118, 127, 131, 133, 134, 137, 141n, 153, 155, 156, 197, 200, 202, 204, 205, 211, 212, 226, 227, 228, 229n, 231, 231n, 239, 241, 248, 253n, 266, 274, 275, 281, 282n, 287, 297, 310; occupied by Allies, 102

332

Index

Corfu, Protocol of, 143
Corriere della Sera, 54
Corriere Italiano, 102n
Corti, Major, 22, 24
Council of Five, 10n
Council of Foreign Ministers, 10n, 12
Council of Four, 10n
Covenant of the League of Nations, 4n, 85, 91, 94, 96, 99, 100, 104, 105, 108, 110, 122, 124, 125, 138, 141n, 158, 165, 166, 174, 185, 205n, 216, 254, 256, 257, 257n, 301, 302, 310, 311, 312
    Article One, 174; Article Ten, 138; Article Eleven, 72; Article Twelve, 89n, 90, 92, 95, 97, 98, 134, 137, 138, 165, 308, 311; Article Fifteen, 72, 83, 84, 89n, 90, 92, 93, 95, 97, 98, 134, 137, 138, 164, 165, 166, 257n, 308; Article Sixteen, 18, 83, 92, 93, 94, 95, 177, 178, 184, 304
Crete, 101, 103n
Crewe, Lord, 122, 122n, 145, 146, 147, 152, 154, 156, 175, 185, 186, 211, 214, 215, 224, 225, 226, 230, 231, 232, 241n, 242, 268-69, 271-72, 275, 277-84, 286-87, 291, 293, 295-96; compromise formula, 232-35, 239-41, 246-49, 306; and Conference's second note, 190-203
Cromwell, Oliver, 288
Crowe, Sir Eyre, 3, 156, 294
Currey, Muriel, 25n
Curzon, Lord, 48, 64, 64n, 85, 86n, 87, 122n, 156, 178, 181, 181n, 184, 186, 202-204, 211, 235, 246, 252, 253, 267, 279, 281, 281n, 282, 282n, 283, 286, 287, 288, 294, 304, 305, 306
    discussion with Poincaré, 113-14; note from Kennard, 89; note to France, 88; supports Greek appeal, 107-12; surmises French position, 89; views on powers of Conference of Ambassadors, 10, 10n, 12; withdraws support from League, 177, 214-16
Cyrenaica, 182

Daily Chronicle, 86n
Daily Mail, 86, 86n, 124, 129
Dalmatia, 68
Daretti, Lt. Lorenzo, 70n
Dartige du Fournet, Admiral Louis, 102
Davis, John W., 11
De Facendis, Domenico, 35, 39
Derby, Lord, 8, 10
Dodecanese Islands, 42, 57, 68, 68n, 69, 70
Don Pacifico Affair, 124
Drin Valley, 22
Drummond, Sir Eric, 150n, 169, 170, 188, 253, 254, 257n, 296, 312
Duce, *see* Mussolini, Benito
Dulles, John Foster, 4
Durazzo, Carlo, 28n

Écho de Paris, 241n
Egypt, 86n, 182, 232, 233
Eleftheron Vima, 60
Emmanuel III, King Victor, 57, 58, 71, 100n, 173n
England, *see* Great Britain
Epirus, 42, 143, 190, 191, 213, 223, 258; banditry, 21, 30, 32, 38n, 83, 144-45; blockaded, 103n; inquiries in, 118, 270, 270n, 273, 292, 294; Italian Consul, 21
Ethiopia, 303
Euripéos, Petros, 75, 76, 77, 77n
Exarchopoulos, Mr., 26, 27

Fascist, 29, 29n, 42, 45, 53n, 54, 297, 298, 300
Finland, 141n
Fiume Question, 42, 116n
Florence, Protocol of, 16
Florias, Colonel Demosthene, 26, 27, 260, 270n
Formosa, 101
Foschini, Captain Antonio, 68, 69, 74n, 75, 76, 77, 77n, 78, 79n
France, 8, 9, 12, 17, 48, 99, 107, 127, 182, 186n, 200, 220, 228n, 276, 313
    attitude toward Italian Ultimatum, 63; attitude toward League, 113, 122-23, 123n, 153, 178, 179n,

333

Index

300, 302, 303, 304; attitude toward neutralized territory, 104; Balkan policy, 42-43; blockades of foreign ports, 101; bombardment of Fu-cao, 101; Chamber of Deputies, 296n; Italian trade, 177, 178n; occupation of Mytilene, 101; policy in Eastern Europe, 43; Ruhr policy, 49, 62, 87-90, 88n, 108, 112, 113, 115, 116n, 138, 207, 305; sanctions, 179; supports Conference of Ambassadors, 88-89, 115n-16n, 178; supports Italy, 113, 113n, 130-32, 154, 158, 173, 209, 241, 250-51, 253n; Treaties of London, 102, 102n, 103n

Franco, Dr. Alfranio de Mello, 126n
Frank, Rear-Admiral Angelo, 68, 70
Franklin, Count Alberto Martin, 141n, 142n
Fromageot, Henri, 89, 194, 199, 200, 201, 213, 278
Fu-cao, 101

Gabetti, Captain Giovan B., 176
Gallipoli, 67n, 74n
Genoa, 183
George V, King, 180n
George, David Lloyd, 4n, 11
Géraud, Henri, 241n
Germany, 6, 9, 13, 41, 44, 101, 104n, 123, 138, 178, 182, 207, 276, 281, 303, 304, 305, 309
Ghèziri, Thanassi, 22, 24
Gibraltar, 182
Giuriati, Giovanni, 104-106, 122, 128, 139, 139n, 174, 299
Gladstone, William, 233
Gonatas, Colonel Stylianos, 35n, 58, 59n, 80, 117
Graham, Sir Ronald W., 79
Great Britain, 14, 17, 44, 45, 68n, 85-87, 99, 107, 113n, 127, 155, 182, 187n, 207, 226, 227, 228n, 241n, 272, 277, 279, 280, 282, 287
  attitude toward Italy, 112, 183, 184, 202, 241, 243, 253; attitude toward League, 85-87, 109, 111, 112, 122-23, 153, 184-87, 214-18, 283, 300, 302, 303, 304, 306; attitude toward neutralized territory, 104; blockade of Venezuela, 101; bombardments of foreign ports, 101; House of Commons, 296n; Italian trade, 177, 178n; military weakness, 176-81, 305; occupation of Egypt, 232; supports Greek appeal, 108; Treasury opinion, 177, 304; Treaties of London, 102, 102n, 103n; Treaty of Lausanne, 103n

Greco-Bulgarian Incident (1925), 311
Greco-Turkish War (1897), 103n
Greece, 28n, 43, 46, 49, 62, 68, 81-84, 88, 91, 114, 115, 127, 129, 145, 151, 153-57, 159, 163, 167, 172, 183, 183n, 190, 193-202, 204-206, 211-13, 220-23, 225-56, 228, 229n, 233, 235, 237, 241, 243-52, 253n, 265, 269, 272, 275, 277, 279, 280, 284-86, 289, 292, 296, 304, 306, 308
  appeal to League, 66, 72, 83, 90-98, 108, 110-11, 117-18, 124, 128-29, 133-38; blockaded, 103n; borders with Albania, 16-19; Italian Ultimatum, 65-67, 72; League attitude toward, 301; Poincaré's advice, 113; relations with Entente, 102; relations with Italy, 69-70; replies to Conference's notes, 117-22, 133, 144-48, 153, 202, 206-207, 210, 217, 219, 230, 240, 288-90; territorial ambitions, 31; Treaties of London, 102, 102n; Treaty of Lausanne, 103

Grew, Joseph C., 129n, 139
Guani, Alberto, 168, 173
Guariglia, Raffaele, 33, 68n, 106, 106n, 184

Hague Convention, 104n
Hague Court, The, *see* Permanent Court of International Justice at The Hague
Halvorsen, Otto, 142n
Hamel, Dr. Joost-Adrian van, 170
Han Delvinaki, 24
Hanotaux, Gabriel, 89, 91, 98, 130,

Index

132, 138, 150, 150n, 154, 174, 175, 179, 189, 190, 243, 304; compromise formula, 160-67, 173
Harenc, Major R. E., 24n, 258, 259, 260-65, 267, 288, 306
Hitler, Adolf, 298, 300, 303, 313
Hudson, Mr., 239, 240
Hughes, Charles Evans, 152
Hungary, 43, 44, 45
Hymans, Paul, 165, 166, 167, 168, 173, 173n

Il Popolo d'Italia, 54
Imperial Conference, 282, 282n
interim Reparations Committee, 8
Ionian Islands, 102n, 103n, 178n, 275
Ionian Sea, 69
Ireland, 272
Ishii, Viscount Kikujiro, 90, 138, 150n, 154, 157n, 158, 168, 169, 170, 171, 192, 192n, 193, 217, 256, 257n
Italo-Turkish War (1911), 41, 69
Italy, 8, 11, 13, 17, 30, 45, 49, 54, 68, 69, 81, 82, 84, 86, 88, 91, 100, 109, 113, 115, 116n, 118, 124, 126n, 136, 140, 140n, 155, 156, 163, 166, 172, 176, 182, 183, 183n, 184, 185, 187n, 205-207, 211, 215, 216, 218-20, 224-27, 228n, 233, 236-39, 241-44, 247, 250-52, 254-56, 262, 266, 267n, 275, 277, 279, 280, 282, 283, 287, 297, 298, 299, 304-306, 308, 310, 311
  and League, 87, 99, 106-107, 110, 119, 125, 130, 173, 174, 204, 281; anti-British feelings, 111; anti-French demonstrations, 54-55; anti-Greek demonstrations, 54; attitude toward Greek appeal to League, 90-98; Balkan policy, 42-43; blockade of Venezuela, 101; bombardment of San Carlo, 101; British attitude toward, 112, 183, 184, 202, 241, 243, 253n; British trade, 177, 178n; Conference's Second Note, 191-203, 210; French support, 114-15, 125, 130-32, 154, 158, 173, 241, 250-51, 253n; French trade, 177, 178n; General Staff, 181, 182, 183; military weakness, 181-84; Norwegian attitude toward, 142n; occupation costs, 200-202, 212, 230-31, 243, 245, 285; Swedish attitude toward, 141n; Treaties of London, 102-103; Treaty of Lausanne, 103n; United States trade, 177, 178n

Janina, 16, 22, 23, 24, 25, 26, 26n, 33, 51, 59, 240, 258, 259, 265, 266, 267, 274, 275n, 278, 288
Japan, 103n, 153, 192, 192n, 303
Juvenel, Henry de, 179, 179n

Kakavia, 19, 22, 23, 24, 24n, 25, 31, 38n, 261
Kalpaki, 23
Kapishtica Agreement, 16-17
Kemalist, 20, 35
Kennard, Sir Howard W., 89, 130, 156, 184, 203, 204, 214
Keyes, Vice-Admiral Sir Roger, 177, 180, 180n, 181
Koritsa, 17

Lacombe, Colonel, 258, 259, 260, 261, 263, 264, 288, 307
Lambropoulos, Captain, 23
Lansing, Robert, 3, 8, 11
Laroche, Jules, 12, 62, 88, 88n, 113, 115, 143-47, 149, 150, 150n, 151, 158, 160, 211, 215, 220, 223, 224, 225, 227, 231n, 278, 279, 280, 298, 304; compromise formula, 232, 235-39, 246, 247, 249; and Conference's Second Note, 188-203
Lausanne Conference, 35, 36n, 297
Lausanne, Treaty of, 68, 69, 70, 103n
Lauterpacht, H., cited, 59n
League of Nations, 4n, 5, 6, 84, 89, 104, 106, 126n, 142, 151-52, 154-55, 157-59, 176, 184, 203, 205, 207, 210, 224, 226, 234-35, 238, 248, 250, 255, 256, 257n, 275, 281, 283, 290, 296, 297, 301-303, 305-306, 308, 310-13
  British attitude toward, 85-87,

Index

109, 111, 122-23, 153, 184-87, 214-18, 283; competence, 85, 99, 105, 119-22, 130-32, 234-39, 141n, 160-69, 172-74, 185-87, 188-201, 208, 211, 214, 217-18, 254, 307, 309; French attitude toward, 113, 115, 116n, 122, 123, 123n; Greek appeal to, 66, 72, 83, 90-98, 108, 110-11, 117, 118, 124, 128-29, 133-38, 148-49, 202; Italy refuses referral of Corfu question to, 82, 106-107, 110, 124-26, 130, 132; legal status, 15, 15n; Norwegian attitude toward, 142n; problem of Albania's borders, 17, 19; sanctions, 177-79; Secretariat, 150, 150n, 154, 169, 170; Secretary General, 5, 18, 90, 169, 170, 188, 253, 254, 257n, 296, 312; Swedish attitude toward, 141n; Swiss attitude toward, 89n
Le Matin, 219n
Leros, 69, 70
Libya, 41
Like, Mr., 142n
Limperany, Captain de, 26n, 33, 49
Lindsay, Sir Ronald, 109, 184n, 266, 267, 267n
Little Entente, 88, 187n, 228n
Liverani, Andrea, 26
Livorno, 183
London Conference (1922), 297
London Daily Telegraph, 295n
London Protocols, 102n
London, Treaty of (1915), 41
London, Treaty of (1864), 102, 103n, 114
London, Treaty of (1863), 102n
Longare, Count Lelio Bonin, 8, 10, 140n

Makino, Baron, 3
Malta, 180, 181, 182, 183, 183n
Manchuria, 303, 312
Marcilly, Henri de, 278
Massigli, René, 12n, 89, 199
Matsui, Mr., 8
Matteoti, Giacomo, 29, 30
Mediterranean Sea, 35, 41, 42, 68n, 180, 180n, 184, 187, 250, 305

Melas, Léon, 285, 286, 295n
Menam, 101
Messaggero, 111
Millerand, Alexander, 9-10
Modica, Baron, 21, 259
Montagna, Giulio Cesare, 28n, 33, 34, 55, 56, 64, 82, 254; delivers ultimatum, 57-58, 60, 66-67; and Greek note, 118-19, 119n; protests to Greeks, 50-53; relations with Greece, 35-36, 36n, 37n; reports to Mussolini, 37-39; transmits Corfu Proclamation, 81
Motta, Giuseppe, 89, 89n
Munich, 123
Murray, Sir Oswyn, 180n
Mussolini, Benito, 28n, 29, 30, 32, 35-38, 55, 68n, 73, 80, 82, 88n, 102, 104, 113, 115, 115n, 116n, 122, 126n, 128, 129, 133, 153, 154, 155, 173n, 174, 176, 181, 181n, 182, 183, 191, 202-204, 207, 209, 214, 215, 218, 227, 228, 229, 230, 236, 240-43, 249, 250-52, 254-56, 265-67, 277, 279-81, 281n, 282n, 291, 293, 294, 297, 303, 304, 307, 310, 313, 314

attitude toward Conference of Ambassadors' protest note, 61-62, 63; attitude toward League, 84-85, 93, 99, 100, 114, 124-25, 135, 139-40, 173-74, 204, 205n; cites precedents for Corfu action, 101-102; and competence of Ambassadors' Conference, 98, 130-32, 204; conversation with Giuriati, 105-106; Corfu Proclamation, 71-72, 81, 85, 100, 110; and Dodecanese Islands, 68-69; foreign policy aims, 40-43; French attitude toward, 88; instructions to Solari, 74; Kennard conversations, 130, 204, 204n, 205n; knows French position, 89-90; Politis' overtures to, 92; protest to England, 86; qualified acceptance of Conference's note, 221-26; reaction to Conference's second note, 210-12; reaction to Corfu bombardment, 79, 79n; reaction to Tellini

Index

murder, 33, 33n, 34, 39, 40; relations with Italian Foreign Ministry, 44-46, 298, 300; supported by Salandra, 84; ultimatum to Greece, 56-58, 60, 71
Mytilene, 101, 200

Nancy Incident (1913), 147
Nansen, Fridtjof, 105, 140, 140n, 141, 141n, 142n, 175
Napoleon III, 288
Neuilly, Treaty of, 43, 138
Nicoglou, Stephan Ph., 186n
Nicolson, Sir Harold, cited, 59n, 109, 181, 184n
Ninčić, Momčilo, 116n
North Sea, 182

Ortega y Gasset, José, 72
Otchiai, Mr., 3
Otranto, Strait of, 42
Ottoman Empire, see Turkey

Pagliano, Professor, 8
Palmerston, Lord, 124, 288
Panourias, Naos, 28n
Paris Conference (1923), 297
Passau-Ingolstadt, Incident of, 147, 151
Patras, 57
Paxo, 102
Peretti de la Rocca, 48, 49, 50, 62, 63
Permanent Court of International Justice at The Hague, 100n, 139, 154, 155, 159, 194, 196, 202, 209, 212, 231, 237, 243, 244, 245, 248, 268, 280, 281, 282n, 284, 285, 286, 286n, 290, 291
Perrone, Colonel Ferdinando, 40, 56, 59, 59n, 66, 70n, 79, 127, 144, 147, 209
Pertinax, 241n
Pessoa, Dr. Epitacio, 126n
Petit Parisien, 70n, 241n
Philippe, Albert, 103n
Phillips, William, 8n, 87
Phipps, Sir Eric, 50, 60, 61, 62, 242
Pichon, Stephen, 8
Plastiras, Colonel Nikolaos, 35n, 80, 81n

Platis, Colonel, 23n, 26, 27, 28, 270n
Poincaré, Raymond, 49, 58, 60, 62, 63, 65, 73, 88, 88n, 89, 112, 143, 144, 154, 155, 174, 175, 179n, 181n, 187, 211, 215, 216, 220, 228n, 242, 243, 251, 276, 304
and Conference of Ambassadors, 116n, 185-87; conversation with Avezzana, 114-15; proposes compromise formula, 130-32; recommendation to Greeks, 113; supports Italy, 114, 138
Poland, 88, 100n
Politis, Nikolaos, 122, 139, 149, 154, 155, 156, 159, 160, 167, 168, 172, 217, 218-19, 286, 286n, 289, 300, 301; and Conference's second note, 205-206; and Greek appeal, 83, 90-98, 119-21, 128-29, 135-38
Polk, Frank L., 8, 8n, 9
Prespa, Lake, 16
Preveza, 57, 127, 159, 193, 195, 210, 221, 223, 230, 247
Preziosi, Gabriele, 294
Price, G. Ward, 124, 125, 129
Prussia, 102, 102n
Psaroudas, Constantinos, 204
Ptelia, 16

Quiñones de León, José Maria, 170, 175, 210; compromise formula, 157-69, 173

Remizio, Farnetti, 22, 24
Revel, Grand Admiral Thaon di, 67, 68, 69, 70, 74n, 75n, 78, 79n, 176, 182, 183, 183n, 242, 291
Rhine, 303
Rhineland, 9, 13
Rhodes, 57
Richelieu, Cardinal, 288
Romanos, Athos, 115n, 152, 153, 205, 206, 219, 220, 225, 231n, 249, 285, 286, 298, 300
Rousseau, Charles, 186n
Royal Sovereign, H.M.S., 180
Russia, 41, 102, 102n, 281, 303, 305
Russo, Baron, 175

337

Index

St. Germain, Treaty of, 138
St. Jean de Maurienne, Treaty of, 41
Salandra, Antonio, 79, 80, 99, 101, 122, 124n, 125, 132, 139n, 140n, 159, 172, 174, 175, 178n, 212, 217, 218, 243, 254, 255, 256, 257
  and Conference's second note, 207-209; and Greek appeal, 90-98, 133-35, 137; notes Nansen's agitation, 105; questions League competence, 93-94, 98-100, 100n, 119, 139, 140, 158-69, 173, 189; recommendations to Mussolini, 84-85; requests private Council meeting, 90-91; sends Giuriati to Rome, 104-106, 107n, 112, 128; studies Covenant, 105, 105n; surmises French position, 89
Salentina Peninsula, 183
Salsbury, Lord, 233
San Carlo, 101
Santi Quaranta (Sarandë), 21, 223, 230
Sardinia, 183
Sato, Mr. Nantake, 147, 191, 192, 193, 201, 271, 278
Satow, Sir Ernest M., cited, 59n
Schelini, Mr., 76
Scialoja, Vittorio, 4, 10, 11, 105, 105n, 139
Scutari, 101
Sèvres, Treaty of, 12, 102n
Sforza, Count Carlo, 30, 44n, 46n
Shanghai, 312
Shibouya, Colonel, 193, 212, 213, 234, 307; Commission of Inquiry, 258-61, 263, 264, 288, 292
Sicily, 182, 183, 272
Smuts, Jan Christaan, 112
Solari, Admiral Emilio, 67, 67n, 68-71, 74, 74n, 75-79, 79n
Spain, 175
Sportive, H.M.S., 180
Spyropoulos, Captain, 23
Stamfordham, Lord, 180n
Stefani Agency, 210n
Stack, Sir Lee, 86n
state responsibility, 150, 150n, 161-62, 169-71, 189-90

Storting, Mr., 142n
Stresa front, 303
Stylos, Cape, 16
Sudetenland, 296
Supreme Council, 3, 4, 6-9, 12
Sweden, 141n
Switzerland, 89n, 155, 190, 308

Tampico Incident, 102n
Taranto, 68, 69, 70, 70n
Taranto, Gulf of, 67n
Tardieu, André, 3, 6
Tellini, General Enrico, 62, 72, 127, 143, 259, 270, 273, 274, 274n; arrival in Albania, 20; Mission, 19, 27, 32, 33, 39, 48, 49, 53, 61, 65, 69, 184, 272, 308; murder, 21-24, 25n, 33n, 37-38, 39, 49, 50, 52, 53, 53n, 54, 55, 58, 64, 72, 80, 82, 83, 102n, 109, 111, 117, 118, 126, 131, 133-36, 141n, 144, 158, 166, 185, 186n, 190, 194, 197, 212, 236, 244, 263, 291n, 292, 293, 295, 297, 309, 310; murder theories, 29-32, 70n; relations with Greeks, 19; task of delimitation, 22
Times, The (London), 60
Tittoni, Tommaso, 3
Torretta, Marchese Pietro Tomasi della, 47, 48, 49, 50, 62, 63, 64, 64n, 72, 85, 86, 176, 202, 210, 216, 217, 242, 253n, 265, 266, 267, 267n, 298, 300; conversation with Curzon, 109-112, 305
Trapani, 182, 183
Trianon, Treaty of, 138
Trygger, Ernst, 141n, 142n
Tsinganos, Captain, 22
Turin, 70n
Turkey, 41, 69, 101
Tyrrell, Sir William, 47, 48, 62, 63, 64, 64n, 85, 87, 109, 112, 156, 185, 186, 186n, 210. 215, 216, 242, 253n, 265n, 298

United Nations, 309, 310, 312
United Nations Charter, 312
United States, 6, 8, 87, 178, 226, 276, 277, 281, 287, 302, 303, 305; Ital-

Index

ian trade, 177, 178n; occupation of Vera Cruz, 101

Valona, 31
Vanutelli, Count Luigi Rey, 28n, 48, 49, 50, 60, 61, 62, 63, 113, 113n
Vattel Thesis, 48, 62, 64
Venizelos, Eleutherios, 36n, 122n
Vera Cruz, 101, 102n
Versailles Treaty, 3, 4, 4n, 5, 7, 9, 11, 44, 110, 122, 138, 302, 303, 304, 309, 310
Vorovsky, V. V., 170n, 190, 190n

Wallace, Hugh C., 11
Weber, Max, 45
Wheeler, Post, 72, 87, 214
Whitehouse, Sheldon, 115, 115n, 116, 146, 146n, 151, 152, 201, 234, 239, 240n, 248, 249, 272
Wilson, Woodrow, 11
World Court, *see* Permanent Court of International Justice at The Hague

Yugoslavia, 43, 68, 116n, 176, 187n; borders with Albania, 17-19; territorial ambitions, 31, 42

Zaharoff, Sir Basil, 86n
Zahle, Herluf, 140n, 141n
Zepi, 23, 24n, 25, 26